Widening Participation in Higher Education

Issues in Higher Education

Titles include:

Jürgen Enders and Egbert de Weert (*editors*)
THE CHANGING FACE OF ACADEMIC LIFE
Analytical and Comparative Perspectives

John Harpur
INNOVATION, PROFIT AND THE COMMON GOOD IN HIGHER EDUCATION
The New Alchemy

Tamsin Hinton-Smith (*editor*)
WIDENING PARTICIPATION IN HIGHER EDUCATION
Casting the Net Wide?

V. Lynn Meek and Charas Suwanwela (*editors*)
HIGHER EDUCATION, RESEARCH, AND KNOWLEDGE IN THE
ASIA-PACIFIC REGION

Guy Neave, Kjell Blückert and Thorsten Nybom (*editors*)
THE EUROPEAN RESEARCH UNIVERSITY
An Historical Parenthesis?

Guy Neave
THE EVALUATIVE STATE, INSTITUTIONAL AUTONOMY AND RE-ENGINEERING
HIGHER EDUCATION IN WESTERN EUROPE
The Prince and His Pleasure

Mary Ann Danowitz Sagaria (*editor*)
WOMEN, UNIVERSITIES, AND CHANGE
Gender Equality in the European Union and the United States

Snejana Slantcheva and Daniel Levy (*editors*)
PRIVATE HIGHER EDUCATION IN POST-COMMUNIST EUROPE
In Search of Legitimacy

Sverker Sörlin and Hebe Vessuri (*editors*)
KNOWLEDGE SOCIETY VS. KNOWLEDGE ECONOMY
Knowledge, Power, and Politics

Bøjrn Stensaker, Jussi Välimaa, Clàudia Sarrico (*editors*)
MANAGING REFORM IN UNIVERSITIES
The Dynamics of Culture, Identity and Organisational Change

Voldemar Tomusk
THE OPEN WORLD AND CLOSED SOCIETIES
Essays on Higher Education Policies "in Transition"

Issues in Higher Education
Series Standing Order ISBN 978–0–230–57816–6 (hardback)
(*outside North America only*)

You can receive future titles in this series as they are published by placing a standing order. Please contact your bookseller or, in case of difficulty, write to us at the address below with your name and address, the title of the series and the ISBN quoted above.

Customer Services Department, Macmillan Distribution Ltd, Houndmills, Basingstoke, Hampshire RG21 6XS, England

---

Widening Participation in Higher Education

Casting the Net Wide?

Edited by

Tamsin Hinton-Smith
University of Sussex, UK

First published 2012 by
PALGRAVE MACMILLAN

Palgrave Macmillan in the UK is an imprint of Macmillan Publishers Limited,
registered in England, company number 785998, of Houndmills, Basingstoke,
Hampshire RG21 6XS.

Palgrave Macmillan in the US is a division of St Martin's Press LLC,
175 Fifth Avenue, New York, NY 10010.

Palgrave Macmillan is the global academic imprint of the above companies
and has companies and representatives throughout the world.

Palgrave® and Macmillan® are registered trademarks in the United States,
the United Kingdom, Europe and other countries.

ISBN 978–0–230–30061–3

This book is printed on paper suitable for recycling and made from fully
managed and sustained forest sources. Logging, pulping and manufacturing
processes are expected to conform to the environmental regulations of the
country of origin.

A catalogue record for this book is available from the British Library.

A catalog record for this book is available from the Library of Congress.

10   9   8   7   6   5   4   3   2   1
21 20 19 18 17 16 15 14 13 12

Printed and bound in Great Britain by
CPI Antony Rowe, Chippenham and Eastbourne

Contents

Part III   Non-Traditional Students' Experiences in Higher Education

Part IV   Widening Participation in International Contexts

Illustrations

Tables

Figures

Acknowledgements

'Good students, bad pupils: Constructions of "aspiration", "disadvantage" and social class in undergraduate-led widening participation work' © 2008 Yvette Taylor, partially reproduced from a chapter originally published in *Educational Review*, Taylor and Francis, 60 (2): 155–168.

'Wider still and wider? A historical look at the "open-ness" of the Open University of the United Kingdom' © 2010 Alan Woodley, an extended version of ' "Open as to people": The people's response to the Open University of the United Kingdom', published in French in *Éducation et Sociétés* 2 (26): 13–27.

Contributors

Caroline Berggren is Research Fellow in the Department of Education and Special Education, University of Gothenburg, Sweden. Her research interest is trajectories: previously relating to social selection from upper secondary school to higher education and currently graduates' paths to the labour market. Conducted research has been large-scale statistical analyses on Swedish register data, with gender and class perspectives.

Christina Cliffordson is Professor of Education at University West, Sweden, and is currently conducting research on selection and admission in higher education, development of intellectual performance, and grades and grade assignment. The research is based mainly on large-scale longitudinal register data and is being carried out with the use of multivariate analysis methods.

Miriam E. David is Professor Emerita of Sociology of Education at the Institute of Education, University of London, UK, where she was formerly Associate Director (higher education) of the Economic and Social Research Council's (ESRC's) Teaching and Learning Research Programme. She is also Visiting Professor at the Centre for Higher Education and Equity Research (CHEER) at the University of Sussex, UK. She has a world-class reputation for her research on equity, family, feminism, gender and education. Her publications include *Improving Learning by Widening Participation in Higher Education* (2009), and she has edited a special issue of *Contemporary Social Science* 2011 6 (2) on 'Challenge, Change or Crisis in Global Higher Education'.

Sarah Earl-Novell is Research Associate at University of California Berkeley's Center for Studies in Higher Education (CSHE) in California, USA. She also holds an adjunct faculty position at Las Positas College, California, USA, where she teaches the Sociology of Gender. Sarah holds a PhD in sociology from the University of Sussex, UK, and an MSc in sociology from the London School of Economics, UK. Dr Earl-Novell is currently working on 'Men in higher education: Investigating the gendered terrain of University participation, experience and achievement'. Prior to that, she was a staff researcher at CSHE, where she worked on the Andrew W. Mellon Foundation-funded 'Future of Scholarly Communication' project.

John Field is Professor in the School of Education, University of Stirling, UK, and Visiting Professor in Lifelong Learning, Birkbeck, University of

London, UK. He has written widely on the social, economic and historical aspects of adult education and training. His recent books include *Mental Capital and Wellbeing* (2009, edited with Cary Cooper and others) and *Researching Transitions in Lifelong Learning* (2009, edited with Jim Gallacher and Robert Ingram).

Philip Frame is Principal Lecturer in Organisational Development in the Human Resource Management Department of Middlesex University Business School, UK. He is a Fellow of both the Royal Society of Arts and the Higher Education Academy. He researches, publishes and has provided staff development workshops on student induction, work-based learning and managing diversity and employability.

Tamsin Hinton-Smith is a Lecturer in Sociology at the University of Sussex, UK. Her research interests include gender, education and the social inclusion of marginalised groups, particularly mature women students, lone parents and teenage parents, and participation in learning, training and employment. Tamsin has also worked as a parliamentary researcher on issues related to women, families, poverty and welfare. She is the author of *Lone Parents' Experiences as Higher Education Students: Learning to Juggle* (2012).

Catherine Lido joined the Psychology Subject Group at the University of West London (formerly Thames Valley University), UK, in 2004 and is presently the programme leader for the BSc programme. She has headed a number of funded projects in the area of stereotyping, prejudice, education and widening participation, including an Economic and Social Research Council (ESRC) grant, examining the direct effects of the media on thoughts and behaviours related to asylum seekers. Furthermore, she collaborated on two Higher Education Academy (HEA) grants and a further ESRC grant with Professor Mary Stuart in the area of widening participation and the minority ethnic student experience. In addition, she has headed projects funded by West London Lifelong Learning Network and the West Focus Knowledge Exchange.

Anne J. MacLachlan is Senior Researcher at the Center for Studies in Higher Education at the University of California, Berkeley, USA, and in the Department of Molecular and Cell Biology. Her research areas include the access and success of women and underrepresented minorities in science at every level of postsecondary education, from first-year students to faculty, and she has disseminated her findings in over 60 papers and invited talks. She works with state and national agencies and organizations, including the National Institutes of Health, Sloan Foundation, National Science Foundation and the American Association for the Advancement of Science.

Lynda Measor is Reader in Applied Social Sciences in the School of Applied Social Sciences at the University of Brighton, UK. Her research interests are in the problems and issues that face young people in educational settings and in their communities. Her contribution to this volume echoes her similar findings from ESRC-funded research on the difficulties that face young people when they make the transition from primary to secondary school. Her publications include *Changing Schools* (1984, with Peter Woods).

Barbara Merrill is Reader in Lifelong Learning at the Centre for Lifelong Learning, University of Warwick, UK. Her research interests include issues of class and gender in relation to the learning experiences and the learning identity of adult students as well as biographical research approaches. She has published extensively in the field of adult education and biographical research.

Marie-Pierre Moreau is Senior Research Fellow at the University of Bedfordshire, UK. Her research is at the nexus of education, work and equality issues, especially gender. She has published many articles in this field. Her recent book *Les enseignants et le genre: les inégalités hommes-femmes dans l'enseignement du second degré en France et en Angleterre* (2011) is an exploration of gender inequalities in the teaching profession.

Jessica Morgan is Senior Lecturer in the Department of Psychology and Counselling at the University of Greenwich, UK. Her recent publications include research reports on extracurricular activity and graduate employment (for the Higher Education Academy) and students' social identity and cultural capital (for the Economic and Social Research Council). Her research interests also include adult development and well-being, positive psychology as well as motivation and personality.

Natalie Morgan-Klein is Research Fellow in the School of Education, University of Stirling, UK. Her research interests relate to the impact of social and economic disadvantage, and she has published on child policy (contributing chapters to the book *Safeguarding and Protecting Children and Young People,* edited by Stafford and Vincent, 2008) and non-traditional students in higher education (including 'Researching retention and non-traditional learners: Evidence on pre-entry preparation', jointly authored with John Field, 2010).

Louise Morley is Professor of Education and Director of the Centre for Higher Education and Equity Research (CHEER) at the University of Sussex, UK. She has an international profile in the sociology of gender in higher education studies. Recent journal publications include 'Misogyny posing as measurement: Disrupting the feminisation crisis discourse', *Journal of*

Contemporary Social Science 2011; 'Sex, grades and power in higher education in Ghana and Tanzania', *Cambridge Journal of Education* 2011; and 'Gender mainstreaming: Myths and measurement in higher education in Ghana and Tanzania', *Compare: A Journal of Comparative Education* 2010.

M. Teresa Padilla-Carmona is Senior Lecturer in the Department of Research and Assessment Methods in Education, University of Seville, Spain. She has published several books and chapters on career assessment and guidance, and her most recent articles deal with the educational aspirations of secondary school students and higher education students' participation in their learning assessment. Her research interests include gender and education, adults' career guidance and students' participation in higher education.

Mary Stuart is Professor of Higher Education Studies at the University of Lincoln, UK, where she is also Vice-Chancellor. Mary has written extensively on widening participation over the years, including *Collaborating for Change? Managing Widening Participation in Further and Higher Education* (2002). Her latest publications are 'Personal stories – How students' social and cultural life histories interact with the field of higher education', *International Journal of Lifelong Education* (2011, with Catherine Lido and Jessica Morgan), and *Social Mobility and Higher Education* (2012).

Yvette Taylor is Professor in Social and Policy Studies and head of the Weeks Centre, London South Bank University, UK. She has held fellowships at Rutgers University and University of California, Berkeley, in USA. Her books include *Working-Class Lesbian Life* (2007), *Lesbian and Gay Parenting: Securing Social and Educational Capital* (2009) and *Fitting into Place?* (2012). Her edited collections include *Educational Diversity* (2012) and *Theorising Intersectionality and Sexuality* (2010). Yvette is currently working on an ESRC standard grant 'Making space for queer identifying religious youth'.

Paula Wilcox is Lecturer in Criminology at the University of Brighton, UK. She researches and publishes around student engagement in higher education, as well as issues of violence against women or domestic violence. Relevant publications include *Widening Participation and the Role of Social Motivation in Students' Transitional Experiences in Higher Education* (2009), with Hilary McQueen, Dawn Stephen and Carl Walker, and ' "It was nothing to do with the university, it was just the people": The role of social support in the first-year experience of higher education' (journal article, 2005) with Sandra Winn and Marylynn Fyvie-Gauld.

Ruth Woodfield is Reader in Sociology at the University of Sussex, UK. Her research work focuses on gender in the context of science, technology, employment and higher education. She is the author of *Women, Work and Computing* (2000) and *What Women Want from Work: Gender and Occupational Choice in the 21st Century* (2007) and has published widely on the subject of gender differences in experience, engagement and attainment within higher education.

Alan Woodley was for many years Senior Research Fellow at the Institute of Educational Technology of the Open University of the United Kingdom. There he carried out institutional research into various aspects of access and widening participation. Now, newly in retirement, he can look back and consider what has been achieved.

Mantz Yorke is Visiting Professor in the Department of Educational Research, Lancaster University, UK. He has researched various aspects of 'the student experience' and has published widely on higher education. The bulk of his work encompasses the interlinked themes of student success, assessment, employability, widening participation and retention.

Part I

Inclusion, Exclusion: Issues in Widening Participation

1
Introduction

Tamsin Hinton-Smith

Widening participation (WP) in higher education (HE) is a key contemporary social issue. It has been a global concern in supporting the economic and social health of nations for several decades (Delors, 1996). Through its relationship with labour force participation and social inclusion, it is relevant to those engaged with social issues and policy, extending far beyond educational scholars and practitioners. Lifelong learning has been promoted as a recognised means of social inclusion (Jones, 2006: 487), and HE participation is acknowledged to be 'a critical determinant of life chances' (Naidoo and Callender, 2000: 235). The United Kingdom Conservative–Liberal Democrat Alliance Government's 2011 Social Mobility Strategy emphasises the importance of HE participation, including elite higher education institutions (HEIs), for increasing social mobility and life chances amongst socially disadvantaged groups. The importance of WP policies is set to continue in an increasingly globalised labour market, as traditional manufacturing industries decline and economies develop. The ensuing demand for ever-increasing proportions of populations to develop the skills required for employment in more skilled, non-manual occupations in developing knowledge economies inevitably requires increased participation in post-compulsory education, including HE.

Previous efforts to extend HE participation through the 1950s and 1960s concentrated on traditional students. But subsequent demographic shifts, as the post-war baby boom ended and birth rates declined in the United States from the late 1950s and across Europe from the late 1960s, resulting in decreasing numbers of school-leavers, are accredited with informing the necessity for universities to cast the recruitment net wider, looking to previously untargeted populations to meet expanding intake targets (Edwards, 1993; Gallagher *et al.*, 1993). Engaging non-traditional student groups, including women, ethnic minorities, mature and working-class students, and students with disabilities initially functioned as a quota-filling exercise of subsuming previously excluded groups into the existing dominant framework of HE. But generations of students and tutors have

3

experienced, and WP commentators have explicated, the frequent inadequacies of a system designed for educating a privileged minority of young, white, western men without disabilities or without the constraints of employment or dependents to meeting the needs of an increasingly heterogeneous university population. This causes inevitable friction with students' and HEIs' expectations – clashing as square pegs are asked to fit round holes – as HEIs attempt to assimilate non-traditional students with their differently ranging circumstances and needs into the mould created for the 'bachelor boy' model of the traditional ideal university student (Edwards, 1993). Similar to the social model of disability in its assertion that social institutions have a responsibility not merely to open their doors to disabled individuals but to ensure that conditions facilitate full participation by diverse differently abled members (Oliver, 1996; Shakespeare and Watson, 2002; Barnes and Mercer, 2009), WP commentators critique assumptions that WP students can simply be incorporated into HE without addressing their specific needs and tailoring environments accordingly. Without such active facilitation of genuine inclusion, many WP students remain destined to exist as 'deviant tokens', courted to meet the needs of universities and economies, yet remaining outside the dominant framework as second-class students.

Critics have accused the government and the HEI sector of an 'ambivalent attitude' towards non-traditional students, often presenting them in conferences and in policy papers and journal articles (Woodley and Wilson, 2002), but preferring in fact to recruit the easiest students into HE first – being students with high A-level results who thus need the least 'top-up' to get up to good university standard – and then searching for the rest (Watson, 2007). The UK Government is criticised for not valuing the non-traditional students they seek to attract to HE (Jones, 2006), who it is claimed are 'tolerated rather than prized' (Woodley and Wilson, 2002).

The impact of policy developments

WP in HE has been a central aspect of UK educational policy in recent decades. This reflects similar trends in all economically developed societies in an increasingly competitive, globalised marketplace. In the 2003 White Paper, 'The Future of Higher Education', the UK Government stated aims that included a vision of a sector in which we would see 'all HEIs excelling in teaching and reaching out to low participation groups' (2003: 22). There has been hope that allocation of special funds for WP projects would encourage universities to implement high-quality schemes to recruit traditionally excluded students (Callender and Kemp, 2000: 239). But despite increasing student numbers over recent decades, and the efforts to 'ensure that all those with the potential to benefit from HE have the opportunity to do so whatever their background and whenever they need it' (Hefce, 2007: 4), critics have expressed concern that the UK drive to widen HE participation has concentrated on 'how many' as an indicator of equal opportunities in access, at the expense of exploring inequalities in the qualitative experience of underprivileged student groups (Edwards, 1993; Reay, 2003; Laing *et al.*, 2005; Taylor, 2007: 35). A 2007 report from the National Audit Office revealed that although the United Kingdom ranked fifth in the world in terms of student retention, ahead of Germany and the United States, one in five students still dropped out of their courses. The report recommended that 'more support is needed for all students, especially those studying part-time, who face particular challenges and are more likely to drop out' (Hands, Mackay, Ormiston-Smith, Perryman and Wright-Anderson, 2007).

The complexity of the WP debate is compounded by important developments, including changes to student financing in many countries. In the United Kingdom, the move from grants to loans and the introduction of top-up fees have impacted damagingly on HE participation amongst the most vulnerable students. More recently, governments have responded to global recession with broad cuts to public spending, including on education. Critics have for several decades identified a fundamental clash of interests between the drive to widen participation and cuts to student financing (Edwards, 1993; Callender, 2002; Taylor, 2007: 35). In the United Kingdom, the impact of wider global fiscal developments and spending constraints, combined with the 2010 regime change to a conservative-led alliance government determined to reverse the pattern of tax and spending, has accelerated the pre-existing trend towards rising course fees. Faced with 80 per cent spending cuts (Hefce, 2011), the majority of UK HEIs have confirmed the implementation of annual course fees from September 2012 entry at or near the £9,000 ceiling, leaving many students facing being priced out of HE participation. This threatens to undo much of the valuable work achieved in equalising HE access by the WP agenda.

The UK Government's assurance that no student will be required to meet course fees up front is unlikely to assuage students confronting loans of £27,000 for course fees alone for a three-year course. This is exacerbated by the wider context of today's prospective HE students' awareness of a deepening pensions crisis, stringent mortgage lending conditions, unsure labour market outcomes in recompense for HE participation and a retracting welfare safety net delivering a decreasing package of social support under the universal credit introduced in the 2011 Welfare Reform Bill. Poorer prospective university students are likely to be most deterred by the prospect of spiralling debt, given evidence of the impact of socio-economic status in informing debt aversiveness. This group includes many of those targeted by WP including working-class, black and minority ethnic (BME), mature and lone parent students and those with disabilities whose work participation is restricted (Jenkins and Symons, 2001; Reay, 2003). As a spring 2011 Liberal Democrat consultation paper acknowledged, 'financial security makes adults more likely to take productive risks, such as undergoing training... that enhance capabilities. Inequality thus remains self-perpetuating to some extent: it is harder to escape poverty having grown up in it'.

While to some extent we may be able to draw predictions from the US context of an HE sector with a well-established landscape of high fees, the specific impact of their introduction in the United Kingdom as yet remains to be seen. Evidence of student responses already indicate increases in traditional entry-age student applications to the open university (OU), whose historical status as a provider primarily of mature HE may be altered by the comparative modesty of its tuition fees in light of increases in the rest of the sector. Alongside increased applications by UK students to international HEIs, motivated by the same rebalancing of the relative cost of course fees, there is additional evidence that some school leavers plan to defer university entry until they reach 21 years of age and are financially assessed on their own income as independents, rather than being assessed on parental income. It is additionally perceived that the educational top-up offered by a master's course in a progressively competitive graduate marketplace may increase in attractiveness as its cost, relative to a first degree, declines. The features of a rapidly changing HE sector in flux – including these factors, amongst many more – dictate that to an extent up-to-date commentary on the future of HE, including WP, particularly in the United Kingdom, can currently remain little more than hypothesis and conjecture. As this volume goes to press, unsureness remains, even within Westminster, as to the true impact of the course fee rises to be implemented from September 2012 and whether these will result in a drop in student numbers that could close departments *en masse*, force a drop in fees for 2013 entry or simply lead to an influx of wealthy international students to fill the places that cannot be afforded by home students with high grades but low incomes. Universities in the United Kingdom have claimed that the continuing substantial outstripping of supply by demand for university places means that tens of thousands of well-qualified individuals miss out on a place. Recognition of this mismatch prompted the government review into HE that commenced in autumn 2010 to address the rising demand for university places. Fee increases may lead to readjustment of that imbalance, simply weeding out those applicants who feel that they can neither afford the fees nor take on the debt, and in the process threaten WP amongst the most disadvantaged student groups. Whatever the eventual outcomes, it remains clear that the way forward for HE lies increasingly in question.

The potential deterrent effect of the incoming student finance policy is exacerbated by the simultaneous disbandment of the Aimhigher programme. Aimhigher, initially launched as Excellence Challenge in 2001, was commissioned to widen participation in HE by raising awareness, aspirations and attainment amongst under-represented groups (Aimhigher, 2007). Criticisms of perceived failings of the programme to deliver on its targets are seen as resulting from too many other government policies working against 'a more just and equitable distribution of educational goods across society' (*The Guardian*, 2007). Despite over 20 years of government initiatives and increasing student numbers over the last two decades, relative levels of HE participation have persistently remained stubbornly low amongst disadvantaged groups (Christie *et al.*, 2005). Although there have been substantial increases since the mid-2000s in individuals from the most excluded backgrounds entering HE, this has taken place in the context of simultaneous increases in participation by the most advantaged, leaving the disadvantaged still considerably less likely to participate. The United Kingdom is far from unique in these perceived shortcomings. For example the drive to expand HE participation in France is perceived to have failed to deliver hopes of democratisation of access (Deer, 2005). Insights into comparative international policy and experience are facilitated by inclusion in this volume of perspectives from commentators on WP in HE in countries in Europe, Africa and America. These perspectives contribute to the identification of areas of perceived similarity and difference. For example it has been suggested that in Scandinavia education is seen more positively as having succeeded as an instrument of equalisation of social status and experience, rather than as one of selection, when compared with other countries (Komulainen, 2000). Such perceived international differences take place against the backdrop of wider social distribution of equality of income and life chances (Wilkinson and Pickett, 2011), illustrating the complex mutual causality between material resources and educational opportunity.

With regard to the role of Aimhigher in the United Kingdom, whatever its shortcomings in redressing the inequalities of broader policy, the potential to reach out to disenfranchised groups is likely to be substantially further compromised by the replacement of Aimhigher with the National Scholarship Programme (NSP) in 2012, which focuses on providing student bursaries, and unlike Aimhigher, includes no funding for student recruitment outreach work targeting school leavers from financially disadvantaged backgrounds.

The £70 million per annum Aimhigher programme ended in July 2011, with the NSP commencing in September 2012 as a replacement. Alongside fears around the retention repercussions of leaving an entire cohort of the most financially disadvantaged students recruited through Aimhigher stranded without support over the course of the transitional academic year 2011–2012, the absence of outreach work has serious implications. Here the policy stands in stark contrast to the identification of lack of good quality advice as a central factor that negatively affects disadvantaged students' decisions on whether to apply for a selective course or institution, as indicated in the 2010 Harris report 'What more can be done to widen access to highly selective universities?'. Similarly, the 2009 Milburn report 'Unleashing aspiration: The final report on the panel of fair access to the professions' had recommended that universities become more involved in schools as a means to increasing social mobility. The March 2011 guidance to universities from the Higher Education Office for Fair Access (OFFA) accordingly advised universities to focus the WP strategy on outreach work rather than on bursaries, which are evidenced not to affect students' HE choices. Under the NSP, universities must fund outreach work themselves and set their own targets. This is of particular concern in the context of the previously discussed cuts facing UK HEIs. The criterion for adequate outreach provision is a spending of £900 of each £9,000 of course fee on access activities, rather than on any element of evaluation by success. A further concern is that NSP supports students only during their first year of university, raising concerns regarding implications for retention. This is despite the OFFA evidence that bursary awareness and take-up is higher amongst continuing students compared with first-year entrants.

The projected detrimental impact of Aimhigher's replacement with the NSP has simultaneously been exacerbated by the termination of the Educational Maintenance Allowance (EMA) that provided guaranteed support for further-education (FE) participation of all 16–18-year olds from low-income families. EMA will be replaced by discretionary bursaries awarded by individual colleges to some, but not necessarily all, students from low-income households. Vitally students will not be able to find out whether they will be awarded a bursary in advance of taking up an FE course. This is of concern given that EMA is evidenced to have a positive impact on recruitment, retention and achievement, with up to 30 per cent of students in receipt of EMA, indicating that they would not otherwise continue their course. EMA is predominantly taken up by students with low-achievement levels at school, those from BME groups and those from single-parent families, and is credited with having been a vital tool for increasing social mobility.

While access to HE for traditional entry-age WP students looks threatened to be compromised by such developments in educational policy, their mature counterparts with prior labour market experience are challenged by emergent features of broader policy. For example migration from income support to job seeker's allowance (JSA) of lone parents whose youngest children are aged five and six, under the 2011 Welfare Reform Bill, introduces the compulsion for individuals in this group to be available for and actively seeking work through employment-related activities. These are myopically defined in the narrowest sense to exclude participation in HE as preparation for the longer term security of graduate employment. The educational policy is hence criticised for compromising the HE participation of this vulnerable social group at precisely the moment at which many take the step to engage in what may have been a long-held aim, as their youngest child enters full-time school. In addition, mature students indicate worrying about the employment implications of their advancing age in terms of securing graduate employment, providing adequate recompense for their time invested in HE and debts accrued in what they perceive to be an ageist job market.

Many perceive age as impacting more significantly than social class upon the opportunities available to them after graduation (Hinton-Smith, 2012). The justifiability of this concern is corroborated by the evidence of the detrimental impact of age upon graduate employment (Brennan *et al.*, 1999; Merrill, 1999; Woodley and Wilson, 2002: 335).

Diversity and inequalities within widening participation

Non-traditional students' motivations for HE participation capture the complexity of the relationship between intrinsic personal development orientation and instrumental employment-directed outcomes, with the relative balance fluctuating between distinct groups. For example BME students have been documented to enter HE for predominantly career-related reasons compared with white students (Brennan *et al.*, 1999), while the significance of career-related motives for study have also been evidenced to decline relatively with age (Gallagher *et al.*, 1993). This contrast reflects simultaneous tensions inherent in the rationale for WP in HE. While WP is justified in terms of social equity, it is generally seen as being driven by the changing labour force needs of postmodern knowledge economies (Naidoo and Callender, 2000; Wain, 2000). Such an instrumental rationale draws implicitly on human capital theory as developed by Schultz (1961), and later Gary Becker, advancing that education and training raise the productivity of workers by imparting useful knowledge and skills (1964). Human capital rhetoric is critiqued as leading to seeing education as a commodity rather than as a public service (Tomlinson, 2005: 1). The gap between ideological social equity rhetoric and the reality of limits to both HE participation and graduate employment opportunities causes inevitable stress as individuals feel frustrated in finding their attempts to realise their potential through HE participation thwarted by the limitations of available opportunities and support.

The catch-all categories of WP and non-traditional students unhelpfully mask the diversity of experience and need represented by those historically excluded from HE learning. It is often charged that too many WP initiatives have lumped together all non-traditional students at the expense of addressing the unique needs of each group (Edwards, 1993; Reay, 2003; Laing *et al.*, 2005; *The Guardian*, 2006; Taylor, 2007). This volume addresses this identified deficit by introducing perspectives based on research focusing on the particularised HE experiences of different groups of WP students. Different variables of HE inclusion and exclusion intersect importantly, with for example women from disadvantaged backgrounds persistently and substantially more likely to enter HE than their male counterparts.

Another key aspect of the unequal spread of WP students within HE is their concentration in the non-elite institution sector, with the largest increases in non-traditional student numbers mainly taking place within former polytechnic institutions (Jones, 2006). For example, 38.8 per cent of students at the Manchester Metropolitan University come from lower socio-economic groups, compared with 24.7 per cent at the University of Manchester, 12.6 per cent at Cambridge and 11.5 per cent at Oxford (HESA, 2011). While this trend has now been addressed through WP quotas, stubborn inequalities show no sign of retreating, and it is of concern that compliance is largely unmoderated and without sanctions.

Disparities in student demographic profiles persist between institutional types for a number of mutually reinforcing reasons. Disadvantaged students both self-select and are selected out of elite institutions, undermining social mobility. First it is inevitable that local HEIs are frequently 'chosen' by mature students who have jobs as well as families to care for, perhaps with children in schools and partners also in work in the local area, not to mention wider support networks and living arrangements to consider, and all within the context of often-limited financial resources. This leads Reay to identify that many mature learners can find themselves operating within such narrow choices of HEI that these are sometimes effectively distilled to 'a choice of one' (2003: 307). University-fee increases will intensify the propensity for less financially advantaged students to attend their local university, and so, for traditional entry-age students, to avoid incurring additional accommodation and living costs on top of course fees by remaining resident in the parental home while they complete HE. Given that non-traditional students are frequently relatively financially disadvantaged, and that people with fewer financial resources tend to find residence in areas of housing affordability, this acts to cluster non-traditional students within the localities of urban former polytechnics rather than the ancient colleges or leafy campus universities. In addition to the many constraints on their concrete circumstances, WP students are further constrained by the same lack of confidence that may well have both hindered and been created by their experiences of educational engagement in initial schooling. As identified by Egerton, individuals from educationally excluded groups frequently seek to recoup earlier educational disadvantage through HE participation at a mature age (2000: 64). An element of self-censoring frequently takes place, whereby many WP students identify non-elite institutions as those where they can see themselves studying and imagine feeling most comfortable and 'at home', and direct their applications accordingly. This may represent a combination of both assuming elite institutions to be 'above them' – or aimed at other types of students – and rejecting the culture of elite institutions as cold, unwelcoming and ultimately undesirable.

Earlier educational decisions also feed into institutional choices. For example, BME students have higher rates of post-16 education when compared with white British students, but are more likely to attend FE colleges rather than sixth-form colleges (Bhattacharyya *et al.*, 2003). This in turn influences choices of HE subject and institution, with BME students less likely to follow the A-level route, which is ultimately indicated as a factor in lower levels of first classifications achieved by BME students at university (Connor *et al.*, 2004). While one in six UK HE students is BME, this is true of only one in ten students at elite institutions (Kerr, 2011). Similarly, while providing a valuable pathway for providing and preparing for HE access to non-traditional students (Leonard, 1994: 163), access routes also have the potential to disproportionately channel WP non-traditional students – particularly mature working-class women with family responsibilities – into HE courses, and ultimately into careers as nurses, nursing auxiliaries, social workers, teachers and teaching assistants, and the new universities that predominantly offer these courses. These vocations are too often characterised by the same low pay, low status, long hours and high-stress feminised caring work that also dominates the same individuals' lives at home, as they bring up children, ultimately falling short of providing individuals with opportunities to move beyond the constraints of such traditional stereotypes (Jackson, 2004: 14). Further, that university students from A-level routes are far more likely to complete their degrees clashes with attempts to widen participation to include more working-class and BME students through access routes (Leonard, 1994: 163).

That WP students cluster disproportionately outside the elite sector can be couched in positive terms as indicative of a superior emphasis placed on student support by institutions for which teaching is their bread and butter, particularly amongst those institutions with the highest concentrations of non-traditional students that are perhaps most attuned to meeting their needs. WP students may therefore be seen as active agents in their HE learner trajectories, positively identifying those institutions most able to support their educational journeys.

It is, nevertheless, also important alongside acknowledging the role of individuals' choices, however constrained these may be, in informing institutional preference, not to lay all responsibility for the learning pathway, subject and institution choices with WP students themselves, as evidence also shows them to be persistently disadvantaged by discriminatory admission practices (e.g. Burke and McManus, 2010), with 'high tariff' HEIs, in particular, long evidenced to show a bias towards 'traditional' entrants (Purcell *et al.*, 2009). Shiner and Modood have investigated ethnic bias in the allocation of university places (2002). Indeed the highest-ranking HEIs that are most attractive to students can be seen as lacking the impetus to engage enthusiastically with WP, as they are confident that they can fill their places with traditional students who can be seen as 'safer bets' in terms of having higher completion rates (Yorke, 2001; Murphy and Roopchand, 2003; Hands *et al.*, 2007). To some extent, a polarisation of provisions for the needs of WP students can hence be seen as taking place, as less prestigious universities develop facilities such as childcare provision in hope of attracting students, while high-tariff universities that do not need WP students close down the same services.

HE students from non-traditional backgrounds are seen as being frequently perceived as a risk to universities and to the state that invests in them (Leathwood and O'Connell, 2003). Across the UK HE sector, OFFA statistics show that intelligent children from the richest 20 per cent of homes in England are seven times more likely to attend a high-ranking university than intelligent children from the poorest 40 per cent, compared to six times more likely in the mid-1990s. That decreases in the proportion of students from disadvantaged backgrounds attending elite UK institutions have fallen over recent years against the backdrop of WP initiatives demonstrates the challenging environment in which the continuing battle for greater equity is fought. The message conveyed by such inequalities of access within the sector is stark, as Woodley and Wilson observed with regard to mature students: 'because the more elite universities recruit...fewer mature students one might conclude that they [a]re not a highly sought after commodity' (Woodley and Wilson, 2002). This observation is equally true of other WP student groups.

The contemporary move towards more private universities, which set their own fees and are not democratically accountable, will affect WP students, who may be drawn towards competitive course fees, attractive admission requirements or flexible learning arrangements. The detrimental impact of such unmoderated private universities upon some of the most vulnerable HE students is already apparent in the United States, and it is particularly relevant that in the United Kingdom developing private universities will largely offer vocational courses such as teaching, which have high uptake amongst WP student groups.

The chapters

This book draws together the insights of experts on issues in contemporary HE. In doing so, it presents contrasting perspectives on important aspects of the WP agenda, representing the breadth of the UK HEI sector as well as WP groups in their diversity of circumstances. Perspectives from international colleagues and UK scholars of international HE locate the WP agenda in the context of the globalised education marketplace. Commentators utilise their expertise to provide historical context, empirical and statistical evidence as well as theoretical analysis, and to locate developments in WP in the context of up-to-date policy. In particular, realised and projected impacts of recent far-reaching HE policy developments are identified with regard to a range of relevant issues.

The first part addresses broad issues around the inclusion and exclusion of different groups in UK HE. In Chapter 2 Miriam David explores the changing concepts of equity, charting the shift from gender equality, with a focus on women's educational access in the 20th century, to questions of men's participation in the 21st century. These changing concepts of equity are linked to wider social and economic transformations, the expansion of HE and the growth in the knowledge economy, or what has been called 'academic capitalism'. The chapter explores how notions of WP in policy and practice have frequently focused on equity, with a focus on social class, socio-economic disadvantage, ethnicity and race at the expense of gender questions. It draws on research evidence from the Teaching and Learning Research Programme (TLRP), the United Kingdom's largest ever initiative in education research about equity and diversity in UK HE, showing how incorporation of diversity questions has cost the discussion of gender its critical and feminist edge. The chapter concludes by focusing on the future of HE policies and practices in addressing equity and diversity.

Chapter 3, written by Mantz Yorke, addresses the charge that WP leads to an inevitable decline in academic standards, indicated by the simultaneous trends of participation by students with lower academic results, alongside rising university attainment levels. Yorke challenges elitist assumptions of the masses entering HE to take 'Mickey Mouse degrees'. Instead he argues that while it is predominantly the new university sector that has absorbed WP students, it is the elite institutions that have seen the highest relative gains in degree attainment. This leads Yorke to postulate alternative explanations for rising attainment levels and their spread across the sector. These include increased specification of learning outcomes giving students a clearer indication of what is expected of them in terms of assessment and the shift away from formal examinations towards coursework. Yorke further suggests that the academic performance of less financially privileged students is increasingly threatened by employment pressures and that these students are most concentrated in new universities.

In Chapter 4 Alan Woodley looks at how the demographic characteristics of OU students have changed over the institution's 40-year history. He examines how with its distance delivery and its open entry the OU was intended to be 'open as to people', focusing on providing second-chance opportunities to older people. But Woodley argues that contrary to assumptions, growth patterns for some WP groups, including part-time women students and students with disabilities, are actually lower in the OU compared with the HE sector as a whole. Further, he identifies the rising cost of university participation as having informed a 30 per cent increase in OU students aged 18 or 19 over the past year, in contrast to its original focus on students aged over 21. He suggests that this trend is likely to continue as alongside the potential financial benefits of combining paid employment with part-time study, the latest round of course fees announced make the OU an attractive option comparative to other HEIs.

Part II of the book explores issues of access and motivation in students' engagement with HE as non-traditional students. In Chapter 5, Yvette Taylor discusses undergraduate student involvement in WP initiatives at a traditional university, and the ways that students promote and market their university and HE more generally, drawing on a C-SAP[1] research project. She explores the WP messages disseminated by students in their outreach work with school pupils and teachers, the ways that these are taken up and/or resisted, and the interactions between university students and 'local' schools. Taylor identifies the significance of notions of 'us' and 'them' for university student participants in such programmes, suggesting that social class is mobilised in constructions of the 'good student' as against the 'bad pupil', leading her to question the assumptions of the 'all round benefits' of such WP work.

Chapter 6 by Ruth Woodfield explores how research on mature women students' HE participation is too often dominated by a 'discourse of disadvantage'. Without undermining the specific challenges faced by the group, including in terms of caring commitments, finances and extracurricular engagement, Woodfield identifies important areas of HE engagement in which mature students are comparatively more successful than younger students. These include their likelihood of securing a graduate-level job at the end of their degree course. This chapter discusses the extent to which mature women students' enhanced post-degree employability is recognised by commentators, policymakers and mature women students. The discussion draws on quantitative data alongside qualitative interviews with mature women students discussing their motivations for HE participation and awareness of their comparative employability.

Chapter 7 by Tamsin Hinton-Smith explores lone parents' motivations for and hoped for effects of HE participation. The chapter draws on longitudinal qualitative research with 77 lone parents studying at UK HEIs. It identifies the determination and deferred gratification mobilised by lone parent HE students to persist in HE participation despite the extreme deficits of time and financial security they must frequently negotiate to do so. Lone-parent students' narratives are used to demonstrate the complex interweaving of instrumental employment-oriented goals with intrinsic motivations in terms of personal development, giving something back to society and providing a positive role model to children. The chapter identifies how lone parents use HE participation to challenge stigmatised stereotypes of scrounging welfare dependency and poor parenting.

Part III focuses on WP students' experiences once engaged in HE. Chapter 8 by Mary Stuart, Catherine Lido and Jessica Morgan examines how different student groups engage with extracurricular activities at university and how this engagement is perceived by employers, alumni and the students themselves. Such activities are described as including union clubs and societies, volunteering and class representation, part-time work, family commitments and community activities. The authors explain how patterns of participation in extracurricular activities differ according to students' ages, gender, ethnicity and social class, as well as between different types of institutions. Based on a study conducted for the Higher Education

Academy (HEA) in the United Kingdom, the chapter draws on a 'sociology of higher education choice' (Reay *et al.*, 2005) alongside Bourdieu's theory of cultural capital, habitus and taste (Bourdieu and Passeron, 1977; Bourdieu, 1985) to elucidate how different student groups make decisions about their student lifestyle and what implications these 'choices' have on their graduate prospects.

In Chapter 9 Lynda Measor, Paula Wilcox and Philip Frame explore the transition to HE as trauma or transformation for non-traditional students. In doing so they address the question of why after having achieved the required academic proficiency to gain access to HE, non-traditional students do less well than their traditional peers. The chapter draws on recent qualitative empirical research to examine the factors governing non-traditional students' transitions to HE. These factors are located within the frameworks of identity formation and acculturation, centrally invoking the notion of 'status passages', whereby individuals undergo changes in status, identity and sense of self. The authors argue that while the transition to HE is an expected, accepted *rite de passage* for traditional students, non-traditional students' prior experiences are not granted equal status, leaving them less well-equipped to make the transition.

Chapter 10 by Barbara Merrill focuses on the access, retention and drop-out of non-traditional adult students in HE. Drawing on biographical data from a European project, the chapter discusses why some non-traditional adult students 'keep on going on' and complete their undergraduate courses and why others from similar socio-economic backgrounds drop out. Merrill suggests that although some drop out, often for complex reasons, this should not always be seen as negative. In contrast, she argues that for some non-traditional students who do not ultimately complete their course, their participation in HE learning may nevertheless have impacted on them in positive ways. The chapter focuses on issues of class and gender and biographical stories within the framework of Bourdieu's concept of habitus and Honneth's concept of respect.

In Chapter 11 John Field and Natalie Morgan-Klein examine the ways in which non-traditional students view their existing social relations as a resource, while also developing new social relations with fellow students and academic staff. In doing so they build on previous work on social relationships and HE participation, drawing on current research into retention of non-traditional students. They conclude by suggesting that while there is widespread recognition of the importance of the support provided by peer group, family and other connections to HE students, universities rarely explore the implications of access to support networks for students' decisions to leave or persist.

The final part of the book locates developments and debates related to WP in international context, with perspectives from Sweden, France, Spain, Ghana, Tanzania and the United States. Caroline Berggren and Christina

Cliffordson provide a historical overview of WP in Sweden in Chapter 12. They document the changing rationale for WP in Sweden from one of equality to efficiency, by charting the development and impact of national regulations in both HE and compulsory schooling that have influenced the university participation of different groups of students. For example they explore how changes to admissions criteria, including recognition of employment experience, have increased opportunities for an educational second chance for older students. However educational tracks in secondary school have continued to steer working-class men and women into gender-segregated and class-specific vocations, including builders, electricians and child carers, respectively, with their associated long hours and low pay. Berggren and Cliffordson indicate that HE participation by working-class men remains stubbornly low in Sweden, with governmental initiatives to counteract the effects of family background counterbalanced by early educational choices, whereby children as young as 12 years make subject-choice decisions that pivotally steer their future educational and employment options towards or away from HE and professional careers.

In Chapter 13 Marie-Pierre Moreau explores patterns of WP in French HE. Moreau draws on policy documents, key literature and empirical evidence, including national statistics which show the persistence of divides based on social class, gender and ethnicity. She discusses how students' participation and experiences of HE are shaped by these demographic characteristics, arguing that French HE policy and academic discourses have sidelined gender and ethnicity. Moreau documents the way in which the inclusion of working-class students and their access to the most elite segment of the education system have been a topic of interest and concern amongst French policymakers and academics for some time, as exemplified by the work of Pierre Bourdieu. In contrast, she suggests, differences relating to gender and ethnicity have not attracted a similar level of interest or intervention in French HE access.

M. Teresa Padilla-Carmona introduces the Spanish WP context in Chapter 14. She explores the relative newness of debate around WP and non-traditional students in Spanish HE, despite the ever-increasing numbers of students from non-conventional populations entering the system. Padilla-Carmona draws on statistical data as well as the developing body of Spanish WP initiatives and literature to identify trends and advances in participation, and graduate employment outcomes for non-traditional students in Spain. These groups include mature and economically under-privileged students and those with disabilities. Padilla-Carmona explores the experience of non-traditional students in Spanish HE, through research on teacher-training students – a pathway heavily overrepresented by students from non-traditional backgrounds. Exploring the extent to which course provision and WP initiatives meet students' needs and circumstances, Padilla-Carmona further locates her findings within the context of current reform in teacher training, presenting preliminary predictions of their impact on participation by non-traditional students.

In Chapter 15, Louise Morley discusses the impact of WP initiatives in Ghana and Tanzania, drawing on extensive ESRC–DFID[2] funded research, including interviews with students, staff and policymakers. Morley presents evidence of positive and enabling experiences of HE amongst WP students in universities in both countries, including supportive lecturers, well-taught programmes, positive relations with other students and stories of developing networks, self-confidence and self-efficacy. However, she also presents evidence of widely reported negative experiences, including lack of or the poor quality of facilities and resources, large classes, poor pedagogy, lecturers' lack of professionalism, problems with assessment, favouritism, corruption and lack of transparency in admissions procedures and student loan entitlements. Morely explains how in spite of widespread problems, WP students in Ghana and Tanzania remain motivated to persist in HE by its value in enhancing social mobility, status and employability.

Anne J. MacLachlan explores participation in HE in the United States in terms of gender and ethnicity in Chapter 16. She provides evidence that increases in the educational level of the general population since World War II have not produced parity, and that today increasing numbers of Americans are excluded from educational opportunity and related economic mobility as a result of decades of poor public policy and more recent polarising politics. MacLachlan argues that the poverty of excluded groups is sustained by low educational opportunities, leading to low-paid employment. She identifies those most negatively affected as being women of all ethnicities, black Americans, Latinos and native Americans. MacLachlan discusses the detrimental operation of a many-tiered hierarchical HE system in the United States, with access for excluded students concentrated in the lower status echelons, which also have the lowest levels of HE outcomes, with high dropout rates. MacLachlan identifies this as particularly concerning in light of the high cost of HE in the United States, meaning that many of the poorest and most vulnerable students are incurring huge HE debts without ultimately securing a degree qualification.

In Chapter 17 Sarah Earl-Novell explores the success of WP initiatives in contributing to efforts to diversify the undergraduate student body and increase the representation of minority and mature students and those from lower socio-economic backgrounds. She particularly addresses the potential of online provision to widen access to HE opportunities, focusing on the University of California's controversial effort to become one of the first 'elite' institutions to deliver online undergraduate education through the development of a 'virtual university'. Earl-Novell examines how, while extending online HE provision has the potential to increase access, it has generated widespread concerns around the dilution of quality. She investigates the persistence of gendered divisions in HE participation, and considers the potential of online provision to impact upon these and other participation inequalities.

Chapter 18 by Tamsin Hinton-Smith concludes the volume by drawing together the insights provided by the collection's contributors into their countries and specialism on WP perspectives. The chapter takes stock of achievements in WP, acknowledging the importance of the global growth and inevitable diversification of HE participation over the last half century. These achievements are weighed against the persistence of inequalities in access and participation experience, but perhaps most significantly in the perpetuation of elitist ideals around good and bad students, institutions and courses, and the part these play in maintaining exclusion from privilege within the context of WP. The significance of such processes is further considered in relation to HE outcomes for WP students, including issues around non-completion and career progression. The chapter reviews some of the significant diversity in the HE experiences of different demographic WP groups, also considering the impact of contrasting country focus on particular demographic variables in WP work. The role of universities is asserted in promoting, supporting and taking responsibility for WP, including acknowledging and validating the significance of WP students' wider lives for their HE participation. The chapter concludes the volume by considering why WP matters, both in terms of providing a balance against the extension of the neo-liberal project into HE provision and in terms of identifying central elements of good practice that are (increasingly) relevant to all students. In doing so, it finishes by considering priorities for supporting the future of WP.

Notes

1. C-**SAP** is the Higher Education Academy Subject Network for Sociology, Anthropology and Politics.
2. Economic and Social Research Council, and Department for International Development.

Bibliography

Aimhigher (2007) *About Aimhigher* [online] http://www.aimhigher.ac.uk/about_us/about_aimhigher.cfm [accessed 1 August 2007, the website no longer exists].

Barnes, C. and Mercer, G. (2009) *Exploring Disability* (Cambridge: Polity Press).

Becker, G. ([1964]1994) *Human Capital: A Theoretical and Empirical Analysis with Special Reference to Education* (Chicago: The University of Chicago Press).

Bhattacharyya, G., Ison, L. and Blair, M. (2003) *Minority Ethnic Attainment and Participation in Education and Training: The Evidence,* Department for Education and Skills Research Report 01–03.

Bourdieu, P. (1985) 'The Genesis of the Concepts of Habitus and of Field', *Sociocriticism,* 2: 11–24.

Bourdieu, P. and Passeron, J. (1977) *Reproduction in Education, Society and Culture* (London: Sage).

Brennan, J., Mills, J., Shah, T. and Woodley, A. (1999) *Part-Time Students and Employment: Report of a Survey of Students, Graduates and Diplomats* (London: DfEE/HEQE/QSE).

Burke, P. and McManus, J. (2010) *Art for a Few: Exclusion and Misrecognition in Art and Design Higher Education Admissions* (London: National Arts Learning Network).

Callender, C. (2002) 'The Costs of Widening Participation: Contradictions in New Labour's Student Funding Policies', *Social Policy and Society*, 1 (2): 83–94.

Callender, C. and Kemp, M. (2000) *Changing Student Finances: Income, Expenditure and the Take-Up of Student Loans Among Full Time and Part-Time Higher Education Students in 1998-99*. DfEE Research Report, 213 (London: DfEE).

Christie, H., Munro, M. and Wager, F. (2005) 'Day Students in Higher Education: Widening Access Students and Successful Transitions to University Life,' *International Studies in the Sociology of Education*, 15 (1): 3–30.

Connor, H., Tyers, C., Modood, T. and Hillage, J. (2004) *Why the Difference? A Closer Look at Ethnic Minority Students and Graduates?* Research Report No. 552. (London: DfES).

Deer, C. (2005) 'Higher Education Access and Expansion: The French Experience,' *Higher Education Quarterly*, 59 (3): 230–241. [online] http://www.employment-studies.co.uk/news/es6art5.php [accessed 20 August 2007].

Delors, J. (1996) *Learning: The Treasure Within*. Report to UNESCO of the International Commission on Education for the Twenty-First Century [online] http://unesdoc.unesco.org/images/0010/001095/109590eo.pdf [accessed 7 October 2011].

Department for Education and Skills (2003) *The Future of Higher Education* [online] http://www.bis.gov.uk/assets/biscore/corporate/migratedd/publications/f/future_of_he.pdf [accessed 5 June 2011].

Edwards, R. (1993) *Mature Women Students: Separating or Connecting Family and Education* (London: Taylor and Francis).

Egerton, M. (2000) 'Monitoring Contemporary Student Flows and Characteristics: Secondary Analyses Using the Labour Force Survey and the General Household Survey,' *Journal of the Royal Statistical Society, B*, 163 (Part 1): 63–80.

Gallagher, A., Richards, N. and Locke, M. (1993) *Mature Students in Higher Education: How Institutions Can Learn from Experience*, University of East London.

Hands, A., Mackay, J., Ormiston-Smith, N., Perryman, S. and Wright-Anderson, P. (2007) *Staying the Course: The Retention of Students in Higher Education*. National Audit Office Report (London: The Stationary Office).

Hefce (Higher Education Funding Council for England) (2007) *The Hefce Equality Scheme* [online] www.actiononaccess.org/.../files/resources__HEFCE_Equality_scheme.doc [accessed 30 September 2011].

Hefce (2011) *Funding for Universities and Colleges for 2010-11 and 2011-12* [online] http://www.hefce.ac.uk/pubs/circlets/2011/cl05_11/ [accessed 30 September 2011].

HESA (2011) 'Table T1a – Participation of under-represented groups in higher education: young full-time first degree entrants 2010/11', [online] http://www.hesa.ac.uk/index.php?option=com_content&task=view&id=2060&Itemid=141 [accessed 20 August 2012].

Hinton-Smith, T. (2012) *Lone Parents' Experiences as Higher Education Students* (Leicester: Niace).

HM Government (2011) *Opening Doors, Breaking Barriers: A Strategy for Social Mobility* [online] http://download.cabinetoffice.gov.uk/social-mobility/opening-doors-breaking-barriers.pdf [accessed 17 May 2011].

Jackson, S. (2004) *Differently Academic? Developing Lifelong Learning for Women in Higher Education* (Netherlands: Kluwer).

Jenkins, S.P. and Symons, E.J. (2001) 'Childcare Costs and Lone Mothers Employment Rates,' *The Manchester School*, 69 (2): 121–147. March (Blackwell Publishers Ltd and the Victoria University of Manchester.

Jones, K. (2006) 'Valuing Diversity and Widening Participation: The Experiences of ACCESS to Social Work Students in Further and Higher Education', *Social Work Education*, 25 (5): 485–500.

Kerr, S. (2011) ' "Poverty and Ethnicity: Exploring the Connections", National Campaign Director, Race for Opportunity Business in the Community', *Poverty and Ethnicity Seminar*, Joseph Rowntree Foundation, London.

Komulainen, K. (2000) 'The Past is Difference – The Difference Is Past', *Gender and Education*, 12 (4): 449–462.

Laing, C., Chao, K.M. and Robinson, A. (2005) 'Managing the Expectations of Non-Traditional Students: A Process of Negotiation,' *Journal of Further and Higher Education*, 29 (2): 169–179.

Leathwood, C. and O'Connell, P. (2003) ' "It's a Struggle": The Construction of the "New Student" in Higher Education', *Journal of Education Policy*, 18 (6): 597–615.

Leonard, M. (1994) 'Mature Women and Access to HE', in Davies, S., Lubelska, C., and Quinn, J. (eds.) *Changing the Subject: Women in Higher Education* (London: Taylor and Francis, pp. 163–177).

Liberal Democrat Inequality Consultation paper 102 (2011) [online] http://www.libdems.org.uk/siteFiles/resources/PDF/conference/Spr11%20Inequality%20consultation%20paper%20CLEAR%20PRINT.pdf [accessed 7 October 2011].

Merrill, B. (1999) *Gender, Change and Identity: Mature Women Students in Universities* (Aldershot: Ashgate).

Murphy, H. and Roopchand, N. (2003) 'Intrinsic Motivation and Self-Esteem in Traditional and Mature Students at a Post-1992 University in the North-East of England', *Educational Studies*, 29 (2–3): 243–259.

Naidoo, R. and Callender, C. (2000) 'Towards a More Inclusive System of HE? Contemporary Policy Reform in Higher Education', in Dean, H., Sykes, R. and Wood, R. (eds.) *Social Policy Review* 12 (Newcastle: Social Policy Association, Newcastle pp. 224–249).

Oliver, M. (1996) *Understanding Disability: From Theory to Practice* (London: Macmillan).

Panel on Fair Access to the Professions (2009) *Unleashing Aspiration: The Final Report of the Panel on Fair Access to the Professions* (London: The Cabinet Office). [online] http://www.bis.gov.uk/assets/biscore/corporate/migratedd/publications/p/panel-fair-access-to-professions-final-report-21july09.pdf [accessed 13 June 2011].

Purcell, K., Elias, P. and Atfield, G. (2009) *Analysing the Relationship Between Participation and Educational and Career Development Patterns and Outcomes: A New Classification of Higher Education Institutions*. Futuretrack Working Paper 1, IER/HECSU (Warwick: University of Warwick).

Reay, D. (2003) 'A Risky Business? Mature Working-Class Women Students and Access to Higher Education,' *Gender and Education*, 15 (3): 301–317.

Reay, D., David., M. and Ball, S. (2005) *Degrees of Choice Social Class, Race and Gender in Higher Education* (Stoke-on-Trent: Trentham Books).

Schultz, T. (1961) 'Investment in Human Capital', *American Economic Review*, 51 (1): 1–17.

Shakespeare, T.W. and Watson, N. (2002) 'The Social Model of Disability: An Outmoded Ideology', *Research in Social Science and Disability*, 2: 21–28.

Shiner, M. and Modood, T. (2002) 'Help or Hindrance? Higher Education and the Route to Ethnic Equality', *British Journal of Sociology of Education*, 23 (2): 209–232.

Taylor, Y. (2007) 'Going Up Without Going Away? Working-Class Women in Higher Education', *Youth and Policy*, 94: 35–50.

The Guardian (2006) 'The Changing Face of Success', 1 August [online] http://education.guardian.co.uk/higher/news/story/0,,1834155,00.html [accessed 16 Feb 2008].

The Guardian (2007) 'Participation Problems Persist', 26 June [online] http://education.guardian.co.uk/higher/comment/story/0,,2110973,00.html [accessed 2 August 2007].

Tomlinson, S. (2005) *Education in a Post-Welfare Society* (Maidenhead: Open University Press).

Wain, K. (2000) 'The Learning Society: Postmodern Politics,' *International Journal of Lifelong Education*, 19: 36–53.

Watson, D. (2007) *Keynote Address,* Centre for Higher Education and Equity Research (CHEER) Launch, University of Sussex, 15th November 2007.

Wilkinson, R. and Pickett, K. (2011) *The Spirit Level* (London: Penguin).

Woodley, A. and Wilson, J. (2002) 'British Higher Education and Its Older Clients,' *Higher Education*, 44: 329–347.

Yorke, M. (2001) 'Outside Benchmark Expectations? Variation in Non-completion Rates in English Higher Education', *Journal of Higher Education Policy and Management*, 23 (2): 147–158.

2
Changing Policy Discourses on Equity and Diversity in UK Higher Education: What Is the Evidence?

Miriam E. David

Introduction

Widening participation in higher education (HE) became a major policy discourse in the United Kingdom at the beginning of the 21st century, although it had its origins in the expansions of educational opportunity in the last third of the 20th century. As the second decade of the 21st century opened, the policy discourses around widening participation shifted towards a concern with social mobility rather than equity and diversity that underpinned previous policy agendas. This chapter considers these changing policy discourses on widening participation to HE and also reviews some of the policy evidence-base on which changes have been developed. The focus is on the social and educational research undertaken in England commissioned by the UK government to underpin the new Labour policy initiatives around the notion of widening participation or 'fair' access to HE (David, 2009a). All these developments have taken place in a changing socio-economic and political context, in which HE has played an increasingly important role: the so-called global knowledge economy or 'academic capitalism' (Slaughter and Rhoades, 2004; David, 2011).

Changing political and social contexts

During the last third of the 20th century, United Kingdom and global HE expanded inexorably in response to economic and social changes, although the form and types of the system varied greatly. The principle of equality of educational opportunity had underpinned post-war expansions of education, initially in terms of the development of 'secondary education for all', regardless of family backgrounds of poverty or privilege (David, 1980). This principle was subsequently extended to post-compulsory education and different forms of educational provision in colleges and forms of HE including universities. Initially, the focus of the policy discourse was for the expansion to include provisions for various social groups such as those from socio-economically disadvantaged family backgrounds or social classes, and it became increasingly finely nuanced and specified, linked to developing subjects and the changing economy. Notions of merit or abilities to participate in HE also bore on the changing provisions (David, 2009a).

Expansion of post-war educational opportunities also began to include the question of both male and female participation as a response to changing patterns of women's involvement in family, the economy and labour markets. The questions of educational opportunities for women, especially, became an explicit component of the policy discourses in the 1970s, partly as a response to changing economic circumstances and also as a response to women's involvement and activism especially through the emerging feminist movement, linked to wider social, civil and human rights movements for change (see, for example, David, 2003). However, during the 1980s, in the United Kingdom under Thatcherism, policy discourses about educational and social expansion became increasingly contested and challenging, linked as they were to questions of the changing needs of the economy and the ideological moves towards a renewed economic liberalism, by contrast with previous social democracy and liberalism (David, 2003).

Thatcherite expansions of education were increasingly linked to economic needs, including computing and information technology expansions, and continued perforce under the subsequent Major administrations. Neo-liberalism became the mantra of these Conservative administrations, although it remains debatable the extent to which Thatcherism embraced both forms of economic liberalism with social authoritarianism or neo-conservatism across the varied areas of social policy. Most academic commentators agree that in the arena of educational policies, the critical emphasis has been on the development of marketisation and privatisation, leading to the creation of educational markets, choice and competition balanced with quality standards and controls. However, the processes of educational expansion continued under Thatcher's administrations and indeed the first coinage of the term 'widening participation' in the HE policy arena began with her as Secretary of State for Education in the Heath government of 1970–1974. Thatcher's policy was to widen access for mature students (David, 1993).

It is also the case that in a paradoxical fashion post-war educational policies and practices, linked to social changes, meant that in the era of Thatcherism, the gender gap in schooling closed, and in many areas was reversed. As we argued in *Closing the Gender Gap: postwar education and social change* (1999), drawing on Thatcher's own autobiography:

> She found herself in a contradictory position, and found it very hard to impose Victorian family values and indeed she appeared to accomplish the very opposite ... [and] enhance the advancement of women's educational and public achievements such that 'ordinary' girls began to desert the traditionally female educational avenues directed towards family life ...
>
> (1999: 42–47)

We concluded:

> In the UK, schooling appears to have broken with the traditions of the gender order. It is this decisive break with the social and educational past that lies behind the closing of the gender gap.
>
> (Arnot *et al.*, 1999: 156)

We were, however, perhaps overly optimistic about the trends towards the closing of the gender gap across all social classes and its political implications. A policy backlash, given the trends towards neo-liberalism, developed such that feminist values were made invisible across the polity.

Indeed, the rise of the new Labour government in 1997 did not challenge the economic developments towards markets and individualisation but shifted some of the policy discourses around the expansion and the necessity of HE as part of the economic landscape. It was under the new Labour government that the discourse of widening participation in HE came to its zenith. This was about participation and fair access to HE, largely in terms of disadvantaged social groups, although broadly defined, and including social class, gender, ethnicity, disability and race. Indeed, a keynote transformation under the new Labour regime was the recreation of an equality agenda and the creation of legislative principles about ensuring equality duties, which were nevertheless on individualistic grounds. Over the 13 years of new Labour administrations, HE was a major policy discourse, amassing the policy evidence-base and the process of implementation, especially around widening participation, linked to the emerging discourse about the knowledge economy, as illustrated below.

Nevertheless, these policy developments remained firmly rooted in an individualistic neo-liberal policy discourse, increasingly linked to an economic agenda, and concern with the rising costs of HE, a major legacy of Thatcherism. Towards the end of the third Labour administration, in 2009, the name of the government department responsible for HE was changed to the Department for Innovation, Universities and Skills (DIUS) and was separated from the departments for children, schools and families, and also business and industry, illustrating the changing policy terrain. Moreover, the terms of the debate were changed with the commissioning of a report about how to provide sustainable HE by the then Secretary of State for DIUS, Lord Peter Mandelson. The Browne Committee, however, did not report until after the general election in May 2010 (Browne Report, 2010).

Under the newly elected coalition government in May 2010, the policy discourse again took forward a more individualistic agenda around social mobility, as had been pre-empted by the Milburn Inquiry for the new Labour government (2009). During the first year, the coalition government consolidated a narrowing of the policy discourse, through the creation of yet another newly configured Department for Business, Innovation and Skills (BIS) and arguments about the necessity of an austerity culture. This department under a Liberal Democrat Secretary of State Vince Cable and his Universities Minister David Willetts has been pro-active in transforming the HE policy agenda towards an even more individualistic and financially focused one, without much regard to equalities on the agenda or the research evidence for the policies. By June 2011, the coalition government launched its social mobility strategy through HE transforming the policy discourses about equity and diversity. I turn now to illustrate these changing policy and ideological approaches, whereby inequalities in access to and participation in HE have become increasingly contested and challenging issues, within a neo-liberal political context. I will return to discuss the reformed policy discourses in the conclusion of this chapter.

Policy discourses about equity and diversity: Evidence from the Teaching and Learning Research Programme

The new Labour government policies developed around competing and divergent concepts of equity and widening participation, although the focus was largely on access to HE rather than participation throughout HE leading to equity in academic achievements. The Higher Education Act 2004 altered the financing of student participation in higher education through student fees, with higher education institutions (HEIs) able to charge an array of fees for undergraduate study. At the same time, an Office for Fair Access (OFFA) was created to act as a form of quality control on the operation of institutional measures on bursaries and plans for widening access and participation. Aimhigher,[1] a scheme targeted at schoolchildren to try to raise their aspirations and expectations about particular forms of HE, was also inaugurated.

In 2005, this government, through its Higher Education Funding Council for England (HEFCE) and the Economic and Social Research Council (ESRC), commissioned the Teaching and Learning Research Programme (TLRP) to undertake seven projects on widening participation in HE. Our work, in keeping with UK policy developments, was largely around socio-economic disadvantage or working-class students rather than gender. There was a huge debate about which were the key new groups to be the focus of attention – those from low social classes (such as the working class) or socially disadvantaged as low socio-economic group or status (SES) or other markers of socio-economic position such as income or employment (David, 2009a). Questions were raised about parental education as well as parental employment, concentrating attention on school leavers and young people rather than those who are non-traditional students in terms of age of potential participation and access. The policy debate was also narrowly focused upon a particular way of conceptualising lack of participation, ignoring wider cultural issues, such as ethnicity or race. Gender, however, did not enter this debate despite feminist contestation (Morley, 2003; Evans, 2004; Hey, 2004; Leathwood and Read, 2009; Morley and David, 2009), because there was a growing assumption in mainstream UK public policies that gender equality has been 'achieved' for women students and that the problem is now one of male disadvantage (HEFCE, 2005; Bekhradnia, 2009).

Whilst there was intensive debate about which types of individuals and HEIs to include, there was no question about concern focusing on initial undergraduate or first-degree student participation. Wakeling and Kyriacou (2010) made this point strongly in their recent UK research synthesis: What is the research evidence drawn from seven interdisciplinary projects commissioned by HEFCE on the UK government's policies to widen access to, and participation within, HE, as presented in *Improving Learning by Widening Participation in Higher Education* (David, 2009a)?

No one concept of equity underpinned all the studies, although concepts about learners' identities and backgrounds of social class, socio-economic disadvantage, ethnicity, increasingly multi-cultural communities and gender were used. Given the English policy focus, definitions of widening participation concentrated upon socio-economic disadvantage, SES or working class and diversity rather than more multi-cultural questions about ethnicity, race or the newly emerging issues concerning international students, whether from Africa, Asia, Europe or the other nations of the United Kingdom. UK public policy concerns about 'working class' entry to elite universities (defined in terms of international university league tables) underpinned the initial research focus and designs.

The findings from across all seven projects emphasise the diversity of student participation in a diverse, inequitable and stratified HE system. We addressed participation across the life course, questioning the international league table approach to higher learning and the relevance of HE to people across their lives. We also addressed the appropriate national and international policy contexts for post-compulsory education for a more equitable system across a diversity of subjects and HEIs in the 21st century, given the expansions of academic capitalism. It is amply demonstrated that recent UK government policies have led to increasing, if not widening, opportunities for learners from diverse families and disadvantaged socio-economic backgrounds (David, 2009a).

The policies have not led to fair access or recruitment to all types of HE or to equal benefits in the graduate or professional labour markets in contexts of academic capitalism. Nevertheless, we show, in our summary chapters, that policies have also provided opportunities for new institutional practices and pedagogies to engage diverse students, including gendered and racialised students for the 21st century (David, 2009a: 180–201). We see how influential critical and feminist pedagogies have been and what the potential for inclusive pedagogies might be in a changed policy environment.

The research team, led by Parry (David, 2009a: 31–47), studied policies to broaden participation by offering HE in further education (FE) colleges and provided the contextualisation of these policies, practices and strategies. In England, the higher and FE sectors have different and separate funding and quality regimes. Government policy has expanded HE in the FE sector to make it easier for colleges to operate within two funding systems. Rather than identify a special or specific mission for colleges in HE, these compete and collaborate with universities in the same markets for college students.

We linked English policies on widening participation and institutional differentiation to wider international debates about the role of lower tier colleges in the democratisation of access and the diversion of demand. We showed that English policies militate against such new open systems, given the asymmetries of power and advantage. We provided a clear map of systemic and systematic differentiation in HE and demonstrate how this leads away from equalising opportunities and outcomes for diverse gendered and racialised students towards different regimes of practice.

Having presented detailed contextual evidence from Parry's team's project, we went on to consider undergraduate students' pathways into and through HE (David, 2009a: 47–95). Parry's team also considered student progress and progression around 'seamlessness and separation' between HE offered in further and HEIs (David, 2009a). A 'seamless' system of tertiary education may be desirable and possible, but our research evidence suggests that institutions, staff and students treat FE and HE as separate enterprises, affecting the practices of students and tutors at various stages in the student lifecycle and the imagined futures at the end of college study. The 'logic of practice' throughout these various stages is related to implicit and explicit awareness of the gendered, stratified and differentiated nature of HE. Here, the critique of seamlessness, and the emphasis on separation between the more privileged HEIs, such as Russell group universities, is at the expense of the less privileged and lower status colleges.

Similarly, three other projects focused on access and retention of individual undergraduate students. Vignoles' team (David, 2009a: 47–62 and 124–132) undertook a large-scale quantitative cohort study (young people aged 16 in state schools in 2004–2005) of students' access, participation and disadvantage in HE using an innovative linkage of newly available official datasets and sophisticated modelling techniques. Access to UK HE has increased dramatically: women especially have increased their participation relative to 'traditional' students, defined as male, white and middle class, and now outnumber men. This team focused particularly on the extent to which differences in university participation between advantaged and disadvantaged students are driven by their very different prior educational experiences. Male and female children from poor (low SES) backgrounds remain far less likely to go to university than more advantaged children. Controlling for individual characteristics, such as gender, however, reduces the gap, and once prior attainment is controlled for, the disparity disappears. In other words, females have higher attainment than males whatever the SES and are more likely to participate in HE. When poor students, mainly female, participate, they attend lower status universities (in league table terms).

The socio-economic gap in HE participation is because poorer (or socioeconomically disadvantaged) pupils do not achieve as highly in state secondary school as their more socio-economically advantaged counterparts (and this ignores the most privileged students studying in private and independent schools). Controlling for socio-economic background, most ethnic minority students are significantly more likely to participate in HE than their white British peers, confirming the success of long-standing policy measures to widen participation to ethnic minority groups (David, 2009a: 60–61). Vignoles' team showed that the issue of equal or fair access to old and research-intensive universities does not have its origins in HE recruitment, but rather in the prior educational experiences in different types of state schools.

In order to reap the rewards from a university education in the labour market, poorer students need to secure a good class of first degree. The English university system has historically had low levels of student dropout (retention), but as it has expanded, non-completion has risen (David, 2009a: 124–132). Socio-economically disadvantaged male and female recruits to HE have a lower probability of retention, taking full account of their level of prior achievement. However, mature students, the majority of whom, in the United Kingdom, are women, appear less likely to drop out than their younger peers, and are more likely to achieve a higher class of degree result. Clearly, it is critical that if educational inequalities emerge early in the education system (certainly by age 11), it is necessary to raise children's expectations, especially boys' from disadvantaged families, as they are found to be amongst the least likely to continue.

Hayward's team (David, 2009a: 75–88) looked at learners' transitions from Vocational Education and Training (VET) to HE and demonstrates similar gendered patterns of recruitment, retention and results. This analysis revealed that the proportion of students entering full-time HE with vocational qualifications rather than the General Certificate of Education (GCE) Advanced-level qualifications increased between 1995 and 2004 from 18 to 25 per cent. This growth was due to an increase in those combining vocational and academic qualifications, up from 4 to 14 per cent. Over the same period, the proportion of students entering full-time HE with only vocational qualifications decreased from 14 to 10 per cent. Including students from VET backgrounds widens instead of simply increasing participation, that is it alters the SES composition of the student population; but compared with traditional A-level students, those with VET qualifications have a much higher risk of not obtaining a place and of dropping out after their first year.

The majority of these students are young men, and these VET students are heavily under-represented in higher status universities. This uneven distribution is a result of individual and institutional processes. First-year students who had undertaken VET before they started HE describe their transition into university as a complex, often difficult, process including family commitments (especially for the women) and the jobs needed to finance their studies. Students need to be able to draw on support to overcome these difficulties, but existing mechanisms of retention are often not appropriate to deal with the complexity of issues faced by students with a VET background (who are often mature students).

Crozier's team studied how socio-economic circumstances influence the challenges facing working-class students entering university, where the majority are women (David, 2009a: 62–75). Their students (defined as either first in the family to go to HE or through their parents' occupations) were at four contrasting 'colleges' or universities (an elite, a high status, a new university and a FE college). The students were studying a range of subjects – law, engineering, history, chemistry, English and economics at the three universities, and performing arts, arboriculture and early childhood studies at the FE college. For the mainly female, working-class students, not only were their financial resources limited but so too was their route map through HE. Whilst the predominantly female students are not richly endowed with 'cultural capital' (Bourdieu, 1992), they are resourceful, determined, persevering and strongly focused. Having overcome significant challenges to get to university, such women students are determined to succeed and achieve good degree results.

Two projects concentrated on pedagogies and equitable practices for diverse gendered and racialised students (David, 2009a: 95–124). Hockings' team focused on teachers' strategies to engage diverse students, especially learning and teaching for social diversity. Using the concepts of 'academic engagement' and 'ways of knowing', they explore the conditions under which students engage with or disengage from learning in two contrasting universities (a high status and a new university) and across six different subjects – bioscience, business, computing, history, nursing and social work. They found that student diversity is multi-faceted, and students do not fit simplistic constructions of being 'traditional' or 'non-traditional' but come from a range of social, cultural and educational backgrounds, in which the majority are women and mature students. Drawing on data from classroom videos, interviews, focus groups and questionnaires, similarities and differences in teachers' pedagogic practices were found. These differences were influenced by the teachers' beliefs about their students, their own educational experiences and the ways of knowledge generation in their subject and professional communities. Student-centred and inclusive pedagogies were found to engage thoughtfully with student diversity (David, 2009a: 95–109).

Williams' team (David, 2009a: 109–124) focused on how diverse students learn mathematics for university study of science, technology, engineering or medicine (STEM). They showed how mathematics is inflected slightly differently from VET around student identities and questions of pedagogy. They found a picture of students 'aiming higher' with high expectations of going to university. Their subject choices, however, were gendered, classed and subject to strong ethnic trends. Students used ideological values to present themselves as certain kinds of people. Although the team found that the majority aspired to university, the choice of institution and kind of HE was culturally influenced, with white, British working-class and Asian female students indicating preferences for staying in their local areas. Students' decisions to participate in post-compulsory education were strategic: mathematics must be 'useful' and meaningful. A measure of success, somehow construed as 'value' by the gendered student, is an essential outcome if students are to persist in recruitment to universities.

The study also showed that different pedagogies can make a real difference to students. An inclusive approach to mathematics involves mathematicians literally devaluing mathematics as an abstract approach and making it more social. For use value, these propositions or concepts are the opposite: engaging socially in shared consumption of mathematics as a communicative practice can be satisfying for learners and teachers and can even become a pleasure shared. Thus a 'connectionist' teaching approach by contrast with a 'transmissionist' (teaching to the test) pedagogy is of more value to students' dispositions and understanding (especially for those with lower grades). The former is akin to reflexive and critical pedagogies as opposed to ones which, with the current cultures of performativity in colleges, can be damaging to students. There are also fewer female learners' narratives of mathematical success at college.

Fuller's team (David, 2009a: 132–147) uniquely focused on non-participation in HE and how adults think about their educational and social identities, given that they are qualified to participate in HE but do not all choose to participate. They looked at social networks, or 'networks of intimacy', that influence individuals' decisions about participation across the life course. They questioned how decisions are made within families and social networks about study at university, and when this decision is made, using a critical and feminist framework. Those adults with the qualifications to enter HE but who have not yet chosen to do so are seen as 'potentially recruitable' and as a pool to be tapped to deliver government participation targets. Research has not focused on mature adult decision-making about education and careers, and little is known about their values about formal learning or the relevance of HE to their lives. Fuller's team showed that, although the 'potentially recruitable' men and women might be likely to participate, given the example of their younger 'participation pioneers', they are living comfortable, stable lives and usually see little need for HE. However, the mature (women) learners want high-quality work-related and employer-supported provision and the recognised qualifications that offer economic and social returns. Choices are then clearly related not only to employment or economic benefits but also to the fit with family lives and circumstances.

These studies demonstrated how equity and diversity were currently played out in the processes of diverse UK HE, leading to inequitable pathways for individual, diverse or disadvantaged (low SES) and mainly female students through highly stratified systems of HE (defined in terms of international league tables). Nevertheless, the pedagogies and institutional practices can lead to meaningful educational engagements across the life course. The diverse practices and pedagogies across subjects may sustain or reverse patterns of differentiation and inequity. The learning outcomes through and across the life course illustrate that HE can be meaningful in people's lives – authentic, practical and relevant – as social as well as work or economic experiences. Nevertheless, policies for equity and widening participation in UK HE have not achieved either fair access or equal participation, and achieving degrees results in a diversified and highly stratified system of HE.

Changing policy discourses around gender equality

There has been a 'closing of the gender gap' (Arnot *et al.*, 1999) not only in UK HE enrolments but also in participation across UK HE (HEFCE, 2005; Bekhradnia, 2009). Bekhradnia (2009) argues that on average more women than men participate as undergraduate and first-degree students in UK HE. Altbach shows that this is also part of a global phenomenon (2010: 50):

'Widening access opens HE to people from an array of social class and educational backgrounds, but one of the most dramatic results of greater access is the expansion of enrolments by women, who now comprise a majority in many countries.'

In policy discourses, the question of how to deal with this evidence is raised simplistically as about the reverse 'gender gap': how to ensure male access and attainment rather than female equality in participation and attainment in HE. A traditional student in elite universities was not clearly typified, but the evidence of David *et al.* showed one as a 'young, white and middle class man' (David, 2009a: 13). Whilst the question of gender or women's participation had been the original concern in the United Kingdom, particularly through feminist campaigning and research, the policy debates have recently been normalised to be about working-class men (Morley and David, 2009).

As governments have increasingly sought to embed HE or universities in their policies for national developments, this focus on male students is a serious policy shift. One example was the new Labour government's White Paper published in November 2009 titled 'Higher Ambitions: The Future of Universities in a Knowledge Economy' to show how transformative universities could be for policy purposes (David, 2009b). A report of a UK Government Cabinet Office committee, a few months previously, also showed how limited UK universities had been in achieving social mobility especially into graduate professions and extending opportunities for women's participation (Milburn Report, summer 2009). Milburn argued that there remained a glass ceiling for women in graduate professions.

The coalition government has taken forward the emphasis on social mobility rather than social and gender equity in access and participation. This is most evident in the recent White Paper from BIS, 'Higher Education: Students at the Heart of the System' (June 2011). The government argues that 'higher education can be a powerful engine of social mobility, enabling able young people from low-income backgrounds to earn more than their parents'. The paper sets out two definitions of social mobility (BIS, 2011: 54) as 'inter-generational' (the extent to which people's success in life is determined by who their parents are) or 'intra-generational' (i.e. the extent to which individuals improve their position during their working lives, irrespective of where they started off). They continue:

> It can be 'relative', which refers to the comparative chances of people with different backgrounds ending up in certain social or income groups, or 'absolute' which refers to the extent to which all people are able to do better than their parents. Our focus is on relative social mobility. For any given level of skill and ambition, regardless of a person's background, everyone should have a fair chance of getting the job they want or reaching a higher income bracket.

In developing this reformed discourse, the government was highly selective in its evidence-base. First, its focus was on the completely instrumental idea of HE being about access to graduate (and potentially high-earning) jobs or earning rather than learning. There is no concern with groups whether they are social class, ethnicity, race or gender. Indeed, the government's new advocate for HE access, Simon Hughes, MP, in launching his report (July 2011) to 'improve access to higher education', which contained 33 recommendations, focused on the centrality of 'the graduate premium' to encourage disadvantaged young people into HE.

Secondly, David Willetts, Minister for Universities, in launching the White Paper blamed the entry of women into the workplace and universities for the lack of progress for men. 'Feminism trumped egalitarianism', adding that women who would otherwise have been housewives had taken university places and well-paid jobs that could have gone to ambitious working-class men. He went on to say that:

> One of the things that happened over that period was that the entirely admirable transformation of opportunities for women meant that with a lot of the expansion of education in the 1960s, 1970s and 1980s, the first beneficiaries were the daughters of middle-class families who had previously been excluded from educational opportunities...And if you put that with what is called 'assortative mating' – that well-educated women marry well-educated men – this transformation of opportunities for women ended up magnifying social divides. It is delicate territory because it is not a bad thing that women had these opportunities, but it widened the gap in household incomes because you suddenly had two-earner couples, both of whom were well-educated, compared with often workless households where nobody was educated.

Thus, the coalition government has attended selectively to the complex evidence about how to ensure equity in an expanded and diversified HE system. The government's emphasis is now firmly on ensuring an increasingly stratified system through the new provisions in the White Paper. Three different types of undergraduates are linked to different types of university or HEI – namely top students, cheap students and the rump – defined in relation to the institution and the type of student they may wish to recruit, rather than the fee they bring. So, in fact, it is differential levels of fees that are at the heart of the proposals rather than students. Elite institutions, such as the Russell group, may continue to charge the originally proposed £9,000 per annum so long as they aim to recruit the very best students as regards A levels (i.e. AAB). Indeed they are offered the carrot of more student numbers, with a total of 20,000 to bid for. Cheap students are those choosing to go to an HEI that charges under £7,000 per annum, and here again inducements to HEI are offered to increase numbers of them. Finally, new private or

FE institutions will be allowed into the marketplace, although with limited numbers.

Conclusions

It is not merely the acknowledgement of equity and gender that is important but how gender and feminist perspectives could contribute to reducing socio-economic and ethnic inequalities, and how they are based upon ethical principles that value and respect contributions from a diversity of people. The ways in which the policy discourses have developed in the United Kingdom over the last 30 years have been to use social research evidence selectively and for ideological or political purposes that do not value diversity but focus on power and privilege in an increasingly individualistic marketised system of neo-liberalism. If we value diversity and inclusion, this would not only entail the production of knowledge or research evidence, such as that from the TLRP, for policy but collaborative approaches for the 21st century, including incorporating a diversity of women in the processes of ensuring that the inclusive and flexible curricula have a strong impact upon learning outcomes and success.

If we value inclusion, teachers, practitioners and policymakers should maintain high expectations of all students, as learners, whilst recognising the diversity of their needs, cultures and identities. A vision for the global academy would surely include women's diverse perspectives on pedagogies and institutional as well as cultural perspectives. These feminist pedagogies, including inclusive, collaborative or connectionist, critical and personal pedagogies, would ensure that diverse people's lives across the life course are enhanced.

Note

1. Aimhigher ended in 2011, being replaced by the National Scholarship Programme (NSP). The NSP includes no funding for school outreach work, with ensuing ramifications predicted for promoting university participation amongst disadvantaged groups.

Bibliography

Altbach, P. (2010) 'Trouble with Numbers', *Times Higher Education*, 23 September 2010, pp. 48–50.

Arnot, M., David, M. and Weiner, G. (1999) *Closing the Gender Gap: Postwar Education and Social Change* (Cambridge: Polity Press).

Bekhradnia, B. (2009) *Male and Female Participation and Progression in Higher Education* (Oxford: Higher Education Policy Institute). [online] http://www.hepi.ac.uk/466-1850/Male-and-female-participation-and-progression-in-Higher-Education–further-analysis.html [accessed 19 September 2011].

BIS (Department for Business, Innovation and Skills) (2011) *Higher Education: Putting Students at the Heart of the System* [online] http://www.bis.gov.uk/news/ topstories/2011/Jun/he-white-paper-students-at-the-heart-of-the-system [accessed 19 September 2011].

BIS (Department for Business, Innovation and Skills) (2009) *Higher Ambitions: The Future of Universities in a Knowledge Economy* [online] http://bis.ecgroup. net/Publications/HigherEducation/HEStrategyReports/091447.aspx [accessed 20 August 2012].

Bourdieu, P. (1992) *An Invitation to Reflexive Sociology* (Cambridge: Polity Press).

Brown, P., Lauder, H. and Ashton, D. (2011) *The Global Auction: The Broken Promise of Education, Jobs, and Incomes* (New York: Oxford University Press).

Browne, J. (2010) *Securing a Sustainable Future for Higher Education*. An Independent Review of Higher Education Funding & Student Finance [online] http:// webarchive.nationalarchives.gov.uk/+/hereview.independent.gov.uk/hereview/ [accessed 20 August 2012].

Cabinet Office Strategy Unit (2009) *Unleashing Aspiration: Summary and Recommendations of the Full Report*. The Panel on Fair Access to the Professions (Milburn report).

David, M. (2011) 'Overview of Researching Global Higher Education: Challenge, Change or Crisis?' *Contemporary Social Science*, 6 (2): 147–165.

David, M. (ed.) with Bathmaker, A.-M., Crozier, G., Davis, P., Ertl, H., Fuller, A., Hayward, G., Heath, S., Hockings, C., Parry, G., Reay, D., Vignoles, A. and Williams, J. (2009a) *Improving Learning by Widening Participation in Higher Education* (London: Routledge).

David, M. (2009b) *Transforming Global Higher Education: A Feminist Perspective*, An Inaugural Professorial Lecture Institute of Education, London.

David, M. (2003) *Personal and Political: Feminisms, Sociology and Family Lives* (Stoke on Trent: Trentham Books).

David, M. (1993) *Parents, Gender and Education Reform* (Cambridge: Polity Press).

David, M. (1980) *The State, The Family and Education* (London: Routledge).

Equality Challenge Unit (2010) *Accelerating Equality in Higher Education*, Conference 17–18 November, London.

Evans, M. (2004) *Killing Thinking: The Death of the Universities* (London: Continuum).

Gale, T., Hattam, R., Comber, B., Tranter, D., Bills, D., Sellar, S. and Parker, S. (2010) *Interventions Early in School as a Means to Improve Higher Education Outcomes for Disadvantaged Students*. National Centre for Student Equity in Higher Education, University of South Australia, Adelaide, SA, Australia.

Halsey, A.H., Lauder, H., Brown, P. and Wells, A.S. (eds) (2000) *Education: Culture, Economy and Society* (Oxford: Oxford University Press).

Hey, V. (2004) 'Perverse Pleasures: Identity Work and the Paradoxes of Greedy Institutions', *Journal of International Women's Studies*, 5 (3): 33–43.

Higher Education Funding Council for England (HEFCE) (2005) *Young Participation in Higher Education* (London: HMSO).

Hughes Report (2011) *Improving Access to Higher Education* [online] http:// simonhughes.org.uk/en/article/2011/503533/simon-hughes-publishes-final-report-of-the-advocate-for-access-to-education [accessed 19 September 2011].

Leathwood, C. and Read, B. (2009) *Gender and the Changing Face of Higher Education* (Maidenhead Berks: SRHE and McGrawHill/Open University Press).

Morley, L. (2003) *Quality and Power in Higher Education* (Buckingham: SRHE and Open University Press).

Morley, L. and David, M. (2009) 'Introduction: Celebrations and Challenges: Gender in Higher Education', *Higher Education Policy*, 22: 1–2.

Slaughter, S. and Rhoades, G. (2004) *Academic Capitalism and the New Economy. Markets, State and Higher Education* (Baltimore, MA: The John Hopkins University Press).

Wakeling, P. and Kyriacou, C. (2010) *Widening Participation from Undergraduate to Postgraduate Research Degrees: A Research Synthesis* (National Coordinating Centre for Public Engagement & Economic and Social Research Council University of York).

Weiler, K. and David, M.E. (2008) 'The Personal and Political: Second Wave Feminism and Educational Research: Introduction', *Discourse*, 29 (4): 433–435.

Willetts, D. (2011) Wikipedia [online] http://en.wikipedia.org/wiki/David_Willetts [accessed 19 September 2011].

3
Widening Participation in Universities in England and Wales: Is There a Connection with Honours Degree Achievement?

Mantz Yorke

The problem: Context

The novelist Kingsley Amis once asserted forcefully, with respect to the expansion of the higher education (HE) system in the United Kingdom, that 'more will mean worse' (Amis, 1960: 9, emphasis as in original). This was at a time when the participation rate of young people was around 6 per cent. Currently, the participation rate across the United Kingdom is not far short of an order of magnitude higher. Students from traditionally disadvantaged backgrounds tend to enter HE with weaker academic qualifications and, hence, to enter the less prestigious institutions.

Whilst some choose to argue that the current level of participation in HE in the United Kingdom is too high, trends in the labour market are pointing towards the need for higher levels of expertise in the workforce (e.g. Leitch, 2006; European Commission, 2009) and, hence, to the desirability of high levels of participation. Many jobs, once routine and the province of those with limited educational qualifications, are increasingly requiring a breadth of view and a standard of professionalism associated with higher levels of education. McMahon (2009: 110) gives an example of this kind of shift:

> Janitors were normally illiterate early in the history of the United States and European Union countries […] But in the United States now they are called building custodians, and most have high school and even college degrees. They can do many things in maintaining and protecting buildings that the illiterates before them could not do, can see what needs to be done and do it on their own, and have more responsibility and more equipment to maintain.

In the national economic interest, it is difficult to argue against widened participation in HE, let alone argue for lower levels of participation.

Ball (1990), making a play on Amis' assertion but pressing for the widening of participation in the United Kingdom, argued instead that 'more means different'. A massified system should not be a larger scale replication of the elite system of the 1960s but should be qualitatively different because of the need to fulfil a broader collection of national needs. Curricula evolved as a consequence, as did approaches to the assessment of student achievement. Greater attention was given to the need to develop the employability of graduates and, hence, to what some have termed 'generic skills'.

The 'more will mean worse' line of thinking has latterly been transmuted into attacks on so-called 'Mickey Mouse degrees'[1] or 'absurd degrees like golf course studies'.[2] Sloganistic thinking of this sort overlooks the significance of the generic in contemporary HE and probably harks back to elitist conceptions of what HE should be. For around half the graduate-level jobs advertised in the United Kingdom, the subject of study is of little relevance – it is the generic capabilities of graduates that are key to their employability. Other jobs, of course, require a blend of subject-specific expertise and the generic.

Between the academic years 1994–1995 and 2006–2007 there was, in England, Wales and Northern Ireland, a fairly widespread uplift in the honours degree classifications awarded to bachelor's level students. The increase has typically been presented in the press in terms of the percentage of first-class honours degrees and has led to claims of 'grade inflation'. There is a paradox that can best be expressed in the form of a question: if HE has over the years enrolled students with weaker academic qualifications, how is it that honours degree classifications have risen – especially since research[3] confirms the strong association between entry qualifications and degree performance?

Could the widening of participation in the United Kingdom have anything to do with the uplift in honours degree awards? Publicly available data allow an initial, and necessarily circumstantial, exploration of the issue to be undertaken.

Boundaries

This chapter is limited to institutions in England and Wales that had gained the title of 'university' by 2007.[4] Specialist institutions were excluded because their profiles of entrants are often out of kilter with those of multi-disciplinary universities.

Data from the two universities in Northern Ireland were also excluded because the profile of demographic backgrounds of students in the numerically small provision of HE in that country is markedly different from those of other countries in the United Kingdom.

In Scotland, the general pattern is that young students enter HE at the age of 17; non-honours programmes are three years long; and the award of honours is typically related to a fourth year of full-time study. This differentiation from the rest of the United Kingdom, where the typical young entrant to HE enrols at 18 or 19 years of age and the bulk of honours-level programmes are three years long, means that data from Scottish institutions do not align with those from the rest of the United Kingdom, and hence Scottish universities are excluded from the analyses presented here.

Widening participation

The disparity between social groupings regarding access to HE is historically documented, as is the widening of access between 1960 – when only 5.4 per cent of school-leavers entered HE – and the mid-1990s (Robertson and Hillman, 1997). National and institutional data available from the Higher Education Statistics Agency (HESA) in the United Kingdom show that, in respect of the widening of participation in England and Wales, there was a modest advance between 2002–2003 and 2006–2007 in the enrolment of young people on full-time first-degree programmes, though not in Scotland or Northern Ireland (Table 3.1). Data for the percentage of entrants from low-participation neighbourhoods are not included in Table 3.1, because a change in the method of their determination means that the figures for the two selected years are not directly comparable. The state school entrance data are unhelpful where widening participation (WP) is concerned because of the high percentage of school students they encompass, though they have obvious value where the focus of concern is on students entering HE from private (i.e. fee-paying) schools.

The Labour government (1997–2010) sought not only to increase participation in HE (it did, as is evident below) but also to see a greater proportion of young people from relatively disadvantaged backgrounds entering elite universities. On the latter policy point, the level of success has been modest, where the criterion is the percentage of entrants from lower socio-economic groups (Harris, 2010, Annex C). Figure 3.1 shows, for universities in England and Wales, the trends in the enrolment of young people from lower socio-economic groups on first-degree programmes. The data are discontinuous because of a shift in the method of categorising social groups from the Registrar-General's classification to the National Statistics Socio-Economic Classification (NS-SEC). This shift may account for the slight uplift between the earlier and the later data.

Table 3.1 Participation of under-represented groups in higher education: Young full-time first-degree entrants

Country	Percentage from state schools or colleges	Percentage from NS-SEC classes 4, 5, 6 and 7
England, 2002–2003	86.4	27.9
England, 2006–2007	87.2	29.8
Scotland, 2002–2003	87.5	28.0
Scotland, 2006–2007	86.6	25.9
Wales, 2002–2003	91.9	29.8
Wales, 2006–2007	93.1	30.1
Northern Ireland, 2002–2003	99.9	41.3
Northern Ireland, 2006–2007	99.6	41.7

Note: National Statistics Socio-Economic Classifications (NS-SEC) 4, 5, 6 and 7 refer to entrants from the following backgrounds: small employers and own account workers (4), lower supervisory and technical occupations (5), semi-routine occupations (6) and routine occupations (7).
Source: www.hesa.ac.uk/index.php/content/category/2/32/141/.

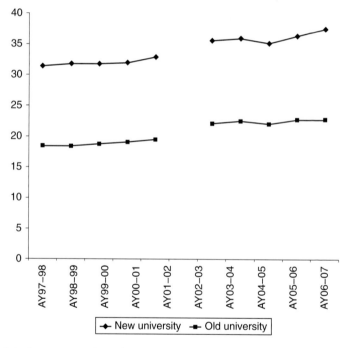

Figure 3.1 Percentage of students from lower socio-economic groups (y-axis), academic years from 1997–1998 to 2006–2007 (x-axis), from universities in England and Wales. The breaks in the lines mark a change in the way in which 'lower socio-economic groups' were classified
Source: www.hefce.ac.uk/learning/perfind/ and www.hesa.ac.uk/index.php/content/category/2/32/141/.

The figures in Table 3.1 do not show the disparity between institutional types as regards young people who could be classified as entrants from NS-SEC categories 4, 5, 6 and 7 (hereafter, 'lower socio-economic groups'). Whereas in 2006–2007, the median percentage of entrants from lower socio-economic groups entering institutions that had become multi-disciplinary universities in England and Wales by 2007 (hereafter, the new universities) was 37.7 (range 28.6–51.3), for the longer established universities (the old universities) it was 22.0 (range 9.8–49.0). The difference between the two types of university is shown more clearly in the two frequency charts in Figure 3.2. A similar picture, albeit based on a different methodology, is evidenced in the study of Harris (2010, Annex C).

In 2001, the Higher Education Funding Council for England (HEFCE) introduced three years of 'aspiration funding' in addition to increasing the 'postcode premium' that had been designed to encourage applications from areas of low participation. The aspiration funding stream was explicitly intended to help institutions with fewer than 80 per cent of their

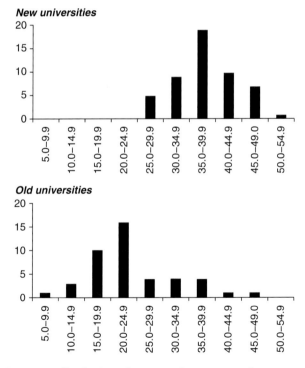

Figure 3.2 Frequency distributions, by range of percentage of young entrants from lower socio-economic groups (x-axis), for 51 new universities and 44 old universities (first-degree programmes, academic year 2006–2007)

students from state schools (decoded, this referred to elite universities) to encourage applications from such students.[5] In doing so, it reflected the impact on the government policy of the highly publicised rejection by Oxford University in the preceding year of a potentially well-qualified student from a state school who had applied to study medicine and had been interviewed at Magdalen College (see Yorke, 2003). The student's rejection probably also catalysed, later in the same year, a switch in the attention of the broadsheet (quality) press from dropout rates (which had dominated commentary on the publication of institutional performance indicators in 1999) towards issues relating to equity in access to HE.[6]

Data for England show that there was, across all social backgrounds, a steady rise in young people's participation in HE between academic years 1994–1995 and 2006–2007. The rise was, however, markedly differentiated by social background. Whereas the percentage of young people entering HE from the most advantaged areas rose from roughly 50 per cent in 1994–1995 to 55 per cent in 2006–2007, the corresponding percentages for the least advantaged areas were 13 and 16 (HEFCE, 2010: 23). There was also a differentiation in respect of gender, with women enrolling in a greater proportion than men.

Rising grades

Between the academic year 1994–1995, when statistics for HE in the United Kingdom were first collated by the HESA, and 2006–2007 there was an overall rise in grades awarded for students' work, which becomes publicly visible in the classification of bachelor's degree awards. For a host of technical reasons, the honours degree classification is deeply flawed as an indicator of student achievement (Yorke, 2008); nevertheless, it is the only index of achievement available at the sectoral level and perforce has to be used in this chapter. A convenient statistic for present purposes is the percentage of 'good honours degrees' awarded: 'good honours degrees' subsumes first-class and upper second-class awards, and the percentage is calculated with reference to the totality of honours degree awards.[7] In some subject areas (nursing, business and management and design studies), the trend was essentially flat, whereas in others (politics, civil engineering, electronic and electrical engineering) there was a fairly consistent rise (for a detailed analysis, see Yorke, 2009). The rising trends tended to be concentrated in the period up to 2001–2002.

Coalescing subject-based data at the level of the institution (or worse, as has been done in some press reports, at the level of the sector) is misleading, because of the marked differences between subject areas. The rising trend in classifications has often been reported in terms of 'grade inflation' (e.g. Attwood, 2008; Paton, 2011) and parallels similar rhetoric from the United

States about the rise in grade-point averages (GPAs) over the years (e.g. Rosovsky and Hartley, 2002; Johnson, 2003).

The reality, on both sides of the Atlantic, is more complex. In the United States, Adelman (2004: 77ff) showed, through a detailed analysis of transcript data for students who entered HE in 1972, 1982 and 1992, that there was no systematic rise in GPAs across the spectrum of higher education institutions (HEIs). GPAs had in fact dipped for the middle cohort. Adelman pointed out that there had been changes over the period of the three cohorts, which muddied the waters for the interpreter: e.g. there was a marked increase in the percentage of pass grades between the two later cohorts (such grades, whilst counting as credit towards the degree, are not included in computations of GPA[8]) and also in the percentage of withdrawals and no-credit repeats combined. (Adelman, 2004) As the title of his chapter signalled, any rigorous analysis of undergraduate grades is necessarily a complex undertaking (Adelman, 2004).

Data from universities in England and Wales show that the percentages of 'good honours degrees' awarded between the academic years 2002–2003 and 2006–2007 in eight subjects common to both old and new universities remained fairly steady, despite the earlier rises (Figure 3.3). Biology in new universities showed an upward trend, but against this a number of other subjects tended to exhibit a falling trend. As one might expect from the positive relationship between A-level grades and university degree awards (HEFCE, 2003, 2005; Kirkup et al., 2010), the degree award profiles for the old universities are raised in comparison with the profiles for the new universities, with the exception of nursing where the profiles in the two categories of university are very similar. The reasons for the 'nursing anomaly' are unclear, but may reflect, inter alia, the practical nature of the programmes and the particular professional body requirements for nursing curricula.[9]

In considering data relating to honours degree awards, it is necessary not to lose sight of the fact that the awards pertain, of course, only to those students who completed their programmes of study. The exclusion of those who did not complete their programme introduces a bias into the data, which is greater in institutions for which retention and completion rates are relatively low. In general, as the performance indicators published by HEFCE and HESA have consistently shown, rates of retention and completion are lower in new universities than in old universities.

So could widening participation have anything to do with the uplift in classifications?

In the new universities between 2002–2003 and 2006–2007, the percentage of entrants from lower socio-economic groups rose slightly, whereas on the whole the profile of awards was flat. On the rather heroic assumption that

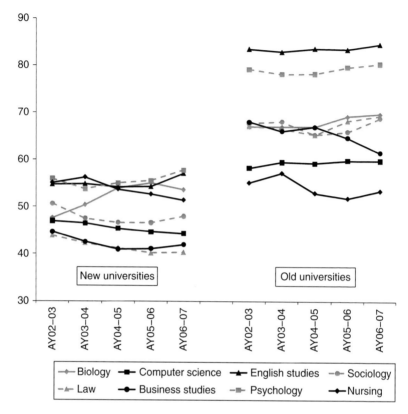

Figure 3.3 A comparison of the percentages of 'good honours degrees' awarded in eight subject areas by old and new universities (y-axis), academic years 2002–2003 to 2006–2007 (x-axis)

the WP data for whole institutions can be applied to subject areas within institutions,[10] there are no grounds in the data analysed for this chapter for suggesting that WP from lower socio-economic groups has led to an uplift in classifications. In the old universities, over the same period, both measures were broadly flat.[11]

Looking further back, between 1994–1995 and 2001–2002, there was across England, Wales and Northern Ireland a general rise in the percentage of 'good honours degrees' awarded, though with a few exceptions in particular subject areas (Yorke, 2008, chapter 4). The rises tended to be strongest in the elite 'Russell Group' of universities and weakest in the new universities, with old universities outside the Russell Group in between. Figure 3.2 shows that, between 1997–1998 and 2001–2002, the percentage of entrants from lower socio-economic groups rose only very slightly in both old and new universities. Again, there is nothing in the data to encourage the view that WP has had a direct influence on honours degree classifications.

The analysis presented in this chapter is necessarily limited. Its conclusions are suggestive rather than definitive. The percentage from lower socio-economic groups is an imperfect index of WP, as it pays only indirect attention to areas of particularly low participation and deals poorly with other factors bearing upon participation, such as ethnicity. It is, arguably, the 'least worst' option amongst the indexes that are readily to hand.

On the available (and necessarily circumstantial) evidence, the conclusion has to be that the widening of participation cannot be said to have had a direct influence on the trends in the percentage of 'good honours degrees' over the period of ten academic years 1997–1998 to 2006–2007. The only way in which a sharper picture could be obtained would be to analyse in considerable detail data from the individual student records held at the national level. It is doubtful that the outcomes of such an analysis would justify the costs involved.

The analysis presented in this chapter does not eliminate the possibility of indirect influences of WP on honours degree awards. To illustrate the point, one hypothetical (and improbable) example of an indirect effect would be if some of the more selective institutions were to wish to preserve their relative advantage over the less selective in 'league tables' by adjusting their method for determining honours classifications. Indirect effects are, by their very nature, formidably difficult to identify.

If widening participation has not influenced the rise in classifications, what might have done?

The following are some of influences that may have, directly or indirectly, encouraged an uplift in honours degree classifications:

- Improved quality of teaching
- Greater diligence on the part of students
- Students making 'strategic' choices within programmes of study
- Curricula framed in terms of intended learning outcomes and specific assessment criteria
- The way in which student work is marked
- Greater reliance on coursework in assessment requirements
- Changes in the way that honours degree classifications are determined
- 'League tables' or rankings of institutions in the media.

Some of these possible influences are pernicious; others are not. Other influences could have had an opposite effect, such as students' engagement in part-time work and the distraction from teaching stemming from the need for academic staff to demonstrate achievements in research for the (roughly quinquennial) research assessment exercises. The effects, if any, of yet other possible influences, such as changes in institutions' provision of programmes in some subject areas and national demographic changes, are difficult to assess.

Three of the possible influences can be argued to have been the likeliest to have had the greatest effect on classifications, though, in respect of the first, substantial empirical evidence is lacking.

1. The specification of curricula in terms of intended learning outcomes, and the consequent explicitness of assessment criteria, came to prominence as institutions constructed their curricula along modular lines, mainly during the 1990s. Such curricula gave students a clearer indication of what was expected of them (especially as regards assessment tasks); as a consequence, students' performances and hence their grades improved. Whether their all-round learning improved to the same extent is a moot point.

2. Roughly contemporaneously, the balance of summative assessment demand shifted away from formal examinations towards coursework of various kinds depending on the nature of the subject. Coursework tends to attract higher grades than do examinations (e.g. Bridges et al., 1999, 2002; Yorke et al., 2000; Simonite, 2003) for various reasons, some praiseworthy but others not. Properly handled, coursework can provide a better index of a student's capabilities than an examination, so it is not the case that coursework is necessarily an 'easier' option for the student, nor that it is necessarily related to perceptions of a decline in academic standards.

3. As the financial pressures on students have increased, part-time employment has become an increasingly significant aspect of the lives of many full-time students. Students from less advantaged backgrounds are more likely to be affected in this way. A survey of full-time students in the United Kingdom in 2006 showed that students from managerial and professional backgrounds undertook on average fewer hours per week of part-time employment than students from more 'working class' backgrounds (Yorke, 2008: 99). As Figures 3.1 and 3.2 illustrate, the latter are to be found in greater proportions in the new universities. There is evidence that a large commitment to part-time employment can affect academic performance adversely (Barke et al., 2000; Brennan et al., 2005; Pascarella and Terenzini, 2005; Salamonson and Andrew, 2006). The net result is likely to be some depression of award levels (as well as the widely known decreased likelihood of completion), particularly in the new universities.

Elton (1998: 37) summed up the likely impact of the first two of these potential influences:

…the increasing use of assessment methods which test other skills has enabled proportionally more students to attain higher marks. As the class boundaries have been left unchanged, this has also meant that, on average, they obtained better classes, but not necessarily that their performance was better. In other words, the measuring instrument has been changed and, until we have calibrated the changed instrument, we cannot say anything about what it is measuring, i.e. about student achievement.

Elton signalled indirectly an often unacknowledged change in HE in the United Kingdom as it has evolved from the elite system of the 1960s to the massified system of the present day. What is expected of graduates has evolved over the years, becoming more overtly concerned with employability-oriented achievements. The consequence has been that the focus of, and approach to, assessment has changed.

Concluding comments

The honours degree classification

It is evident from the analysis and discussion in this chapter that the uplift in honours degree awards has complex causes. Whilst those inside HE may have an appreciation of the effects of changes to both curricula and assessment on the national profile of honours degree awards, the 'outside world' typically does not. It probably makes the general assumption that honours degree classifications 'work' in the way they always have done, overlooking the changes that have stemmed from the massification of the HE system. The Measuring and Recording Student Achievement Scoping Group – charged with opening up the issue of how student achievement was (and might be) presented – concluded that 'the existing honours degree classification system has outlived its usefulness and is no longer fit for purpose' (UUK and SCoP, 2004: 4). It follows that the index is of very limited value as a vehicle for public information. Yet it is set to continue in existence for the indefinite future.

Funding and access

Following the general election of 2010, the Conservative-Liberal Democrat Coalition Government's changes to the funding of students (a major increase in tuition fees) and its cutbacks to the funding of HEIs have radically altered the HE landscape in England. Aftershocks will be felt elsewhere in the United Kingdom – and beyond. The profile of HE in England can be expected to undergo significant changes in terms of both the programmes on offer (the arts, humanities and social sciences bearing the brunt of funding cutbacks) and student participation (due to perceptions of the impact of high levels of indebtedness). The latter is likely to obtain to a greater extent in respect of students from relatively disadvantaged backgrounds, despite the access agreements that the government expects to be struck between the Office for Fair Access (OFFA) and institutions in respect of the admission of students from under-represented groups.[12]

The implementation of the new funding arrangements will introduce – perhaps sharply – discontinuities into the trends discussed in this chapter which, at the time of writing, are difficult to estimate and will only become apparent in the medium term. As the financial services sector is wont to warn (and as the banking crisis vividly illustrated), past performance is not necessarily to be taken as an indication of what the future will hold.

Acknowledgements

I am grateful to Mark Gittoes and Mark Corver of HEFCE for pointing to me some sources relevant to this chapter. The use I have made of the material is, of course, entirely my responsibility.

Notes

1. Margaret Hodge, then Minister for Higher Education in the UK Government, was quoted as having used the term (see Woodward, 2003).
2. Melanie Phillips (2003), a columnist in the conservative-leaning Daily Mail.
3. See HEFCE (2003, 2005; Kirkup et al., 2010).
4. Institutions gaining university status relatively recently were little different in general character from the 'new universities' that had gained the title following the legislation in 1992. Their inclusion gives extra weight to the analysis.
5. See HEFCE (2001, para 5).
6. See Yorke (2003) for an account of the press treatment of the first few years of published institutional performance data.
7. There are some minor problems associated with the calculation of the percentage of 'good honours degrees', but these are of no consequence for this chapter. See Yorke (2009) for details.
8. 'Strategic' students may opt to go for only a pass grade in a minority of study units. When these units are known to be difficult, choosing to go only for a pass avoids prejudicing their GPA.
9. Whereas there are pressures towards commonality in respect of nursing, curricula within the same broad subject heading can differ substantially both between and within institutional types. This is a matter that cannot be addressed within this chapter.
10. The matter cannot be pursued in this chapter because of the unavailability of data on widening participation that are disaggregated by subject area.
11. However, in findings that were an aside from the main thrust of their study, Kirkup et al. (2010: 26) noted that a student with average entry qualifications was more likely to achieve a higher class of degree where the university did not fall into a group that could be categorised as being highly selective regarding entrance. The authors are cautious about pressing the findings too far because of various methodological difficulties with their analyses.

12. For details, see Guidance to the Director of Fair Access issued in February 2011 by the Secretary of State for Business, Innovation and Skills and the Minister for Universities and Science, at www.bis.gov.uk/assets/biscore/higher-education/docs/g/11-728-guidance-to-director-fair-access (accessed 15 July 2011).

Bibliography

Adelman, C. (2004) *Principal Indicators of Student Academic Histories in Postsecondary Education, 1972-2000* (Washington, DC: U.S. Department of Education).

Amis, K. (1960) 'Lone Voices', *Encounter XV* (July): 6–11.

Attwood, R. (2008) 'Rise in Proportion of Firsts to 13% Renews Inflation Debate', *The Times Higher Education*, 17 January, [online] http://www.timeshighereducation.co.uk/story.asp?sectioncode=26&storycode=400190&c=1 [accessed 14 July 2011].

Ball, C. (1990) *More Means Different: Widening Access to Higher Education* (London: Royal Society of Arts).

Barke, M., Braidford, P., Houston, M., Hunt, A., Lincoln, I., Morphet, C., Stone, I. and Walker, A. (2000) *Students in the Labour Market: Nature, Extent and Implications of Term-Time Employment Among University of Northumbria Undergraduates [Research Report 215]* (London: Department for Education and Skills).

Brennan, J., Duaso, A., Little, B., Callender, C. and van Dyck, R. (2005) *Survey of Higher Education Students' Attitudes to Debt and Term-Time Working and Their Impact on Attainment* (London: Universities UK).

Bridges, P., Bourdillon, B., Collymore, D., Cooper, A., Fox, W., Haines, C., Turner, D., Woolf, H. and Yorke, M. (1999) 'Discipline-Related Marking Behaviour Using Percentages: A Potential Cause of Inequity in Assessment', *Assessment and Evaluation in Higher Education*, 24 (3): 285–300.

Bridges, P., Cooper, A., Evanson, P., Haines, C., Jenkins, D., Scurry, D., Woolf, H. and Yorke, M. (2002) 'Coursework Marks High, Examination Marks Low: Discuss', *Assessment and Evaluation in Higher Education*, 27 (1): 35–48.

Elton, L. (1998) 'Are UK Degree Standards Going Up, Down or Sideways?', *Studies in Higher Education*, 23 (1): 35–42.

European Commission (2009) '*New Skills for New Jobs – Anticipating and Matching Labour Market and Skills Needs (20/04/2009)*', [online] http://ec.europa.eu/social/main.jsp?catId=568&langId=en&pubId=98&type=2&furtherPubs=yes [accessed 15 July 2011].

Harris, M. (2010) *What More Can Be Done to Widen Access to Highly Selective Universities?* (London: Office for Fair Access), [online] http://www.offa.org.uk/wp-content/uploads/2010/05/Sir-Martin-Harris-Fair-Access-report-web-version.pdf [accessed 15 July 2011].

HEFCE (2001) *Widening Participation in Higher Education: Funding Decisions for 2001–02 to 2003–04* (Bristol: Higher Education Funding Council for England).

HEFCE (2003) *Schooling Effects on Higher Education Achievement [Report 2003/32]* (Bristol: Higher Education Funding Council for England).

HEFCE (2005) *Schooling Effects on Higher Education Achievement: Further Analysis – Entry at 19 [Report 2005/09]* (Bristol: Higher Education Funding Council for England).

HEFCE (2010) *Trends in Young Participation in Higher Education: Core Results for England [Report 2010/03]* (Bristol: Higher Education Funding Council for England).

Johnson, V.E. (2003) *Grade Inflation: A Crisis in College Education* (New York, NY: Springer).

Kirkup, C., Wheater, R., Morrison, J., Durbin, B. and Pomati, N. (2010) *Use of an Aptitude Test in University Entrance: A Validity Study* (Slough: National Foundation for Educational Research).

Leitch, S. (2006) *Prosperity for All in the Global Economy – World Class Skills [Final Report of the Leitch Review of Skills]* (Norwich: Her Majesty's Stationery Office).

McMahon, W.W. (2009) *Higher Learning, Greater Good. The Private and Social Benefits of Higher Education* (Baltimore, MD: Johns Hopkins University Press).

Pascarella, E.T. and Terenzini, P.T. (2005) *How College Affects Students: A Third Decade of Research* (San Francisco, CA: Jossey-Bass).

Paton, G. (2011) 'Warning Over "Grade Inflation" as More Students Gain Top Degrees', *The Daily Telegraph*, 13 January, [online] www.telegraph.co.uk/education/educationnews/8257808/Warning-over-grade-inflation-as-more-students-gain-top-degrees.html [accessed 15 July 2011].

Phillips, M. (2003) 'Eat Your Heart Out, Matthew Arnold', *Daily Mail*, 23 January, [online] www.melaniephillips.com/eat-your-heart-out-matthew-arnold [accessed 15 July 2011].

Robertson, D. and Hillman, J. (1997) 'Widening Participation in Higher Education by Students from Lower Socio-Economic Groups and Students with Disabilities. Report 6', in: National Committee of Inquiry into Higher Education, *Higher Education in the Learning Society, Reports 5–9* (Norwich: Her Majesty's Stationery Office, pp. 31–81).

Rosovsky, H. and Hartley, M. (2002) *Evaluation and the Academy: Are We Doing the Right Thing?* (Cambridge, MA: American Academy of Arts and Sciences).

Salamonson, Y. and Andrew, S. (2006) 'Academic Performance in Nursing Students: Influence of Part-Time Employment, Age and Ethnicity', *Journal of Advanced Nursing*, 55 (3): 342–351.

Simonite, V. (2003) 'The Impact of Coursework on Degree Classifications and the Performance of Individual Students', *Assessment and Evaluation in Higher Education*, 28 (3): 459–470.

UUK and SCoP (2004) *Measuring and Recording Student Achievement* (London: Universities UK and Standing Conference of Principals), [online] http://www.universitiesuk.ac.uk/Publications/Pages/Publication-216.aspx [accessed 15 July 2011].

Woodward, W. (2003) ' "Mickey Mouse" Courses Jibe Angers Students', *The Guardian*, 14 January, [online] http://education.guardian.co.uk/higher/news/story/0,9830,874230,00.html [accessed 15 July 2011].

Yorke, M. (2003) 'The Prejudicial Papers? Press Treatment of UK Higher Education Performance Indicators, 1999–2001'. in Tight, M. (ed.) *Access and Exclusion* (Amsterdam: JAI/Elsevier, pp. 159–184).

Yorke, M. (2008) *Grading Student Achievement in Higher Education: Signals and Shortcomings* (Abingdon: Routledge).

Yorke, M. (2009) *'Trends in Honours Degree Classifications, 1994–95 to 2006–07, for England, Wales and Northern Ireland'*, [online] www.heacademy.ac.uk/assets/York/documents/resources/publications/Yorke_Trends.doc [accessed 15 July 2011].

Yorke, M., Bridges, P. and Woolf, H. (2000) 'Mark Distributions and Marking Practices in UK Higher Education', *Active Learning in Higher Education*, 1 (1): 7–27.

4
Wider and Still Wider? A Historical Look at the 'Open-Ness' of the Open University of the United Kingdom

Alan Woodley

Introduction

When the United Kingdom Open University (OU) began to teach in 1971 with its ambition to be 'open as to people', it had the potential to have a great impact on the nature of British higher education (HE) and its student population.

- It was big enough to have a national impact. It started with 25,000 students and currently has around 200,000 registrations per year.
- Through the use of distance education it enabled people to study at home and to continue in employment.
- Its multi-media system improved upon correspondence education by using broadcasting, local tutorials, residential schools, etc.
- The credit-based system allowed flexible study patterns.

However, its defining characteristic was that there were to be no entry qualifications. Anybody aged 21 or over (later lowered to 18 and then 16) and living in the United Kingdom would be entitled to register and places would be offered on a first-come, first-served basis.

To put this in context, the Robbins Committee on Higher Education (Great Britain, 1963) had shown that in 1962 only 8.5 per cent of the 18–20 age group entered full-time HE: 4.0 per cent went to universities, 2.5 per cent into training colleges to become teachers and 2.0 per cent into advanced courses in further education. Robbins felt that the so-called 'pool of ability' was not being tapped and that there was 'impressive evidence that large numbers of able young people do not at present enter HE' (op. cit.: 52). In particular, they noted that 'of grammar-school leavers with a given measured ability at the age of 11, the proportion obtaining the qualifications for entry to HE varies widely according to their social background' (op. cit.: 52).

The children of manual workers were much less successful, largely because they left school earlier.

Thus, at least in the early days, the OU was in a position to offer HE to the many people in society who were capable of study at that level but who were denied the opportunity by their lack of entry qualifications, the lack of places or by various personal and social barriers. The Labour Party's manifesto for the general election of March 1966 announced that the OU would mean 'genuine equality of opportunity to millions of people for the first time' (Labour Party, 1966). However, since the Robbins report there has been a massive increase in HE student numbers, and the current participation rate stands at around 40 per cent. There have also been determined efforts to widen participation among certain disadvantaged groups. In this chapter, we look at the characteristics of OU undergraduates and, wherever possible, compare them with those of students in what could be termed 'conventional' HE. What has the OU's contribution to widening participation been and how has it changed over time?

Women

Universities in the United Kingdom began as male domains. In the case of Cambridge, the first women's college was not opened until 1869, and women became full members of the university with the right to gain degrees only in 1947. The situation improved after the Second World War, but, as noted by Robbins, women still only represented one in four university students in 1962–1963 (Great Britain, 1963).

Thus, one might have expected the OU to be inundated by women applicants, at least by those who were qualified for entry but not able to gain full-time places. In fact, three out of four new OU students in 1971 were men, much as in conventional universities. Nevertheless, the proportion of women then proceeded to increase fairly steadily and has now risen to slightly over 60 per cent (Figure 4.1).

This is a notable achievement. The OU has provided opportunities for thousands of women, many of whom would not otherwise have been able to study. This includes women with caring responsibilities, or in part-time work where day-release is not possible, or living a long way from a university. However, the figures have to be placed in the context of society and HE in general. When we look at the data of recent years in Figure 4.2, we see that the growth patterns for women at the OU are almost identical to those for full-time HE and are actually slightly below those for others studying part time. Thus, rather than trail-blazing, the OU appears to be following a common trend for higher levels of participation by women. In fact, the lower average attainment of boys in schools and higher female participation and progression rates in HE has led several observers to consider men rather

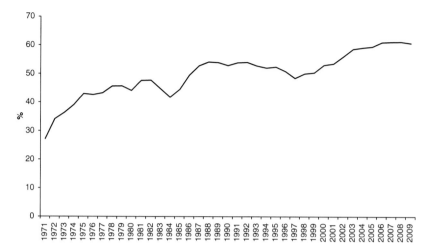

Figure 4.1 The percentage of women among new OU undergraduates (1972–2009)
Sources: Higher Education Statistics Agency and Open University Statistics.

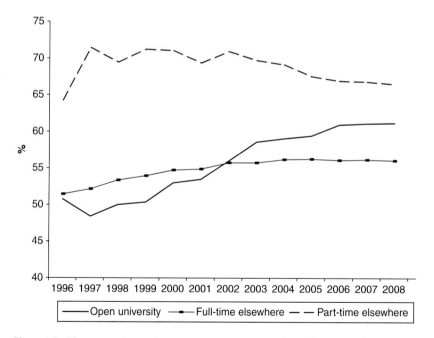

Figure 4.2 The percentage of women among new undergraduates at the OU and elsewhere (1996–2008)
Sources: Higher Education Statistics Agency and Open University Statistics.

than women to be the disadvantaged group in today's educational system (Vincent-Lancrin, 2008; HEPI, 2009).

Older students

British full-time degree courses continue to be dominated by school-leavers and those who have had a 'gap year' or two, as can be seen from the first column in Table 4.1.

The OU originally set its entry age at 21 and aimed at 'mature' students who would be benefiting from a 'second chance'. However, this was also partly because the OU needed the co-operation of conventional universities and could not be seen to be poaching younger students from them (Perry, 1976). The age limit was soon dropped to 18.This was justified not only because 18 had become the age of 'adulthood' but also because the OU needed more students of all ages to sustain its growth and because conventional universities themselves were becoming more interested in recruiting mature students.

The OU has succeeded in recruiting older students. Some six out of ten new OU undergraduates were aged 30 or over in 2006–2007 (Table 4.1), which again was broadly in line with the general part-time HE position.

Figure 4.3 breaks down each intake of OU students into age bands, and there is actually evidence of a surge in younger students over the last five or six years. In 2009, those aged under 25 formed a quarter of the new OU intake, nearly the largest single age group. It appears that many young people are considering the benefits of paid employment plus part-time OU study over those of full-time study with its attendant loans and debts. However, another reason for the very large increase in the number of under 21-year-olds is the Young Applicants in Schools Scheme (YASS) where students can

Table 4.1   First-year undergraduates by qualification aim, mode of study and age (2006–2007)

Age	Full time			Part time			
	First degree (%)	Other undergraduate (%)	Total (%)	First degree (%)	Other UG (%)	Total (%)	OU (%)
18–20	79	45	74	7	8	8	
21–24	10	18	11	15	11	12	
Under 25	89	63	86	23	19	20	22
25–29	4	12	5	18	15	15	19
30 and over	7	26	9	59	66	65	58
	100	100	100	100	100	100	100

Sources: Higher Education Statistics Agency and Open University statistics.

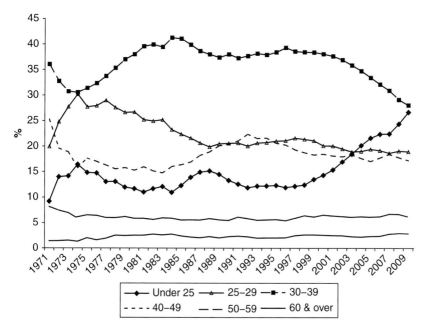

Figure 4.3   The age on entry among new OU undergraduates (1971–2009)
Source: Open University Statistics.

study OU modules alongside their A levels or school-leaving exams. Here the OU is actually helping young people who are already on the track for educational success.

Interestingly, there has not been a drop-off among the highest age groups with those aged 50 and over forming a constant 10 per cent. The fall has been mainly in the 30–39 age band, normally the OU's prime market. Consequently, the median age on entry has remained in the early 30s ever since the first intake in 1971.

Ethnicity

The 1991 census was the first time that ethnic origin was measured in the United Kingdom on a national basis, and the OU followed suit in 1992. As Figure 4.4 shows, the OU was not very successful at attracting black and minority ethnic (BME) students at that time, but the figures have steadily improved, and they now stand slightly above the national population figures.

However, despite the fact that BME groups show a disadvantage across a broad range of national indicators, Figure 4.4 shows that they are in fact over-represented in HE in general and particularly in the full-time

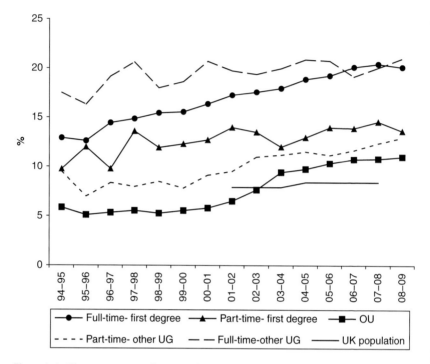

Figure 4.4 The percentage of new undergraduates from black and ethnic minorities (1994–2008)

Sources: Higher Education Statistics Agency and Open University Statistics.

mode. Thus, as with gender, the OU cannot claim a major breakthrough in percentage terms. Again though, the flexible study pattern may have opened up educational opportunities for many BME students unable to study through a conventional full-time or part-time route for cultural or other reasons.

People with disabilities

The OU with its distance education would seem to offer access to people with disabilities that make campus attendance difficult or impossible. The OU also takes pride in its provisions for students with disabilities, such as audio recordings and 3D diagrams for the visually impaired, scripts for the hearing impaired, and adapted information technology (IT) equipment for those with motor or visual disabilities. However, as can be seen from Figure 4.5, the percentage of students with disabilities in full-time HE appears to greatly exceed that at the OU. The OU is also falling behind the figure for all part-time HE.

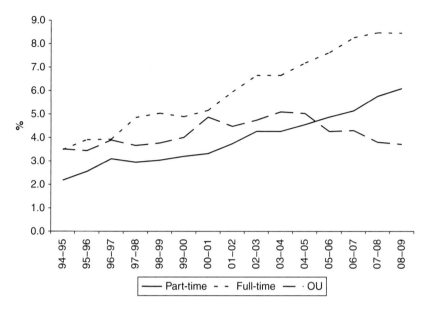

Figure 4.5 The percentage of new undergraduates with disabilities (1994–2008)
Sources: Higher Education Statistics Agency and Open University Statistics.

Richardson (2010) recorded a higher percentage of OU students with disabilities than is reported here, one that is similar to the rest of the United Kingdom HE sector. This appears to be because he analysed all students rather than just new students, and students with disabilities appear to persist longer with their OU studies.

'Disability' is a highly complex concept that is difficult to measure. It covers a broad range of physical and mental conditions and within each there are varying degrees of severity. The statistical results on offer indicate the type of disability that a student has on the basis of their own self-assessment. Students are not obliged to notify a disability, and so the reporting agency 'advises that the figures reported in the analyses are derived from a subset that may not be representative of the total student population' (HESA, 2007). This might have a differential impact on OU students, but the direction is not clear. One could argue that distance students are likely to have a higher level of 'concealed' disability because they are less likely to deem that it affects their study, or because it is not visible to teaching staff. Contrastingly, one might expect higher levels of disability merely because of the OU's higher age profile.

As Table 4.2 shows, the distribution of specific disabilities at the OU is very different from that recorded for the rest of UK HE. In particular, the OU has a very high proportion of students with 'multiple disabilities'. This may be because for many people with multiple disabilities resulting from

Table 4.2   Types of disability among HE students (2006–2007)

Disability	First degree		Other undergraduate		OU (%)
	Full time (%)	Part time (%)	Full time (%)	Part time (%)	
Dyslexia or other specific learning difficulty	52	24	54	25	16
Blind or partially sighted	2	2	2	3	2
Deaf or hard of hearing	4	4	4	9	2
Restricted mobility	3	4	2	7	2
Mental health difficulties	4	10	5	7	11
Autistic spectrum disorder	1	0	1	0	0
An unseen disability	14	13	15	18	2
Multiple disabilities	9	30	5	16	54
Other disability	11	12	12	14	10

Sources: Higher Education Statistics Agency and Open University Statistics.

chronic illness, distance learning is the only practical means of access to HE (Newell and Debenham, 2009). The OU has a relatively low proportion of students with dyslexia and other specific learning difficulties. Again this may be due to differences in occurrence or reporting. It may be that people with dyslexia are less likely to opt for a text-based distance-learning mode. Or as Richardson and Wydell (2003) suggest, it may reflect the increased identification of young people with such disabilities as they progress through the school system.

Previous educational qualifications

Table 4.3 shows that the majority of those entering full-time degree courses in 2006–2007 did so on the basis of A levels, the standard school-leaving exams, or their Scottish equivalent. Some already had a previous HE qualification, but only a handful entered with low or no qualifications. The situation at the OU was very different. Only one in five had A levels as their highest previous qualification. Four in ten already had an HE qualification, and a similar number did not possess the standard HE entry requirement of A levels or their equivalent.

The qualifications of other part-time HE students were, on average, higher than at the OU. However, it seems that at least in the case of 'other undergraduate' courses many of them are very short refresher or personal interest

Table 4.3 The previous educational qualifications held by HE entrants (2006–2007)

Previous qualification	First degree		Other undergraduate		OU
	Full time (%)	Part time (%)	Full time (%)	Part time (%)	
Higher education	11	50	21	59	40
A level or equivalent	84	26	58	17	21
O level or equivalent	5	18	17	14	36
None held/required	1	5	4	10	3
	100	100	100	100	100

Sources: Higher Education Statistics Agency and Open University Statistics.

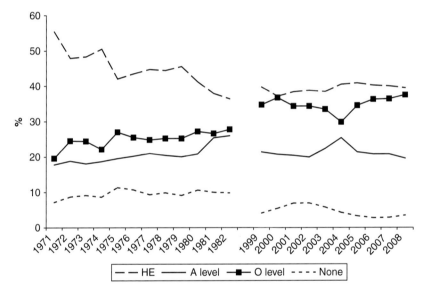

Figure 4.6 The previous educational qualifications of new OU undergraduates (1971–1980 & 1999–2008)
Source: Open University Statistics.

courses. These were formerly known as extra-mural classes, but universities have re-badged them and attached credit to them in order to continue to receive government funding.

The percentage of OU students with previous HE experience was very high in 1971 but then declined over the following 10 years (Figure 4.6). The situation over the last 10 years has remained relatively static.

In terms of widening participation, the position is rather confusing. The OU, with its large share of under-qualified entrants, could be described as more open than conventional universities. From another perspective, it could be described as less open because many of its participants have already experienced some form of HE.

Social background

Finally, we turn to the topic that so concerned Robbins, the question of a student's social background or class. Hopes were high for many that by opening its doors the OU would attract lots of 'working-class' students. From the researchers' point of view, this created the problem of how to measure the class or social background of the students.

In the early years, all applicants were asked to self-code themselves into one of fourteen 'occupational categories' based on their current status. Three of these categories were for people not in employment. In 1971, only 10 per cent were not in employment, but this had risen to one in five by 1980. Throughout this period, women looking after the home or family – 'housewives' as they were called at the time – formed the great majority of this group.

Students are now asked separately about their 'occupational statuses'. For those students choosing to declare their occupational status, Table 4.4 shows that over the last five years there has been a fall in numbers in full-time paid work and a rise for those not in paid work. 'Housewives' no longer form the

Table 4.4   The labour market status of new OU undergraduates (2005–2009)

	2005 (%)	2006 (%)	2007 (%)	2008 (%)	2009 (%)
In full-time work/ self-employed	64	61	61	58	53
In part-time work/ self-employed	14	14	15	14	14
Looking after the home/family	8	9	8	8	9
Retired from paid work	3	2	3	3	3
Doing unpaid voluntary work	1	1	1	1	1
Unable to work: long-term sickness/ disability	3	3	3	3	4
Unemployed and looking for a job	4	4	4	4	7
Not in paid work for some other reason	4	5	6	8	10
All 'Not in paid work'	22	25	25	28	33

Source: Open University Statistics.

majority of this group, and there has been a marked increase among those not in paid work 'for some other reason'. By definition, the latter would appear to include, among other categories, those in prison, full-time students elsewhere and refugees or asylum seekers without work permits, but it is not apparent where the increase is coming from and merits further investigation.

When the OU began, teachers, both primary and secondary, formed by far the biggest single occupational group. These were people with teaching certificates, who needed a degree to progress in their career. Their numbers diminished as the pool of non-graduate teachers disappeared, but they were not replaced by any particular other occupational group.

Here, we attempt to look in general terms at occupational prestige or ranking and search for changes over time. We take early data where students allocated themselves to particular occupational groups based on the Registrar-General's very broad categories (e.g. communications and transport would contain both airline pilots and truck-drivers) and compare it with recent findings where students used the Registrar-General's self-rating scale, which relates more to status (Table 4.5).

The comparisons are not exact, but they do suggest a large degree of consistency over the years. Around one in ten OU students work in classic 'working-class' routine and semi-routine jobs and a third in lower-level white-collar jobs. Slightly over a half were professionals, managers or administrators.

In national terms, the Higher Education Statistical Agency found that although student numbers had increased in recent years, the social background of those entering had not changed. Fifty per cent of the 2009 intake had managerial or professional backgrounds, with only 4 per cent from backgrounds of (working-class) routine occupations (*Independent,* 2009). These are very similar to the findings for the OU in Table 4.5. However, they are based on the parental occupations of young students, whereas the OU figures are for the students' own occupations.

In a survey of OU students carried out in 2005, they were asked the following three questions:

(1) At the time that you were leaving school, how would you have described your father's social class?
(2) At the time that you were leaving school, how would you have described your mother's social class?
(3) How would you describe your own social class today?

The results presented in Table 4.6 show that around half of OU students would categorise their parents as working class. Thus, as was found with the first intake of OU students (McIntosh *et al.*, 1976), many came from a working-class background but had been upwardly mobile before entering the OU. However, the changing class structure of British society over the

62

Table 4.5 The occupation of new OU undergraduates (1971–1975 & 2005–2009)

	1971 (%)	1972 (%)	1973 (%)	1974 (%)	1975 (%)	2005 (%)	2006 (%)	2007 (%)	2008 (%)	2009 (%)	
Administrators and managers	6	6	5	5	6	28	29	30	28	29	Modern professional occupations
Teachers	43	35	36	37	30	15	16	16	15	13	Traditional professional occupations
Professions & arts	10	14	12	13	13	14	12	14	15	11	Senior managers or administrators
Qualified scientists & engineers	8	5	5	5	4						
'High status'	67	61	59	59	53	57	56	59	57	53	'High status'
Technicians	14	15	15	14	13	9	9	9	9	9	Middle or junior managers
Armed forces	2	2	3	4	4	18	18	17	18	19	Clerical and intermediate occupations

Clerical & office	8	10	10	11	15	6	6	6	6	6	Technical and craft occupations
Sales & service	4	5	5	4	6						
'Medium status'	28	32	33	34	38	33	31	33	32	35	'Medium status'
Electrical, machines & allied trades	2	3	4	3	4	5	5	5	5	6	Semi-routine manual and service occupations
Farming, mining, construction & other manufacturing	2	2	2	2	3	5	5	5	6	6	Routine manual and service occupations
Communication & transport	1	1	2	2	2						
'Low status'	5	7	8	7	10	10	9	11	11	12	'Low status'
	100	100	100	100	100	100	100	100	100	100	

Source: Open University Statistics.

Table 4.6 The class of OU students and their parents as perceived by the students (2005)

	Father's class (%)	Mother's class (%)	Class of self (%)
Upper class	0.2	0.6	0.5
Upper middle class	6.3	5.8	10.3
Middle class	25.0	26.5	42.5
Lower middle class	12.9	14.4	15.7
Upper working class	13.0	12.5	9.1
Working class	27.4	25.7	8.5
Lower working class	2.0	2.9	0.2
Other (please write in)	0.7	0.6	1.9
I do not recognise social classes	7.0	6.8	11.2
Father/mother not alive then	3.6	2.5	
I don't know	1.9	1.8	
Working class as % of declared	48.4	46.2	20.2

Source: Open University survey.

last 40 years means that a smaller proportion of workers are now in manual occupations. So, apparently static figures over time could be interpreted as a relative success.

Other measures of open-ness

So far we have looked at the profile of new OU students but clearly an institution's success or otherwise in widening participation cannot be judged solely on this one criterion. A comprehensive approach would look at further indicators including the academic progress made by the different student groups, their experience of the courses, graduation rates, degree classifications, the acquisition of competences and occupational outcomes.

There have been a number of studies that looked at particular OU student groups against one or more of these criteria. Some evidenced negative outcomes. For example, Woodley (1987) showed that those with low previous educational qualifications were less likely to pass their first courses, and Richardson (2009) demonstrated that BME graduates were less likely to gain 'good' honours degrees. On the other hand, a study by Woodley and Simpson (2001) indicated that women OU graduates achieved relatively higher earnings than did men. In other studies, the results were mixed or inconclusive. For example, Richardson *et al.* (2004) found that the impact of a hearing loss on engagement in distance education, as measured by scores on an abbreviated version of the Academic Engagement Form, was relatively slight.

Table 4.7 The percentage of new students who gained a course credit on the science and social sciences foundation courses analysed by year and previous educational qualifications

Previous qualifications	1976	1977	1978	2006	2007	2008
(a) Science foundation course						
High	65	65	64	64	64	64
None	29	34	25	36	36	41
EDF	2.3	1.9	2.5	1.8	1.8	1.6
High minus none %	36	31	38	28	27	23
Previous qualifications	**1976**	**1977**	**1978**	**2006**	**2007**	**2008**
(b) Social sciences foundation course						
High	69	71	64	62	64	69
None	33	34	29	45	45	39
EDF	2.1	2.1	2.2	1.4	1.4	1.8
High minus none %	36	37	35	17	19	30

Source: Open University Statistics.

What has been missing from these analyses is any systematic attempt to measure changes over time. Has the OU's performance improved or deteriorated? Inevitably, such an analysis is difficult because valid time series data are hard to obtain. Definitions, questions, academic regulations and course provision all change. Here, I have attempted to make a comparison over a thirty-year period between the academic performance of those who entered the OU with no previous educational qualifications and those who already held some HE qualification (Table 4.7). The analysis is based on two courses, the science course and the social science foundation course. An educational discrimination factor (EDF) was calculated, which is the ratio of the pass rates for the two groups.

The table shows that, in general, the performance of those with no qualifications had improved relative to that of those with previous experience of HE. The EDFs were lower, and the absolute gap in performance had also narrowed. Thus, it could be claimed that the OU is now doing better in its aim to widening participation.

There was no clear-cut difference by subject. In four of the six years examined, science was more discriminatory against those with no qualifications than was social science. However, in two years the reverse was true.

Conclusions

The OU has admitted nearly two million students and so has clearly expanded educational opportunities for many adults. They have received

HE through the OU because places were not available elsewhere or because those available did not provide adequate flexibility. Some of these students have come from traditionally disadvantaged groups, and so participation has been widened in a purely numeric sense. However, more rigorous standards are required if the OU is to be declared truly 'Open as to people'. I would contend that for the OU to be considered a success it should attract more individuals from disadvantaged groups than does the rest of HE; that these students should make comparable academic progress; that they should derive similar benefits from study; and that in each case these figures should improve over time.

The present results show that, compared with other universities, the OU has attracted a large number of students from working-class backgrounds and/or without the normal educational entry requirements for HE. When it comes to ethnicity and disability, the OU appears to be improving but tends to under-perform when compared with the rest of HE in terms of the percentage of these groups in the new student profile. Women have been attracted to the OU in increasing numbers, but this can be seen as part of a national trend for more women to go to university.

Perhaps, the biggest difference is that OU students are on average 10–15 years older than conventional full-time students. In the time between leaving school and entering the OU, many have been upwardly mobile, both educationally and occupationally. With increasing age would also seem to come increasing disabilities, contributing to the discussed overrepresentation of multiple disabilities amongst OU students.

Apart from the results themselves, this analysis has brought to the surface some of the inherent problems in measuring an institution's success or failure in widening access. There is no single unique variable to be used. Here, we have considered gender, age, ethnicity, disability, previous educational qualifications and social background. In different circumstances, and with different data sources, we might have considered further identifiers including geographic regions, religious belief, income and sexual orientation. This raises questions of how one prioritises these variables in terms of which are deemed to be most significant. Furthermore, there may be sub-groups involving two or more of these variables that need special attention such as, for example, Asian women or young working-class men.

Many of these characteristics entail particular measurement problems. In the case of self-reported 'disability', for example, it might lead to under-reporting in distance education, because the disabilities are less visible or because students see them as less relevant. Certain disabilities such as dyslexia are now much more likely to be recognised while a person is at school. Measuring social class has long been a contentious issue, but with mature students there is the added problem of whether to determine it from the student's own occupation, if indeed they have one, or from that of their parents.

A given characteristic may have knock-on effects on other measures of widening participation, age being a case in point. The apparent surge in the number of younger OU students, presumably due to the increased costs of full-time study, has interesting ramifications. Back in the 1970s, the OU was compelled by the government to pilot the admission of school-leavers (Woodley and McIntosh, 1980). The OU opposed this because it was seen as counter to its aims of providing second-chance opportunities to older people. Now younger students are welcomed as a useful boost to overall demand, but they will also improve measures of widening participation. Because they have had less time to take higher level courses, they will supplement the numbers entering with low previous qualifications. However, they are also less likely to display the 'disabilities' associated with increasing age such as hearing impairment and mobility problems, and traditionally younger OU students fare less well academically.

The OU does not have a selection policy. When there are more applicants than places a 'first-come, first-served' mechanism is used. It is not therefore in a position to adjust the nature of its student population by favouring certain disadvantaged groups via the admissions process. To become more open it must attract a broader cross-section of the population. Removing entry qualifications is not enough in itself to make a university truly open. As a minimum, to attract disadvantaged groups, it must be visible, it must offer appropriate teaching and support, and it must be affordable. On the first count, market research has shown that the OU is well known amongst the general public. Widespread advertising and links to British Broadcasting Corporation (BBC) television programmes are designed to consolidate this position. Teaching standards can be adduced from the fact that 93 per cent of OU students say that they are satisfied with the overall quality of their course. This placed the OU in third position among the 152 HE institutions surveyed in 2010 as part of the National Student Survey (BBC, 2010). However, this survey is only completed by students who reach the end of their course. Paying the tuition fees can be a problem for some people, but in recent years, the OU has paid the fees of one in four new students because they are on low incomes.

The OU remains committed to widening participation. This aim features in all of its policy statements, there is a university department with this remit, the University continues to set admission targets for certain groups, and its teaching has expanded into sub-degree 'openings' courses for people who require preparation for study. However, if there are to be major changes in this area, they are likely to be provoked, for better or worse, by events and policies in the wider society.

In 2007 the OU, along with other universities, was faced with strong external pressure to widen participation still further. The then Labour government announced that it was phasing out funding for the majority of students in England studying for a qualification that was equivalent to, or lower than, a qualification that they had already achieved. They said that the money spent on so-called equivalent or lower qualifications (ELQ) students needed to be diverted to support those who were entering HE for the first time. In effect, this meant that the OU would have to replace funding for 29,000 ELQ students, possibly by attracting more students with low previous qualifications. The vice chancellor of the OU announced that doing by this, through the recruitment and retention of a similar number of hard-to-reach (and hard-to-keep) students will be a major and costly undertaking, and filling such a large number of places in such a short space of time an almost impossible task. We will nevertheless give it our best efforts (Gourley, 2008).

The OU campaigned hard against the ELQ policy, arguing that many people with HE qualifications needed to re-train to make career changes, and the Higher Education Funding Council for England (HEFCE) decided to make no changes to the funding method for part-time study until after the independent review of HE fees and funding due to report in 2010. That review was completed in 2010 in the form of the Browne report (Browne, 2010), and the current Coalition government has recently issued a White Paper titled 'Higher Education: Students at the Heart of the System' (BIS, 2011). Following further consultation, a HE bill will be presented to the parliament in 2012. The contents of the bill will have direct effects on widening participation at the OU, and there are also likely to be knock-on effects caused by changes, both chosen and imposed, in conventional universities. Some outcomes for conventional universities are already clear:

- The teaching grant that the government pays to universities will be greatly reduced.
- Universities will be expected to make up the difference by increasing student tuition fees.
- The majority of universities have announced plans to increase their fees by the maximum amount allowed, namely from £3,000 to £9,000.

The White Paper stresses that nobody should be put off HE because they cannot afford it, and a new framework for widening participation and fair access is outlined. However, other observers believe that many potential students will be put off by the size of the student loans that they would have to take out. If they decide to pursue HE, other things being equal, they might well opt for part-time study at the OU in order to continue in employment and so minimise their dependence on loans.

The OU is also subject to changes. On the positive side, the White Paper confirms Browne's recommendation that part-time students, unlike now, will be entitled to take out government-backed student loans to pay for their tuition fees. However, the OU is also experiencing the same level of funding cuts as conventional universities, and it is using the new availability of loans as an opportunity to increase its own fees. It has announced that the fees in

England will be £5,000, which is proportionately similar to the increase proposed by other universities. How this will affect the OU and its openness can only be surmised, but there are already certain pointers.

The White Paper makes no mention of ELQ. It appears that this issue has been resolved by the new fees. Those with previous HE will be able to study at the OU by paying the high un-subsidised fees. However, it is almost certain that they will not qualify for student loans if they have already benefited from them on previous courses. Therefore, it seems that many of them will be deterred from OU study for financial reasons.

Surveys of representative samples of current OU students suggest that large numbers of them would not continue with their studies if the fees rose to the proposed level, even if they were entitled to student loans (Woodley, 2011). This was particularly true of older students and those who had formerly had their OU fees paid for them through financial assistance funds. The impact on the profile of OU students and on widening participation will be affected by the extent to which the OU can provide alternatives to loans to low-income students. Those who want to test the water with a short course will require special support because student loans will not be available to those studying fewer than 30 credit points.

Young adults appear to be less concerned by loans. However, even they seem averse to the size of loans needed for conventional universities. The OU has seen a 30 per cent increase in students aged 18 or 19 over the past year (OU, 2011). Some of these will be school pupils improving their portfolio of qualifications, but others appear to be rejecting the full-time HE route. Whether this is 'widening participation' at the OU will require careful analysis. The younger students will not have HE qualifications, but, historically, they have been shown to make poorer student progress (Woodley and McIntosh, 1980). Time will tell whether their social and demographic profile confirms that the OU is continuing to offer opportunities to disadvantaged groups, despite them being considerably younger.

Bibliography

BBC (2010) *Student Satisfaction Rate Stalls at 82%, Survey Finds* [online] http://www.bbc.co.uk/news/education-11001891 [accessed 24 August 2011].

BIS (2011) *Students at the Heart of the System* [online] http://www.bis.gov.uk/news/topstories/2011/Jun/he-white-paper-students-at-the-heart-of-the-system [accessed 24 August 2011].

Browne, J. (2010) *An Independent Review of Higher Education & Student Finance in England. Securing a Sustainable Future for Higher Education in England* [online] http://webarchive.nationalarchives.gov.uk/+/hereview.independent.gov.uk/hereview/ [accessed18 August 2011].

Gourley, B. (2008) *The Outcome of the ELQ Debate* [online] https://msds.open.ac.uk/events/shbulletins/200847_56900_nr.pdf [accessed18 August 2011].

Great Britain, Committee on higher education (1963) *Higher Education.* Report of the Committee Appointed by the Prime Minister under the Chairmanship of Lord Robbins 1961–1963 (London: Her Majesty's Stationery Office).

HEPI (Higher Education Policy Institute) (2009) *Male and Female Participation and Progression in Higher Education* [online] http://www.hepi.ac.uk/files/41Maleand femaleparticipation.pdf [accessed 24 August 2011].

HESA (2007) *Press Release 110 Higher Education Statistical Agency* [online] http://www. hesa.ac.uk/index.php/content/view/153/161/ [accessed 24 August 2011].

Labour Party (1966) *Time for Decision,* Manifesto of the Labour Party, General Election, 1966.

McIntosh, N.E. *et al.* (1976) *A Degree of Difference* (London: Society for Research into Higher Education).

Newell, C. and Debenham, M. (2009) 'Disability, Chronic Illness and Distance Education', in Rogers, P., Berg, G., Boettcher, J., Howard, C., Justice, L., and Shenk, K. (eds) *Encyclopedia of Distance Learning*, 2nd ed., vol. 2 (Hershey, PA: Information Science Reference, pp. 646–654).

OU (2011) *The Open University Continues to See a Rise in the Number of Young Students* [online] http://www3.open.ac.uk/media/fullstory.aspx?id=21827 [accessed 24 August 2011].

Perry, W. (1976) *Open University: A personal Account by the First Vice-Chancellor Milton Keynes* (Milton Keynes: Open University Press).

Richardson, J. (2010) 'Course Completion and Attainment in Disabled Students Taking Courses with the Open University UK', *Open Learning*, 25–2: 81–94.

Richardson, J. (2009) 'The Role of Ethnicity in the Attainment and Experiences of Graduates in Distance Education', *Higher Education*, 58 (3): 321–338.

Richardson, J., Long, G. and Foster, S. (2004) 'Academic Engagement in Students with a Hearing Loss in Distance Education', *Journal of Deaf Studies and Deaf Education*, 9 (1): 68–85.

Richardson, J. and Wydell, T. (2003) 'The Representation and Attainment of Students with Dyslexia in UK Higher Education', *Reading and Writing*, 16–5: 475–503.

The Independent (2009) *Colleges Told: Raise Standards If You Want More Cash* [online] http://www.independent.co.uk/news/education/education-news/colleges-told-raise-standards-if-you-want-more-cash-1809140.html [accessed 24 August 2011].

Vincent-Lancrin, S. (2008), 'The Reversal of Gender Inequalities in Higher Education: An On-Going Trend', in *Higher Education to 2030 Volume 1: Demography* (OECD) (Paris: Centre for Educational Research and Innovation) [online] www.oecd.org/dataoecd/48/28/41939699.pdf [accessed 24 August 2011].

Woodley, A. (2011) 'Browne Sky Thinking: Estimating the Impact of Proposed Changes to the Fees System on Part-Time Higher Education Students', *Widening Participation and Lifelong Learning*, 13 (1): 27–38. [online] http://dx.doi.org/10.5456/WPLL.13.1.27 [accessed 24 August 2011].

Woodley, A. and Simpson, C. (2001) 'Learning and Earning: Measuring "Rates of Return" Among Mature Graduates from Part-time', *Distance Courses Higher Education Quarterly*, 55 (1): 28–41.

Woodley, A. (1987) 'Has the Open University Been an Unqualified Success?' *Journal of Access Studies*, 2 (2): 7–14.

Woodley, A. and McIntosh, N. (1980) *The Door Stood Open – An Evaluation of The Open University Younger Students Pilot Scheme* (Lewes: The Falmer Press).

Part II

Engaging with Higher Education as a Non-Traditional Student: Access and Motivation

5
Good Students, Bad Pupils: Constructions of 'Aspiration', 'Disadvantage' and Social Class in Undergraduate-Led Widening Participation Work

Yvette Taylor

In this chapter, I explore undergraduate student involvement in widening participation initiatives at a traditional university and the ways that students promote and market their university and higher education (HE) more generally. I seek to uncover widening participation messages disseminated by students in their work with pupils and teachers, the ways that these are taken up and/or resisted, and the interactions between university students and local school pupils. The idea of peer-led discussion, whereby 'sameness' is encouraged and endorsed, is positively promoted within student-tutoring programmes. However, this study found a sharpening of notions of 'us' and 'them' amongst many student participants and a vocalisation of educational success stories versus educational failures. While involvement in such programmes may be a way that students can contribute to their locality and foster career skills, this study interrogates the scope of 'all-round benefits' in widening participation and suggests that social class is mobilised in constructions of the 'good student' as against the 'bad pupil'. Widening participation initiatives need to engage with – and beyond – such interpersonal positioning in order to erode continued structured inequalities.

Widening participation: Motivations and practices

At a time of international 'crises' on the future and sustainability of HE (e.g. the 2010 Browne Report in the United Kingdom; the European Union's 2020 Strategy), widening participation in HE remains on social policy and academic agendas, now used to justify maximum top-up fees (Taylor and Scurry, 2011). Widening participation is generally taken to mean extending and enhancing access to and experience of HE for people from under-represented groups (Leathwood and O'Connell, 2003). The 'culture of leaving at 16', the increasingly questionable pathway of those supposedly failing to make appropriate, even educated, transitions through school to university, is heavily coded as a working-class problem (Quinn, 2002; Archer *et al.*, 2003; Modood, 2004). Many HE institutes now variously operate a range of widening participation initiatives, often utilising existing students in their attempts to reach out beyond the university to the wider community. Drives to increase post-16 education and reduce and replace educational disaffection with educational affection exist in institutional initiatives in both new and traditional universities. Their targets are primarily local schools and pupils, whereby the term 'locals' is seemingly used rather euphemistically to refer to non-traditional, disadvantaged working-class groups. Initiatives aimed at raising working-class pupils' 'desire to participate' beyond compulsory education and into HE are seemingly contradictory in so far as participation is prompted as attractive and attainable for all, while this sentiment is not structurally supported or resourced. In such circumstances, attainment becomes a matter of choice, deeply individualised and de-contextualised.

In fact, as Archer and Hutchings (2000) suggest, widening participation initiatives, by targeting supposedly faulty motivations, may be based on stereotypes of social groups rather than an assessment of concrete social and economic factors. In contrast to non-participation being an individualised motivational issue, working-class pupils account for non-participation in terms of real economic and social risk. For young people from working-class backgrounds, 'debt aversion' is a very real structural dis-incentive rather than something that they personally have to conquer and 'get over' (Lynch and O'Neil, 1994). The risks and benefits associated with HE participation are unequally distributed across social class and, as such, HE often remains a more difficult, 'risky' and costly choice for working-class students. Nonetheless, many formal initiatives draw on meritocratic discourses, identifying ability to participate solely in terms of academic achievement, motivations and desires. Such notions are present within the widening participation programme, which this chapter explores.

Methods

In order to focus upon students' own constructions of educational inequalities, one-to-one interviews were completed with students who had taken part in various widening participation schemes at a traditional university. The Students into Schools scheme allows over 600 students to work as tutors each year alongside teachers and pupils in regional schools and colleges. University students are encouraged to participate in this scheme, with 10-week placements, as a way of gaining key skills and thus enhancing employability. The university, which features as a Case Study 1, has a range of widening participation initiatives, utilising a range of strategies to encourage applications from non-traditional cohorts. There are a range of campus-based events that include shadowing and campus tours. Summer schools target year 10 and 11 pupils in local schools, offering educational and leisure activities over the summer. Another two-week-long summer school, offered to locally linked schools, makes guaranteed university offers in the fulfilment of lower grades plus summer school attendance. The range of prospectuses and other printed material, as well as university web pages, may also be considered as recruiting devises in the drive to widen participation, containing information on university courses, facilities, accommodation, finances and opportunities to volunteer. Seven participants of the Students into Schools programme were interviewed for this study: six of whom self-identified as middle-class and one as working-class. A focus group was also conducted with six other students, all of whom identified as working-class, which looked at more general issues of educational advantages and disadvantages. All students were undergraduates, ranging in age between 19 and 29 years.

The key questions of this research project, conducted from March to September 2006, were how do students 'market' their university? What devices and/or stories do they deploy when explaining 'why you should come to university' and how do they promote the worth of studying and the experience of students? Within this I was interested in finding out which students actually participated in the student-tutoring programme and what their motivations in doing so were. In the context of peer-led information, how do students negotiate sameness and difference with their audiences? I was also interested in whether 'local' students were becoming, or could become, 'success stories' and effective marketers or mentors and the extent to which students' own personal stories or transitions were mobilised in re-telling educational journeys, successes and failures? Many of these questions remain while others have been explored and tentatively answered in this small-scale research project.

All-round benefits?

Widening participation initiatives have many laudable aims, supported by genuine, interested and passionate student engagements. Yet engagements with the programmes were facilitated by a range of varied and potentially classed notions of what it was to be a 'good student', to have an 'interesting' curriculum vitae (CV), to make the degree count beyond the educational market and into the job market (Archer *et al.*, 2003). For many, participation was seen as a way to enhance employability, to 'help themselves' at the same time as 'helping others', combining altruism with a sense of instrumentalism. Yet in meeting with local pupils, interviewees often embraced ideas of the 'good student' versus the 'bad pupil', which cemented an 'us' and 'them', an embodied sense of difference as opposed to promoted 'sameness' via peer dissemination and understanding (Taylor, 2005; Taylor and Scurry, 2011).

State schools that take part in widening participation programmes are often spatially distinct in terms of being 'inner city', or they are on the geographical margins, situated on peripheral estates. In engaging in tutoring programmes, students had to travel to often unfamiliar places, demonstrating and often reinforcing a spatial, material and subjective distance between students in cosmopolitan city space, and 'locals' in peripheral space (Taylor, 2011). In similarity with Reay's (2004) research, students spoke of their school placements located within 'sink' estates, hosting 'rough' pupils. Often interviewees described participating schools as 'local' which, at times, seemed to be a euphemistic substitution for 'troubled', 'marginal', 'over there', 'outside': a spatialised segregation of the local against the achieving, well-placed and centred beacon of enlightened education, which were good schools (Taylor and Scurry, 2011).

All interviewees and focus group participants spoke of the benefits of widening participation, yet there was also much discussion of its disadvantages and an awareness that such initiatives do not necessarily go far enough in tackling educational inequalities. This was most vivid in terms of students stating that university was not for everyone and that alternative pathways should be equally recognised and validated. Further, there was an acute awareness of the continued inequalities within – rather than outside of – the higher educational environment and thus a certain cynicism towards the idea that educational opportunity could be evened out simply by opening the university door that bit wider (Taylor, 2006a, 2007, 2009). This research begins to unpack the complexities of widening participation agendas and practices and broader educational disadvantages or advantages, as articulated by students themselves. Students were positioned (and self-positioned) as mentors, even marketers, and were acutely aware of market-based principles of competitiveness and consumerism slipping into and shaping the university experience. In fact, it was the competitive need to be a good, well-rounded student that motivated much of their engagements with widening participation, again raising the question of who stands to gain – and who stands to lose out?

Motivations, entertainments and distractions

All students who directly participated in the Students into Schools programme said that the experience positively benefited them, in terms of accumulating skills, knowledge and experiences, adding to the all-important CV. In several cases, volunteering in such programmes was seen to facilitate access into the Postgraduate Certificate in Education (PGCE). Time and time again, students echoed the mantra that getting a degree was 'not enough':

> ...because like having a degree, everyone has got a degree now, so it is like you need something else to give you that little bit edge, something that everyone is really aware of, like all the opportunities needed to build on that CV.
>
> (Beth, 19 years old)

One respondent, Rose (20 years old), described the accumulated benefits to herself and others in terms of 'killing two birds with one stone', those being the immediate need for experience and the desired need to tackled educational inequality. Neil specifically named the gathering of CV snippets as a bit cynical but was still keen to point out the ways in which in participating he was helping himself and others at the same time:

> ...but when you're a student at the university, you're very much a student at the university aren't you? You get treated as if you're a 'rah', really hated and it was really nice to go to this school and having the kids kind of automatically assume you're a teacher, it was really refreshing to be treated like a grown up it was really nice. My main reservation would probably have been the fact that you can't get onto a PGCE unless you've got the experience on your CV of working in a school environment so again that's a little bit cynical and certainly my main reservation was I knew I had to get that experience and this seemed like an ideal opportunity.
>
> (Neil, 23 years old)

Interestingly, it's Neil's desire to challenge the limitations of his student identity or position (a rather specific, classed one at that – as a 'rah'), which proves motivating. Neil is not positioned as the 'same' and the automatic positioning of him as a teacher and a 'grown up' is described as quite refreshing. Others also emphasised the 'all-round benefits' of widening participation schemes, of raising their own and others' 'aspirations'. Yet Lynn emphatically speaks of 'our' skills and 'our' futures, not in the broad sense but as something that accrues particularly to student participants (rather than school pupils):

> ...basically they get you all involved with teaching and tutoring at schools, and the more you get into it, the more you develop, your personality evolves as well as your skills. They aim to first of all raise aspirations around schools, which is what we help for. But apart from that, they give you the opportunity to have interviews, presentations...This is a really

good thing for us as well, because it helps us to develop our skills and what we need for our future, so its really, really good.

(Lynn, 20 years old)

To turn to the classroom setting, there was at times a rather definite positioning between student 'sameness' (anyone can get to university) versus pupil difference, even disorder, as pupils and schools were placed as 'naughty', 'rough' and 'poor'. There was a tendency to even medicalise some of the social problems which pupils in disadvantaged schools faced. Here students reported on uncontrollable pupils with attention deficit and hyperactivity disorder (ADHD) and other 'little horrors' – presumably not the type that they would align themselves with. This sense of difference also became apparent when discussing their own schooling experiences and progression to university, as against the pupils' anticipated, failing journeys. Several stated that their experiences had been educational 'eye openers', encounters into previously unknown territories:

I don't know, I mean, I got the train there from Hill Bank down to Park Terrace every morning and it's only a short walk from the train station but all the kids got the train also and as soon as they got off the train they lit cigarettes, which isn't surprising. I remember one morning I was walking along the road to school and there was this kid and he must have been about fourteen years old and it was about 8:20 in the morning and he had this can of Fosters in his hand! . . . the school was quite rough and I remember seeing on the news the other night that [it] was a hot spot for arson and things. I mean, of course some of the kids are going to go down the wrong path, but then they have good features, and hopefully teachers can minimise it.

(Neil, 23 years old)

Neil identifies 'problem kids' who display quite rough behaviours that are in need of reformation, recuperation and minimisation through educational intervention.

Students engaging in the Students into Schools programme are required to undertake a training programme, which briefs them on the potential, even likely dangers and scenarios, including pupil disruption, drink and drug use. Interactions between university students and school pupils at times pointed to the divergent attitudes, hopes and behaviours, as opposed to seamless peer 'sameness'. Nonetheless, the 'us' and 'them' division was not one way, and pupils were reported as being very much the ones on top in many classroom situations:

. . . I used to worry, 'cause I used to look out the window every time – they were obsessed with my car. They would say, 'Miss I saw you at the weekend in your car', I was like 'Where?', like, 'This place', I was like 'I wasn't there at the weekend, I live in the centre'. They would always say, 'I saw you drunk in the gutter at the weekend', I was like 'No you didn't'. They tried and have a laugh.

(Clare, 19 years old)

Clare refutes these allegations as they are not only behaviourally, but spatially unlikely – she is another, different person, in another, different location. The descriptions of 'having a laugh' resonates with Willis' account whereby humour and transgression is seen to represent strategies amongst working-class 'lads', to deal with alienating educational systems (Willis, 1977; Taylor, 2006b). In actually resisting the schooling process, working-class students reproduce themselves inside social class relations, as different and other, ultimately 'failing'.

In contrast to interviewees' own remembered academic preparations and progressions often via well-equipped school guidance systems, all participants noted the inadequate provisions and resources in local schools. Further, lessons were often condemned as not properly academic (Clare spoke of 16-year-olds making Xmas cards and watching Romeo and Juliet on television – rather than reading the 'proper' version), meaning that only the good few' ever stood a chance of educational achievement and accreditation:

... there were kids who you had to sell university to, and they couldn't even spell university. There was one child who was looking through the Universities and Colleges Admissions Service (UCAS) website, and they didn't know what eligible meant. There was another girl who decided that, off the top of her head, she would go and do Child Psychology, once she realised you had to get 3 As for it, and she is predicted Ds and Es, and that's terrible, because what do you say? It is difficult trying to promote it to everybody.

(Rose, 20 years old)

The mismatch between promotional messages and educational realities leaves at least one pupil stuck with nowhere to go, further troubled by knowing she does not match up to the required standard. Worryingly, but perhaps not surprisingly so, Rose anticipates that schools are able to recognise future university candidates from year 5. Several special exceptions in failing schools are then singled out, while the failure of other pupils is then projected onto anticipated futures:

I think in the top set, there was one little girl, it was a shame for her really, because her mum was an accountant and she was in the bottom set of maths ... You could tell which kids will probably go onto university, some definitely had the ability....I could probably pick out 10 kids at least, who would go onto university. There was one boy in particular who was very intelligent and the kids always wanted him on their team when they were playing maths games. Whenever he had a spare second he would get out his pencil and start drawing, he was really good at art and he was a really good all rounder...I'd be very surprised if he didn't go to university. But then at the same token, some people, I'd be very surprised if they did.

(Rose, 20 years old)

Rose confers pity upon a single student, perhaps as a result of her departure both from the norm both in terms of unusual parental, middle-class status within the 'local' working-class school, and from all which that usually transfers and conveys (Ball, 2003). Conversely, Neil (23 years old) spoke of his 'triumph' with one 15-year-old pupil, with whom he had spent a lot of time given her removal from most lessons. Despite the classroom success, Neil has remaining doubts about her future: 'I don't know, I'm sure she's burnt down a church or something by now (laughs) but you know on that day she was a lovely kid and we made progress so that's nice.'

The idea of making good progress, increasing aspirations and motivations lies at the heart of many widening participation initiatives. Further, in sending students into schools there is the idea – or hope – that perceptions about who students are and, therefore, who university is for, can be challenged. Lynn narrates a tale of struggle, survival and success, overcoming barriers and fulfilling potential via educated transitions:

We had situations when the students were, 'Well I can't get into university, and only rich people only get into university, everyone that goes to university is posh, everyone has money', all these things...I contrast their things, the things that they have in mind with the things that actually are, in reality...one of my best friends here, she is on a loan, she is working two jobs, and university work as well, she is struggling. But that is what her target is and that's why she wants to do it. It is all about having an aim in your life and saying 'I will do this' and being very into it...I have evidence to prove that to them. So that more and more, 'Oops, ok I was mistaken'. So they get the real idea how it works.

(Lynn, 22 years old)

Lynn's sense of possibility is not entirely idealised or removed from the necessities of negotiating both economic and cultural barriers. Her aims are firm in charting feasible potential for rich and poor students alike, yet those on the wrong side of the university fence may not understand or experience inequality as a relatively benign 'variation'

'There is a variety of people from many ethnicities, many backgrounds, get loans'

(Lynn, 22 years old)

Moreover, the ability to impact upon perceptions may be a case of 'too little too late' as Neil (23 years old) highlights

Well hopefully it changed it, not that it changed it massively at all but, you know, hopefully the few kids that I spoke to about that sort of thing... But for a few of them it was too late they were, well not too late at all, but too late for that kind of year.

(Neil, 23 years old)

Most interviewees' who participated in the Students into Schools programme had sustained expectations and supports to get to university – their own schooling experiences and environments were often reported as protective bubbles, as opposed to the rather hazardous, even dangerous, battlefields of their school placements. In several cases, this sense of certainty seemed to provide a sense of security and a related willingness to take gap years out, to acquire debt and to move from home localities to university (Heath and Cleaver, 2003). Their own transitions did not seem to be marked out as particularly risky or even debatable, even if they were not linear in the recommended straight-from-school-to-university (Taylor, 2005; Taylor and Scurry, 2011). With the expectation, the resources and the support of 'always knowing' they were going to achieve academically, there was not the imminent danger of being marked as a 'failure' should they not (yet) access university (Reay, 1998; Taylor, 2007).

Several interviewees spoke of the need to 'scale down' pupils' expectations – perhaps rather ironically given that such expectations had already been described as low. In relation to the aim of widening participation, Clare noted that perhaps the ultimate endeavour should not be solely about increasing access to HE but instead to make apparent the range of opportunities and possibilities, more finely tuning motivations, aspirations and likely outcomes:

I don't know if I made a difference to be honest.... But then I suppose you can work within their views, and say that okay you want to be a mechanic, but you have got to get your General Certificate of Secondary Education's (GCSE) first and you have got to be able to read and write to do that. I suppose you could like scale it down to their aspirations, but to raise their aspirations into going to university is probably, a bit too much for one person. Whereas the ones that probably will go to university, would have always gone to university whether you'd been there or not.

(Clare, 19 years old)

'Scaling down' and 'pulling up': Widening participation as too much or not enough

Most interviewees argued for the need to extend all widening participation initiatives backwards, to primary school years, while others mentioned the need to target educational aspirations beyond the school environment, particularly focusing on the family environment of 'troubled' students with 'low aspirations' (Reay, 2004). However, operating alongside the promotion of educational achievement and credentialism were many critical commentaries that challenged the appropriateness of widening participation to all situations and to all people. To paraphrase Rose, it is not a case of either/or – of 'University or McDonalds':

> I suppose at school [placement] you always get the impression it is either university or McDonalds and I think there needs to be some more middle ground. The kids that don't want to go to university I imagine they feel like second best all the time to the ones that do. I think there needs to be something else for them. Those kids need to hear about university, of course, but they don't need to be told how great it is and how they are missing out, how their lives are not going to be complete and fulfilled if they don't go to university . . .
>
> (Rose, 20 years old)

The message of success via university entrance may at times serve to inscribe impossibility and failure, creating a difficult balancing act for those students seeking to encourage and not to deflate, to promote without prescribing. Neil also reflects a similar sentiment, speaking for the need to manage a balancing act between promotion, possibility and realism:

> It's a bit extreme that at some schools it's automatically expected that 99 per cent of the kids in the sixth form are going to go to university. Whereas in other schools like this one it's the complete opposite and it's just not expected of the kids. And I wouldn't suggest that everyone at B Sixth Form should have gone to university but they should be able to think at a realistic level you know, you can go to university and your parents don't have to be rich to afford your course fees.
>
> (Neil, 23 years old)

Neil's comments, like those of others, conveys the message that university can be affordable, yet with this comes the proviso that university still has to be worth it, it still has to pay off in monetary and personal gains: CV building for the future and social and leisure provision in the here and now. Campus-based events were seen by all interviewees and focus group participants as a way of generating interest in accessing university, portraying the reality of life at university in a very practical manner. Lynn describes feedback from campus-based events, as immediately dissolving preconceptions, offering up a more inclusive actuality:

> We get things like, 'it has been fantastic, we had great time, we really want to go to university now, it made us think more that we can actually become what we want to do, and can do anything we want' ... 'University life is not just for clever students'. So all these rumours and stories in their heads just dissolved, so they have the real thing in front of them.
>
> (Lynn, 22 years old)

In charting the possibilities on offer, there is a risk that other pathways, other locations and other people are marginalised.

Speaking of widening participation programmes and the previous New Labour government backed 'Aimhigher'[1] initiative, focus group participants discuss the ways that achievement is often solely discussed in terms of access to HE, potentially sharpening the dichotomy between achievement and success and non-participation and failure. Speaking of the university-promoting pamphlet which asked 'How proud can you be?', focus group participants were quick to challenge the equation between pride, worth and (non)attendance:

> It should be more like 'it is great' and you should be really proud of it but that shouldn't be the only aspect to it not 'How proud can you be to get a degree and be at the university', I don't think that would help to encourage more people, it might but I don't think it will help in altering the whole feel, or atmosphere, of university.
>
> (Sarah, 21 years old)

> I think that as well really, I don't just think it's about the hot shot with the degree.
>
> (Angie, 29 years old)

> What does it mean like 'How proud ... ?' I don't know.
>
> (Kate, 22 years old)

> Like, aim higher and achieve.
>
> (Angie, 29 years old)

> If you got your degree, how proud would you be kind of thing.
>
> (Lisa, 19 years old)

> So they're kinda equating being proud with uni.
>
> (Ann, 21 years old)

I don't think you necessarily have to be part of the institution to, before you can be proud of yourself. But you should have the same opportunities to develop your skills and belong to the university or the city.

(Angie, 29 years old)

Within the focus group, there was much discussion of the university's own efforts at recruitment and targeting different audiences, in advertising the 'real thing'. As actual university participants, students were reading university messages critically, apparently aware of how messages of prestige and exclusivity may be read differently by different audiences. While they all spoke of the benefits of promoting their university in particular and more generally, there was a certain scepticism about the applicability of the message for local audiences. In quoting from the prospectus, these official messages are derided for their implicit exclusions:

'A great night out', it's got all the stuff on night life. I think as well if you're not in Halls or if you're not in student accommodation then you have to be involved. If you were a local student and you lived locally you might feel a bit out of it, you should feel just as involved, I think... So I think from the point of view of local students they might be put off from it and feel that they should move away to get the student lifestyle.

(Lisa, 19 years old, focus group)

Further, focus group participants identify the slippage between potentiality in access and the transformations needed and valued therein. The glossy prospectus itself alludes to cultural transformations within the local area, while keeping its exclusivity and tradition intact:

There's lots of things in it [university prospectus], like 'transforming horizons',

'transforming culture', is that the culture of the North? 'Make it happen'! (laughs).

(Ann, 21 years old)

They can appeal to people. You've got students studying and then a picture of the [the city] and the old building? Which building is that, the old building? So you've got the old and the new, the idea that the city is changing.

(Sarah, 21 years old)

It's got a glossy feel to it, quality paper! (laughs)

(Angie, 29 years old)

That one shows you night life and everything and the bridge, the city lights. It's quite appealing to look at I think. It makes you want to sit down and read them and flick through.

(Lisa, 19 years old)

...I mean people from [here] know what the city looks like. It seems there's a divide between making it more accessible and keeping it, well with different cultural things to do, as a highly acclaimed place, with lots of things to do and relax there but as well as making it accessible, like all this 'transforming', is it a useful transformation?

(Ann, 21 years old)

Yeah, will they, the students who come, will they end of transforming the environment? But at the same time it's saying 'Yes, you can do it, it is possible'.

(Kate, 22 years old)

It's quite hard to find a balance.

(Ann, 21 years old, focus group)

Ann nicely speaks to the potential tension in promoting her university versus promoting education in itself; the message is one of differentiating and elevating particular university standards, even top-class status – the experience on offer being marketed as different, even exclusive. The certain image projected in university pamphlets and prospectuses is further discussed, whereby the image on the cover is seen to matter in more ways than one (Maguire *et al.*, 1999):

...it's promoting students not just from here but from overseas as well.

(Lisa, 19 years old)

It doesn't show a 'rah'.

(Kate, 22 years old)

Or a 'pov'!

(Angie, 29 years old)

There should be one of each! (laughs) Is she a 'rah' or is she a 'pov'?!

(Lisa, 19 years old, focus group)

'Rah' is used to describe upper- and middle-class students, while 'pov' is used to describe local, disadvantaged and working-class groups in university (Taylor and Scurry, 2011). While the absence of both groups is commented on, these descriptions begin to point to the huge differences in student access and experience. These comments raise the issue of what is the 'real' university experience, when both accessing HE and continuing within it seems to be experienced much differently between diverse student groups. Many interviewees were explicit in naming these coded phrases (rahs and povs) in classed terms:

> I think it's quite interesting how I'd never heard of the term 'rah' before I came here. And I think it's something that other universities have, but it's definitely here, to refer to people who are kinda middle-class or upper-class, I think specifically girls as well become known as 'rahs'. And I heard a while ago that they had terms for people who didn't have much money or didn't dress quite the same way and that was 'povs'.
>
> (Kate, 22 years old)

> ...You go in with an open mind that there is a certain type of person and I don't like to categorise. But I do think it's mostly middle-class students.
>
> (Sarah, 21 years old, focus group)

The ongoing class inequalities within the HE environment again highlights the conflict in promotional and widening participation messages of peer 'sameness'; the distinctions between 'rahs' and 'povs' mirror the distinctions and constructions of 'good' students versus 'bad' and 'rough' pupils. These binary constructions effect everyday perceptions and interactions between pupils and students (and amongst students), whereby notions of peer sameness and difference are both utilised and challenged, in a way that suggests that educational benefits are far from 'all round' in their scope and effects (Taylor, 2005; Taylor and Scurry, 2011).

Conclusion

Interviewees' engaging in the Students into Schools programme spoke convincingly of the urgent self-benefits and instrumental reasons for their involvement in widening participation schemes, including hoped-for access into post-graduate courses. In an educational climate where getting a degree becomes an investment that must pay off, there is perhaps less scope to engage in such programmes in an altruistic manner. New divisions emerge based upon the good experienced student and those without experience; this is troubling in that voluntary experience may be accumulated without real benefit to others. The official and promoted message of 'peer sameness' vividly contrasts with voiced differences between students as educational 'successes' and local, working-class school pupils as educational failures (Taylor, 2006a, 2007). Social class and classed locale is mobilised in constructions of the 'good student' as against the 'bad pupil'.

Interviewees own educational journeys from school to university were often smooth, linear and entirely expected, particularly amongst those participating in student tutoring, contrasting somewhat with focus group interviewees. Given that it was the former group that had direct contact with school pupils, the 'urban myths' of what constitutes stereotypical students may be reinforced rather than challenged (Archer and Hutchings, 2000). In terms of changing the delivery of Students into Schools programmes, participants could perhaps be encouraged to think more critically about their own positioning within HE and established ideas of normal post-school transitions.

However, at present, training programmes offered to student partici-pants seemingly reinforced, rather than challenged, notions of 'us' and 'them' in presenting an array of, often quite dangerous and disturbing, likely classroom scenarios, including the expectation of bad behaviour, lazi-ness and disrupted families. A point of tension lies in negotiating contact with 'peers' when these pupils or students are situated in very differ-ent places (whether this is a real or imagined difference). It would seem appropriate to ensure that students from working-class backgrounds are also recruited into tutoring, with the potential to erode student–pupil dis-identifications and the sense of accessing unfamiliar territory. Yet, this strategy comes with a warning against over-burdening working-class stu-dents with the responsibility of promoting education or representing them as tokenistic success stories, especially given that they may well be expe-riencing continued inequalities within the HE system (Taylor and Scurry, 2011).

There was a degree of scepticism about the effectiveness of widening participation initiatives alone. At times, this was articulated through a sense that local, disadvantaged students had insurmountable barriers against them, including the lack of parental and/or school support. However, other dis-incentives, such as tuition fees and the elitist climate within universities, were also discussed, featuring as structural dis-incentives operating above and beyond individual motivations. Focus group interviewees seemed par-ticularly alert to the messages and signals that their university was sending out via pamphlets and prospectuses. Indeed, the images, buildings, locations and activities featured in the prospectus were understood to appeal to more middle-class students. The university prospectus remains a signifier of insti-tutional status and student composition and is read differently by different student or pupil groups, with the effects of including and excluding (Maguire *et al.*, 1999).

Working-class pupils continue to be identified as 'at risk' of dropping out of education, while there is a lack of infrastructure and funding to facili-tate participation amongst traditionally excluded groups (Reay, 1997, 1998; Quinn, 2002; Archer *et al.*, 2003). If the abolition of the grant meant a very real threat to the presence of non-traditional students in higher education institutions (HEIs), then the introduction of tuition fees and top-up fees potentially cements and entrenches existing classed exclusions, which seems to be in contradiction to educational inclusion and widening participation. Such structural dis-incentives have arguably reinforced classed exclusion, situating non-participation in terms of individual motivations and aspirations, rather than the ability to pay (Archer *et al.*, 2003). In seeking to 'raise aspirations', widening participation initiatives rather problematically situate educational disadvantage as one of motivation alone, which is reflected in and challenged by students' own involvement with, and feelings about, such initiatives. Many HEIs now have widening participation targets to meet. This can lead to 'local', 'disadvantaged' students being seen as a potentially new market, and whilst this may have many positive aspects to it, it potentially leads to elite universities being in competition, rather than partnership with post-1992 'new' universities, where local students are more likely to attend. Finally, issues of widening participation and educational disadvantage and advantage are not simply admission issues, which necessitates an expanded definition and approach to what 'widening participation' means.

Acknowledgements

I would like to thank C-SAP for funding the research project 'All-Round Benefits? Student Involvement in Widening Participation Programmes'.

Notes

1. The National Scholarship Programme (NSP) is to replace Aimhigher in 2012 (see http://www.hefce.ac.uk/pubs/hefce/2011/11_10/). While controversial, the Aimhigher programme did allow 'outreach' work (see Evans, 2010): in the NSP the focus is on bursaries for stimulating participation from 'disadvantaged' groups. Universities are required to provide outreach work as part of their institutional widening participation strategies, but post-1992 universities will be more vulnerable in this respect, lacking funding, despite their success in securing diverse university cohorts: in contrast 'elite' universities may well be marketing themselves as 'diverse' and 'inclusive' via NSP on the back of rather tokenistic measures that do not alter their middle-class, white compositions (see Taylor, forthcoming, 2012).
2. This research was conducted in an established red-brick university, which is a member of the elite UK Russell group. Widening participation issues are different in 'new' post-1992 universities, but in this new educational climate of Conservative-Liberal fees, it is these institutions that have long-standing commitments to 'widening participation' as a tangible everyday reality that are now rendered more vulnerable. In contrast, elite universities may be in a position to offer limited student bursaries through the NSP, without altering their overall white, middle-class composition. Indeed, elite institutions may now be in the curious position of marketing their own 'elitism' and 'diversity', while post-1992 institutions are positioned as 'failing' to deliver on what is now a strange brand of 'diverse' elitism (see Taylor, 2011 and forthcoming, 2012).

Bibliography

Archer, L. and Hutchings, M. (2000) ' "Bettering Yourself? Discourses of Risk, Cost and Benefit in Ethnically Diverse, Young Working Class Non-participants" Constructions of HE', *British Journal of Sociology of Education*, 21: 555–574.

Archer, L., Ross, A., Hutchings, M., with Leathwood, C., Gilchrist, R. and Phillips, D. (2003) *Higher Education and Social Class: Issues of Exclusion and Inclusion* (London: Routledge Falmer).

Ball, S. (2003) *Class Strategies and the Education Market: The Middle Class and Social Advantage* (London: Routledge Falmer).

Browne Report (2010) *Securing a Sustainable Future for Higher Education* [online] http://www.bis.gov.uk/assets/biscore/corporate/docs/s/10-1208-securing-sustainable-higher-education-browne-report [accessed June 2012].

European Union's 2020 Strategy [online] http://ec.europa.eu/europe2020/index_en.htm [accessed January 2011].

Evans, S. (2010) 'Becoming "Somebody": Examining Class and Gender Through Higher Education', in Taylor, Y. (ed.) *Classed Intersections: Spaces, Selves, Knowledges* (Farham: Ashgate, pp. 53–72).

Heath, S. and Cleaver, E. (2003) *Young, Free and Single? Twenty-Somethings and Household Change* (London: Palgrave Macmillan).

Leathwood, C. and O'Connell, P. (2003) ' "It's a Struggle": The Construction of the "New Student" in Higher Education', *Journal of Education Policy*, 18 (6): 597–615.

Lynch, K. and O'Neil, C. (1994) 'The Colonisation of Social Class in Education', *British Journal of the Sociology of Education*, 15 (2): 307–342.

Maguire, M., Ball, S. and MacRae, S. (1999) 'Promotion, Persuasion and Class-Taste: Marketing (in) the UK Post-Compulsory Sector', *British Journal of Sociology of Education*, 20 (3): 291–308.

Modood, T. (2004) 'Capitals, Ethnic Identity and Educational Qualifications', *Cultural Trends*, 13 (2): 37–105.

Quinn, J. (2002) *Social Class and Participation in HE: Case Studies Update* (London: UUK).

Reay, D. (2004) ' "Mostly Roughs and Toughs": Social Class, Race and Representation in Inner City Schooling', *Sociology*, 38 (5): 1005–1023.

Reay, D. (2001) 'Finding or Losing Yourself? Working Class Relationships to Education', *Journal of Education Policy*, 16 (4): 333–346.

Reay, D. (1998) ' "Always Knowing" and "Never Being Sure": Familial and Institutional Habituses in Higher Educational Choice', *Journal of Educational Policy*, 13 (4): 519–529.

Reay, D. (1997) 'The Double-Bind of the "Working-class" Feminist Academic: The Success of Failure or the Failure of Success?', in Mahony, P. and Zmroczek, C. (eds.) *Class Matters. 'Working-Class' Women's Perspectives on Social Class* (London: Taylor and Francis, pp. 18–30).

Taylor, Y. (ed.) (forthcoming, 2012) *Educational Diversity: The Subject of Difference and Different Subjects* (London: Palgrave Macmillan).

Taylor, Y. (2011) 'Accessions: Researching, Designing Higher Education', *Gender and Education*, 23 (6): 777–782.

Taylor, Y. (2009) 'Facts, Fictions, Identity Constrictions: Sexuality, Gender and Class in Higher Education', *Lesbian & Gay Psychology Review*, Special Issue 10 (1): 38–47.

Taylor, Y. (2007) 'Brushed Behind the Bike Shed: Class and Sexuality in School', *British Journal of the Sociology of Education*, 28 (3): 349–362.

Taylor, Y. (2006a) 'Intersections of Class and Sexuality in the Classroom', *Gender and Education*, 18 (4): 447–452.

Taylor, Y. (2006b). *All Round Benefits? Student Involvement in Widening Participation Initiatives*, CSAP report [online] http://www.c-sap.bham.ac.uk/inclusion/completed-projects?view= project&id= 192 [accessed June 2012].

Taylor, Y. (2005) 'What Now? Working-Class Lesbians' Post-School Transitions', *Youth and Policy*, 87: 29–43.

Taylor, Y. and Scurry, T. (2011) 'International and Widening Participation Students' Experience of Higher Education, UK', *European Societies*, 13 (4): 583–606.

Willis, P. (1977) *Learning to Labour: How Working Class Kids Get Working Class Jobs* (Farnborough: Saxon House).

6
Mature Women Students, Study Motivation and Employability

Ruth Woodfield

Introduction: Mature students and employability – Key themes in the literature

The move to mass higher education (HE) prompted increased debate about the relationship between earning a degree and employability. Some commentators have claimed that the UK economy cannot supply enough jobs for the graduate 'glut' (Brown and Hesketh, 2004), whilst others have claimed that the link between graduation and enhanced employment prospects remains strong (Brennan *et al.*, 2001; Purcell and Elias, 2004). What is relatively uncontested, however, is that, in the context of increasing competition for graduate jobs, some students 'are better placed than others' (see also Elias *et al.*, 1999; Redmond, 2006: 120; Purcell *et al.*, 2007).

It is also widely acknowledged, however, that comparatively little academic research has examined the relationship between graduates and their post-degree employment, and so there is only a minimal evidential basis for exploring which graduates are better placed than others in the competition for jobs. Very little research indeed has focused on the employment outcomes of mature versus traditional-entry graduates and less still on the relative performance of more specific categories, such as mature female students[1] (Adnett and Coates, 2000; Egerton, 2001; Egerton and Parry, 2001; Woodley and Wilson, 2002; Purcell and Elias, 2004; Redmond, 2006; Woodfield, 2011).

Mature students comprise over a fifth of full-time degree entrants and the majority of all undergraduate students (HESA, 2009/10). Their proportionate presence within the UK HE system has increased rapidly under its expansion (Egerton, 2000). Prominent within the academic and policy literature on mature students' HE experience is what has been called a 'narrative of disadvantage' (Woodfield, 2011: 410). Such literature is usually explicitly or implicitly suggestive of mature students' experience comparing less well with that of their traditional-entry counterparts – identifying that they find themselves under more financial and caring constraints, are more socially isolated, and understand and fit the HE 'system' less well (Weil, 1986; Brine and Waller, 2004; Redmond, 2006). This characterisation has been particularly associated with discussions of the experiences of mature female students (Reay, 2003; Hinton-Smith, 2009). Of course, there are good reasons for this discursive trend in the literature – mature students undoubtedly do experience significantly different profiles and constraints than traditional-entry students, and this is reflected in their higher levels of non-completion (Yorke, 2001). Equally, mature women students often bear the burdens of primary caring responsibilities, work and study. The default assumption in much literature is that these differences always translate into disadvantage,[2] however, and this is suggested to be the case even in the context of minimal empirical exploration.

In line with this overarching perspective, the majority of research looking at mature students' employability suggests that they experience a significant disadvantage in the graduate labour market when compared with their younger counterparts, and that, therefore, their degree represents less added value for them in employment terms (Purcell and Pitcher, 1996; Connor *et al.*, 1997; Elias *et al.*, 1999; Egerton, 2000, 2001; Egerton and Parry, 2001; Blasko *et al.*, 2002; Woodley and Wilson, 2002; Purcell and Elias, 2004; Redmond, 2006; Purcell *et al.*, 2007). It has been claimed that women, in particular, struggle to match the investment returns enjoyed by their traditional-entry counterparts (Purcell and Elias, 2004). Set against this is a much smaller amount of research that has suggested that mature graduates may be moderately advantaged in the labour market (see, for instance, Woodley and Simpson, 2001; Brennan and Shah, 2003; Feinstein *et al.*, 2007; Woodfield, 2011). Some research has suggested that those 'younger mature' students, aged under 30, may have favourable long-term employment outcomes. Crucially, however, they conclude that mature graduates from courses tailored to their particular needs (e.g. at the Open University and Birkbeck) significantly improve the overall mature performance (see Woodley and Simpson, 2001; Feinstein *et al.*, 2007). A recent analysis of an entire cohort of UK graduates has concluded that regardless of whether mature students studied part- or full-time, this group secured paid work, graduate-level work and a higher salary more frequently than their traditional-aged counterparts. Furthermore, mature women students had more employment success than their younger female and male counterparts, with mature women who had completed a science degree performing especially well (Woodfield, 2011).

This chapter will further explore the relative employability of mature women graduates through analysis of the 2006 and 2009 cohorts of UK graduates. It will then discuss the findings of ten in-depth interviews with mature female graduates. The aims of the chapter are further to explore the extent to which the participants of this group are aware of their membership of a comparatively advantaged set, in terms of post-degree employment, and to assess the role that employability plays in motivating them initially to undertake a degree.

Mature graduates and the career motive

Research has shown that mature students themselves often have comparatively little confidence with regard to whether their educational investment will pay off in terms of enhanced employability (Egerton, 2001; Davies *et al.*, 2002; Brine and Waller, 2004; Hinton-Smith, 2009), but very little, if any, literature has sought to explore whether this reflects the reality of their employment prospects. As we have seen previously, much general commentary is pessimistic and involves what Woodley and Wilson (2002: 331) have called 'crude hypotheses based upon a stereotype of a graduate aged 35–40 from a full-time course who is aiming for a career change'. Such hypotheses include the suggestions that mature graduates are less employable because they bring age-associated background disadvantages into HE with them, that they are vulnerable to age discrimination by employers and that they are more likely to return to previous employers; the assumption being that this represents less opportunity for graduate-level career development. Typically, projections become progressively more pessimistic as students age. Indeed, as Egerton has suggested, 'it is widely believed that older mature graduates have poor prospects in the labour market' (Egerton, 2001: 141).

Nevertheless, it has also been suggested that mature students are likely to have 'taken their courses with a clear intention of enhancing their employment opportunities' (Purcell *et al.*, 2007: 61). Such statements rarely compare the motives of mature students with the motives of younger students for whom career concerns must also be salient, if not as immediate and explicit, but the assumption is that, for mature students, the employment motive is primary. Mullen's work on US students provides a useful body of data in relation to this and concludes that middle-class, traditional-age students who attend prestigious universities, as part of an expected life trajectory, readily articulate their commitment to education as intrinsic and see 'the end value of education in the journey' (2010: 142). Accordingly, they frequently pursue a liberal arts programme and do so explicitly to enhance their personal development. By contrast, older and less well-off students attending public colleges seek pre-professional programmes and enhanced employability and firmly 'set their sights on the destination' (2010: 142). They engage less with the all-round experience of university and personal development beyond those related directly to building enhanced employability.

The dovetailing of enhanced employment motivation and poorer employment prospects for mature students would seem to be particularly concerning as this group is also more likely to come from socially disadvantaged backgrounds. This means that HE investment 'entails considerable economic costs and material risks' (Brine and Waller, 2004: 107; see also Egerton, 2001;

Egerton and Parry, 2001). This combination of factors has been cited as part of the reason that the decision-making surrounding investing in a degree course is arguably more 'complex' and 'fragile' than for traditional-entry students (Osbourne *et al.*, 2004: 294; see also Egerton, 2000; Davies *et al.*, 2002; Reay, 2003; Purcell and Elias, 2004; Purcell *et al.*, 2007).

Reay's work with working-class mature women students on access to HE courses (2003) has not only confirmed the fragility of their decision-making in relation to undertaking a degree but also challenges the view that enhanced employability for the individual is a primary motive. In contrast with Mullen's participants, these participants, despite their disadvantage, were focused on the learning itself rather than what specific objective it could lead to

> For all 12 women students it would appear that it was the doing of a degree that was important rather than instrumental goal orientation. This prioritising of the process rather than the outcome highlights a distinction between the mature students and their younger female counterparts aged 17 and 18.
>
> (Reay, 2003: 304)

Moreover, Reay's participants, in their desire to pursue education for education's sake, were not, however, pursuing it in order to become 'what one is'. Self-realisation was consequently 'not at the core of these women's educational projects' (2003: 304) in the way it can be for many middle-class and younger students (Reay, 2003: 304: see also Mullen, 2010). Reay's participants' commitment to 'education for its own sake' was strongly linked to a further commitment to 'give something back' (2003: 301) and to 'make a contribution to society' (2003: 304). Where employment goals were discussed, it was in relation to the desire to pursue careers in teaching or social work that could facilitate the contribution to participants' communities. Desires to access HE were articulated in the context of pressing family and work commitments as desires to give back to family and community: ' "giving back" was their rationale for justifying what they clearly perceived to be an essentially selfish act' (Reay, 2003: 305). Reay concludes that her participants manifest 'collective rather than individualised motivations for returning to education' (2003: 309), and those collectivist motivations 'allow women to occupy the acceptable space of authentic femininity' (2003: 309).

Mature women graduates' employability re-examined

Data and participants

The data on which the chapter is based initially comprises the results of an analysis of the employment status of the 2006 and 2009 cohort of graduates

Table 6.1 Graduates' employment success by gender and age (2006 & 2009)

Year	Student group	Employed full-time (%)	Employed part-time (%)	Self-employed (%)	Total in paid employment (%)	Unemployed and looking for ESorT (%)	Employed in graduate-level* role (%)
2006							
	All men	59	9	3	71	7	56
	All women	59	13	2	74	5	54
	Mature men	60	8	5	73	8	61
	Mature women	57	16	3	76	6	65
2009							
	All men	47	13	4	64	11	66
	All women	51	17	2	70	7	65
	Mature men	54	10	5	69	10	76
	Mature women	56	17	3	76	6	78

*Note: Woodfield undertook the categorisation of occupations into 'graduate-level work' in the 2006 dataset using Elias and Purcell's typology. In the case of the 2009 dataset, the categorisation was undertaken by Higher Education Statistics Agency (HESA) data services.

in the United Kingdom,[3] six months after graduation. After this quantitative picture is explicated, further data will be explored, comprising interviews with ten mature women graduates; all interview and participants completed their degrees between 2004 and 2008 at the University of Sussex. Five were interviewed whilst on their courses (aged 25, 27, 29, 33 and 50), five after graduation (aged 22, 23, 40, 47 and 50[4]). Of those who had graduated, five had secured employment or further study with three having secured employment they considered to require a degree to undertake successfully, one was employed in what she described as a non-graduate job and the fifth had been self-employed as a property developer. Participants studied from a range of disciplines including biology, cognitive psychology, law, sociology and art history.

Interview questions focused on initial motivations for HE study, participants' employment histories, aspirations and experience of seeking employment after graduation. They also sought to elicit a sense of participants' awareness of employability issues, including their own employability and its relationship to their having undertaken a degree. Interviews lasted approximately an hour and were undertaken in private in rooms at the University of Sussex. Interview data was transcribed and coded by hand to identify recurring and salient themes in relation to study motivation and the significance of employment, and personal and general graduate employability issues.

The quantitative picture

In previous literature, measures of employment success after graduation have often comprised solely or primarily the securing of full-time work (Egerton and Parry, 2001; Woodley and Wilson, 2002; Furlong and Cartmel, 2005). This ignores the possibility that graduates have secured part-time work intentionally. It further assumes that part-time work is by definition a less favourable outcome in other respects (that it may be less likely to be graduate-level employment, for instance) and ignores generally acknowledged gendered patterns of employment, whereby women are far more likely to seek and/or be constrained to undertake part-time work for care reasons. Mature women graduates are the groups most likely to take up part-time employment for caring reasons. In defining those in part-time employment as unsuccessful, such research ignores salient features of the UK labour market and potentially produces a negatively skewed picture of mature women graduates' employability. In the research under consideration here, those achieving part-time paid employment after graduation have been included in the sample when calculating employment success and the definition of successful graduate employment centres on the 'graduate' element and not the part- or full-time status.

The categorisation of employment as 'graduate-level' or 'non-graduate-level' is determined using the specifically designed classification system developed by Elias and Purcell (2004): Social Occupational Classification

(Higher Education), SOC(HE). In this typology, five distinct occupational groups are identified (2004: 4):

1. Traditional graduate occupations (e.g. solicitors, doctors)
2. Modern graduate occupations (e.g. information technology (IT) professionals, teachers)
3. New graduate occupations (e.g. occupational therapists, management accountants)
4. Niche graduate occupations (e.g. planning engineers, hotel managers)
5. Non-graduate occupations

For the purposes of this analysis, categories 1–4 have been collapse together to comprise 'graduate-level employment', and category 5 comprises 'non-graduate employment'.[5]

As can be seen from Table 6.1, mature female graduates are more likely than mature male, as well as traditional-aged male and female graduates, to secure paid employment overall. This measure includes employment that is full-time, part-time and self-employment. Seventy-six per cent of mature women graduates do so. Additionally, they are also more likely than other groups of graduates to secure graduate-level employment. Seventy-eight per cent of mature women graduates secure such employment within six months of graduating.

Mature women are also more likely to be in employment with a permanent or open-ended contract. In 2009, for instance, 55 per cent of them secured this type of employment as against 51 per cent of mature men, 40 per cent of traditional-aged men and 43 per cent of traditional-aged women.

Mature women graduates were less likely than traditional-aged men and mature men to be unemployed six months after graduation in 2006 and the least likely to be unemployed in 2009.

Mature women graduates' perceptions of their employability

A key finding from the qualitative data was participants' misperceptions in relation to the employment prospects of mature graduates and how their prospects fared when compared with traditional-aged graduates. No participants distinguished between male and female graduates when talking about the employability of mature graduates generally, indicating that they assumed these two groups' employment prospects would be the same. Five of the participants believed that mature graduates would be disadvantaged in the labour market, with four of these participants being in the group that had already graduated:

I don't have any prior information on this [mature graduates' employ-ability] but I would think it would be worse...Ageism is still very rife in this country although it's very much denied and I think when you say 'mature' it depends on the level of maturity...I think someone that's going to be mid-50s coming out is going to have a heck of a job.

(Participant 1, aged 48, graduate)

If they want to improve their job opportunities I would say they need to really be more focused on what career they want at the end of it and speak to someone about what's the best degree to do and what the chances are of them getting a job being a mature graduate at the end of it...the other thing to think about as well, you've got this big debt at the end of it and you're middle aged, so to speak...I don't know that I regret it necessarily, I enjoyed it. But...I think in hindsight it won't change my job opportunities very much at all. If I'd spent 4 years perhaps concentrating more on my career I'd be in a better position.

(Participant 5, aged 30, student)

The problem is...your age stops you getting the normal graduate level jobs...a normal graduate in Art History will have probably the same dif-ficulties getting a job in an Art History career but they could get a job in another degree level area...a company that do graduate training, but they don't want to take on mature students because they think they have to pay you too much money or that you're not as quick at learning. There is still a lot of bias.

(Participant 4, aged 33, graduate)

Three of the participants believed mature students could expect the same treatment as younger graduates and two believed that mature students might be slightly advantaged. These latter two participants claimed that mature students, including themselves, were probably more employable because they had 'been around the block a bit more', 'had life skills' 'and would be more loyal'. No participant indicated awareness that mature women's graduate employment prospects were comparatively strong.

The anticipation of disadvantage shared by four of the graduate partici-pants was sometimes related to their own employment searches or success. In one case, a participant had struggled to secure graduate-level employment in social service (or related) administration, despite achieving a first in soci-ology and having a long pre-entry working history that had provided her with excellent office and administrative skills:

What I thought was, I mean I knew that I was limited because of my home life...and also because of my age. I thought 'I've got to be real-istic', but what I thought was that it would make me employable in that small area that I wanted to be employed in...But it didn't happen at all...The reality was that nobody could give a **** basically. They absolutely couldn't. I mean, a degree was just worth nothing, absolutely nothing. I was applying for all sorts of things...constant interviews.

(Participant 3, aged 50, graduate)

This participant cited three reasons for her negative experiences applying for work after graduating. She believed that a lack of specific and direct work experience related to her chosen career was held against her, as was the fact she had not undertaken a pre-professional training degree at HE level, such as social work. Lastly, she believed that employer ageism was in evidence in interviews and discussions with organisational members before and after interviews:

I think that...having a degree at my age isn't taken seriously. One job I went for was some poxy typing job. I could have done it in my sleep, and one of the women on the interview panel said 'what did you do a degree in?' and I said 'sociology' and she said 'Oh yes, lots of older women do that don't they?'

It is worth noting in relation to the perceived lack of prospects for graduates without more vocationally oriented degrees expressed by this participant that graduates of science degrees also shared the belief that their employability had not necessarily been enhanced by HE study:

I think you need to be aware of the reality of it really, if you want a house, a career, then a degree in biology isn't necessarily going to do it for you. Not even in commercial biology.

(Participant 9, aged 29, graduate)

The journey versus the destination: Self-development and the employment motive

Another key finding from the qualitative data was that only two participants cited clear employment goals as a main initial motivation for their HE study, with a further two reporting vague aspirations that HE would 'open a few more doors'. Six, however, were explicit that their motives to undertake a degree were not related to future employment. Of the two who cited career goals as a main motivation, both subsequently changed these initial plans early on in their studies. One participant had suffered a stroke 'which devastated my career' (Participant 1, aged 47, Student) and had emerged from her rehabilitation with eyes fixed on a clear career path into a pre-professional degree and its associated career:

So I applied to college to do an access course with a very straight view of where I was going – social work – that was it for me. I knew exactly what

I was doing.... I had very much a career plan which was to keep improving my fitness through the university degree and then go into social work with a view to perhaps running older people's departments.

These plans were disrupted, however, when she 'fell in love' with sociology:

On day we had a social theory lecture with an amazing tutor, and I'd never heard of these concepts and perspectives and I just fell in love with it... then of course, because of this change of heart, I had to think where will I go with this if I do sociology? And I didn't really know. I just knew I wanted to do it.... My tutor said... 'have you not thought about teaching?' and I said 'No'. He said 'I think you'd be great because you're so enthusiastic' and I said 'well, can I do that from this degree?' and he said 'yes, you can'.

The second participant motivated by a career choice that necessitated undertaking a science degree also changed her plans. The further two participants who reported that employment prospects had been considered in relation to the decision to study suggested that it was jobs undertaken in the past that played a role rather than careers imagined in the future. In both cases, participants described a growing awareness emerging in the course of working in a previous job that clarified that they did not want to remain in the same work in the long term:

I just worked at Sainsbury's. Still work there now but obviously there was all the 'come and be a manager, come and do this and do that' and I think that was the reality check. Do I want to spend the rest of my life being a manager at Sainsbury's or do I want to go and do something that I've always wanted to do?

(Participant 7, aged 23, student)

As with the majority of Reay's participants, all ten participants here, including the four cited above, shared a strong motivation to study: the intrinsic love of learning and of the subject being read. Six of them cited this as the only motive for undertaking a degree, or the motive that eclipsed all others. This desire to learn was articulated as something they re-engaged with and which dated from an earlier halted educational trajectory because of negative educational experiences, low self-expectations and/or caring priorities:

Since I was knee-high to a grasshopper I've always wanted to go to university... it didn't happen straight away because of being put down by teachers in A levels and all they said was I was too thick to go to university... 'go to secretarial school'.

(Participant 8, aged 27, graduate)

University wasn't expected out of me really. I grew up on the estate across the road, so it wasn't something we did... but it was something that had been scratching at my head for a long time when I'd done GCSEs in the evening and done other part time courses.

(Participant 9, aged 29, graduate)

I got my A levels and then I was planning to go to university straight off, but I suppose it was more personal circumstances that stopped me. I decided to have a year out... but then my best friend got pregnant, had a baby and her mum kicked her out and she ended up living with me, which obviously took my mind off it completely.

(Participant 7, aged 23, student)

Eight participants reported that deferred HE aspirations re-emerged from the crucible of a significant personal crisis triggered by events in their personal or employment histories. These triggers ranged from bereavements, significant changes in relationships and serious illness through to being made redundant, and sometimes more than one of these, and led to a period of reflection about themselves and their priorities and aspirations for personal development:

One of the major decision-making things was I was marrying and had a catastrophic event with my health, so it wasn't as if I did it for employability reasons, the reasons were more personal really, largely to prove to myself that I could do it really and to force some change in my life.

(Participant 9, aged 29, graduate)

I moved down to Brighton...the weekend I moved down here I fell pregnant...while I was pregnant with my daughter I thought 'this is such a life-changing thing...well maybe now's the time to actually follow my dream. I've kind of got one of my dreams which is to be a mum, maybe it's time to follow that great big dream that's right up there'. I remember actually driving to the hospital while I was in labour saying to my daughter's dad 'I think I'm going to start studying'...three days before I had [my daughter] I became a lone parent so it was all a bit...I don't do things by halves. It was all or nothing. I thought 'right, well, if I can do that then I can do anything...it's me and you now girl'.

(Participant 6, aged 40, student)

The overwhelming majority of commentary on why these women returned to their education was therefore more strongly related to self-realisation than employment. Two participants went so far as to report being surprised that their degree had enhanced their career prospects and employability in the context of being extremely gratified at the personal development it had facilitated:

> I've actually been the richest in my life when I was a student. You gain so much insight... I just love studying, so, for me, I could sit and study for the rest of my life.... Doing a degree was a personal pleasure, was personal achievement, enjoyment. I never related it to getting a job afterwards, or, you know, what it could do for me beyond... if I hadn't come to work here [in current job]... it would have just been something 'oh well, I've got a degree' and just trundled on and never thought about the skills that I've now got.
>
> (Participant 8, aged 27, graduate)

Additionally, disciplinary areas studied were chosen by all participants because of prior interest in the material they covered rather than for employability reasons. Even where a particular career was aspired to initially, this had been identified because of an intrinsic interest in the subject it was related to rather than because of the financial or lifestyle characteristics with which it was associated. This general pattern included those who had chosen to study pre-professional disciplines, such as law:

> I don't know, it's hard to explain [why I chose law]. It's just a passion I suppose, it just interests me and I get bored easily with a lot of subjects and this is the one subject that has sort of kept me wanting to know more... I wouldn't say it's because I wanted to be a barrister or solicitor... It's just the subject as a core thing that's just done it for me.
>
> (Participant 7, aged 23, student)

> I've got a degree that's not worth a lot at the moment but there you go. I remember... [someone saying] 'you do realise that you're studying the worst degree for getting a job statistically out of any other degree', but, you know, it was my interest and passion so it's just one of those things.
>
> (Participant 4, aged 33, graduate)

All participants, including those expressing disappointment at their graduate careers, declared that their degree had not disappointed these personal development motivations and had delivered significant benefits:

I thoroughly enjoyed the actual learning process so from a personal point of view I don't regret it.

(Participant 3, aged 50, graduate)

I gained so much out of it not just in terms of specialist knowledge and the ability to explore different ideas. I met so many people and I just broadened my expectations of myself...it broadened by worldview, I think, my global view. And certainly I travelled more after I went to university whereas I never did before.

(Participant 9, aged 29, graduate)

Individual and community

The mature women interviewed here were not focused on career goals. They did, occasionally, however, briefly mention careers they might be happy to pursue. Following Reay's participants, these careers were often in education, social work or related occupations, and health support occupations, i.e. in those occupational areas often associated with altruistic motivations on the part of the employee. It should be noted, however, that by contrast with Reay's mature women, the participants for this project did not articulate a strong collectivist motivation or project future community-oriented careers. It should be noted in this regard that the occupational areas cited by them were precisely those dominated by women generally, were likely therefore to be familiar to them, and confirming of their gender and gender-associated traits and skills (Gottfredson, 1981; Blackburn and Jarman, 2006; Woodfield, 2007).

Also, in contrast with Reay's participants, the mature women interviewed in this study did not indicate that they were struggling to explain 'an essentially selfish act' (Reay, 2003: 305), when explaining their choice to go to university, nor did they narrate their desire to access HE within a discourse that allowed them to 'occupy the acceptable space of authentic femininity' (2003: 309). To be sure, participants did mention their children as beneficiaries of their decision to take a degree, and especially the importance of their having role-modelled educational aspiration, success and resilience for their children by doing so. However, their salient motivation was reported as self-realisation, personal development and enjoyment.

Concluding discussion

The findings presented here contribute to our understanding of the neglected relationship between age and graduate employability and do so via an analysis of two recent cohorts of graduates and ten in-depth interviews with mature women either undertaking a degree or after the completion of a degree.

The key findings from the quantitative data suggest that what I have called the 'discourse of disadvantage', replicated in much mature student research, and which extends to mature students' graduate employability, is not warranted in the latter case. Indeed, the findings from the quantitative picture indicate that mature students are advantaged when it comes to securing paid employment and graduate-level employment in particular. Mature women secure a higher rate of graduate-level employment than mature male graduates, and male and female traditional-aged students.

The research therefore confirms the reasonably optimistic findings of a small amount of earlier research identifying younger matures as being slightly advantaged and matures as a whole as being so (see, for instance, Woodley and Simpson, 2001; Brennan and Shah, 2003; Feinstein *et al.*, 2007). It presents a wholly different picture from that outlined in most related research work, however, which has claimed that mature students are disadvantaged in the graduate labour market and that their degree represents less added value for them in employment terms (Connor *et al.*, 1997; Elias *et al.*, 1999; Egerton, 2000, 2001; Egerton and Parry, 2001; Blasko *et al.*, 2002; Purcell and Elias, 2004; Redmond, 2006). The findings outlined here challenge previous literature that has claimed women, in particular, are particularly vulnerable to poor rates of return on their degree investment (Blasko *et al.*, 2002; Purcell and Elias, 2004; Redmond, 2006). Overall, the findings here tell an affirmative story and should give confidence to those mature students making the undoubtedly difficult decision to commit to a degree.

The second key finding, however, is that this success story would not seem to have been disseminated into the population of prospective, existing and past students. None of the mature women interviewed here was aware that they were part of an advantaged group when it comes to employability.

Finally, a key finding to emerge here is that the majority of the mature women interviewed did not undertake study at the HE level to improve their employability. Their reasons for undertaking a degree were far more clearly related to a range of personal development priorities: from satisfying a passion for a specific subject to confirming that they were capable of achieving a degree-level education following negative or interrupted earlier educational experiences. In contrast with Mullen's (2010) US non-traditional participants, these women were focused on the journey and not the destination – the self-realisation and not the employment outcomes.

In the context of these findings, it is interesting to speculate whether higher numbers of mature women would be persuaded to undertake a degree if the graduate employability rates of this group were more widely known and whether the focus on self-development would have been more muted if the link between employability and graduation had been more clearly understood by the participants of this study. Given the changing funding landscape of HE, it is also important to consider whether the women interviewed here would have committed to a degree in the context of the partial or inaccurate knowledge they held about what this qualification would do for their employability.

Notes

1. The term 'mature' designates students over the age of 21 on entry to HE, whilst 'traditional-entry' or 'young' designates those under the age of 21. See author's: Widening participation of under-represented groups – definitions (Tables T1 and T2) available on http://www.hesa.ac.uk/index.php?option= com_content& task=view&id=2061&Itemid=141 for further information [accessed 30 September 2011].
2. The notable exception is research focused on mature students' good academic achievement rates at the HE level, e.g. Richardson and Woodley (2003).
3. The HESA datasets that formed the basis of the results presented here comprised 232,063 UK- and EU-domiciled students who completed an honours degree in UK HE institutions in 2006, and 299,152 UK- and EU-domiciled students who completed an honours degree in UK HEIs in 2009, and for which HESA also have Destinations of Leavers of Higher Education data. The bespoke datasets (ref: 27322 and 31214, respectively) comprised 44 raw categorical variables, including employment information of graduating students, as well as information on a range of background and on-course factors. Students' age on entry was grouped as: 17 and under; 18–20; 21–24; 25–29; 30–39; 40–49; 50–59; 60 and over.
4. The ages of graduates are given at the point of graduation rather than interview.
5. When assessing the percentages of those securing 'graduate-level employment', students declaring that they were in full-time study were excluded.

Bibliography

Adnett, N. and Coates, C. (2000) 'Mature Female Entrants to Higher Education: Closing the Gender Gap in the UK Labour Market', *Higher Education Quarterly*, 54 (2): 187–201.

Blackburn, R.M. and Jarman, J. (2006) 'Gendered Occupations: Exploring the Relationship Between Gender Segregation and Inequality', *International Sociology*, 21 (2): 289–315.

Blasko, Z., Brennan, J. and Shah, T. (2002) *Access to What: Analysis of Factors Determining Graduate Employability*. Report to HEFCE by the Centre for Higher Education Research and Information (CHERI).

Brennan, J. and Shah, T. (2003) *Access to What? Converting Education Opportunity into Employment Opportunity* (London: Centre for Higher Education Research and Information).

Brennan, J., Little, B., Shah, T. and Woodley, A. (2001) *The Employment of UK Graduates: Comparisons with Europe and Japan*. A Report to the HEFCE by the Centre for Higher Education Research and Information, Open University.

Brine, J. and Waller, R. (2004) 'Working-Class Women on an Access Course: Risk, Opportunity and (Re)constructing Identities', *Gender and Education*, 16 (1): 97–113.

Brown, P. and Hesketh, A. (2004) *The Mismanagement of Talent: Employability and Jobs in the Knowledge Economy* (Oxford: OUP).

Connor, H., La Valle, I., Pollard, E. and Millmore, B. (1997) *What Do Graduates Do Next?* (Brighton, UK: Institute for Employment Studies).

Davies, P., Osborne, M. and Williams, J. (2002) *For Me or Not for Me, That Is the Question. A Study of Mature Students' Decision-Making and Higher Education* (London: DfES (DfES Research Briefing No. 297)).

Egerton, M. (2001) 'Mature Graduates I: Occupational Attainment and the Effects of Labour Market Duration', *Oxford Review of Education*, 27 (1): 135–150.

Egerton, M. (2000) 'Monitoring Contemporary Student Flows and Characteristics: Secondary Analyses Using the Labour Force Survey and the General Household Survey', *Journal of the Royal Statistical Society*, A 163/1: 63–80.

Egerton, M. and Parry, G. (2001) 'Lifelong Debt: Rates of Return to Mature Study', *Higher Education Quarterly*, 55 (1): 4–27.

Elias, P., McKnight, A., Pitcher, J., Purcell, K. and Simm, C. (1999) *Moving on: Graduate Careers Three Years after Graduation – Short Report* (Manchester: CSU).

Elias, P. and Purcell, K. (2004) SOC(HE): 'A Classification of Occupations for Studying the Graduate Labour Market. Graduate Careers Seven Years On', Working Paper No. 6 (Coventry: University of Warwick).

Feinstein, L., Anderson, T.M., Hammond, C., Jamieson, A. and Woodley, A. (2007), *The Social and Economic Benefits of Part-Time, Mature Study at Birkbeck College and The Open University*, The Open University/Birkbeck, University of London.

Furlong, A. and Cartmel, F. (2005) *Graduates from Disadvantaged Families, Early Labour Market Experiences*, Joseph Rowntree Foundation Ref: 0505.

Gottfredson, L.S. (1981) 'Circumscription and Compromise: A Developmental Theory of Occupational Aspirations', *Journal of Counselling Psychology (Monograph)*, 28 (6): 545–579.

HESA (2009/10) *Performance Indicators: Widening Participation of Under-Represented Group (Tables T1, T2)*, Table T2a – Participation of Under-Represented Groups in Higher Education: Mature Full-Time Undergraduate Entrants 2009/10 and Table T2b – Participation of Under-Represented Groups in Higher Education: Part-Time Undergraduate Entrants 2009/10 [online] http://www.hesa.ac.uk/index.php?option=com_content&task=view&id=2060&Itemid=141 [accessed 30 September 2011].

Hinton-Smith, T. (2009) *Lone Parents as Higher Education Students: A Longitudinal Qualitative Email Study*. Unpublished doctoral thesis, University of Sussex, Brighton.

Mullen, A.L. (2010) *Degrees of Inequality: Culture, Class and Gender in American Higher Education* (Maryland: The Johns Hopkins University Press).

Office for National Statistics (ONS) (11/2/2009) *Correction Notice*, Labour market Statistics, February 2009.

Osbourne, M., Marks, A. and Turner, E. (2004) 'Becoming a Mature Student: How Adult Applicants Weigh the Advantages and Disadvantages of Higher Education', *The International Journal of Higher Education and Educational Planning*, 48 (3): 291–315.

Purcell, K. and Elias, P. (2004) *Graduate Careers Seven Years On: Short Report* (Manchester: HECSU).

Purcell, K. and Hogarth, T. (1999) *Graduate Opportunities, Social Class and Age: Employers' Recruitment Strategies in the New Graduate Labour Market* (London: Council for Industry and Higher Education).

Purcell, K. and Pitcher, J. (1996) *Great Expectations: The New Diversity of Graduate Skills and Aspirations* (Manchester: Higher Education Careers Services Unit).

Purcell, K., Wilton, N. and Elias, P. (2007) 'Hard Lessons for Lifelong Learners? Age and Experience in the Graduate Labour Market', *Higher Education Quarterly*, 61 (1): 57–82.

Reay, D. (2003) 'A Risky Business? Mature Working Class Women Students and Access to Higher Education', *Gender and Education*, 15 (3): 301–317.

Redmond, P. (2006) 'Outcasts on the Inside: Graduates, Employability and Widening Participation', *Tertiary Education and Management*, 12 (2): 119–135.

Richardson, J.T.E. and Woodley, A. (2003) 'Another Look at the Role of Age, Gender and Subject as Predictors of Academic Attainment in Higher Education', *Studies in Higher Education*, 28 (4): 475–493.

Weil, S.W. (1986) 'Non-Traditional Learners within Traditional Higher Education Institutions: Discovery and Disappointment', *Studies in Higher Education*, 11: 219–235.

Woodfield, R. (2011) 'The Relationship between Age and First Destination Employability for UK Graduates: Are Mature Students Disadvantaged?' *Studies in Higher Education*, 36 (5): 409–425.

Woodfield, R. (2007) *What Women Want from Work. Gender and Occupational Choice in the 21st Century* (Baginstoke: Palgrave Macmillan).

Woodley, A. and Simpson, C. (2001) 'Learning and Earning: Measuring Rates of Return among Mature Graduates from Part-Time Distance Courses', *Higher Education Quarterly*, 55 (1): 28–41.

Woodley, A. and Wilson, J. (2002) 'British Higher Education and Its Older Clients', *Higher Education*, 44 (3–4): 329–347.

Yorke, M. (2001) 'Outside Benchmark Expectations? Variation in Non-Completion Rates in English Higher Education', *Journal of Higher Education Policy and Management*, 23 (2): 147–158.

7
Lone Parent Students' Motivations for and Hopes of Higher Education Engagement

Tamsin Hinton-Smith

Introduction

Lone parents are a key educationally excluded group targeted by widening participating (WP) agendas. Yet it has been argued that the distinct needs of students with parental responsibilities have been largely ignored by WP strategies, despite evidence that the group is increasing and facing a range of issues (Moreau, 2011). This chapter explores the motivations and aspirations of lone mothers studying at UK Higher Education Institutions (HEIs). Lone fathers have been omitted from the discussion due to low response rates in the research on which this chapter draws. Nevertheless, the rich longitudinal narratives provided by those lone fathers who participated suggested that in many key respects, lone parent status transcends gendered experiences, with lone mothers and lone fathers describing a broad commonality of higher education (HE) motivations, priorities and challenges.

The research draws on rich qualitative self-report data from 77 lone mothers, collected longitudinally over a year through regular email contact. The lone mothers researched represented the breadth of the UK HE sector, studying a broad range of academic and vocational courses at institutions from post-1992 universities to Oxbridge colleges. The participants' stage of study ranged from pre-entry open course students and first-year undergraduates through to postgraduate finalists. The learning trajectories of lone parents who contributed to the insights in this research further represent the increasing blurring of the boundaries between further education (FE) and HE, through including lone parents studying towards HE qualifications franchised from universities to FE colleges and also those studying towards pre-entry or open courses at HEIs.

This breadth facilitates insight on a wide range of issues around motivation and aspiration. Lone mothers discuss their motivations to engage with HE in order to improve the long-term prospects of themselves and their children. This includes both instrumental goals in terms of financial stability and freedom from welfare dependency and intrinsic motivations in terms of developing self-esteem and providing a positive role model for children. As lone parents draw towards the end of their HE studies, their aspirations become more concretely defined in terms of professional and material goals, and these are discussed within the context of lone parents' self-reported awareness of the potential challenges and limitations to their ambitions.

National context

While lone parenthood is a persistent demographic trend internationally, the United Kingdom has particularly high numbers, with lone parents caring for almost one in four children (Policy Research Institute, 2007: 8). It is important to increase the understanding of lone parents' motivations to pursue professional and personal development through HE participation. Much research on lone parents is informed by a social policy perspective, focusing on the groups' status as welfare recipients and problematising this persistent social trend of late modernity. Hence, the majority of relevant work addresses lone parents' participation in work and training (Bradshaw and Millar, 1991; Ford, 1996; Kiernan et al., 1998; Land and Lewis, 1998; Duncan and Edwards, 1999; Millar and Rowlingson, 2001; Klett-Davies, 2007). This focus sits alongside policy emphasis on tackling welfare dependency, located in a broader socio-cultural context of stereotypes that have long vilified lone parents as lazy, feckless and responsible for a range of social ills, from draining public resources to failing to provide a moral example for their children (Polakow et al., 2004; Cappleman-Morgan, 2005; Freud, 2007; Klett-Davies, 2007). The narratives of lone mothers included in this chapter evidence that far from this caricature, they are frequently highly motivated to improve the lives of themselves and their children, within the context of the structural constraints they face (e.g. Hyatt and Parry-Crooke, 1990: 6; Zachry, 2005: 2582). For many, this path follows the route of improving their educational qualifications, including through HE participation. Alongside inter-generational benefits for children, employment engagement for lone parents is associated with higher qualifications, while persistent welfare dependency is associated with a qualification deficit (CESI, 2007). There is a further demonstrated relationship between long-term employment and level of qualification for lone parents (Polakow et al., 2004: 9), and HE completion is further evidenced to impact positively upon wage level for the group (Jenkins and Symons, 2001: 129; Horne and Hardie, 2002). Despite such evidence, the United Kingdom continues to spend less than many other European countries investing in addressing the gap between the qualification levels of lone and partnered mothers, despite the presence of a larger gap than in many other countries (Gingerbread, 2007: 3).

Lone parents as mature university students: Similarities and differences

The most comprehensive statistical data providing insight into lone parents' HE participation was undertaken for the Scottish Executive in 2005. The data hence refer only to Scottish students but is nevertheless useful in illustrating trends. In 2005, 8 per cent of all Scottish HE students had dependent children (Callender et al., 2005: 26), of whom 61 per cent were lone parents (2005: 67). While some lone parent HE students are as young as traditional post-school entrants, the vast majority are mature women students. Similarly, while some mature women students do not have children (Scott et al., 1996: 235), they are nevertheless understandably more likely to do so, compared with traditional entry-age students (Merrill, 1999: 159). Lone parents, hence, share many important elements of experience with the broader group of mature women students, whose HE experiences have been much more extensively documented (e.g. Hyatt and Parry-Crooke, 1990; Edwards, 1993; Pascall and Cox, 1993; Davies et al., 1994; Wisker, 1996; Merrill, 1999; Parr, 2000; Jackson, 2004). Much work on mature women students identifies the salience of socio-economic status in informing experience, and this also is relevant to lone parent students (Hinton-Smith, 2012). Further, much research on mature women students' experiences as HE learners inevitably focuses on the challenges encountered in simultaneously managing the demands of family, university and often also paid work (e.g. Yorke and Longden, 2004: 106). This juggling act is a pervasive facet of experience shared by all student parents, but in many ways intensified for those who are lone parents (Hinton-Smith, 2009: 120). Similarly, lone parent learners share with mature students, more broadly, important aspects of experience including increased risk of financial hardship (Jackson, 2004, 52), lack of geographical mobility (Yorke and Longden, 2004: 106) and problems integrating into both academic and social dimensions of university life (Christie et al., 2005: 3, 13). These factors are all deterministic of the motivations and hopes surrounding lone parents' HE participation, as discussed in this chapter. The important aspects in which lone parent students' experiences are amplified or re-directed by their status as sole carers, rather than primary carers, inform the need for targeted investigation.

Despite a wealth of literature addressing mature students' HE learning experiences, investigation of students' backgrounds and successes is frequently prioritised over increasing understanding of personal experiences (Wisker, 1996: 6). This research addresses this persistently relevant identified deficit in focus by specifically investigating lone parent students' motivations and hopes around HE participation, explicating the relationship between these and their concrete circumstances.

Lone parents higher education motivations

Financial motivation

In 2007, the Freud report identified that eight out of ten lone parents wanted to work (2007: 16). However, UK lone parent employment rates have remained well below the national average (Leitch Report, 2006: 360), as well as lone mothers having low employment relative to married mothers (Jenkins and Symons, 2001: 121), and lagging behind much of the rest of Europe (Freud, 2007: 16). A number of cumulative factors, including UK lone parents' comparatively low educational levels (Millar and Rowlingson, 2001: 28), combined with some of the highest childcare costs in the OECD (2011), and that lone parents must meet this cost from one wage mean that it is often only financially feasible for lone parents to be in employment if they are in well-paying and hence well-qualified jobs (Millar and Rowlingson, 2001: 28; Horne and Hardie, 2002; Shaw and Woolhead, 2006; Klett-Davies, 2007). For many lone parents, building on their current level of educational qualification is their only means to accessing sufficiently well-remunerated work to meet childcare costs. This balance is exacerbated by changes to childcare assistance introduced in the UK Welfare Reform Bill, meaning that lone parents are now only able to recover up to 60 per cent of childcare costs from governmental assistance dependent on income, compared with up to 80 per cent previously. Combined with other changes, this is projected to lead to up to a ten-fold increase in childcare costs for some families (Family Action, 2011).

Research with mature students acknowledges the extent to which motivations for educational engagement vary between vocational reasons and personal development (Edwards, 1993; Leonard, 1994; Woodley and Wilson, 2002). Such diversity of motivation is inevitable given the heterogeneity of mature HE students as a group. Male and ethnic minority students have been documented to enter HE for predominantly career-related reasons when compared with women, white and older students (Edwards, 1993; Brennan et al., 1999). The significance of career-related motives for study decline with age; for students under 30 years of age, vocational reasons prevail, after which they become of equal value to personal motivations. For students over 35 years, personal reasons dominate (Gallagher et al., 1993). The well-documented prevalence of personal satisfaction motives for HE participation amongst mature students as a whole (Woodley and Wilson, 2002; Murphy and Roopchand, 2003; Reay, 2003) translate into successful learning outcomes, with intrinsically motivated students demonstrated to perform better in HE (Byrne and Flood, 2005: 11).

Despite over-representation of mature, white women participants in this research, the corresponding prevalence of intrinsic motivations for HE engagement amongst this group observed extensively elsewhere (Edwards,

1993; Gallagher et al., 1993; Leonard, 1994: 167; Brennan et al., 1999; Murphy and Roopchand, 2003; Reay, 2003) did not emerge. Existing research on lone parents has identified the significance of instrumental motivations for educational participation amongst the group (Wisker, 1996; Polakow et al., 2004: 116). The narratives of lone parents in this research indicate hoped-for future career development, financial stability and enhanced material opportunities as a result of their HE participation to be primary educational motivators, even if these goals accompany desires for intrinsic satisfactions. Hence, lone parent students share the utilitarian motivational agenda of potential impact upon earning capacity, rather than one of social justice or personal development, that also informs policy justifications for supporting the group's participation in adult learning.

Lone parent status informs the particular instrumental and intrinsic goals individuals hope to achieve through HE participation. The majority of lone parents' motivations for educational engagement map onto one or more of the three key areas dominating the group's experiences of HE participation: time, finances and childcare. Key motivations include job prospects, earning potential, improved personal circumstances, providing for dependants, setting a positive example for children, doing something for oneself, escaping the house, meeting new people and getting off state benefits, thus illustrating the extent to which intrinsic and instrumental goals are complexly interwoven for lone parent HE learners.

Course choice

Lone parent status further impacts upon the HE courses individuals choose to study. Many lone mothers attribute their enrolment in social science courses to interest in issues around social justice, stemming from their own experiences as lone parents, chiming with findings that mature women students' interest in social sciences is frequently informed by life experience (Edwards, 1993: 83). Instrumental goals lead large numbers of lone parents to opt for teacher training courses, perceiving a particular compatibility between teaching as a career and their responsibilities as sole parents. Several lone parents described embarking on teacher training to provide a future career that would both offer a stable salary and maximise time with their children after school each day and during school holidays, representing the combination of instrumental and intrinsic motivations. Lone parent students describe hoping that HE participation will ultimately facilitate a future with more time and financial security and less reliance on childcare than in their existing lives as lone parents. For some lone parents, these motivating benefits of HE participation must not all be deferred for future gratification, with some instead being realised in the immediate term. For many, the flexibility of HE participation combined with entitlement to financial assistance, however inadequate this may be deemed to be, in fact, offers a preferable alternative to combining paid work with the responsibilities of lone parenthood (also Klett-Davies, 2007: 60).

Risk and deferred gratification

While instrumental gratification for lone parents' HE participation must largely be deferred at least until completion of their studies, the intrinsic gratification of HE participation contributing to nurturing of the self and perceived quality of parenting is frequently immediate:

> Student life can be tough but is a massive improvement to being on the dole; more women should be encouraged to study while bringing up their kids. There is nothing more miserable than staring at the wall all day till the children get home.
>
> (MSc history of science, 35 years old, 12-year-old child)

Nevertheless, belief in the future rewards of HE participation frequently does demand strong commitment to deferred gratification, particularly for those without family experiences or support to draw on in validating long-term benefits of educational participation. For some, individual belief in the value of deferred gratification stands in stark contrast to childhood parental pressure to leave school early and take up paid employment. The importance of deferred gratification runs throughout lone parents' narratives of their experiences as HE learners. For example, many describe feeling aware that other students are out socialising while they stay at home studying but assuage themselves that sacrificing social activity to prioritise their studies in the short-term will ultimately repay them with a more comfortable life, the rewards of which will include increased social opportunities. In the immediate term, however, the very problems in terms of finances, time and childcare that lone parents seek to alleviate through HE completion are frequently magnified for the duration of their studies. For example, while lone parents training to be teachers are often motivated by hopes of enjoying hours of work and holidays that fit better with children's schooling than other occupations, undertaking teacher training frequently engenders particular problems for lone parents in terms of travelling long distances to training placements, early start times and long working days.

Given the increased risk-aversiveness documented amongst non-traditional students including lone parents (Reay, 2003), it can be difficult for individuals to embrace the opportunities offered by HE participation when this entails leaving the relative certainty of the welfare state safety net (Hinton-Smith, 2008: 67). Risk aversion is shown to correlate negatively with income – those with the lowest incomes are the most risk-averse, and lone parents are characterised by poverty (Jenkins and Symons, 2001: 139). Reay's research with mature working-class women students evidenced that going to university is often considered too financially 'risky' a process, ultimately leading to decisions not to engage for many of those who would otherwise like to do so (2003: 303, 312). This has important implications for the vast rise in UK HE fees introduced in 2010, suggesting that the most financially vulnerable students targeted by WP programmes are likely to be put off enrolling in HE by the prospect of hefty debts, regardless of the government's assurances that no one will be excluded by being required to pay fees up front.

Intrinsic motivation and lone parents' higher education outcomes

Alongside instrumental goals, lone parents frequently describe a further important motivation for HE participation as being securing employment which is more interesting, challenging or useful to society. This is particularly the case for those training in nursing, teaching and social work – areas in which lone parents and mature women students generally proliferate – and chimes with research on mature working-class women students who indicate the desire to 'give something back' to society (Reay, 2003: 301). For lone mothers in this research, the change in values and perspectives entailed in the experience of becoming a parent was often indicated to have catalysed the development of an interest in political and environmental concerns, as observed by Edwards with regard to mature women students (1993).

While lone parent students' narratives are dominated by motivational hopes that persisting in completing their HE studies in the face of the considerable challenges they inevitably face will ultimately be recompensed by providing a secure future for themselves and their children, this is counterbalanced by an evident wavering of confidence amongst many as they move towards and beyond graduation. This is notably apparent amongst the substantial number of lone parents pursuing teacher training courses, for whom the vocational orientation of their studies reflected particularly highly primarily instrumental, career-oriented HE motivations:

> To tackle your final point about whether my reward reflects my efforts, well, I guess if I had managed to get a full time teaching position then yes, I would say it would have been worth all of the effort but as yet, things are still a little precarious and as such I'm not entirely sure. On one level, it was definitely worth the hassle, i.e. personal development, etc., but the amount of debt that I now have really does need to have some financial reward associated with it and as yet, I don't have that so I suppose the jury is still out on that one!
>
> (PG Dip HE, 29 years old, three
> children aged 12–17 years)

Research on mature women students has found only a minority to succeed in entering the type of paid work that they had hoped to and perceived as a suitable reward for their HE participation; and that for many, securing graduate work is a case of doing whatever fits in with family responsibilities (Edwards, 1993: 149). The relevance of this experience to lone parents was corroborated by findings in this research. But the research also highlighted that given the balance of priorities juggled by lone parents, the relative advantages of HE study experienced may be deemed a satisfactory, if not ideal, outcome, with lone parents often reflecting that, on balance, their HE studies have been worthwhile even if they have not resulted in hoped-for enhanced financial circumstances.

Triggers for higher education engagement

Researchers of adult learners have frequently identified the significance of pivotal moments in individuals' life trajectories in triggering (re)engagement with education. Such moments have been variously conceptualised as 'critical incidents', 'fateful', 'trigger' or 'epiphany' moments (Gallagher et al., 1993: 6; Leonard, 1994; Komulainen, 2000; Merrill, 1999; Parr, 2000; Crossan et al., 2003; Brine and Waller, 2004; Jones, 2006; Hyde, 2007). Crompton and Harris' further identification of such epiphanic moments as informing women's engagement with paid employment is similarly relevant to understanding the motivations of lone parent HE learners (1999: 139). The occurrence of such critical trigger moments emerged as central to the trajectories of many of the lone mothers in this research, resonating with findings of participation in adult learning as frequently either responding to life change or seeking it (Jones, 2006: 496).

Specific educational triggers documented in this research include availability of funding, fear of or actual redundancy, reduction in childcare commitments, relationship breakdown, geographical move, illness or bereavement, or realisation of the need to provide that is inherent in becoming a parent or a lone parent (see also Gallagher et al., 1993: 6; Leonard, 1994). Exemplifying the way in which such concrete circumstances can inform HE engagement, one lone parent explained: 'I could not study on my course if I was at work full time, no way! Neither could I do this if [my daughter] was under school-age' (43 years old, 3rd year BSc clinical nursing, having seven-year-old child). Further important triggers for educational engagement can include experiencing discrimination (Woodfield, 2007: 71) or the shedding of constricting traditionally stereotyped gender roles (for example, through divorce) (Komulainen, 2000: 457). These areas of experience are particularly relevant to lone parents and were frequently indicated as relevant motivating factors for HE engagement by participants in this research. This contributes to understanding of why the change in circumstances of becoming a lone parent is so frequently documented as being the overall motivator for HE participation. Existing research has identified a strong impact of parent status upon overall educational motivation for both young students (Zachry, 2005) and mature learners (Edwards, 1993). Indeed, in this research, becoming a parent or lone parent was indicated to be, by far, the dominant motivator for educational engagement, with more than half of those who described events leading to their entry into HE, citing becoming a parent or becoming a lone parent as the key factor.

Becoming a parent or lone parent can act as the catalyst for the return to learning that individuals have long put off embarking on, representing an example of the acknowledged way in which major change can lead to an individual's reassessment of life and priorities, creating the conditions to fulfil a long-gestated ambition to return to learning (Parr, 2000; Brine and Waller, 2004: 101). Many lone parents in this research reflected that they would probably not have enrolled in HE at all had they not become lone parents:

> My being a single parent has meant that in some ways I can be more selfish when it comes to study, as I don't have a partner to consider or set aside time for. If I hadn't become a single parent I would still have had the desire to return to study but would have been less likely to act on it, as would have been more stuck in the rut of work, financial success, promotional and career ladders, etc. So I am very happy that I decided to go back to study and think that every cloud definitely has a silver lining, becoming a single parent forced me to go back to a simpler way of life and to do some of the things that make me more secure and happy.
>
> (Year 1 MBA, having two children)

The longitudinal dimension and inclusion of individuals at varied stages of their HE learner journeys charted reflective development in lone parents' subjective interpretations of the motivating factors, informing their HE engagement. This included individuals' changing perceptions of the triggers underlying their educational engagement, as indicated by the following:

> It's pretty clear to me now that university provided the perfect 'way out' of the bad relationship without needing to go down the route of finding a great job (with a good salary) and the struggle of childcare. At the time, that wasn't necessarily how I viewed it! It was more that I felt with [my son] being at school, the time for postgrad study was right.
>
> (Year 2 PhD archaeology, 33 years old,
> 8-year-old child)

That HE engagement can coincide with exiting an unsatisfactory relationship was a recurring theme. Lone mothers' reflections suggest that separation from a partner, who may have dominated family life and decision making in various ways, can lead to an increased sense of autonomy, free time, self-confidence and closeness with friends, which can underpin and catalyse the feeling that there is space in life for something else alongside parenting.

A particularly salient area of pivotal moments in informing educational re-engagement is traumatic experiences, or 'mega trauma'. Such events can be central to informing individuals' desire to change their identity through engaging with education (Parr, 2000) and are often relevant in the trajectories described by lone parents. Such critical incidents, or 'status passages', are seen as marking the entry to changes in role, status or identity (Crossan et al., 2003), sometimes constituting a 'metamorphosis' of the self (Komulainen, 2000: 453). For example, one lone parent through bereavement reflected that they would probably not have taken up studying had family life remained 'normal'.

Support

The influence of a key person who is pivotal in building a learner's self-esteem has been identified as central to engagement with adult learning (Weil, 1986: 224). Factors including the relationship an individual has with a partner and the direction of family support can intersect to critically impact upon the determining effect that events such as becoming pregnant or a lucky break in getting a job have on an individual's life (Procter and Padfield, 1998: 246). Alongside lone parent status, level of support is the other key motivating factor for HE participation cited by lone mothers in this research. Individuals described the negative impact of lack of educational support and encouragement from teachers, parents and partners. They also stressed the significance of encouragement from supportive individuals in childhood or adulthood as being pivotal in informing their HE engagement (also Hyde, 2007). For example, one research participant described how her motivation for HE participation had been the role model provided by a good friend:

> College was never mentioned at home or school. I come from a rough area where most girls get pregnant and most men get jobs in factories or get into crime. In fact me and my sister are the only people in my entire family to have gone to uni, we have a huge extended family so it's quite strange that no one else has. Although no one in my family has returned to education, my oldest friend of 22 years has returned to uni. She has been my best mate for so long she is like family and she is the reason I came to uni as she inspired me and made me believe I could do it.
>
> (Year 2 BA developmental psychology, 29 years old,
> children aged 7 and 8 years)

Some lone mothers' attribution of their HE engagement to the availability of access routes chimes with findings that without the support of access tutors, mature learners often feel that they would not have had the confidence to apply to university (Leonard, 1994: 168). Illustrating the two primary educational motivators of lone parenting status and networks of support, another lone mother reflected that

> I was very encouraged by the positive feedback from the tutors on my access course and to be honest I'm not at all sure what I would have done in my life had I not become a parent when I was 21.
>
> (MA primary education with QTS, 34 years old, 12-year-old child)

Filling a void

The potential of HE participation to re-mediate the dissatisfactions and inequalities of individuals consigned to domestic, childcare roles, the majority of whom have been women, has long been acknowledged. In 1965, Betty Friedan advocated HE participation as the solution to what she called 'the problem that has no name' – the isolation and dissatisfaction of 'wifing' and mothering roles. Edwards has drawn on this legacy to suggest that adult educational engagement can be a political instrument for, and of, power, offering a way out of inequality and oppression for groups who are powerless. For women especially, it is claimed that education can be an escape route from domestic life and second-class citizenship into the public sphere (Edwards, 1993: 1). Such dissatisfaction is not necessarily exclusively feminine but may relate primarily to the under-valued primary parenting role. Lone parents describe experiencing dissatisfaction and 'boredom' with their role (Greif, 1992: 267), and this can be a motivating factor for educational engagement. The opportunity to be alone, an individual, independent, and to take a break from the responsibilities of parenthood represents aspects of the rewards mature learners experience from HE participation.

Trajectories documenting the role of HE participation in fostering a sense of freedom and time for oneself can be seen as representing what we contemporarily conceive as 'personal development', with lone mothers frequently describing their motivation to participate in HE in terms of 'broadening horizons'. Several lone parents indicated hoping that their university participation would address absences in their lives beyond the academic remit of studentship. For example, many hoped that HE engagement would additionally create opportunities to expand social horizons.

Child-oriented motivations for higher education engagement

Children of lone parents have been evidenced to be at increased risk of academic failure (Lipman and Boyle, 2005: 1451). In contrast, daughters of lone parents who work are more likely to do well at school and less likely to become lone parents themselves (Shaw and Woolhead, 2006: 178). One of the key potential net gains of investing in supporting lone parents to fulfil their potential through HE participation and achieve financial independence is the 'spill-over' effect in terms of encouraging both present and future generations to participate in and value education. Hence, lone parents can be seen as holding the key to influencing the attitude of future generations to education, work and state dependence through acting as role models for their children (Scott et al., 1996: 234; Horne and Hardie, 2002).

The needs and futures of lone parents' children are ever-present in narratives of educational motivation, with hopes for children's futures a key recurring theme, discussed by a third of research participants. Motivational factors for HE engagement including new opportunities, career advancement, providing a better future and improved quality of life are all discussed by lone parent students in terms of benefiting their children. Family-oriented instrumental and intrinsic motivations are tightly interwoven in lone parent HE learners' motivational trajectories, with individuals hoping that HE participation will help them to meet their children's needs financially, practically and in terms of becoming 'better' parents. The key theme is that of hoping to have more time for their children in future, either because of no longer having to study or because individuals are studying towards occupations including teaching that they anticipate will fit better with children's school lives. The desire to achieve financial stability is a key motivation for HE engagement and is frequently explicitly linked to the importance of earning enough to support a family as a lone parent:

> I remember growing up and being bullied for not having a mum at home and for never having the new, trendy clothes, etc. There are bigger motivations than money, but I guess as a parent it is a natural feeling to want to be able to look after your children. I know it must have been very difficult for my dad as a single-parent to bring up two girls, and I will always love and respect him for doing the best he could. In a way, I want to learn from him and do things differently. Things like being able to take my son abroad, to broaden his understanding of the world, which I never had the opportunity to do as a child. I would also like to be able to save some money for when he is an adult, for either university, or a deposit for a house, or to travel. For whatever he needs.
>
> (BA sociology, business and management, one child)

One in seven lone parent students researched described hoping that their completion of HE studies would benefit their children by enabling them to provide a more materially comfortable lifestyle. This included, for example, the hope that increased income would facilitate dreams of buying one's own home, as well as improving family quality of life, including allowing more holidays and other treats for children. For some lone parent students, it is important that HE completion is perceived as enabling them to provide a better childhood for their children than their parents had been able to give them: 'I am determined still to give my children a better childhood than mine and even now go out of my way to make things happen for them' (Year 2 BA Ed studies and IT, g children aged 9 and 13 years).

Lone parent students often perceive their educational participation as enhancing the quality of their parenting skills, as other commentaries have observed of parents generally (Duckworth, 2005; Eccles and Daris-Kean, 2005; Shaw and Woolhead, 2006). A strong intrinsic motivation to provide a positive model to children is further significant for lone parent HE learners (also Scott et al., 1996: 234; Horne and Hardie, 2002). Parents' educational participation is evidenced to provide important parenting skills that impact fundamentally on children's academic performance independently of socio-economic status (Duckworth, 2005: 240), attesting to the significance of positive inter-generational outcomes from lone mothers' HE participation, despite not always favourable employment outcomes. The following quote encapsulates the co-existing intrinsic and instrumental HE motivations for many lone parent learners:

> The single mum status did influence my decision to train as a lawyer – no one else to help me to pay the bills! I want my children to be able to stand up in class at school and say my mummy is a lawyer – and be proud of me rather than saying my mum just stays at home.
>
> (Year 3 LLB, 27 years old, four-year-old twins)

Women with children are evidenced to see their engagement with learning in terms of helping their children achieve educationally, positioning themselves within a framework that articulates responsibility as 'good parents' and seeing themselves as passing on their education to their children in a variety of ways. The desire to act as positive role models for children is seen to represent a particularly strong aspect of this motivation (Reay, 2003; Zachry, 2005: 2566). The overwhelming key benefit lone parents perceive of their HE participation upon their children's futures is to encourage children to strive to fulfil their own academic potential. Despite not being directly questioned about it, almost a third of lone parent students researched indicated hoping that their studies would inspire their children in their own educational journeys, to study to the best of their abilities and develop an intellectually inquisitive approach to life:

> To me it is important that I set an example to [my child] through what I do and I did not feel staying at home on benefits would do that. I think that by going to university instead and hopefully becoming a teacher I can show her that despite the odds she can achieve what she wants.
>
> (Year 2 BA development studies, 23 years old, one-year-old child)

As I have all girls, I've been very keen to let them know that they must equip themselves with skills and knowledge so that they do not have to rely on anyone else to survive, I'd hate for them to have confidence and issues that I had and still have.

(PG Dip HE, 39 years old, three children aged 12–17 years)

Beyond these hopes for their children's futures, lone parents hope that their successful participation in HE will make their children proud of them. But despite themselves having risen to the challenge of participating in HE as lone parents, they often indicated hoping that their children would learn from witnessing their parent's experience to live their lives differently, not to have children young or alone and to go to university before settling down with responsibilities.

Freedom from stigma

The complex range of motives for lone parents' engagement with HE learning sit uncomfortably alongside their dominant perception of others' opinions of them as scroungers, and freeing themselves from this perceived stigma is an important motivation for lone parents' HE participation (NUS, 2009: 20, 22). Lone parents describe the need to prove to themselves and others that they can succeed. Among others citing the desire for freedom from welfare dependency, two described their motivations: 'to not be on benefits anymore. I would say my self-esteem is much higher being a "psychology undergraduate" rather than a single mum on the social' (Year 1 psychology, one child) and 'to lose the stigma attached to lone parent that will still never truly disappear. But really, and more importantly, I did it for the security for the future for me and my daughter' (PGCE history, 26 years old, 8-year-old child).

Discussion

This chapter has highlighted the complex interweaving of intrinsic and instrumental motivation for lone mothers' HE engagement. The unique position of sole responsibility for meeting both the material and emotional needs of children disrupts the breadwinner model of women as secondary wage earners and primarily responsible for children's practical and emotional care that remains deeply entrenched in both social policy and underlying socio-cultural values. Lone parents' responsibilities as sole breadwinners, or as one lone mother described, 'having to be mother and father … and fulfil two roles (multi-tasking to the extreme)' (Year 2social sciences and human biology, four children), stand them apart from other mature students for whom intrinsic educational motivations dominate. Instead, lone parents frequently feel forced to think instrumentally about providing for their families' present and future material needs, acting as what Crompton and Harris have termed 'careerists by necessity' (1999: 138).

Comparing lone parents' motivations and experiences to literature on mature students as a whole illustrates how parenting alone heightens the intensity of priorities that are relevant to all parents. Hence, both instrumental and intrinsic motivations for HE engagement appear to be felt particularly acutely by lone parents. This impact of breadwinning pressure upon the prevalence of intrinsic or instrumental motivations for HE engagement fits with documented social-class differences in motivational orientation amongst mature male and female students with caring responsibilities, whereby working-class learners report increased instrumental motivation, compared with prioritisation of intrinsic motivation amongst middle-class learners (Cappleman-Morgan, 2005: 5).

The relationship between lone parents' HE engagement and gratification resulting from this is similarly complex. Financial gratification must largely be deferred, projected by lone parents' instrumental motivations to use university participation as a means to achieving greater economic security as sole providers for their families. Yet in the meantime, becoming an HE student has been evidenced to inform both additional short-term intrinsic hardships including time for children and care of the self and immediate advantages in terms of personal development and perceived parenting ability.

This chapter has relayed lone parent HE students' frequently high levels of motivation to succeed in completing HE for the benefit of both themselves and their children, in the face of considerable practical constraints. Further, mature learners as a whole have been evidenced elsewhere to 'make exceptional students who are very motivated and who perform well academically' (Scott et al., 1996: 233). In addition, students who are mothers (both partnered and single) have been shown to achieve grades higher than both school-leaver students and mature students as a whole. Student mothers also report higher gains in confidence, ability, intelligence and competence than mature students generally (Burns and Scott, 1993: 40; Scott et al., 1996). Evidence of such strength of motivation sits uncomfortably with documented high incidences of non-completion amongst lone mothers, leading to the question of why such highly motivated learners with so much to gain also have such a high incidence of non-completion, representing a loss not only for the individuals affected but also for society (Scott et al., 1996: 234). Lone mothers' HE learning narratives as contributed to this research locate their strong intrinsic and instrumental motivation to participate successfully in HE within the context of recognition of the very real challenges they routinely face in doing so. These challenges mediate and often override the strength of lone parent learners' motivation. This informs the need for increased support provision in the form of family-friendly policies, at both institutional and governmental levels, to facilitate the HE learning journeys of these highly motivated WP learners and realise the long-term benefits for this wide and vulnerable social group and their children.

Bibliography

Bradshaw, J. and Millar, J. (1991) *Lone Parent Families in the UK* (Great Britain: Department of Social Security, H.M.S.O.). Docs/DSS-RR 6.

Brennan, J., Mills, J., Shah, T. and Woodley, A. (1999) *Part-Time Students and Employment: Report of a Survey of Students, Graduates and Diplomats* (London: DfEE/HEQE/QSE).

Brine, J. and Waller, R. (2004) 'Working-Class Women on an Access Course: Risk, Opportunity and (Re)constructing Identities', *Gender and Education*, 16 (1): 97–113.

Burns, A. and Scott, C. (1993) 'Career Trajectories of Single and Married Mothers Who Complete Tertiary Study as Mature Age Students', *Education and Society*, 11: 39–50.

Byrne, M. and Flood, B. (2005) 'A Study of Accounting Students' Motives, Expectations and Preparedness for Higher Education', *Journal of Further and Higher Education*, 29 (2): 111–124.

Callender, C., Wilkinson, D., MacKinnon, K. and Vegeris, S. (2005) *Research Report on Higher and Further Education Students' Income, Expenditure and Debt in Scotland 2004–2005* (London: Policy Studies Institute) [online] http://www.scotland.gov.uk/Publications/2005/10/26105054/50552 [accessed 25 January 2008].

Cappleman-Morgan, J. (2005) 'Obstacle Courses? Mature Students' Experiences of Combining Higher Education with Caring Responsibilities', *The Higher Education Academy: Sociology, Anthropology, Politics*. [online] www.c-sap.bham.ac.uk/media/com_projectlog/docs/PG_04_16.pdf [accessed 20 August 2012].

CESI (Centre for Economic and Social Inclusion) (2007) *Lone Parents and Employment Seminar*, 19 September.

Christie, H., Munro, M. and Wager, F. (2005) 'Day Students in Higher Education: Widening Access Students and Successful Transitions to University Life', *International Studies in the Sociology of Education*, 15 (1): 3–30.

Crompton, R. and Harris, F. (1999) 'Employment, Careers, and Families: The Significance of Choice and Constraint in Women's Lives', in Crompton, R. (ed.) *Restructuring Gender Relations and Employment: The Decline of the Male Breadwinner* (Oxford: Oxford University Press, pp. 128–149).

Crossan, B., Field, J., Gallacher, J. and Merrill, B. (2003) 'Understanding Participation in Learning for Non-Traditional Adult Learners: Learning Careers and the Construction of Learning Identities,' *British Journal of Sociology of Education*, 24 (1): 55–67.

Davies, S., Lubelska, C. and Quinn, J. (eds) (1994) *Changing the Subject: Women in Higher Education* (London: Taylor and Francis, pp. 163–177).

Duckworth, K. (2005) 'Effects of Mothers' Education on Parenting: An Investigation Across Three Generations', *London Review of Education*, 3 (3): 239–264.

Duncan, S. and Edwards R. (1999) *Lone Mothers, Paid Work and Gendered Moral Rationalities*, Basingstoke: Macmillan.

Eccles, J.S. and Daris-Kean, P.E. (2005) 'Influences of Parents' Education on Their Children's Educational Attainments: The Role of Parent and Child Perceptions', *London Review of Education*, 3 (3): 191–204.

Edwards, R. (1993) *Mature Women Students: Separating or Connecting Family and Education* (London: Taylor and Francis).

Family Action (2011) *Welfare That Works Better – 10 Recommendations for Improving the Universal Credit* [online] http://www.family-action.org.uk/section.aspx?id= 13397 [accessed 8 June 2011].

Ford, R. (1996) *Childcare in the Balance: How Lone Parents Make Decisions about Work* (London: P.S.I).

Freud, D. (2007) *Reducing Dependency, Increasing Opportunity: Options for the Future of Welfare to Work*. An Independent Report to the Department for Work and Pensions, Corporate Document Services.

Gallagher, A., Richards, N. and Locke, M. (1993) *Mature Students in Higher Education: How Institutions Can Learn from Experience*, University of East London.

Gingerbread/One Parent Families (2007) Reducing Dependency, Increasing Opportunity: Options for the Future of Welfare to Work. *A Response to David Freud's Review from One Parent Families* (London: One Parent Families).

Greif, G.L. (1992) 'Lone Fathers in the United States: An Overview and Practice Implications', *British Journal of Social Work*, 22: 565–574.

Hinton-Smith, T. (2012) *Lone Parents' Experiences as Higher Education Students* (Leicester: Niace).

Hinton-Smith, T. (2009) 'Lone Parents as Higher Education Students: A Qualitative Email Study', in Merrill, B. (ed.) *Learning to Change? The Role of Identity and Learning Careers in Adult Education* (Oxford: Peter Lang, pp. 113–127).

Hinton-Smith, T. (2008) 'Lone Parents as Higher Education Students', in Johnson, R. (Ed.) University life uncovered: making sense of the student experience. (Southampton: SWAP, pp. 66–75) http://www.swap.ac.uk/resources/publs/monographs.html [accessed 20 August 2012].

Horne, M. and Hardie, C. (2002) 'From Welfare to Higher Education: A Study of Lone Parent Students at Queen Margaret University College,' *Edinburgh Journal of Adult and Continuing Education*, 8 (1): 60–72.

Hyatt, J. and Parry-Crooke, G. (1990) *Barriers to Work: A Study of Lone Parent's Training and Employment Needs* (London: The Council).

Hyde, S. (18 May 2007) 'An Absence of Gender in the Workplace Learning Agenda? Reflections on a Life History Project with Workplace Learners', *Gendered Choices and Transitions: Part-Time Pathways, Full-Time Live,* Birkbeck College, London.

Jackson, S. (2004) *Differently Academic? Developing Lifelong Learning for Women in Higher Education* (Netherlands: Kluwer).

Jenkins, S.P. and Symons, E.J. (March 2001) 'Childcare Costs and Lone Mothers Employment Rates,' *The Manchester School*, 69 (2) pp. 121–147. Blackwell Publishers Ltd and the Victoria University of Manchester.

Jones, K. (2006) 'Valuing Diversity and Widening Participation: The Experiences of Access to Social Work Students in Further and Higher Education', *Social work education*, 25 (5): 485–500.

Kiernan, K., Land, H. and Lewis, J. (1998) *Lone Motherhood in Twentieth-Century Britain: From Footnote to Frontpage* (Oxford: OUP).

Klett-Davies, M. (2007) *Going It Alone? Lone Motherhood in Late Modernity* (Hampshire: Ashgate).

Komulainen, K. (2000) 'The Past Is Difference – The Difference Is Past', *Gender and Education*, 12 (4): 449–462.

Land, H. and Lewis, J. (1998) 'The Problem of Lone Parenthood in the British Context', in Ford, R. and Millar, J. (eds) *Private Lives and Public Responses* (London: Policy Studies Institute, pp. 141–153).

Leitch, S. (2006) *Prosperity for All in the Global Economy: World Class Skill* (London: HM Treasury).

Leonard, M. (1994) 'Mature Women and Access to HE', in Davies, S., Lubelska, C. and Quinn, J. (eds) *Changing the Subject: Women in Higher Education* (London: Taylor and Francis, pp. 163–177).

Lipman, E. L., and Boyle, M. H. (2005) 'Social support and education groups for single mothers: a randomized controlled trial of a community-based program', *Canadian Medical Association Journal*, 173 (12): 1451–1456.

Merrill, B. (1999) *Gender, Change and Identity: Mature Women Students in Universities* (Aldershot: Ashgate).

Millar, J. and Rowlingson, K. (2001) *Lone Parents, Employment and Social Policy: Cross-National Comparisons* (Bristol: Policy Press).

Moreau, M.P. (2011) 'Supporting Student Parents in Higher Education: A Policy Perspective', Nuffield Foundation Research. *British Educational Research Association (BERA) Conference* Presentation, 8th September, Institute of Education, London.

Murphy, H. and Roopchand, N. (2003) 'Intrinsic Motivation and Self-Esteem in Traditional and Mature Students at a Post-1992 University in the North-East of England', *Educational Studies*, 29 (2–3): 243–259.

NUS (2009) *Meet the Parents: The Experience of Students with Children in Further and Higher Education* (London: NUS) [online] http://www.nus.org.uk/PageFiles/5386/NUS_SP_report_web.pdf [accessed 17 May 2011].

OECD (2011) 'Doing Better for Families', [online] www.oecd.org/dataoecd/61/32/47701096.pdf [accessed 14 June 2012].

Parr, J. (2000) *Identity and Education: The Links for Mature Women Students* (Aldershot: Ashgate).

Pascall, G. and Cox, R. (1993) *Women Returning to Higher Education* (Buckingham: The Society for Research into Higher Education and The Open University Press).

Polakow, V., Butler, S.S., Stormer Deprez, L. and Kahn, P. (eds) (2004) *Shut Out: Low Income Mothers and Higher Education in Post-Welfare America* (Albany, NY: State University of New York Press).

Policy Research Institute, Leeds Metropolitan University (2007) *Towards Skills for Jobs: What Works in Tackling Worklessness?* Rapid review of Evidence Coventry: Learning and Skills Council.

Procter, I. and Padfield, M. (1998) *Young Adult Women, Work and Family: Living a Contradiction* (London: Mansell).

Reay, D. (2003) 'A Risky Business? Mature Working-Class Women Students and Access to Higher Education,' *Gender and Education*, 15 (3): 301–317.

Scott, C., Burns, A. and Cooney, G. (1996) 'Reasons for Discontinuing Study: The Case of Mature Age Female Students with Children', *Higher Education*, 31 (2): 233–253.

Shaw, M. and Woolhead, G. (2006) 'Supporting Young Mothers into Education, Employment and Training: Assessing Progress Towards the Target', *Health and Social Care in the Community*, 14 (2): 177–184.

Weil, S. (1986) 'Non-traditional Learners Within Traditional Higher Education: Discovery and Disappointment', *Studies in Higher Education*, 11 (3): 219–235.

Welfare Reform Bill (2011) [online] http://www.publications.parliament.uk/pa/cm201011/cmbills/154/11154.i-v.html [accessed 2 March 2011].

Wisker, G. (1996) *Empowering Women in Higher Education* (London: Kogan Page).

Woodfield, R. (2007) *What Women Want from Work: Gender and Occupational Choice in the Twenty-First Century* (Basingstoke: Palgrave Macmillan).

Woodley, A. and Wilson, J. (2002) 'British Higher Education and Its Older Clients', *Higher Education*, 44: 329–347.

Yorke, M. and Longden, B. (2004) *Retention and Student Success in Higher Education* (Maidenhead: Open University Press).

Zachry, E.M. (2005) 'Getting My Education: Teen Mothers' Experiences in School before and after Motherhood', *Teacher's College Record*, 107 (12): 2566–2598.

Part III

Non-Traditional Students' Experiences in Higher Education

8
Choosing a Student Lifestyle? Questions of Taste, Cultural Capital and Gaining a Graduate Job

Mary Stuart, Catherine Lido and Jessica Morgan

Students, choice, social mobility and higher education

Higher education (HE) participation is increasingly pervasive across the United Kingdom. Participation rates are at about 43 per cent of young people entering HE. Much of the debate over the last 10 years has focused on widening participation (WP) for young people from lower socio-economic groups, but, more recently, a debate has opened up, which focuses on how socially mobile our society is (Milburn, 2009; Clegg, 2011), and HE is seen to be a key component of creating upward social mobility.

Little (2006) points out that there is a real diversity of student experience developing in institutions for students from different backgrounds, which will create different employment outcomes, and Pearson (2006) highlights that there are no longer any 'typical' graduates, although employers still have a rather blinkered view of what a 'good graduate' is. Barber and Hill (2005) highlight that overemphasis on graduates who come from a small pool of universities with certain characteristics restricts choice and limits graduate opportunities.

Recent government reports have suggested that access to professional careers has become more difficult for people from lower socio-economic backgrounds. Milburn argues that 'access to society's top jobs and professions has become less, not more, socially representative over time' (Milburn, 2009: 18). This concern has been taken up by the current government which has set out a social mobility strategy led by the deputy prime minister in the United Kingdom, Nick Clegg. Research has suggested that the United Kingdom does not compare favourably with other developed countries in the level of social openness (Jäntti *et al.*, 2006). Enabling the most creative and talented people in society to succeed is seen to be vital to a successful economy and society (Goldthorpe *et al.*, 1987); hence, the issue of social mobility has become a key element in social policy over the last five years.

Social scientists divide social mobility between absolute and relative mobility. Absolute mobility is about the shape of society, the size of different groupings or classes. Certainly the middle classes have grown substantially over the last 100 years, and the working class has shrunk. This is because the employment needs of the society have changed, but several social scientists (Goldthorpe *et al.*, 1987 and Savage, 2000) argue strongly that relative mobility has not changed at all during this time. Blanden *et al.* (2005, 2010) argue that relative mobility has actually declined, but this is contested by other theorists suggesting that Blanden's work has focused on income data only rather than a fuller view of class. While there is considerable debate about social mobility between different social scientists (Blanden *et al.*, 2005; Erikson and Goldthorpe, 2010; Saunders, 2010), particularly whether there has been a decline in relative upward social mobility as opposed to a slowing of absolute upward social mobility, social mobility is 'the principal goal of the government's social policy' (2010 5).

The government's strategy places considerable weight on the role of HE in getting working-class students into HE, but while WP may be a precursor to upward social mobility, it does not automatically create it. Concerns about HE's role in social mobility are more sharply focused as policy on the costs and value of a degree are debated as government grants to HE decrease, and institutions replace this funding with higher tuition fees. HE is being tasked with providing young people from working class backgrounds with the ability to move into professional occupations by gaining a degree. However, the Milburn report highlighted that while it is true that many more professional jobs

> now require at least an undergraduate degree... employers said they found it increasingly hard to fill graduate vacancies because students fail to match academic achievement with leadership, team working and communication skills.... There is good evidence that young people develop these skills through extra-curricular activity and participation in clubs and societies.
>
> (2009: 44)

In research undertaken for the Higher Education Academy (HEA) (2007–2008), we also found that employers valued and used graduates' range of interests and activities as an important part of their selection process. Many of the employers said that the class of degree was used as a minimum requirement of attainment. Particularly in large firms where there was often a high academic standard, class of degree acted as a filter at the first stage of the selection process by determining which students would be selected for interview:

> The qualification is the first thing you notice, the degree they studied and the mark. The class of degree you tend to look at, and we consider all people ranging from a 2:2 and above.
>
> (Ross, IT consultancy firm)

However, these employers also conceded that the large number of graduates applying with a good degree meant that there was little variation in the applicants' levels of degree attainment. Therefore, class of degree on its own was an insufficient criterion with which to compare applicants. In these circumstances, extra-curricular activities became more important as a source of additional information:

> A 2:1 is important for getting into the interview but because all students have a 2:1 it's become pretty meaningless in the sense that we almost take it as a given. So that's where the other activities come in as an indicator of what they can do.
>
> (Hannah, public relations firm)

> Some of them seem to think a 2:1 is enough, which may be true for some companies but not for ours. They don't understand that we're viewing 1,000's of applicants with a 2:1 and they need something extra to stand out from the crowd.
>
> (Luke, accountancy firm)

Hence, for employers once a graduate has demonstrated a sufficient academic standard for a graduate job, then they use a variety of other measures to assess their suitability for the job. Employers were particularly keen on extra-curricular activities that demonstrate their communication, teamworking and organisational skills, which favour particular extra-curricular activities. However, despite the importance of these other activities for graduate employment, there is little research which examines what students do beyond their 'classrooms'. Given the variation in the student demography in HE and the variation of resources and facilities at higher education institutions (HEIs), students will be engaged in a wide variety of activities, including clubs and societies, sporting activities, volunteering, religious and cultural activities, as well as part-time work and caring responsibilities. The particular environment of the university undergraduate experience creates a specifically challenging milieu, for many the first time away from home, for others balancing attendance at and expectations from university while living at home with different commitments. This means that their 'lifestyle choices' could potentially have differing effects on their future lives. In other words, the issue of WP in HE is only part of the story: what happens to students from poorer backgrounds once they enter HE and what effects their student lifestyle choices have on their future prospects is the other important part of the debate that has not as yet been fully explored.

Based on research for the HEA in the United Kingdom, this chapter examines different students' engagement with extra-curricular activities while in HE and how these lifestyle choices are affected by the particular circumstances of students. The chapter argues that 'choice' 'taste' and lifestyle in HE is not simple but is shaped by the social and cultural context and therefore has implications for the potential of HE to contribute to the development of a more socially mobile society. The following section explores the evidence on different student groups' employment prospects once they have left HE.

Student diversity and graduate outcomes

There is considerable variation in outcomes, both in terms of degree outcomes and in terms of employment outcomes for different groups of students in HE. Graduates with better-qualified parents are more likely to obtain a first-class honours degree, but those with less-qualified parents are more likely to hold an upper second-class degree, leading to similar proportions of students with a good degree (2:1 or above) across socio-economic backgrounds (Blasko, 2002).

Graduates with parents in partly skilled occupations were found to be 30 per cent more likely than others to have a non-graduate job 18 months after graduation, and this risk increased to 80 per cent for graduates who had no employed parents. Graduates from higher socio-economic groups were also shown to move into occupations with salaries 1–3 per cent higher than those from lower socio-economic groups (Smith and Naylor, 2001). However, while social mobility debates have particularly focused on class, other social divisions are also worth considering. Most recently, there has been a debate about the role of women in class mobility (Saunders, 2010); hence gender is an issue that needs to be explored in discussing mobility between groups in society.

Women are more likely than their male peers to obtain a good degree (Rudd, 1984; Smith and Naylor, 2001; Richardson and Woodley, 2003; HESA, 2007; Richardson, 2008b). Female graduates were more likely than male graduates to have entered employment or further study six months after leaving UK HE (Connor *et al.*, 2004). For first-generation graduates, males reported less job satisfaction, whereas females were more likely to report that their qualification was unnecessary for their graduate job (Blasko, 2002). However, male UK graduates were found to be earning 12 per cent more than their female counterparts (Chevalier, 2004).

Recently, there has been considerable concern about outcomes for minority ethnic students in HE in the United Kingdom. Despite their increasing participation levels in UK HE, ethnic minority students in UK HE are less likely to obtain a "good" degree (2:1 or above) than their white counterparts (Connor *et al.*, 1996, 2004; Owen *et al.*, 2000; Naylor and Smith, 2004; Leslie, 2005; Purcell *et al.*, 2005; Elias and Jones, 2006; Broeke and Nicholls, 2007; Richardson, 2008a).

Connor *et al.* (2004) found that six months after leaving UK HE in 2000, 94 per cent of white students had obtained 'successful' graduate outcomes (success being defined as either entering employment or further study), closely followed by the Indian, black Caribbean and black other groups (90–91per cent range); but the black African group had the lowest success rate (84 per cent). Ethnic minority graduates were found to face greater difficulties in obtaining an initial job and were more likely than white graduates to obtain graduate level positions after a longer time period (Blasko, 2002; Brennan and Shah, 2003). Asian graduates were the most likely to be in professional or managerial positions, although these positive employment outcomes were not reflected in higher salaries or greater job satisfaction (Blasko, 2002). Mature students are generally less likely than younger students to enter university with A-level qualifications, which often has a separate negative effect on labour market opportunities (Blasko, 2002) as A levels are still used as an important part of the selection process for graduate jobs, even if an individual has a higher level qualification. Graduates who entered UK HE at the age of 26–29 years were 4 per cent more likely than younger graduates to be working in a non-graduate job 18 months after graduation (DfES, 1999).

Hence, there is considerable variation between different student groups' opportunities for upward social mobility, and some of these differences in outcome may well be related to issues in wider society, and some may relate to their experiences while in HE. A number of theorists (Thomas, 2002; Reay *et al.*, 2005 and Archer *et al.*, 2003) have argued (Bourdieu, 1984) that HE is a distinctive 'field' where some students feel comfortable and others whose prior experiences do not fit with the HE field feel less at home. This sense of feeling comfortable will affect how engaged you feel you can be in any environment, and it is this theme that is explored in the following section.

Cultural capital, lifestyles and issues for different student groups

One of the key reasons why extra-curricular activities are important is that it is often related to an individual's access to 'cultural capital' (Bourdieu, 1977, 1984). An individual's lifestyle choices develop in response to the determining structures and the external conditions or fields that they encounter, and it is a useful framework within which to examine the impact of extra-curricular activities on students' degree and employment outcomes. In other words, engagement in extra-curricular activities is not context-neutral. Students participate (or not participate) as 'a matter of taste', structured by prior background, cultural experiences or by constraints on their economic and social circumstances. As Bourdieu argues:

> It is to be found in all the properties...with which individuals and groups surround themselves, houses, furniture, paintings, books, cars,...and in the practices they manifest their distinction, sports, games, entertainments, only because it is in the synthetic unity of the habitus....
>
> (1984: 173)

Several researchers have identified habitus as an issue for 'non-traditional' students (Reay *et al.*, 2002). Studies have found that decisions of working-class students to attend university are largely based on the social, economic and cultural capital available to them, such as their knowledge and information about HE (Hutchings, 2006a), access routes into university (Leathwood and Hutchings, 2006), student funding (Hutchings, 2006b) and social identity concerns in relation to participation (Archer and Leathwood, 2006). The value of HE is differently structured across class, ethnicity and gender, and research shows that there are greater risks and more uncertain rewards for working-class students. These students frame the value of HE in more ambiguous terms, in light of the low-status institutions accessible to them, the risk of non-completion, and the limited types of graduate opportunities available to them (Archer, 2006).

Bennett *et al.* (2010) indicate that people's preferences for certain activities and attitudes 'cluster' together; hence, 'taste' and choice of lifestyle are seen to relate to particular groups of people linked to the social divisions in society. This work suggests that contextualising engagement in extra-curricular activities for students within their life histories is rooted in socio-economic, political and cultural experiences. These experiences will impact not only on students' time at university but beyond into the workplace and in wider society.

What are students doing after class?

Six hundred and thirty-one students studying at four different UK HE institutions completed a questionnaire looking at their extra-curricular activities. The first institution is a large city-based post-1992 institution with mostly young students, half of whom are white and half from ethnic minority backgrounds, largely doing vocationally focused programmes. The second institution chosen is a 1960s campus-based university in the south of England and has predominantly young white students largely doing academically focused courses. The third is a 1960s campus-based university in Scotland with mostly white Scottish students and a notable proportion of mature students, doing a mixture of vocational and academic degrees. The final institution that took part in the research is an older Russell group university in the north of England with mostly young white students doing academically focused courses. The students demographic from the four institutions therefore offered a diverse set of student groups enabling a comprehensive appreciation of what students did 'after class'. Focus groups were then conducted with 59 students from the overall sample where students expressed an interest in participating. The focus groups provided insight into students' motivation for their choices and their own explanation for these choices.

Overall, students were sampled from a diverse range of ethnic and religious backgrounds, different social and cultural backgrounds, gender and age but this varies by institution. The relationship between educational attainment and social class has been documented widely as the most significant indicator of propensity to undertake HE study (Blanden *et al.*, 2010).

Different activities for different students

Socialising with friends

The most significant activity identified by the students surveyed was being with their friends. Almost all students who completed the questionnaire spent time seeing their friends (98 per cent). However, there were differences in who these friends were and where the students socialised. For example, some students, particularly the younger students at the older universities, socialised with their housemates from halls in bars, pubs, clubs and parties.

> Me and my housemates go out together, sometimes there're quizzes in the bar, flat parties in Halls. Last year especially there were lots of students getting drunk and stealing road cones.
>
> (Tracey, sociology, 1960s campus-based
> university, England)

Others, particularly the mature students, socialised with their families and friends at home:

> We have friends round for lunch and dinner a lot and we love to eat and cook a lot and socialise with our friends. I can't leave the kids so it's easier to do stuff at home.
>
> (Marion, education, 1960s campus-based
> university, Scotland)

Clubs and societies

Forty six per cent of the students who completed the questionnaire were engaged in extra-curricular clubs and societies. Some of these students were in clubs that were affiliated to the university in some way, and many involved team sports, particularly at the older universities. Many students joined established students' union clubs, whilst some others set up their own university societies around their hobbies and interests. Those who chose to join their official university sports teams found that this took up a lot of their time:

> The rowing team does take a lot of commitment, outside the race meets we're at the gym and circuit training six times a week. But there's other less intense options for people as well, for example, you don't have to be on the main teams, you can just set up your own social 5-aside football team that doesn't train as much but meets afterwards in the pub.
>
> (Suzy, economics, Russell group university, England)

Other students joined societies that were based around their chosen subject of study. These societies often involved socialising within their subject groups. Those who accepted positions of responsibility in their societies found that this took up a lot of their time.

> I'm part of PsyTech, for maths, engineering, physics and computer science students. I organised the casino ball in December, we had card tables and a jazz band which was good. I organise the pub crawls, that kind of thing. A lot of work goes into it and it takes up a lot of my time.
>
> (Becky, maths, 1960s campus-based university, Scotland)

Councils and committees

Thirteen per cent of students who completed the questionnaire were involved in councils and committees. Younger students were more involved in university or students' union committees, whereas older students were more likely to sit on committees in their local community:

> I belong to my residents committee; I'm one of the directors. It involves running the finance and day-to-day management of the block of flats where I live, collecting rent and arrears and coming up with solutions for making things run more smoothly.
>
> (Parvati, nursing, post-1992 institution, England)

> I'm on the union council and a few university committees, I'm in the LGBT, the model UN, and I'm running couple of campaigns at the moment like the sponsored silence against homophobia.
>
> (Abi, media, 1960s campus-based university, England)

Paid employment

Fifty per cent of students who completed the questionnaire were engaged in part-time work whilst they were studying, although the amount of paid employment that they undertook varied. Some students, particularly mature students and those at the post-1992 city university, needed a job to fund their course or support their families, and so worked more hours. For these students, paid work took priority over other extra-curricular activities and sometimes conflicted with their studies:

> I don't have the social life of a typical student because I'm so busy and do so much other stuff … always worrying about the bills tomorrow, how am I going to pay rent, electricity, where will I sleep, but this is what I worry about. My job ain't a choice for me like it is for some students.
>
> (Liberty, nursing, post-1992 institution, England)

This contrasted with students who had less of a financial need for paid work. They saw their paid work more as a choice rather than a necessity. Some felt it provided them with much needed 'time out' from studying or some extra pocket money for socialising:

> I've got a part-time job doing agency work for [football club], it's not regular work and it's not so much a necessity, just because I support them and really enjoy being a part of it. I can always say I'm not working an event if I'm too busy.
>
> (Rosie, politics, Russell-group institution, England)

Family commitments

Sixty eight per cent of students spend time with their families, although the amount of time spent and the types of family commitment varied. Younger students who lived at home (as did a large proportion at the post-1992 city university) spent time with their parents or relatives and helped around the house, sometimes in caring roles.

> I am very family orientated, if there are issues that have to be sorted out at home then I like to get involved. Just this morning they came to fit our heater and sort out the gas bill so I had to arrange all that myself.
>
> (Kwame, law, post-1992 institution, England)

Other students were older with young families, particularly at the post-1992 university, and they spent most of their time looking after their children.

> Most evenings I just go home, look after my baby and go to bed.
>
> (Olivia, nursing, post-1992 institution, England)

For these students their childcare took priority over other activities, and sometimes conflicted with their studies:

> I try to do all the things I would normally do with the kids and then do my coursework really late at night, so I can be up doing an essay till 1 or 2 o clock.
>
> (Marion, education, 1960s campus-based
> university, Scotland)

Student 'choices', lifestyles and constraints – The university environment

One way to frame these patterns of participation in extra-curricular activities is to consider the university environments in which they occur. Both the physical and social university environment seemed to play a role in the sorts of activities that were on offer and accessible to the students. While there were differences between city- and campus-based institutions, it is the case that the old versus new university divide was more significant in engagement in activities than whether the university was in a city or out of town.

> I think [...] sports programme is awful, the sport isn't held on any of the actual campuses, this really deterred me from going, and there's no university bus to get there, you really have to plan in advance and leave lots of time.
>
> (Hayley, law, post-1992 institution, England)

> Everything is quite close together on two nearby campuses and very easily accessible by transport links so it's easy to get involved in these things.
>
> (Suzy, economics, Russell–group, England)

A high proportion of the city, post-1992 university students lived at home, and this also prevented them from participating in campus activities:

> I went to a few of the group readings last year but I find that now that I'm living at home it takes two hours to get home. Especially when it's on a day that I'm not in University anyway I tend not to come in anymore.
>
> (Gus, english literature, post-1992 institution, England)

This contrasted with the old university students who described a more integrated and active student body and a political ideology that united many of their activities.

The uni [university] is quite politically active, there's always somebody outside handing out flyers for some campaign, and we get regular emails about the sorts of political campaigns going on.

(Rosie, politics, Russell group university, England)

Student lifestyles – University for fun or university for work

As well as different universities offering different opportunities for engagement in extra-curricular activities, there were also broadly two different student lifestyles at the different universities. Students at the older universities were much more likely to frame the benefits of their extra-curricular activities in terms of personal development and enjoyment and crucial to the overall student experience, whereas students at the new universities, which had a much more diverse student body, whose engagement in extra-curricular activities was more constrained saw such engagement as not central to their experience.

University for fun

There was a general consensus among more middle-class, young white students that learning at university should be primarily about having fun, gaining new experiences and developing as a person:

There's no point being here and having a great degree but no good memories. So I wouldn't sacrifice my good time.

(Abi, media, 1960s campus-based university, England)

I'd definitely say uni [university] is about the experience, yes it would be good to get a first or a 2:1 but ultimately it's about the experience, going out, having fun and meeting loads of people.

(Suzy, economics, Russell group university, England)

Students at the two older universities with a higher proportion of white middle-class students were generally more confident about their employment prospects. Consequently, they were more likely to talk about participating in activities 'just for fun' and were less focused on the employment benefits of these activities:

I only ever get involved with things because I want to...the things I do are for enjoyment reasons. I'm sure some people get involved with things because they feel they should, but for me that's not the point of doing activities...I see this course as an apprenticeship and it will definitely lead to a good job, we're in a great position really.

(Siobhan, medicine, 1960s campus-based university, England)

Generally, my outside interests aren't so much related to my course, they're more to relax and have time out, to do something a bit different... my future employability isn't something which overly scares me (Rosie, politics, Russell group university, England).

University for work

The second lifestyle focused very much on study and working part time to support their studying. These students tended also to live at home and sometimes had caring responsibilities. They prioritised their studies over their social life and 'having fun', saying that the university experience for them was more about getting an education and qualifications. Students whose lifestyle 'choice' focused on work and study were clustered in the post-1992 university. These students tended to be mature, from minority ethnic backgrounds and from lower socio-economic groups, although not exclusively.

> My university life tips towards the studying about 80:20 because I rarely go out. I'm happy with that as it's for a very good cause; this is going towards a very good degree and a very good job at the end of it. And there's a time for everything, now it's to study.
>
> (Kwame, law, post-1992 institution, England)

Mature students were less likely to have financial support from their parents, and many of them had families to support. In this context, they saw their university education much more as a personal investment.

> I want this education badly, so I have to make the decisions to balance out my time. I have a family to support and yes I need the money from my part time job but we must also think long term and concentrate on our studies to go further.
>
> (Mercy, nursing, post-1992 institution, England)

Some students were less involved in socialising around the university because of financial reasons. Age and social class were obviously relevant here, with younger working-class students and mature students, particularly those with families to support, being more likely to report financial hardship:

> I think my financial situation plays a large part in my lack of socialising here. One of my reasons for not going out so much is that this is my second degree and I don't get any government funding. So whatever money I do mange to save, it has to concentrate on books and travelling and food and paying rent rather than actually going out.
>
> (Safiya, pharmacy, post-1992 institution, England)

The problems of choice and lifestyle

As outlined earlier in the chapter, graduate outcomes vary between different student groups, and we have argued here that the choices that students make while at university may contribute to these differing outcomes. We suggest that choosing a student lifestyle has consequences for different students' outcomes both in terms of grades and in their future job prospects, but these 'choices' must be contextualised by life experience, cultural background and social and economic constraints. Choice as an idea is not value neutral. Equally as Denzin (1990) points out the notion of rationality in 'choice' is problematic. It suggests that

> In order for a rational choice to be made, an actor knows [how] an end affects other plans, knows the desirable and undesirable consequences of any givenness ... and knows how these means affect other means and other goals.
>
> (1990: 174)

Such knowledge is seldom obtained, but in the context of students from different backgrounds with different accesses to different levels of cultural capital, decisions and choice is even more problematic. Choice of lifestyle should be contextualised in relation to the constraints placed on groups and individuals. 'Students' choices' are therefore shaped by their social position, education, familial and social experiences and their economic conditions. What we perceive as our 'choice' is therefore made up of a range of factors related to our own background and current conditions. As Reay *et al.* (2005) argue

> Choice is rooted in fine discriminations and classificatory judgements of places for us and places for others.... A sociological view of choice must recognise both obviousness (what people like us do) and neces- sity (the limitations of social and spatial horizons) and the complex and sophisticated nature of individual and familial decision making.
>
> (2005: 160)

In other words, questions of preferences or 'taste' are developed socially, through experience and engagement with family, school, peers and seeing one's place in society. Choice, taste and preference grow out of individ- uals' life experiences which continue to be constrained differentially for different social divisions in society, through their access to economic, social and cultural capital. From this research, it is clear that students are not experiencing the same HE, often due to personal constraints grown out of those social divisions such as class, gender, ethnicity, age and so on because their relationship to the 'field' of HE is different depending on their family background. Sometimes they are making choices themselves based on the cultural capital they have acquired over their lives and sometimes their choices are constrained by institutions' facilities and provision or due to personal constraints related to their circumstances.

Bennett *et al.* found that particular 'tastes' often related to a 'confidence to pass judgements or hold views or not' (2010: 71). This can be seen in the attitudes of the middle-class white students who had confidence that the purpose of university was to have fun and that gaining a graduate job beyond that was not an issue, whereas the students from minority ethnic and working-class backgrounds were less confident and focused on study believing that was the most significant aspect of their life at university. Student 'lifestyle choices' have significant implications for future life prospects. As Bennett *et al.* point out

> Possession of cultural capital is still a route to personal advantage and distinction, with the most profitable portfolio combining educational qualifications...and appropriate forms of embodiment. Culture is not a matter of indifference for the powerful, and for some sections of the middle classes it remains critical...'Good taste'...continues to create, mark and consolidate social divisions.
>
> (2010: 259)

Students from white middle-class backgrounds at 'old universities' are much more able to gain access not only to the qualifications necessary as Bennett *et al.* (2010) highlight but also the 'appropriate forms of embodiment', as opposed to those students from working-class backgrounds who live at home, work longer part-time hours or have caring responsibilities and cannot, or do not 'choose' to, access the wider resources of HE. Social mobility has been a significant concern in the United Kingdom as internationally we do not score as well as other developed countries (Jäntti *et al.*, 2006), and as HE could play a role in offering opportunity for upward social mobility, we need to understand what conditions in HE can offer real opportunities for upward social mobility.

The debate on WP has tended to focus on entry into HE, entry to certain types of universities and attainment of different student groups, but this is only part of the story. Ensuring that students who get into HE have access to graduate outcomes is surely the next issue for WP research to explore. The research discussed in this chapter suggests that HE needs to pay greater attention to what opportunities are available to students beyond the classroom and what students are actually doing after class. Equally, re-framing the WP debate from who gets into HE to what additional resources students get while studying and what impact this has on different student groups once they graduate will support greater understanding of the role that HE can play in supporting upward social mobility in the future.

Bibliography

Archer, L. (2006) 'The Value of Higher Education', in Archer, L., Hutchings, M. and Ross, A. (eds) *Higher Education and Social Class: Issues of Exclusion and Inclusion* (London: Routledge Falmer, pp. 119–137).

Archer, L. and Leathwood, C. (2006) 'Identities, Inequalities, and Higher Education', in Archer, L., Hutchings, M. and Ross, A. (eds) *Higher Education and Social Class: Issues of Exclusion and Inclusion* (London: Routledge Falmer, pp. 175–193).

Archer, L., Hutchings, M. and Ross, A. (2003) *Higher Education and Social Class: Issues of Exclusion and Inclusion* (London: Routledge Falmer).

Barber, L. and Hill, D. (2005) *Is Graduate Recruitment Meeting Business Needs?* (Brighton: IES and CIHE).

Bennett, T., Savage, M., Silva, E., Wade, A., Gayo-Cal, M. and Wright, D. (2010) *Culture, Class, Distinction* (London: Routledge).

Blanden, J., Gregg, P. and Machin, S. (2005) 'Social Mobility in Britain: Low and Falling', *Centrepiece*, Spring 2005: 17–20. [online] http://cep.lse.ac.uk/centrepiece/v10i1/blanden.pdf [accessed 10 January 2011].

Blanden, J., Gregg, P. and MacMillan, L., (2010) *Intergenerational Persistence in Income and Social Class: The Impact of Within-Group Inequality* (Bristol The Centre for Market and Public Organisation Working Paper 10/230). [online] http://www.bristol.ac.uk/cmpo/publications/papers/2010/wp230.pdf [accessed 5 May 2011].

Blasko, Z. (2002) *Access to What? Analysis of Factors Determining Graduate Employability* (Bristol: HEFCE).

Bourdieu, P. (1985) 'The Genesis of the Concepts of Habitus and of Field', *Sociocriticism*, 2: 11–24.

Bourdieu, P. (1984) *Distinction: A Social Critique of the Judgement of Taste* (London: Routledge).

Bourdieu, P. (1977) *Outline of a Theory* (Cambridge: Cambridge University Press).

Bourdieu, P. and Passeron, J. (1977) *Reproduction in Education, Society and Culture* (London: Sage).

Brennan, J. (2004) 'Graduate Employment Issues for Debate and Enquiry', *International Higher Education*, Winter 34: 12–20.

Brennan, J. and Shah, T. (2003) *Access to What? Converting Educational Opportunity into Employment Opportunity* (London: CHERI Open University Press).

Broeke, S. and Nicholls, T. (2007) *Ethnicity and Degree Attainment* (DfES Research Report RW92).

Chevalier, A. (2004) *Motivation, Expectations and the Gender Pay Gap for UK Graduates*. Discussion Paper No. 1101 [online] http://www.iza.org/en/webcontent/publications/papers/viewAbstract?dp_id= 1101 [accessed June 2012].

Christie, H., Munro, M. and Fisher, T. (2004) 'Leaving University Early: Exploring the Differences Between Continuing and Non-continuing Students', *Studies in Higher Education*, 29 (5): 617–631.

Clegg, N. (2011) *Opening Doors, Breaking Barriers: A Strategy for Social Mobility* (London: Cabinet Office). [online] http://download.cabinetoffice.gov.uk/social-mobility/opening-doors-breaking-barriers.pdf [accessed 7 May 2011].

Connor, H., La Valle, I., Tackey, N. and Perryman, S. (1996) *Ethnic Minority Graduates: Differences by Degrees*. Report No. 309 (Brighton: Institute for Employment Studies).

Connor, H., Tyers, C., Modood, T. and Hillage, J. (2004) *Why the Difference? A Closer Look at Higher Education Minority Ethnic Students and Graduates*. Research Report No. 552 (London: DfES).

Denzin, N. (2 April 1990) 'Reading Rational Choice Theory', *Rationality and Society*, 2: 172–189.

DfEE, CSU, AGAS, IER (1999) Moving On: Graduate Careers Three Years after Graduation. Warwick: IER.

Elias, P. and Jones, P. (2006) *Representation of Ethnic Groups in Chemistry and Physics* (London: Royal Society of Chemistry and Institute of Physics).

Erikson, R. and Goldthorpe, J. (June 2010) 'Has Social Mobility in Britain Decreased? Reconciling Divergent Findings on Income and Class Mobility', *British Journal of Sociology*, 61 (2): 211–230.

Goldthorpe, J., Llewellyn, C. and Payne, C. (1987) *Social Mobility and Class Structure in Modern Britain* (Oxford: Oxford University Press).

Higher Education Statistics Agency (2007) *Students in Higher Education Institutions 2005/06* (Cheltenham: HESA).

Hutchings, M. (2006a) 'Information, Advice and Cultural Discourses of Higher Education', in Archer, L., Hutchings, M. and Ross, A. (eds) *Higher Education and Social Class: Issues of Exclusion and Inclusion* (London: Routledge Falmer, pp. 97–119).

Hutchings, M. (2006b) 'Financial Barriers to Participation', in Archer, L., Hutchings, M. and Ross, A. (eds) *Higher Education and Social Class: Issues of Exclusion and Inclusion* (London: Routledge Falmer, pp. 155–175).

Jäntti, M., Bratsberg, B., Røed, K., Raaum, O., Naylor, R., Osterbacka, E., Bjorklund, A. and Eriksson, T. (2006) *American Exceptionalism in a New Light: A Comparison of Intergenerational Earnings Mobility in the Nordic Countries, the United Kingdom and the United States*. Discussion Paper No. 1938 (Bonn: IZA).

Leathwood, C. and Hutchings, M. (2006) 'Entry Routes to Higher Education: Pathways, Qualifications and Social Class', in Archer, L., Hutchings, M. and Ross, A. (eds) *Higher Education and Social Class: Issues of Exclusion and Inclusion* (London: Routledge Falmer, pp. 137–155).

Leslie, D. (2005) 'Why People from the UK's Minority Ethnic Communities Achieve Weaker Degree Results Than Whites', *Applied economics*, 37: 619–632.

Little, B. (2006) 'The Student Experience and the Impact of Social Capital', in McNay, I. (ed.) *Beyond Mass Higher Education* (Maidenhead: SRHE, Open University Press, pp. 57–67).

Milburn, A. (2009) *Unleashing Potential: The Final Report of the Panel on Fair Access to the Professions* (London: Cabinet Office).

Naylor, R.A. and Smith, J.P. (2004) 'Determinants of Educational Success on Higher Education', in Johnes, G. and Johnes, J. (eds) *International Handbook on the Economics of Education* (Cheltenham: Edward Elgar, pp. 415–461).

Owen, D., Green, A., Pitcher, J. and Maguire, M. (2000) *Minority Ethnic Participation and Achievements in Education, Training and the Labour Market*. Research Report No. 225 (London: DfES).

Pearson, R. (2006) 'The Demise of the Graduate Labour Market', in McNay, I. (ed.) *Beyond Mass Higher Education* (Maidenhead: SRHE, Open University Press, pp. 68–78).

Purcell, K.P., Elias, P., Davies, R. and Wilton, N. (2005) *The Class of '99: A Study of the Early Labour Market Experience of Recent Graduate*. Research Report No. RR691 RTP01-03 (London: DfES).

Reay, D., David, M. and Ball, S.J. (2002) 'Making a Difference? Institutional Habituses and Higher Education Choice', *Sociological Research Online*, 5 (4), [online] http://www.socresonline.org.uk/5/4/reay.html [accessed 5 December 2005].

Reay, D., David, M. and Ball, S. (2005) *Degrees of Choice Social Class, Race and Gender in Higher Education* (Stoke-on-Trent: Trentham Books).

Reay, D., Davies, J., David, M. and Ball, S.J. (2001) 'Choices of Degree or Degrees of Choice? Class, Race and the Higher Education Process', *Sociology*, 35 (4): 855–870.

Reay, D., Luke, M. and Ball, S.J. (2001) 'A Difference? Institutional Habituses and Higher Education Choice', *Sociological Research*, 5 (4). [online] http://www.socresonline.org.uk/5/4/reay.html [accessed 5 December 2005].

Richardson, T.E. (2008a) 'The Attainment of Ethnic Minority Students in UK Higher Education', *Studies in Higher Education*, 33 (1): 33–48.

Richardson, T.E. (2008b) *Degree Attainment, Ethnicity and Gender: A Literature Review*. Report for the Equality Challenge Unit and the Higher Education Academy. [online] http://www.heacademy.ac.uk/assets/York/documents/ourwork/research/J_Richardson_literature_review_Jan08.pdf [accessed 8 June 2008].

Richardson, J.T.E. and Woodley, A. (2003) 'Another Look at the Role of Age, Gender and Subject as Predictors of Academic Attainment in Higher Education', *Studies in Higher Education*, 28: 475–493.

Rudd, E. (1984) 'A Comparison Between the Results Achieved by Women and Men Studying for First Degrees in British Universities', *Studies in Higher Education*, 9: 47–57.

Saunders, P. (2010) *Social Mobility Myths* (London: Civitas).

Savage, M. (2000) *Social Class and Social Transformation* (Milton Keynes: Open University Press).

Smith, J. and Naylor, R. (2001) 'Determinants of Degree Performance in UK Universities: A Statistical Analysis of the 1993 Student Cohort', *Oxford Bulletin of Economics and Statistics*, 63: 29–60.

Smith, J., McKnight, A. and Naylor, R. (2000) 'Graduate Employability: Policy and Performance in HE in the UK', *Economic Journal*, 110: 382–411.

Thomas, L. (2002) 'Student Retention in Higher Education: The Role of Institutional Habitus', *Journal of Education Policy*, 17 (4): 174–190.

9
Transformation or Trauma: The Transition to Higher Education of Non-Traditional Students

Lynda Measor, Paula Wilcox and Philip Frame

Introduction

We focus in this chapter on the transition between school or college and higher education (HE) in England. While interested in the experience for all students, we have particular concerns for those who can be defined as non-traditional, as representing diversity, although we do not include specific consideration of disability issues. In recent years, completing this transition effectively in a 'good enough' fashion has been identified as important for a successful university career. Recognising the significance of transition also has consequences for the policy, practice and organisation of universities (Yorke and Longden, 2008).

As members of the research community and practising university teachers, we consider that there is still insufficient information about the transition to HE. In this chapter, we not only consider existing literature on transition to HE but also draw on theoretical models from research into other educational transfers (Measor and Woods, 1984). We present a discussion of recent qualitative research to examine student experiences of the transition to HE. We argue that the focus on qualitative data increases understandings of student experiences of transition and the factors that influence successful transition and enables precise recommendations for practice to be made (Frame, 2008). All the data presented in this chapter are taken from the University of Brighton empirical studies (Wilcox *et al.*, 2005; McQueen *et al.*, 2009).

Educational transitions

Theoretical frameworks on identity formation and acculturation developed over 50 years of research into the transition from primary to secondary school (Nisbet and Entwhistle, 1969; Hamblin, 1978; Measor and Woods, 1984; Galton *et al.*, 1999) have important implications for understandings of the transition to HE. Policies and practices developed to 'ease' the transfer between primary and secondary schools have been heavily scrutinised and are pertinent to improving student experiences in HE.

The concept of 'status passage' (Van Gennep, 1960; Glaser and Strauss, 1968) applied to the primary–secondary transition phase is useful for understanding the HE transfer. 'The concept refers to transitions in life where people undergo a change in status' (Measor and Woods, 1984: 159). While this is rather 'grand theory' to apply to educational transitions, we argue they do involve complicated issues for those undergoing them.

Van Gennep suggested three stages in status passages: separation, transition and reincorporation (1960). The first two phases are characterised by marginality or liminality. People have left one status but are not yet fully secure in the other 'neither here nor there, betwixt and between' (Turner, 1969: 95). Extensive anxieties are associated with these phases of separation and transition, and '*rites de passage*' accompany them. Status passages involve a shift to a new status, a new stage of life and place in life, and the transition to HE relates to significant matters in the lifecycle. We want to stress the degree of personal change the status passage between academic levels implies and involves.

There is not much theory to guide us. Van Gennep (1960) was more interested in the structural aspects of status passages. Glaser and Strauss considered their subjective properties but did not venture into 'identity theory', which is important because status passage usually implies some degree of 'threat to the self', and specifically to the self that has been established in the old status (Measor and Woods, 1984: 162; Wilcox *et al.*, 2005: 712). Traditional students aged 18–19 years face the transition to 'independent' life – to living in student accommodation – and to caring for themselves. Their transition is to a more independent and more 'autonomous' stage of life.

The transfer for traditional students occurs at a time of significant change in the lifecycle having implications for identity as well as status, but has repercussions for non-traditional students too. At its core, it entails shifts in the 'story' one tells oneself about oneself. 'It involves questions about "what sort of person one is to become, what sort of self is in the making"' (Dewey, 1922: 127). Identity development does not begin, or end, at transfer to the status of the 'HE student', but this stage may be highly significant in building a sense of who one *is* in the world. It involves qualifications that lead to decisions not only about what one will *do* in the world but also about who and what one will *be*. The implications are more profound than we may originally suspect and include issues of 'be' 'coming'. Values, appearance and beliefs are only some of the more obvious aspects of what is crucial. Bourdieu's concern for the place of 'identity formation' in students' successful acculturation to the 'habitus' (Bourdieu, 1977) has relevance and draws our attention to the role of the receiving 'habitus' and our role as 'acculturaters' (Frame, 2008: 1). Students articulated their feelings about the shifts involved.

> I feel a lot more ready for grown-up life, even though it's a scary thought, because I know I've, I'm independent, I've got the skills to be independent.
>
> (Cathy, 2nd year, 20)

> Erm, ... it kind of, it meant I could be a lot more independent because I actually see myself as quite an independent person anyway now.
>
> (Vicki, 2nd year, 20)

We are fully aware that our student cohorts include increasing numbers of non-traditional students who are older and already live independently from their families of origin or, by contrast, continue to live at home with their family of origin. Others come from families with class or ethnicity affiliations, which have a significant impact on their accommodation to university (Frame, 2008: 3). Andrews (2007) asserts that mature, non-traditional students tend to have a more fully developed identity on entry, so the formation role of HE for adolescents becoming adults is less applicable. This is not to say that they do not face 'multiple status passage' challenges, but they may be different from those of the traditional student. HE, nevertheless, is likely to produce a number of issues that relate to status passage in the terms we discussed earlier of the stimulus to a 'new' self. We want to argue, therefore, that non-traditional students too have to undergo transition; they may carry a different set of freight with them as they begin the journey through that transition, but there are significant status passages to be made for them.

Multiple status passages

Glaser and Strauss (1968) argue that status passage involves a multiple set of concerns that affect different areas of the individual's life and experiences. In the context of transition to HE, the first aspect of the passage relates to the 'formal culture' of the new institution. The 'formal' culture is defined as that geared to staff expectations and expressed through official policies. Secondly and simultaneously, students face a transfer within the informal culture of the university, geared to student expectations and relationships amongst one's peers. The formal culture is introduced from 'above' by those who staff the organisation and by the statutes and policies guiding them. They set the parameters within which it is formed, the criteria by which it is defined and initiate its inception. The informal culture is 'pressed up from below' by peer cultures and more pervasive youth cultures generally

(Measor and Woods, 1984). The two cultures intermingle, of course, at times in harmony and at others in conflict, but informal cultures can influence, complicate and aid (or hinder) the adaptations of students.

Academic work on transition from primary to secondary school aids our understanding. Galton *et al.* (1999) argue that to facilitate effective transition to secondary school, consideration needs to be given to five aspects, which he terms the 'Five Bridges'. The new entrant must cross each of them to 'pass' to the new 'status'. The first is the bureaucratic bridge relating to formal relationships between educational institutions. Second is the social and emotional bridge involving the development of relationships between peers and between students and staff in the new institution and corresponds to Glaser and Strauss' analysis of 'informal' aspects of the passage. The third bridge concerns academic matters and issues of curriculum. The fourth bridge involves pedagogy, and the fifth considers the management of learning (Galton *et al.*, 1999). Relatively few universities have provisions in place to aid progress over each of these bridges, and this chapter argues the importance of developing transition schemes that support the multiple status passages that face students.

In the following section of this chapter, we mobilise Galton *et al.'s* framework to make an analytic sense of the data generated in the Brighton University study and for practical guidance in developing the policy and practice dimensions of the five bridges.

The bureaucratic 'bridge' of transition

The first bridge, concerning bureaucracy, considers building communication bridges between institutions at different academic levels. Its focus is outside the research projects represented in this chapter, which dealt with student reactions to transition and is not therefore directly considered.

The social and emotional 'bridge' of transition

The majority of students interviewed in the Brighton research spoke about the 'shock of the new' they experienced at the beginning of their transition (Wilcox *et al.*, 2005).

> The first year was different and it could be that because it was new that's why it could be harder.
>
> (Jenny, 1st year, 19)

Both traditional and non-traditional students felt that they had to adapt to distinctively new circumstances and it involved a number of challenges.

> And I think last year it was a new surrounding, I didn't know what to expect, I didn't have any expectations, so things were just hitting me from different directions and it was really hard to begin with.
>
> (Beatrice, 2nd year, 27)

For many mature students, the experience was described as particularly difficult.

> I felt quite nervous because as a mature student, I haven't been in an educational establishment for quite a long time, so I was quite nervous for what I was in for. I was quite overawed by it in the first few days as everyone was saying things and it just seemed too much for me I think that the emphasis at the beginning on 'Don't worry about it too much' would have been useful.
>
> (John, 2nd year, 54)

Friends, 'tribes' and family

The key challenge in coping with the new circumstances and completing an effective transition was making a network of friends in the new institutional setting. Traditional students interviewed in the Brighton study were clear about the critical significance of 'having good friends'. It stood at the heart of their adjustment to university:

> ... because at home you have got the support of your family and stuff and your friends aren't so important I guess. But like here your friends are like your friends and your family and everything really ....
>
> (Beth, 1st year, 20)

The recognition that friends now stand in for family as the core support structure in the new environment is clear in this quote. Other students looked back at the time before they had a network of friends and remembered intense difficulties.

> Looking back now I think why did I get so upset? Because you do feel really lonely and I think that really plays on your mind, so that you feel so bad, that you feel so, you know, you are just so desperate to go home. I went home I remember driving back thinking 'Please crash the car or something' so that I didn't have to go back and that's how bad it was.
>
> (Zoe, 2nd year, 20 years old)

The data indicate the critical importance of having friends, but they need to count as 'proper' friends.

> But yes I guess making good friends is really important, rather than making like loads and loads of friends it's making ones that you really care about.
>
> (Beth, 1st year, 20)

Having 'good friends' reduces anxiety provoked by the status passage, creating a new sense of 'belonging' and allowing progress through the status passage. One factor that turns transition into trauma occurs when friendships are not formed. Students can suffer extreme feelings of isolation and threats to their identity. Mackie (2001) and Bennett (2003) explored student retention or progression in the context of developing connections, integration and identification with the campus community as a significant factor in student success.

Diversity and transition

It is important to question the appropriateness of this analysis for non-traditional students. The samples for many of the studies of transition have been young, full-time, campus-based, mainly middle-class school leavers (Frame, 2008: 2). The experience of students from diverse backgrounds may be distinctly different. In the first place, they may continue to live in their family of origin. A survey of 3,262 students (age not specified) in the northwest of England indicated that almost a quarter continued to live at home. The proportion was much higher in post- than pre-1992 HE institutions in the area (29 per cent compared with 18 per cent) (Patiniotis and Holdsworth, 2005). Statistically significant predictors other than type of university included having a caring role, father's occupation and parental level of education. The quality of these students' integration with university and the nature of their status passage may be somewhat different from the traditional student patterns we outlined previously. Data generated with mature students indicate that making friends is still important for a successful transition.

> I was feeling fine but I was disappointed that I hadn't made any friends. I emailed my god mother – she had always encouraged me to go back into education and said I felt a bit isolated and everything and I was starting to think did I make a mistake and she said just to hang in there and it will get better it is going to be daunting and it is so big so it is going to be different from college.
>
> (Sally, 1st year, 33)

For these learners, nevertheless, identity was more embedded in a community outside the campus, where people kept their affiliations and drew on them for support as an alternative to the people and to the formal structures and processes in the university. By not moving location to attend a place of study, their existing support networks external to the university remained in place – although we do not know what strains and stresses they came under. Such students juggled their lives inside the university community with their commitments outside it, which were of equal or greater importance (Frame, 2008). What quantitative research (Patiniotis and Holdsworth, 2005) cannot tell us, however, is how the different patterns of attachment and integration felt to the students involved and whether they escaped the challenges of the status passage entirely. We suspect they did not but recognise further, and qualitative research is needed on the topic.

Tutors and staff

Crossing the social and emotional bridge to university is affected by relationships not only with peers but also with tutors. It is clear from the data generated in the Brighton study that cool, distant and uninvolved staff can act as a significant block to students developing a sense of 'comfort' in their new space/place.

> Mmm, very important thing is comfort and – also – with the staff as well, the..., it's,...it almost feels like us and them, and I feel very strange because we're all adults, we're not kids. You know if it was like I'm a teacher, and 50, and you're a student, you're 10, it's different, but I've found that, you know, and it could be a cultural thing as well, because what I've noticed being here, British people are not very, they're very conservative and they don't like people coming into their spaces whereas I'm from [home country], you talk to everyone, and you're friendly with everyone.
>
> (Beatrice, 2nd year, 27, international)

The data generated with this mature international student alert us to the significance academic staff can have in easing the 'formal' but also the informal aspects of the transition. The use of the word 'comfort' is interesting and is echoed throughout this study.

Frame (2008) speculates that while supportive relationships with tutors are highly valued, reliability and predictability are particularly important in allowing students to feel 'comfort'. The following quote indicates the specific significance of supportive relationships:

> There are um several academic staff actually who have been particularly. um, ... that I've really sort of looked up to and just have been a real help and a real source of support.
>
> (Jane, 2nd year, 20)

The interviewer presses for an account of specific actions or 'ways of being' a tutor that are helpful. It is significant this student finds it quite difficult to put into words what the particular 'helping' qualities were.

> Well I suppose, I dunno.... Maybe...it's something that I see in myself and that's like a real desire to help people get on. Yes they expect you to have a certain amount of initiative and a certain amount of drive, um,

but once they see that they're more than willing to actually encourage it and to sort of guide you and point you in the right direction. I dunno, maybe if it fulfils something in them.

(Jane)

The data allow us to see how as staff we can reduce the setbacks for the new student in moving from the liminal state to an incorporated status passage. Frame (2008) suggests that continuity in social relations is important in affirming a successful transition and as Kantanis (2000: 8) argues, 'the role of social transition issues underscoring the success of academic transition cannot be underestimated'.

We have discussed the importance of new students developing bonds of friendship with their peers, but we develop from this data the sense that interpersonal connections with tutors or at least some tutors are also a significant bridging point. They all can act as what Koizumi identifies as an anchor point. An anchor point is

an element of a person-in-environment system which facilitates transaction between the person and the environment [and] can be information, knowledge, skills, family, friends, physical bases for activities, institutions, organizations, etc.

(2000: 176)

When entering a new environment, anchor points are likely to be sought that enable the person to find links with it. The data presented here indicate strategies that the students deployed. Some related to informal processes, specifically the development of solid friendship structures, which support the development of the new self as the individual negotiates the transition. Others involve the positioning and involvement of formal agents such as tutors and administrative staff in progress through the status passage. Others are internal to the individual and involve drawing on previous experiences of changing schools or starting a new job. Whatever the strategy selected to aid the movement across the social and emotional bridges, finding resources to do so successfully is essential for the psychic health of our students in the status passage of transition.

The non-traditional students who were the focus of Andrews' work (2007) had engagement with university that was conditional, pragmatic and strategic. He argues that 'anchor points' may or may not be associated with the campus or the university and calls into the question the requirement to be socially and academically integrated into a university to make a successful transition to it and to be successful educationally at it. Andrews asserts that non-traditional students had different strategies. They used one another to manage common dissatisfactions. They did not seek identification as 'Balliol Man' or equivalent but sought service delivery as and when needed by identifying people within the institution who were bridges to that service. This suggests that non-traditional students have worked out their own ways of dealing with the traditional challenges and accommodations to university. While Andrew's study was confined to mature learners, Frame (2008) suspects that much the same is likely to apply to any student studying at a metropolitan university who has a different social loci. We would want, nevertheless, to argue that while non-traditional students have a status passage to complete, its pathways and its challenges may be differently configured and they may have a different route map, but elements of the need for individual and probably psychic change remains.

The social and emotional bridge is central to successful transition to HE. As academics in HE, we need an understanding of the emotional aspects involved in the move to university. Such research allows for the development of evidence-based decision making and programmes that manage the early experience of all students entering HE to foster their social and emotional progress.

The 'academic', 'pedagogic' and 'management of learning' bridges

Galton *et al.* (1999) argue that the third, fourth and fifth bridges of transition concern academic matters of curriculum, pedagogy and management of learning, and it is to these that we now turn. The data from the Brighton study suggest that accommodating to unfamiliar academic approaches involves challenges for both traditional and non-traditional students.

The key characteristic of contemporary academic approaches in universities relates to independent learning; the curriculum specifically calls for it, and pedagogy is fashioned by it. They have implications for new students entering university and require all students to move towards independence quite rapidly. This element of the status passage is traversed equally by non-traditional and traditional students. Frame (2008) notes that students are expected to move seamlessly from patterns of full-time teaching (work or other mode) to managing their own time for learning at the same time, as they are constructing crucial social and emotional bridges. They must cross from crowded curriculum to curriculum 'lite' and from structure to lack of structure. Suddenly, the 'care and control' patterns of school or college are gone. Students at university need to develop significant autonomy and to 'manage' without input from teachers who were personally involved in prompting actions, reminding about deadlines and 'looking over your shoulder'. Previous studies have found that secondary school 'pupils who are coached to deal with the demands of A levels may not be best equipped for the greater level of independence expected in HE' (Yorke and Longden, 2008: 29).

The contact time with tutors offered to students in universities is a controversial matter and is liable to become more so in the context of the new fees structures. One non-traditional student was clear about the difficulties he faced adjusting to the loss of full-time teaching.

> The Access course, was full-time, mean...um...a lot more attendance than a degree, a full-time degree. The degree I've taken doesn't involve as much study time, tutorial time and contact time – attendance time whereas attending the Access course involved more or less every day, all day every day, um, attendance and lessons, etc. I think it was, there were 26 modules in a year, 26 different subjects so um it was very, very high pressure.
>
> (Ian, 3rd year, 43)

This student acknowledged that the pattern of full-time attendance had worked well for him, and the new curriculum arrangements meant that

> I found the University quite difficult to adjust to.
>
> (Ian)

For him the new system meant a loss of 'feeling at ease' and knowing what was expected. The notion of 'comfort' appears again in the data.

> I felt more comfortable with that than I did when I began my first year because I had to arrange my own time..., um..., I had to attend maybe two hours a day for possibly three days a week which gave me an awful lot of time to myself when I had to actually figure out what it is I needed to do.
>
> (Ian)

The student recognised the scale of the adjustment he had to make and understood that it had taken him a significant sector of his first year to work through it. The underpinning issue is that of independent learning. We have selected only two data sections to represent the perspectives of many students who did not understand or know how to go about managing learning independently, which the new curriculum arrangements and pedagogic assumptions demand. Many do not understand what they are newly responsible for and feel resentful about what seems not only unfamiliar but also opaque and possibly uncaring. One traditional student made the same point and was explicitly critical of what he found in HE.

> I expected it to be this difficult but I didn't expect it to be so un-organised.
>
> (James, 1st year, 20)

He went on to make the following point:

> We can't learn if we don't even know what hours we're doing, you know.
>
> (James)

It is not the level of academic difficulty of the work that the students point to but the lack of 'comfort' in the profoundly new arrangements and the focus on independence, autonomy and the management of the self. Elements of status passage appear to be involved in adjustment to the new academic arrangements in addition to those we identified in the discussion of social and emotional bridges. These data support research that indicates that there can be stark contrasts between the expectations and realities of both students and lecturing staff in HE (Parmar and Trotter, 2004). There are few curriculum or pedagogy bridges between secondary and higher educational practices, and Frame (2008) argues that most universities do not seek to build gradually, or even explicitly, on the learning skills that students bring or introduce new patterns gradually.

Learning issues

Students offered commentary on the extent of the difficulties they had in adjusting to the very new patterns of independent learning.

> I like going to, I like the library actually. If I'm in the right frame of mind I like going to the top floor of the library near where the journals are? Because I like the journals, I've discovered them and I quite like them. Um, yeah, that's quite a nice space because it's the sort of thing that if you go to the silent zone, you can sit, you can lay all your work out. It's not too busy, you won't chat and if I get bored then I can look out the window for quite a while.
>
> (Cathy, 2nd year, 20)

Cathy indicates her developing strategies for independent learning. She also, significantly makes a reference to being in the 'right frame of mind' before she can go to the library. The data remind us that formal and informal status passages are linked, and emotional states have impact for the learning processes. The data also indicate that 'comfort' grew when students found their 'corner' – their 'place' in the library.

Pedagogy

The reduced hours of contact in comparison with school or college courses mean that the quality of teaching becomes very important, and the tutor's ability to provide opportunities for positive learning interactions was identified in the data as significant.

Generally, it's probably more the seminar tutor really makes a difference to how it goes, and who's in the group as well.

(Marie, 2nd year, 21)

The interviewer encouraged students to identify specific factors they consider important,

Is there anything that makes it go particularly well?

Um, I think one who's got kind of a plan for the session. We've had some tutors who just kind of turn up and just kind of ask how was the lecture, have you got anything you want to ask about the lecture you don't understand and nobody ever seems to like want to? Um well.

(Gavin, 2nd year, 20)

Is that a short seminar?

They can, they have been pretty short. Yeah and they then just say 'Oh spend some time working on your assignment' type of thing and then you go off into groups and he's supposed to come round and um talk to you but it's just a waste of time really, you could be doing that anywhere really.

(Gavin)

The student feels that tutors who offer structured opportunities to learn create improved learning experiences. Tutors who offer their knowledge and expertise to the student are what counts as quality education. Working alone or in a group is not valued as important, independent learning; it is the tutor input that is prized particularly, but not only, in the first year.

Personal and individual factors relating to tutors and their style of teaching is identified as an important factor in the accounts students gave in the Brighton research. Those tutors who can foster active learning are welcomed.

I'm liking it at the moment, I'm doing critical social theory this semester, and I like the way that's panned out because although I'm in one of the lecture halls, I've got R for it, and it's quite nice because even though it's kind of a lecture he makes it quite interactive and people are saying things, and talking about their experiences and that I'm finding really, really good but I think just in general I'd prefer seminars. I mean I find lectures helpful, but they're not as interactive because I really do learn best by interacting I'd like more seminars in general, just because that's how I learn best.

(Cathy, 2nd year, 20)

The Brighton research indicated that new students found the transition to new methods of teaching difficult. This was not characteristic only of the early part of the year or a feeling that faded as the first year progressed. Ridley (2004) identified how puzzling many non-traditional students find HE. These data indicated that both traditional and non-traditional students struggled throughout the year with the multiple new demands and experienced the 'institutional practice of mystery' that Lillis discussed (2001: 53).

A further issue is that students felt that the emphasis on independent learning meant they felt less able to ask for support.

> At college I found you got more support, as opposed to here where they just sort of let you get on with it and I think this is normal for university life, you know you can't have people standing over your back telling you do this do that. I think I found that I had to work ten times harder.
>
> (Tamara, 1st year, 19)

Others said that while some tutors had been helpful not all were uniformly so.

> In the first year, I did approach a couple of tutors once and a couple of times, and they weren't very. I felt like they didn't have enough time, and I just sort of gave up. Now I seek help from my husband, he is the person who provides support.
>
> (Beatrice, 2nd year, 27, international)

Beatrice's account reveals a multiplicity of reactions; she is resentful about the lack of support while at the same time she feels she 'should' be able to manage her learning alone in the new system. As a non-traditional international student these difficulties are intense. It is interesting she chooses to gather support from her own informal family settings in the way Andrews (2007) argued is characteristic of non-traditional students.

Making the transition to 'be-coming' a university learner and developing new independent learner status varies with individuals, and they use a variety of strategies. If we seek to ease the transition to HE for students, we need to find ways they can recognise and adjust to the new management of learning expected of them. New approaches need to be built, and students offered explicit explanation and guidance.

Assessment

The new learning culture has particular implications for assessment. Teachers in school and college typically take significant responsibility for shepherding students and ensuring they know when work has to be submitted and where it has to be delivered. It is perhaps assessment that represents the most difficult challenge to the successful status passage. Frame (2008) points out that university procedures mean that there is, usually, only one chance at producing a successful assignment. From the General Certificate of Secondary Education (GCSE), students have been accustomed to producing drafts for tutor comment and being allowed to submit work on several occasions to improve their grade. Students in the Brighton research felt the loss of support on assessed work was difficult to adjust to.

> I felt a lot of the time that I was stumbling around in the dark, that I didn't know what was required of me, um, you know a lot of the times I didn't know if I was doing it right or wrong or, ... (sighs).
>
> (Amy, 3rd year, 41)

Both traditional and non-traditional students expressed a wish for:

> Well! someone I could at least turn to say you're going in the right direction. Sometimes I often, when I write my essays I often go down the wrong route, like I just got one back and it said you should have been doing this rather than that, it was a bit muddled, and I feel like if I had a little more support, because this subject is new to me, then I would be more on track. I'd rather get better grades.
>
> (Gill, 2nd year, 20)

We argue that this aspect of the transition affects traditional and non-traditional students equally, and the assessment bridge is the most fearsome of the five to cross. As one traditional student said:

> I have to be honest yes, it's ... m ..., it's er ... d, it's quite painful to experience.
>
> (Cathy, 2nd year, 20)

Another non-traditional student expressed very similar reactions:

> I have a big fear of failure, Yeah I do, I'm putting more effort in than I did at college.
>
> (Ken, 3rd year, 31)

Ramsden tells us that 'good teaching means seeing learning through the learner's eyes' (1988: 3). We need to question the extent to which this represents a guiding principle in HE and acts as a blockage to successful transition. Organisational and structural issues can create barriers to learning. Unsupported transition to HE learning can undermine good work:

> We get taught about Maslow's law don't we, the hierarchy of needs. It's like hang on a minute, we haven't even got the bottom rung yet, how can we move up that pyramid?
>
> (Mark, 2nd year, 20)

Green (2006) suggests that HE fails to build effective links with the student's previous academic experiences and strengths:

> Unless the locus of students is clearly understood, targeted and effective, pedagogical thinking cannot take place, to the detriment of both lecturers (who will continue to be frustrated by what they perceive as deficits of skill and knowledge in their students) and the students themselves (who will struggle to realign their existing skills and knowledge within an imperfectly understood paradigm of subject and of study environment.
>
> (2006: 285)

It is important that we recognise, respect and celebrate the resources and build on the responses that students have amassed in their progress through 13 years of formal education received before coming to university.

It is crucial we recognise that not all students wear the same lens when 'eying' HE. We have already discussed ways that non-traditional students may access support in their own rather than the university community in the context of the social and emotional bridges involved in the transition. The data presented here, nevertheless, suggest that both traditional and non-traditional students face very similar challenges, quandaries and lack of 'comfort' in relation to the academic bridges they must cross to complete the status passages of their transition. Traditional students seem, however, to find ways of adapting more rapidly and more successfully. Research has shown that non-traditional students, having achieved the required academic proficiency to gain access to HE, do less well than their traditional peers (Archer and Leathwood, 2003). We do not have a clear understanding of the configurations of those differences.

Conclusions and ways forward

The data presented here indicate the changes students feel they are asked to make in crossing the 'Five Bridges' to university. As academics, we suggest we have a responsibility to offer specific support for students in the transition. Research that enhances the understanding of the student perspective has a significant role in developing transition schemes. We discuss the issues involved in building sensitive and effective transition schemes in a further article (Frame *et al.*, forthcoming). There we consider what needs to be provided to address the complex issues and offer support across the multiple status passages. Creating more effective transition schemes involves both internal and external innovation. The provision we make for transition for traditional and non-traditional students needs to involve some different elements. Much educational transition research focuses on the impact of new institutional structures on those who join it rather than questioning the structure itself. The assumption is that the student must adapt, and there is little research attention given to the question of adaptation by the university. We argue that equal attention needs to be paid to the ways the 'receiving institution does and can respond' (Frame, 2008: 1).

Bibliography

Andrews, M. (2007) *Access Policy and Practice in F&HE: Investigating 'Success' as Access Turns into Widening Participation*. Unpublished PhD thesis, University of Greenwich, London.

Archer, L. and Leathwood, C. (2003) 'Identities, Inequalities and HE', in Archer, L., Hutchings, M. and Ross, V. (eds) *HE and Social Class: Issues of Exclusion and Inclusion* (London: Routledge, pp. 175–192).

Bennett, R. (2003) 'Determinants of Undergraduate Student Drop Out Rates in a University Business Studies Department', *Journal of Further and HE*, 27 (2): 123–139.

Bourdieu, P. (1977) *Outline of a Theory of Practice* (Cambridge: Cambridge University Press).

Dewey, J. (1922) *Human Nature and Conduct* (New York: Henry Holt).

Frame, P. (2008) *NTFS Projects 2008–09: Stage Two Project Bid* (pp. 1–31).

Frame, P. (2001) 'Managing the Induction Crisis: Students Can Make a Difference', in Frame, P. (ed.) *Student Induction in Practice* (Birmingham: SEDA, Paper 113, p. 104). ISBN 1-902 435-16-8.

Furlong, A., Cartmel, F., Biggart, A., Sweeting, H. and West, P. (2003) *Youth Transitions: Patterns of Vulnerability and Processes of Social Inclusion* (London: The Stationery Office).

Galton, M.J., Gray, J. and Ruddick, J. (1999) *The Impact of School Transitions and Transfers on Pupil Attainment* (London: DfEE).

Glaser, B. and Strauss, A. (1968) *A Time for Dying* (Chicago: Aldine).

Gluckman, M. (1962) 'Les Rites de Passage', in Gluckman, M. (ed.) *Essays on the Ritual of Social Relations* (Manchester: Manchester University Press, pp. 1–52).

Green, A. (2006) 'University Challenge: Dynamic Subject Knowledge, Teaching and Transition', *Arts and Humanities in HE*, 5 (3): 275–290.

Hamblin, D. (1978) *The Teacher and Pastoral Care* (Oxford: Blackwell).

Kantanis, T. (2000) 'The Role of Social Transition in Students' Adjustment to the First-year of University', *Journal of Institutional Research*, 9 (1): 100–110.

Koizumi, R. (2000) 'Anchor Points in Transitions to a New School Environment', *Journal of Primary Prevention*, 20 (3): 175–187.

Lillis, T.M. (2001) *Student Writing: Access, Regulation and Desire* (London: Routledge).

Mackie, S. (2001) 'Jumping the Hurdles – Undergraduate Student Withdrawal Behaviour', *Innovations in Education and Training International*, 38 (3): 265–275.

Frame, P., Measor, L. and Wilcox, P. (Forthcoming) 'Trauma or Transformation: An Analysis of Student Perspectives and Strategies for Improving the Experience of Transition to University'.

McQueen, H., Wilcox, P., Stephen, D. and Walker, C. (2009) *Widening Access and the Role of Social Motivation in Students' Transitional Experiences to and through Higher Education* (Brighton: University of Brighton).

Measor, L. and Woods, P. (1984) *Changing Schools: The Pupils' Perspectives* (Milton Keynes: Open University Press).

Nisbet, J.D. and Entwhistle, N.J. (1969) *The Transition to Secondary Education* (London: London University Press).

Parmar, D. and Trotter, E. (2004) 'Keeping our Students: Identifying Factors that Influence Student Withdrawal and Strategies to Enhance the Experience and Retention of First Year Students', *Learning and Teaching in the Social Sciences*, 1 (3): 149–168.

Patiniotis, J. and Holdsworth, C. (2005) ' "Seize That Chance!" Leaving Home and Transitions to HE', *Journal of Youth Studies*, 8 (1): 81–95.

Ramsden, P. (1988) 'Managing the Effective University', *HE Research and Development*, 17 (3): 347–370.

Ridley, D. (2004) 'Puzzling Experiences in HE: Critical Moments for Conversation', *Studies in HE*, 29 (1): 91–107.

Turner, V.W. (1969) *The Ritual Process* (London: Routledge and Kegan Paul).

Van Gennep, A. (1960) *The Rites of Passage* (London: Routledge and Kegan Paul).

Wilcox, P., Winn, S. and Fyvie-Gauld, M. (2005) ' "It Was Nothing to Do with the University, It Was Just the People": The Role of Social Support in the First Year Experience of HE', *Studies in HE*, 30 (6): 707–722.

Yorke, M. and Longden, B. (2008) *The First-Year Experience of HE in the UK* (London: HE Authority). [online] http://www.heacademy.ac.uk/assets/York/documents/resources/publications/FYEFinalReport.pdf [accessed 19 April 2011].

10

Non-Traditional Adult Students: Access, Dropout, Retention and Developing a Learner Identity

Barbara Merrill

Introduction: A changing higher education

In recent years, the student population in higher education (HE) institutions in the United Kingdom has become more diverse in terms of age, social class and ethnicity as doors have opened to groups previously under-represented. Changes to the student population have been accompanied by social and economic changes as well as policy interventions so that higher education institutions (HEIs) have been subject to the influences of marketisation and neo-liberalism. For Barnett, these factors have brought about 'uncertainties as to what it is to be a student' (2007: 9). Since the 1970s, universities have transformed from being an elite system to a mass HE system not only in the United Kingdom but also across Europe (Trow, 1989). The impact, however, has not been even across the UK HE system, as non-traditional students (both younger and adult) are largely concentrated in the post-1992 universities. Only a small percentage enter the academy of elite universities. The access of non-traditional adult students to universities has been enabled by a period of sustained general growth. However, this may change in the future as the impact of recession is felt by universities together with the recent increase of student fees in the United Kingdom. As a result, new debates have emerged centring on finances, management and the strategic focus of HE at the expense of access and widening participation issues.

It is in this context that the issue of retention and dropout has come to the forefront. Retention and dropout are currently high on the policy agenda of policy-makers in the United Kingdom, and Europe more widely, as they raise questions about the efficiency and effectiveness of HEIs. This chapter discusses the issues of access, retention and dropout by drawing on the findings of a European research project titled 'Access and Retention: Experiences of Non-Traditional Learners in Higher Education' (RANLHE) funded by the European Commission Lifelong Learning Programme. This three-year project involved eight partners from seven countries (England, Germany, Ireland, Poland, Scotland, Spain and Sweden). Using interdisciplinary approaches, the project aimed to examine what limits or promotes the construction of a learner identity amongst non-traditional students (both younger and adult) in becoming, or not, effective learners and how this process may enable or inhibit completion of HE. A key question, therefore, for our research was why some non-traditional students 'keep on going on' despite, in some cases, enormous difficulties and struggles, while others from a similar background in relation to class, gender, ethnicity, age and disability dropout. Although both younger and adult students were interviewed, this chapter focuses on the stories of adult students. The term non-traditional student in relation to adult students was defined as those who are under-represented in HE and whose participation in HE is constrained by structural factors. These groups include first-generation students, those from lower socio-economic backgrounds, minority ethnic groups, adult students and students with disabilities. At the same time, the project team was critical of the term and recognises that non-traditional student is a contested concept but one which is used in literature and by policy makers.

Methodology: Using biographical approaches

This section provides a brief insight into the methodological approaches used. Biographical narrative approaches were central to the research process. Life history and biographical methods have become increasingly popular amongst adult education researchers in Europe (West *et al.*, 2007). Such approaches produce in-depth material for understanding the dialectics of agency and structure in the learning experiences of adult students in HE and how these relate to past experiences of learning and the complex reasons why some students stay and others leave. Importantly, 'such methods offer rich insights into the dynamic interplay of individuals and history, inner and outer worlds, self and other' (Merrill and West, 2009, p.1). Biographies expose the dialectics and the inter-relationship between structure and agency in people's lives for as C. Wright Mills explains 'the personal troubles of milieu' are related to 'the public issues of social structure' (1973: 14). Biographical research often focuses on the individual, but this type of research is also helpful for identifying the collectivities in people's lives such as class and gender as the stories reveal common life experiences (Merrill, 2007). In the feminist tradition, biographical approaches allow the 'voices' of the participants to be heard and place them central to the research process while also breaking down the power relationship between the researcher and the researched.

Lecturers, support staff and senior management were also interviewed to gain insight into the institutional perspective. However, this chapter focuses on the student data. Each partner identified three case study institutions to reflect the different types of universities such as elite, reform or private (the latter is particularly important in Poland). Different cohorts of undergraduate students were interviewed: those in their final year of study, those who leave but later return and those who dropped out, as well as following a cohort from first through the final year of study.

Retention and dropout or non-completion

For non-traditional adult students 'keeping on going on' with their undergraduate study is not always straightforward as other aspects of their lives may intervene such as health or financial and relational issues with partners and family. Integrating into the academic world with its middle-class culture and language is also not easy for some. In Bourdieu's term, some feel 'like fish out of water' as their cultural capital is different to that of lecturers, the younger middle-class students and the institutional culture, particularly in elite universities (Bourdieu and Wacquant, 1992: 127). Sometimes it is an interplay of factors that makes studying and completing both a struggle and a risk but also a changing life experience for those who succeed and complete. As Barnett remarks, 'keeping on going on' for both younger and mature students is

> ... also a project that calls for considerable effort and even anxiety on their parts, and it is a project where success cannot be assured. Yet many millions of individuals do this all over the world and the majority of them succeed.
>
> (2007: 2)

'Dropout' is a term that has negative connotations (Thomas and Quinn, 2007), as it implies failure, placing the blame on the individual rather than the institution. The research team in the RANLHE project preferred to use the term non-completion as many, but not all, of the stories of those who left stated that they had gained educationally, socially and personally from their studies, even though they did not finish their degree. In some cases, therefore, non-completion may be the start of a new transition and stage in their biography, while for others it may indicate a difficult setback in their life. From the institutional perspective, non-completion is a sensitive issue as it has consequences for its status and may also result in loss of finances. Researching retention and non-completion in some institutions can, therefore, be a sensitive issue.

Research and literature on retention and dropout or non-completion has been influenced in the United Kingdom initially by American research and the work of Vincent Tinto in particular. British research has been shaped by the work of, for example, Mantz Yorke, Liz Thomas and Jocey Quinn. Most studies have focused on younger students (Quinn *et al.*, 2005), and some studies have focused on 'traditional' rather than 'non-traditional' students (Tinto, 2003). Other studies have looked at institutional factors and perspectives (Tinto, 2003; Yorke and Thomas, 2003). Tinto (2003), for example, highlights five institutional factors that enhance student retention. First, whether a university has an ethos of expecting students to succeed; secondly, whether there is a wide range of student support available; thirdly, providing quick and in-depth feedback on work; fourthly, student involvement in university activities and finally whether students are engaged and involved in learning. Non-completion, however, is not solely due to institutional factors and cultures. Rather, it is the interaction between institutional issues and external ones such as class, family, health and finance. As Quinn *et al.* argue

> To understand drop-out we need to look beyond student support needs or institutional barriers to cultural narratives and local contexts.
>
> (2005: 57)

In their study, 'First Generation Entry into Higher Education', Thomas and Quinn (2007) employed a socio-cultural approach by examining the role of the family on young first entrants and their experiences of university and the impact of this in terms of whether they complete or not.

As a way of moving towards an interdisciplinary approach and making sense of our biographical data, we chose to employ three key sensitising concepts in helping us to analyse our data and inform our theoretical and conceptual frameworks. These were habitus (Pierre Bourdieu, 1988; Bourdieu and Wacquant, 1989), recognition (Axel Honneth, 1995) and transitional space (Donald Winnicott, 1971). In relation to Bourdieu, we drew on his idea of habitus and his work on social and cultural capital, building on previous work by members of the research team (Peter Alheit, John Field and Barbara Merrill). Bourdieu's work on cultural capital is useful for looking at how working-class adult students learn to cope, or not, with the symbolic and intellectual capitals of the university. More broadly, the concept of habitus provides a powerful tool for revealing the dialectics of agency and structure in people's lives. Bourdieu's work, however, also had its limitations in relation to our study, so other theoretical and conceptual approaches were employed in conjunction with his ideas.

Our second sensitising concept, proposed by Linden West, offers a psychological perspective on non-traditional adult learners. This is the notion of transitional space, which draws on Donald Winnicott's work on human childhood development (1971). This idea was extended to learning in adult life. HE is a

> transitional space in which there is a constant negotiation and re-negotiation of self in relation to others and the cultural world of the university. Basic questions may be asked in entering university... of who

a person is, has been and might want to be. This in turn may provoke intense anxiety about a capacity to cope with change or whether a person is good enough in the eyes of significant people, whether other students or tutors.

(Johnston *et al.*, 2009: 288, 289)

The third sensitising concept is recognition, introduced by the Irish team (Ted Flemming and Fergal Finnegan). This idea straddles, in some ways, the concepts of habitus and transitional space. The concept of recognition derives from critical theory and the Frankfurt School and the work of Axel Honneth. In developing a critical theory of recognition, Honneth focuses on the role of inter-subjectivity in shaping a person's identity (1995). Honneth argues that the individual strives for recognition through developing relationships of self-confidence, self-respect and self-esteem in the family, civil society and the state.

Universities as transitional spaces: A sociological perspective

The concept of 'transitional space', such as in Winnicott's work, is more usually associated with psychology and object relations theory rather than sociology. The stories told by non-traditional students in our research revealed the need to explore and develop transitional space from a socio-logical perspective. Although the term 'space' (Urry, 1996) and 'social space' (Bourdieu, 1989) are discussed sociologically, 'transitional space' remains an underdeveloped concept. In recent years, there has been a growing interest in the concept of 'learning transitions' (Field *et al.*, 2009) in adult education research in the United Kingdom, and there are some links that can be made between transitional space and learning transitions. Both concepts refer and relate to notions of the potential for changing the self through learning. For Ecclestone, transition

... depicts change and shifts in identity and agency as people progress through the education system ... transition is a change process but also a shift from one identity to another.

(2009: 11)

From a sociological perspective, transitional space can be understood as a process of reflecting on one's identity through learning in a particular edu-cational environment. This process may lead to the reworking and changing of one's identity using agency within the boundaries of a particular, tem-porary space, place and time. In the RANLHE study, the space and place is the university campus and its culture and environment, while time refers to the length of study undertaken. Implicit in this is the notion that 'being a student' or 'student-hood' is itself a transitional and temporary identity

(Field *et al.*, 2010). While acknowledging, as Ecclestone (2009) does, the role of agency in reworking identities, there is the need to take into account structure and structural factors. Working-class adult students can find themselves located in a habitus, which is different, in Bourdieu's terms, to what they bring with them to the campus. However, the differences in relation to the students' habitus and that of the university is more pronounced in elite institutions. Identity formation and change becomes a dialectical process between structure and agency. The university can also offer a space for reflection on past life experiences, such as in initial education and the family, and how these impact on current learning experiences and the self at university. It can also lead adult students to reflect upon who they might become in the future. Changes in identity can sometimes be complex and partial rather than a total change in identity. In the transitional space of the university, adult students in the elite university defined themselves as being working class, and, consequently, some felt alienated by some aspects of the middle classness of the institution and some younger students and lecturers. While all recognised, by the end of their degree, that they had changed – some profoundly – none wanted to let go of their working-class identity. A transitional space, therefore, implies being in-between in terms of identity, whereby an individual lets go of part or all of their 'old identity' and transforms to assume a 'new or modified identity'.

Working out their identity and who they want to become is also related to how they and others see them as a student. Adult students strive, and sometimes struggle, for academic success. In seeking a new or changed identity they are also, in Honneth's (1995) terms, looking for recognition and respect from lecturers and other students. As Jenny recalled

> I felt very valued, very much part of it. So it was my desire to pursue my learning and their nurturing, I think, if you like.

The transitional space of a university can also be viewed as both a safe but also a temporary space providing a haven away from life, for example, on a deprived housing estate, poverty or family problems, as the stories in our research illustrate. The campus offers a space where they can leave behind their other life, even if it is only for a few hours a day, and immerse themselves in another and different world – that of academia. As Jane explains

> Some of the highs were when you had a really good lecture and you came out feeling you've got ever so much information – it was like buzzing. And meeting people that I would probably never had met. Just learning. I think it just gave me, absorbed me and gave me another life away from what I had.

Within the transitional space of the university, the campus provides a particular type of social space that is different to the communities in which non-traditional students live. Social space in this context refers to the environment of a university campus such as places for learning, cafes and bars and so on where social interaction with peers and lecturers takes place and where self and identity can be explored and developed in new ways. For non-traditional adult students, entering and learning in HE offers a new biographical experience; and although the transitional space is temporary, it can have a profound effect on their future biographies. As stated, some of the adult students remarked that they do not want to go back to being who they were before entering university. Developing a learner identity can be risky, however. For some, their working-class habitus may make it difficult for them to cope with the culture of the university while others do develop a learner identity and transform themselves while holding on to their working-class identity.

Determination in a transitional space

Biographical stories are important for understanding why most adult students 'keep on going on' and complete their degree and why others do not. As stated above, the reasons are complex and often combine institutional, personal and structural factors. These issues are explored in the next sections through the voices and experiences of the adult student participants. All the students interviewed were working class, most were women and some were single mothers. At one of the other three case study institutions (post-1992 university), the student population was more diverse in terms of ethnicity than the other two.

Being working class was an important aspect of their identity and for those studying in the elite university it raised their awareness of their working classness as they saw themselves as being different to the 'other' middle-class younger students. They talked about their experiences in seminars, for example, particularly in sociology, where they were aware of how their life experiences contrasted with those of the younger students. Language was one way in which class differences were experienced and highlighted:

> I just find it hard. I'm aware of how different I speak. They've got like amazing vocabularies and you just think God you sound brilliant and then I go red. I can't get my words out.
>
> (Anne)

Seminars and lectures also highlighted age differences between them and younger students.

The decision to enter HE was often triggered by a critical incident such as divorce or unemployment, and this decision was encapsulated in the desire to change their lives 'for the better'. Education was viewed as the best option for achieving this (Merrill, 1999). Laura, for example, explained:

> I'd recently become a single parent so I knew I needed to get some qual-
> ifications to get a decent job, as opposed to just working in call centres
> which was on offer at the time. I was looking around.

In a similar way Anne, also a single parent reflected on her work and life situation:

> You just keep thinking am I going to be here for the rest of my life? I had
> kids then moved. When I was younger I thought yes I'm going to do that
> then I thought I'm ending up back where I came from working in a chip
> shop where I worked when I was sixteen. And it was like I'm going to be
> here for the rest of my life if I don't do something. So I thought I've got
> options and when I finish I've got more options.

Anna, an older woman, began a part-time social studies degree:

> Well it all started ten years ago when my husband became ill. I took early
> retirement and I'd had a job that was involved and busy and kept my head
> going all the time.... Then I got bored of just being at home because I was
> his carer. I couldn't sit around doing nothing and all I was doing was jobs
> around the house.... All I was doing was housework and caring and I felt
> as if I was in a situation I didn't want to be in really.

For others, it was about proving that they were capable of learning. Mary, for instance, said: 'I realised that actually it was something that I'd always wanted to do.' Once they began their studies and the learning journey, they talked about being determined to succeed and complete. They did not want to go back to the life they had before. This was related to con-sciously taking the decision to change their lives, to become someone else by changing their identity. Determination was a word used by many partic-ipants to explain why, despite the difficulties experienced, they wanted to finish their studies. Determination was a strong motivating factor. Similarly, Barnett (2007) notes that persistence is key in the students' learning process. At the beginning of their undergraduate studies, many lacked confidence in their learning and were surprised when they progressed to the next year of study. Lack of confidence was also related to issues of class and a feeling that 'I don't belong here'. 'I must have got in by mistake' were phrases uttered by several students. Anne explained that on starting her degree: 'I just felt like a fish out of water, totally out of my comfort zone. I felt like a trampy kid.' However, their determination to succeed increased year by year:

I never actually thought I'd make it to the end, so, each year that went by was quite a shock because I'd got through another year but I was determined to make things different for myself and for my son ... I'd realised that I couldn't make any changes in my personal life unless I really changed ... It is determination that I wanted to change things and make a difference and be able to support us financially and move out of the neighbourhood that I was in too. I just thought I can't afford to drop-out now because I'll have nothing to show for it but I will have lots of student debts.

(Julia)

Mary's determination to keep going stemmed from her unhappy relationship with her father as a child:

There were a few times I thought, 'who the hell do you think you're kidding, what the hell are you playing at thinking you can do a degree?'. But it was always the thought of my dad insulting me when I was younger that always made me get through an essay because I only had to think of him saying 'you'd amount to nothing' and that would spur me on to actually want to finish writing.... Then as the degree went on it was just the determination. I'd made up my mind I was going to do a degree. I couldn't sit and say 'oh I left'. I have to keep doing it until it's done because I've made my mind up.

Sue, a Chinese student, met her English husband in China and then came to live in England. Throughout her degree, she had to struggle with language issues and cultural differences. She explained:

My determination has kept me going. I think that's really my big personality point because to me the opportunity is once in a lifetime but maybe not to others. When I see others drop-out I think why? It's not just you get a degree, you are bettering yourself. Maybe it's a cultural thing but we do treasure education. Not just to say you have a good job. That's part of it of course but education itself is a good thing. That's why I'm doing it.

A small number of those interviewed were asylum seekers. Determination to keep going stemmed from their experiences of being an asylum seeker and trying to establish a new life in a new country. A young adult student from Afghanistan studying at the elite university experienced severe financial problems because of his status as an asylum seeker. Financial and other support that he received from the university made him determined to complete his studies. It was the starting point of a new biography and a new life in a different culture as he stated: 'I don't have anybody back home'. His attitude was mirrored by a female asylum seeker from Ethiopia studying at a post-1992 institution:

> I can't give up now because I've lost everything. I can't go back home. I've lost my mum and dad. I don't have any brothers or sisters. This is my precious thing that I have to have and have to achieve and succeed in life.

Once adult students have taken the decision to enter HE, with all the risk it entails, most are determined to succeed and complete in order to prove to themselves that they are capable of learning and also to improve their life situation and chances. Some, however, find themselves overwhelmed by academia and/or external problems.

The stories of non-completion

Getting through the first term of the first year of study is often a critical period in terms of whether or not a student stays in HE. The longer students (both younger and adult) stay, the less likely they are to leave although this is not always the case. Several students talked about critical points in their learning career when they considered leaving their degree course. Laura's story illustrates the importance of support from lecturers and a personal tutor in helping her at a time when personal issues impacted on her (Laura took a 2+2 social studies degree, which is a four-year course that involves studying at a further education college during the first two years and completing the final two years at the university):

> From year one to year four there's always a time in the year that you feel like jacking it in and it depends on who is around you at that time and who you will ask for help. That makes the big difference and if you just locked yourself away in your room you'd jack it in. After the second year I was about to come up to Warwick when mum died in the July so I'd got no parents. It was almost like I couldn't read because you can't concentrate. So you just think what's the point? By the end of the summer holidays I found that if I just did it day by day or just go with the flow you sort of slot in and muddle through. But by Christmas I was really falling behind with essays and deadlines. I got in touch with my personal tutor and said 'I can't do this – there's no way in the world I can get round this. But funnily enough instead of putting in two class essays I was allowed to do plans and that got me back on track. So long as I was on track I was fine. When I started getting behind I panicked.

Sometimes pressures inside and outside the university build up to an extent that continuing becomes difficult so that some adult students find it necessary to take time out. Emily, a part-time student studying health and social policy decided to take temporary withdrawal rather than not complete. She was not a confident learner and struggled particularly in seminars with younger students. As a result Emily had a fear of seminars:

> I found it very difficult last year. I had a bit of a panic attack in my first module because I think it's the whole thing being at Warwick and not coming through the traditional ways, not having done my A levels and just come from A levels and go straight into academic learning. It's when you come from a different background and you've never had that experience. Then it's very difficult. It's very daunting and it's very intimidating as well when you're with students who, it feels like, they sit there and just answer the questions. They're all very confident. They know what they're talking about and it's really hard because I didn't even do history at GCSE so it's a real start from scratch. Especially with sociology so I missed out on the basics.

At the same time, Emily experienced problems in her life outside university from a neighbour in the block of flats where she lived. The people below played loud music during the night and when she complained she was intimidated by them.

> I took two years out because I nearly had a nervous breakdown. I was very, very, very stressed and I just couldn't cope with that as well. Every day I had trouble from the neighbours.

Although she contacted Environmental Health, the situation was not resolved until they moved out:

> And I felt ready to come back but then again I had the struggle of getting back into study. So it's been a struggle my whole degree from start to finish. I've found it very, very difficult.

Mary, a full-time student, experienced health problems, so she decided to take temporary withdrawal. She enjoyed learning, but at the same time she found studying difficult. However, she was determined to finish

> I deferred for a year due to ill health. At first I was thinking that maybe I just wouldn't be able to continue at all but as soon as I started to feel better I really missed the process. It's like somebody has taken this bit of your life away and you don't know what to fill it with. The second six months of the year was spent looking forward to coming back. I was raring to go again by the time I came back. But once you're back you're up and down the whole time. You have good weeks and you have more difficult

weeks. I think wanting something better, better job opportunities. I think it's something about your personal status as well. You've started so you've got to finish. You'd feel a failure not that you know anyone that would say you were but you personally would feel like a failure for not finishing it.

Returning to study after taking temporary withdrawal can be a struggle but one which is felt to be worth it. The adult students who did not complete did so for different reasons. One was a part-time student who had retired. James chose to do a part-time degree to keep his brain active and he also enjoyed learning. His wife became seriously ill, and he had to become her constant carer. He would like to return to complete his studies in history but does not feel that this will be possible. However, he has kept in contact with staff at the university. Another student, a woman, taking a $2+2$ social studies degree left at the beginning of the final term of her final year. Throughout her career as a student, she had always had panic attacks during the exam period and felt that she would have been alright if the whole course had been fully assessed. Exams made her feel pressurised and stressed so she stopped going to classes and consciously decided not to turn up for her final exams. She was convinced that she would fail her exams and stated that she felt much happier once she had left university. Mary did not view leaving as a negative act as she felt that she had gained personally from studying and had enjoyed learning. She had turned to HE study following a difficult and unpleasant experience at work, which eroded her confidence and left her stressed. During her university life, she gradually regained confidence in herself as a person. While studying full-time she had also had to do paid work for financial reasons, and this had laced another pressure on her. She stated that she had not had any free time for four years. Another female part-time student studying English and cultural studies also left because she could not cope with doing exams:

> I think it's been really good here. I think the fact that I'm giving up, the formal degree course, is more about myself, than, really any fault with the system. I think it's a shame that there aren't higher level courses that an adult student could take without necessarily having to do exams.

Jenny's story illustrates the interplay of factors, which can lead students to not complete. She was in her late 50s and studying a part-time degree in health and social studies. Despite a 'brilliant first year', she then chose a module that she struggled with, and as it was taught during the daytime she studied with younger students, which she found difficult. She stressed that 'I was out of my depth'. The class and age differences undermined her confidence and she felt 'extremely marginalised'. She took temporary withdrawal and had intended to return but:

I started to get butterflies and cold feet. I was full of self-doubt. It's the confidence thing and having to take a seminar (presentation) would just fill me with dread. I knew that there was always going to be a problem and I think I talked myself out of it. I also fell ill that year. But I miss the learning very much but I don't miss the pressure.

She decided to withdraw from her degree despite encouragement from staff for her to return. She said: 'I was very sad to go. I still am. It's been a very difficult time in my personal life.' At home, Jenny felt that her husband 'was very understanding but at the same time I think he would have preferred if I hadn't done it'. Reflecting about her student career, she stated

I do feel knowledgeable. I feel very privileged to have actually done that. I'm pleased with myself that I did well in the first year. I'm not cross but sad that events took the course they did. I know that the confidence issue would have been awful was a problem and I really don't think I could have resolved that one.

These stories, therefore, illustrate a wide range of reasons as to why adults choose not to complete their degree. Reasons for leaving are also often multiple and related but the decision to leave is a considered one. For Mary and Jenny, they believed that their life would be less stressed and more manageable.

Conclusion: Learning in a transitional space

Developing a learner identity largely depended on a determination to succeed as the stories of those interviewed three times over three years illustrated. Once they began their learning career, they made the decision not to go back to their old life but to use studying for a degree and the transitional space of the university as a means of changing to a 'better life' for themselves and their family. Determination to 'keep on going on' was supported by other factors such as support from peers, lecturers and institutions, being recognised as a learner as well as an enjoyment of learning. While their habitus was modified, there was still a strong identity with being working class. They did not feel that they had become middle class but studying did help them to make sense of the world:

I've changed for the better. I'm not as argumentative I don't think. You know the world's not out to get me. I'm not bitter and twisted any more. I can criticise the system. I know a lot of the shortfalls...I can challenge people who say 'these people who sit around on benefits, they don't want to work'. Well it's hard to claim benefits, let alone live off them. I've actually gained the confidence and speaking to strange people, being in strange places, coming out of my comfort zone.

(Laura)

Those that left and did not complete also developed a learner identity which stayed with them after they left, although it was to a different degree to those that completed. The learning journey for both those who completed and those who did not was not always an easy one as life both inside and outside the academy was sometimes a struggle, which led, at times, to self-doubt and a lack of confidence. Being working class and adjusting to the cultural and symbolic capitals of the university had to be constantly worked out. Laura's reflections illustrate the difficulties as well as the positive aspects as experienced by many of those interviewed. 'Keeping on going on', however, was essential for starting a new biographical beginning:

I've never felt good enough. I don't feel like I should be here because I'm not an academic, I haven't got A levels for any subject but what I have got is the motivation and interest that pulled me through the four years. So even though I don't think I should be here I think I've justified my position by working hard enough to stay here because that was really, really difficult. I know a few students think I shouldn't be here and I'm not good enough. It's not an age thing it's a qualification, you know, you're always sitting next to someone brighter than yourself and it wears you down a bit. What I constantly told students and friends was 'look you've worked hard, you work every night after half past eight, every weekend, every minute that you're not with the kids, you've got no life'. And I think that justified my position here. A lot of the time it was easier to carry on than it was to give up. If I'd jacked it in after the second year I'd have had two years knowing I quite liked it but knowing that I couldn't have got a job on the back of it.

(Laura)

Bibliography

Barnett, R. (2007) *A Will to Learn: Being a Student in an Age of Uncertainty* (Maidenhead: Open University Press/ McGraw-Hill Education).

Bourdieu, P. (1989) 'Social Space and Symbolic Power', *Sociological Theory*, 7 (1 Spring): 14–25.

Bourdieu, P. (1988) *Homo Academicus* (Stanford: Stanford University Press).

Bourdieu, P. and Wacquant, L. (1989) 'Towards a Reflexive Sociology. A Workshop with Pierre Bourdieu', *Sociological Theory*, 7: 26–63.

Bourdieu, P. and Wacquant, L.J. (1992) *An Introduction to Reflexive Sociology* (Cambridge: Polity).

Ecclestone, K. (2009) 'Lost and Found in Transition: Educational Implications of Concerns about "Identity", "Agency" and "Structure" ', in Field, J., Gallacher, J. and Ingram, R. (eds) *Researching Transitions in Lifelong Learning* (London: Routledge).

Field, J., Gallacher, J. and Ingram, R. (2009) *Researching Transitions in Lifelong Learning* (London: Routledge).

Field, J., Merrill, B. and Morgan-Klein, N. (2010) *Researching HE Access, Retention and Drop-Out through a European Biographical Approach: Exploring Similarities and Differences Within a Research Team*. Paper Presented at the ESREA Triennial Conference (Linköping).

Honneth, A. (1995) *The Struggle for Recognition: The Moral Grammar of Social Conflict* (Cambridge: Polity Press).

Johnston, R., Merrill, B., Holliday, M., West, L., Fleming, T. and Finnegan, F. (2009) 'Exploring HE Retention and Drop-Out – A European Biographical Research Approach', in Coare, P. and Cecil, L. (eds) *Really Useful Knowledge? Critical Perspectives on Evidence-Based Policy and Practice in Lifelong Learning*. Proceedings of 39th SCUTREA Annual Conference (Brighton: University of Sussex/SCUTREA,).

Merrill, B. (2007) 'Recovering Class and the Collective in the Stories of Adult Learners', in West, L., Alheit, P., Siig Andersen, A. and Merrill, B. (eds) *Using Biographical and Life History Approaches in the Study of Adult and Lifelong European Perspectives* (Frankfurt-am-Main: Peter Lang).

Merrill, B. (1999) *Gender, Change and Identity: Mature Women Students in Universities* (Ashgate: Aldershot).

Merrill, B. and West, L. (2009) *Using Biographical Methods in Social Research* (London: Sage).

Quinn, J., Thomas, L., Slack, K., Casey, L., Thexton, W. and Noble, J. (2005) *From Life Crisis to Lifelong Learning: Rethinking Working Class 'Drop-Out' from Higher Education* (York: Joseph Rowntree Foundation).

Scott, P. (1995) *The Meanings of Mass Higher Education* (Buckingham: Open University Press).

Thomas, L. and Quinn, J. (2007) *First Generation Entry into Higher Education: An International Study* (Maidenhead: Open University Press).

Tinto, V. (2003) *Promoting Student Retention Through Classroom Practice: Using International Policy and Practice*. Presented at International Conference Sponsored by the European Access Network & Institute for Access Studies at Staffordshire University, Amsterdam, 5–7 November.

Trow, M. (1989) 'The Robbins Trap: British Attitudes and the Limits of Expansion', *Higher Education Quarterly*, 43 (1): 55–75.

Urry, J. (1996) *The Sociology of Space and Place* (Oxford: Blackwell).

West, L., Alheit, P., Siig Andersen, A. and Merrill, B. (2007) *Using Biographical and Life History Approaches in the Study of Adult and Lifelong European Perspectives* (Frankfurt-am-Main: Peter Lang).

Winnicott, D. (1971) *Playing and Reality* (London: Routledge).

Wright Mills, C. (1973) *The Sociological Imagination* (Harmondsworth: Penguin).

Yorke, M. and Thomas, L. (May 2003) 'Improving the Retention of Students from Lower Socio-Economic Groups', *Journal of Higher Education Policy and Management*, 25 (1): 63–74.

11
The Importance of Social Support Structures for Retention and Success

John Field and Natalie Morgan-Klein

Introduction

As a policy goal, widening participation (WP) is increasingly associated with retention and completion. For those who are concerned with equity or social mobility, it makes little sense to recruit new types of students if they do not then qualify for a graduate profession. In its strategic plan, the Higher Education Funding Council for England (HEFCE) states that one of its main strategic aims is to promote 'the opportunity of successful participation in HE to everyone who can benefit from it' (HEFCE, 2009: 18). There has also been growing interest in retention among researchers, much of which has centred on the extent to which new students can be helped to integrate into the institution. In the United Kingdom, this focus has been increased through a major programme of research and development on retention, jointly funded by HEFCE and the Paul Hamlyn Foundation, much of which has been concerned with 'promoting academic and social integration into the institution to promote a sense of belonging' (Action on Access, 2009). We are particularly interested here in the ways in which students feel themselves to be legitimate members of the 'imagined community' of higher education (HE), a concept that we have adapted from Anderson's treatment of nationalisms (Anderson, 1991; see also Quinn, 2010).

This chapter is concerned with the social relationships of non-traditional students. While we are certainly interested in the ways in which these can influence integration into the university community, this chapter also explores the ways in which students' networks change through the course of their study. It draws on a research study of retention and non-traditional learners in Scotland, undertaken as part of a wider European research project. Among other things, the project was concerned to identify those factors that can promote retention for non-traditional students, as well as those

This chapter is based on research conducted under the European Commission's Lifelong Learning Programme (project 135230-LLP-1-2007-1-UK-KA1-KA1SCR).

that inhibit retention. We concentrate in this chapter on the ways in which students' social relationships can help or hinder their integration.

Retention and student integration

Students leave courses early for a variety of reasons. The National Audit Office (NAO) summarised the most commonly cited as personal reasons, lack of integration into the institution, dissatisfaction with the course or institution, lack of preparedness, wrong choice of course, financial reasons and to take up a more attractive opportunity (NAO, 2007: 23). In many cases, a combination of different factors influences students' decisions to leave or stay, with different factors having a different weight at different times (Longden, 2004). Perhaps, the most influential author, and certainly the most frequently cited, in this area of study is Vincent Tinto. Brian Longden (2004: 128) has described Tinto's student integration model as having achieved 'near paradigm status' in the field. It has also been widely adapted for policy purposes, with a particular focus on promoting academic and social integration within HE (Stolk *et al.*, 2007: 58).

Tinto (1975, 1987) treats retention as a process that occurs through the lifecycle of student-hood, from pre-university stages through graduation. In this process, he argues that student interaction with the formal and informal dimensions of the university plays a critical role in shaping decisions on departure or persistence. The process starts with the separation stage, during which students prepare to leave their previous environment (home, school or college), and is largely influenced by personal characteristics such as family background and educational ability. This is then followed by the integration stage, in which students start to identify with the institution, and with the wider community of students (and staff), leading them to re-evaluate their institutional commitment and academic expectations. In Tinto's model, the processes of academic integration and social integration are therefore intertwined and, indeed, complement one another.

Hilary McQueen has noted that Tinto's work is itself heavily influenced by Durkheimian notions of social integration (McQueen, 2009: 70–71). While Tinto notes the importance of academic factors in understanding retention and withdrawal, his model also encompasses other aspects of interaction between the institution and student, including the degree to which students see themselves as sharing the norms and values that cement a sense of belonging to the community. In particular, Tinto argues that those who experience 'anomie' – that is, a very low sense of integration into the community, or a feeling of not belonging to the wider whole – are most at risk of dropout. McQueen has further explored the implications of Durkheim's theory to argue that dropout may also be understood as an egoistic response, where students are so excessively integrated into the community that they place its needs above their own destiny, and that it might be seen as an altruistic act, where students withdraw as a result of high integration into an earlier social network, in the hope of preserving their place in their old social world (McQueen, 2009: 76–79).

While Tinto's work has been widely followed, it has also been subjected to critique. Ozga and Sukhandan (1998) suggest that it is too strongly rooted in the educational culture and institutional structures of the United States, though this argument may be losing force as some European HE systems are reformed in ways that bring them closer to the American model. Alternative models take a socio-cultural approach to retention, arguing that it is not just institutional factors that influence retention; rather, withdrawal and persistence – and the very language in which they are debated – are part of a much wider and more complex social and cultural picture (Quinn, 2010). Drawing on the ideas of Pierre Bourdieu about habitus and cultural capital, researchers in this approach have noted that non-traditional students, shaped in a very different social milieu from that of the university, encounter HE as a foreign and unsettling environment, in which they feel themselves 'fish out of water' (Reay *et al.*, 2005: 27–34). In these circumstances, the more pressing question may be why students persist, rather than why they leave.

In both traditions of work, students' social networks emerge as an important factor in understanding students' decisions. Even if Tinto's model is flawed, his work nonetheless encourages us to examine the ways in which non-traditional students can and do negotiate the complex institutional and cultural labyrinths that face any new entrant to higher education institutions (HEIs), and it draws attention to the ways in which they are (or are not) integrated into a new social world. The socio-cultural approach has tended to emphasise the importance of class, gender and race, and the cultural capital acquired in particular social milieus. The social competences required for academic success, according to Bourdieu, are closely associated with educational level, but he believes that they are less likely to be learned consciously, by formal effort, than through the 'unintentional learning made possible by a disposition acquired through domestic or scholastic inculcation of legitimate culture' (Bourdieu, 1984: 28). For Bourdieu, people's social connections are, therefore, a resource, which provide access to information and skills, as well as to other opportunities.

A small but growing body of literature suggests that social support networks play a role both in promoting and inhibiting integration. Research on family support for HE participation is well-established and has shown a wide variety of formal and informal support that students derive from their family connections. Thus, Reay's (1998) work on student habitus emphasised the dynamic interplay of family, peer groups and institutional networks in informing young people's choices. Another study took existing 'affinity groups' among students as the basis for group interviews, leading to findings that largely endorsed Reay's original insights (Jones, 2010; see also Reay *et al.*,

2009). The most extensive study of family ties to date, based on interviews with network members as well as students themselves, concluded that inter-generational relationships were frequently ambivalent, leading some individuals to deliberately broaden their networks, while leading others to fall back on existing ties (Fuller *et al.*, 2011).

A similar ambivalence appears to characterise other social ties, such as friendship groups. Drawing on over 120 life-history interviews, Mary Stuart (2006) demonstrated that friendship groups could help first-generation students bridge the transition into HE, particularly where students lacked access to other resources; however, other students found that existing friendships could lock them into identities and positions that ran counter to adopting a more academic disposition. Yet both strategies can be risky. Other research has found that students who try to build new ties can be penalised for their disloyalty by their former network and treated as probationers or incomers by the new group (Warner *et al.*, 2007). Ironically, the more that entering HE is likely to produce social mobility, the greater the challenge to attempts to maintain existing connections with friends, family and wider community (Jetten *et al.*, 2008).

To date, then, a number of studies have shown that family, institutional networks and peer groups play an important part in students' decision making. As a field of enquiry, though, the role of social networks in student life is still relatively under-developed, and little attention has been paid so far to the ways in which students' networks alter while they are in HE or to the extent to which student agency is a factor in reshaping such networks. Yet these issues are potentially of considerable significance in a society that is characterised by increasing mobility and by an increased probability (perceived and/or real) of transition across and through the life course. They are particularly important with respect to inter-generational social mobility, where HE entrants are likely to be moving from one socio-cultural milieu to another. In each case, social networks appear to help shape student decisions and, thus, affect the outcomes of transitions; yet most research treats social networks as a static property, rather than as dynamic processes that students themselves can reconstruct on a continuing basis as they negotiate a range of educational and other transitions.

The research and its context

Our research was undertaken as part of a European study of access and retention of non-traditional learners in HE.[1] Primarily drawing on life-history interviews with a sample of learners and a range of university staff, the project sought to identify factors that limit or promote the construction of a learner identity among non-traditional adult students in becoming, or not, effective learners, with a view to understanding how this process may enable or inhibit the completion of HE. The main focus of the research was on student experiences and how non-traditional learners perceive themselves as students. Using biographical narratives, we interviewed different cohorts of students – those in their final year, those who leave but return to study later and those who drop out – as well as carrying out two interviews over the course of a year with first or second years. Interviewing those who have dropped out can be challenging and problematic.

Of course, the very language of 'non-traditional' is itself contested. We used the term 'non-traditional adult student' in a simple descriptive sense to denote those who are under-represented in HE and whose participation is constrained by structural factors. This includes first-generation students, those from lower socio-economic strata and ethnic minority groups, mature students and students with disabilities. The project involved partners from seven countries (England, Germany, Ireland, Poland, Scotland, Spain and Sweden). Each partner negotiated access to three types of university, with a view to carrying out research in one highly selective institution, one moderately selective university and one large public institution. We did not include private institutions, as the private sector currently forms a negligible part of the HE system in Britain.

Our own work took place in three Scottish institutions. HE in Scotland has a very long history; the so-called ancient universities are able to trace their roots back to the medieval period. As in many other countries, the system expanded rapidly between the 1960s and the 1990s, but in Scotland there is at least one highly distinctive feature. From the early 1990s, there was a particularly rapid growth in short-cycle HE, in the form of one- or two-year courses leading to a Higher National Certificate or Higher National Diploma; most short-cycle HE is provided in non-university institutions and, particularly, by further education colleges (Gallacher, 2009).

As in the other UK nations, access and participation have been widely debated in Scotland. Following the publication in 2005 of its policy review in wider participation, the Scottish Funding Council (SFC) developed a programme of initiatives designed to strengthen prospects for students from deprived backgrounds and identified a set of measures against which to judge progress. This included work on retention and achievement (SFC, 2005). Subsequently, the SFC has monitored performance annually. The 2010 monitoring report noted that the proportion of pupils entering from schools in the most disadvantaged neighbourhoods has continued to decline, and students from deprived areas are still most likely to discontinue their studies; it also noted that participation in HE had declined steadily since 2001 (SFC, 2010: 47). Against this background, we can grasp the ambivalence of the Scottish Government's claims that on the one hand 'we have made steady progress to widen access' and on the other that WP measures 'have not produced the step change in participation that we would have liked' (Scottish Government, 2010: 13). Tuition fees featured strongly in the 2011 Scottish Parliament elections, with most of the main parties affirming the principle of free HE for full-time undergraduates from Scotland.

Findings: Integration and relationships

The students interviewed were, in the main, highly committed to their studies. Even those who had considered leaving, or found themselves under increasing pressures, generally expressed a determination to complete. They also described enjoying their studies; among mature students in particular, there was often a sense of a new purpose and focus to their lives. However, this positive commitment did not necessarily mean that they felt comfortable or felt an unproblematic sense of belonging, within their institution. Some interviewees expressed a strong sense of belonging to their institution, while others questioned whether they were 'good enough', seeing low grades as an indication that they might not be cut out for university, while high grades might be discounted as flukes or mistakes. Even among those who expressed a strong sense of belonging, a sense of under-performing academically could trigger doubts about legitimacy.

This is not to say that the students simply felt that they were somehow being excluded or marginalised. Rather, their sense of belonging was frequently bounded, ambivalent and contingent. One female mature student said that she worried about going 'back to being plain old me again', while a mature male student described himself as 'absolutely terrified now that I've maybe bitten off more than I can chew', before adding that 'I'd rather have that than be lazy about what I'm doing'. So these students had found ways of negotiating their ambivalent membership of the imagined community of HE. In doing so, students invariably drew on a range of resources, and among these were their relations with others.

Interviewees described a number of social relations as particularly significant. As well as external networks with family, partners, friends and acquaintances, people referred to peer relations with other students and also the quality of their relationships with university staff. Such ties provide support of various kinds, emotional as well as material or social, not only in respect of study itself but also in enabling students to tackle external pressures, from dealing with hardship or finding work to balancing caring responsibilities and navigating such stressful life changes as divorce or bereavement. Such patterns of support are what the social capital literature would lead us to expect, along, of course, with limitations and constraints that can arise from particular types of network bonds (Field, 2008). We explore a number of these issues in turn.

Peer relations

Friendship ties are often critical in helping students develop a sense of legitimacy and belonging within HE (Stuart, 2006). Our sample similarly described peers as providing help through difficult times, particularly in sustaining an individual through periods of self-doubt; in some cases, they had been critical to a student's decision to keep going. One, for instance, told us that in her circle 'there were two or three people who maybe wouldn't be doing a degree today if we hadn't kinda backed each other up' (Pauline). In a number of cases, though, learners expressed discomfort over what they saw as a tension between their new social networks and the ties they had enjoyed before entering HE.

Typically, peer friendships were a key to belonging. Some of our sample entered HE as cohorts from an access course or other similar preparatory programme. Others had made friends at an early stage of their course, whether through social activities, sports or membership of a student society or faith group. Such ties tended to persist through the period of study and, in some cases, could be quite durable. As one second-year student put it, 'it seemed to be this group of mature students that all just seemed to home in on one another as a support network and we've been friends since our access course now' (Helena, studying education). This group of seven women, mostly mature but with one aged 18 years, also socialised outside the university and met during vacations as well as term times. Andrew, another mature student, spoke of 'the fact that we've kind of created a wee community for ourselves among the mature students, the ones that did the access especially, are all still in contact, giving support, advice, etc'.

Not all students presented themselves this way. Some male interviewees described themselves as relatively independent of other students. One man expressed a very strong ethnic identity, with strong friendship ties to others from the same ethnic group across Britain and beyond; he had made a few friends at university, 'but not ones that lasted, sort of come by and go away' (Benjamin). He seemed satisfied with this. Another presented himself as competent and at ease within the university and was frequently uncomfortable with the language of support and help that other interviewees used. As a child-less man, he described himself as 'a wee bit alienated' from the predominantly female students with children he had met on the access course. While he also said that he had found it helpful to meet other mature students informally for chats over coffee and wanted more opportunities to meet mature students on campus, he was at pains to portray himself as independent and not someone who needed support.

Relations with 'traditional students'

Typically, mature students tended to form ties with others who shared their experiences, aspirations and outlook. As one explained, 'It is nice having a network that knows exactly what you're talking about. How you feel as well.' This was less a matter of age *per se* than of having a sense of shared interests and experiences, and of being able to take some things for granted. But while age in itself was not the primary factor in network formation, age-related experiences and attitudes shaped the way that people made new friends, and, in turn, the new ties helped to cement age as a salient and visible factor within the university. Something similar seems to have happened with students from minority ethnic backgrounds; two ethnic minority students found themselves primarily tied to networks that were largely ethnically based, which moreover were largely based outside the university. One described how other students tended to assume she was an immigrant and asked her why she had come to Scotland; when they found out she was born here, they tended to lose interest. As a result, she had found herself socialising with overseas students rather than local peers. By contrast, a Polish immigrant student who had lived and worked in Britain for four years before entering university had established extensive friendships among her fellow students and was spending less time each year visiting her family and friends in Poland.

This process in turn meant that mature students tended to define themselves as 'non-traditional'. Moreover, they often contrasted their university experiences with those of younger students. Frequently, mature students believed that they were more highly motivated than younger people, and therefore they saw themselves as working harder and participating more fully in formal studies. Pauline, a mature student taking a degree in education, kept telling herself 'I think well done, although I know it's happening, it's surreal, it's as if it's not happening.' We can see the interplay of her dispositions as a highly motivated learner, and the new habitus into which she had moved and felt herself an outsider. We can also see how what she described as this 'surreal' experience is connected to the discrepancy between her status as an outsider, who had not pursued the normative route taken by most students: 'I don't think younger, you know, students coming through from school, would be [so thrilled] – 'cos it would just be next step for them.'

Some of the non-traditional students appeared to adopt a stance of humour and ironic distancing as way of describing what they saw as a dominant student culture. Suzie, a first-generation student in her first year of a degree in design, expressed her sense of distance from her fellow students: 'When I came in here, they all looked like stockbrokers. I mean, the girls are so cute and the boys are so smart, I mean it's just so funny.' In this case, the student was saying that she had expected the art college to be a more Bohemian environment but had been surprised to find that she was closer to this stereotype of the art student than the 'normative' students who seemed – at least superficially – much more conventional than she expected. Stella, who was hoping to become a painter, said that she had not even applied to one of the major providers in this area because of the institution's financial policy, which she found exclusionary: 'it's nae [no] riff raff – nae paupers'. This, however, may show how difficult it can be to interpret interview transcripts. Suzie laughed as she talked about her confounded expectations and was talking about *feeling* different, while Stella was solemn and felt excluded by what she saw as the elitist policies of the other institution.

Relations with staff

Relationships with staff were highly significant in students' narratives. Unsurprisingly, helpful, accessible and approachable staff were particularly valued. Perhaps, less obviously, warmth, encouragement and reassurance from staff were also significant. At a time when academic workloads and teaching methods in many universities are developing in ways that reduce direct personal contact with students, it is important to stress the importance of direct staff interventions, particularly at those moments, such as the first days of a course or at moments of crisis, when students' self-doubt and uncertainty were highest (see also Clegg and Rowland, 2010: 727). One particular (male) academic was singled out frequently at one case study university by students, who described him as warm, caring and encouraging. Such staff helped students feel at ease in their new community. More broadly, students talked about a sense of recognition from staff as an important factor in helping to develop a sense of belonging in the imagined community of HE (see Fleming, 2011).

Pastoral support, as it is often known, could be particularly important for students when it came from an academic. Students' narratives were full of examples. Some students found themselves facing a critical juncture where they considered dropping out, whether because of struggles with coursework or for other reasons, and approached staff. Some had made it explicit to staff that they were on the verge of dropping out. However, others had approached staff for help at critical points, though without making the significance clear of their concern. One, for example, had simply asked staff about the timetable prior to the start of semester. In the context of feeling overwhelmed by combining study with being the parent of a young child and doing long hours of paid work to make ends meet, and wondering if she should simply give up, staff responsiveness to her query had been 'a massive help'. What at first sight appears a small and trivial issue can, in fact, be of considerable significance for retention.

Alison, an English studies student, had found herself adrift in seminars tutorials where she lacked the linguistic resources deployed by her tutor and some other students and had seriously considered dropping out. She approached a tutor whom she found to be sympathetic about her difficulty in articulating her ideas in tutorials, and the tutor had empathised and alluded to her strengths. This, together with the support of peers and advice from lecturers about writing essays, had contributed to her capacity to keep going. These experiences indicate that by being supportive when students express concerns, or simply responsive to queries, staff may make a contribution to retention without this being made explicit by students – and conversely that unresponsiveness or unconstructive responses may have a more significant negative impact than might be assumed.

Clegg and Rowland, drawing on their study of third-year social science students in the United Kingdom, characterise such relationships as based less on therapy than on emotional and social capabilities than what they refer to as 'kindness'. Our findings echo their view that 'the affective appears to enhance intellectual achievement' (Clegg and Rowland, 2010: 729). We would also add that the achievement of a relationship with academics can have an important symbolic value. Relationships with staff were particularly important to questions of legitimacy within the institution. The socio-cultural status of academics may well involve a significant degree of stereotyping – just think of the images used to represent lecturers and professors in newspaper cartoons or the standard clichés of 'dons' and 'boffins' that circulate in the popular media. Such stereotypes, which may be particularly deeply rooted for those who have rarely encountered real academics, can sometimes be reinforced rather than challenged by the language, dress codes and performative styles that many academics adopt. In our data, this emerged most commonly in concerns over language. For example, Alison, a particularly un-confident student, found it hard work to understand and use academic language and bridge gaps in her writing skills. She described the process by which she assessed each new academic that took one of her classes: 'I've got to sort of try and suss out my tutor and think, "Right, am I gonnae feel intimidated with them or not".'

Several other students reported challenges with academics' language. For Stella, this was a matter of class. She made it clear that she was talking about fellow students as much as staff and was talking about feeling marginalised and alienated within the dominant culture of the institution:

> middle-class people have a really interesting way of using language where they can say things that might come across that they agree with you or be gentle about things but where the power still remains wi' them. It's a really...I dunno how to describe it – you know, no passion – there's no passion in what they're saying, and this really cold distant calculated use of the English language that I havenae quite managed to grasp yet – thankfully.

Stella was continuing to resist absorption into what she saw as an alien linguistic style that she saw as incompatible with her identity as a Scot and a member of the working class.

Others, though, treated academic language as something that they needed to learn. One education student explained how he had been struck by watching a recording of himself, taken as part of a micro-teaching exercise:

> you see yourself on video, you never speak how you sound, and I seemed to develop into, whilst I'm speaking in front of children, I don't know if it's just children, I've been told it's not, a few friends have said that it's not just children, you do it when you're – when you're speaking to say other people as well, people you don't know well, people who are in a position of authority and should be in a position of respect.... and I seem to develop an accent and a way of speaking that is, is from the streets.

The convoluted sentence structure here conveys something of this person's sense of embarrassment that he 'seemed to talk in quite a rough kind of accent for some reason', and he worried that he might 'come across as being someone who – who – who is maybe dumbing down'. He speculated 'whether subconsciously I thought I would get more engagement from pupils by speaking like them'. Be that as it may, he worried that his accent might damage his career as a teacher. So he found himself emphasising his working-class roots in situations in which others might try to disguise them and was unsure what to make of this.

For students who were initially intimidated by academics and the preconceptions they had about them, the process of un-masking the stereotype took time. As Sandra put it, at the beginning 'they were up on a pedestal as professors and fellows and you think [sharp intake of breath] they're definitely not working-class like the rest of us, they're definitely upper class. And now, you think "They're only human"'. This was the counterpart to academic recognition of students' individuality: through relations with staff, students also came to see academics as individuals whose respect and regard mattered precisely because they were attainable. In some cases, students passed beyond membership of the imagined community of HE to an imagined role for themselves as potential future academics. Graham, a mature history student, saw himself as enjoying 'greater acceptance of me, like you know within the university', and speculated that at some point 'in the future, you can see yourself – doing that type of work. I mean, you think to yourself, "Well, jeeze, you know what? Maybe one day I'll write a history book". You know?' Graham had an acute sense of being under-educated and anxiety about his ability to cope with degree-level study, and he experienced significant challenges related to his disability. He described this sense of being respected and recognised by university staff as leading to a feeling of acceptance by the university and as opening up new aspirations for the future, which in turn kept him going despite the difficulties.

Positive relationships with staff had, then, symbolic, practical and affective value for students. By contributing not only to students' intellectual development but also to a transformation in their learner identities and a growth in their perceptions of their abilities, such 'kind' relationships fostered persistence and resilience rather than the dependency and inadequacy that Ecclestone *et al.* (2005) denounce as the by-products of a therapeutic culture. We will examine later some of the practical implications of this finding, after we have explored some of our evidence on the role of partners and family.

Family values – Negotiating new roles

Since Willy Russell's inspirational play, *Educating Rita*, it has been commonplace to see education as placing a strain on family life. In the play, Rita finds herself losing touch with the socio-cultural milieu of her mother, and falling out of love with her increasingly hostile husband. More broadly, an earlier study by Field notes that as a result of undergoing educational transitions, during which old ties can lose value or even start to become impediments to further progress, some adult learners decide to reshape their intimate networks (Field, 2009). We certainly found cases where people faced challenges from family members or experienced difficulties combining caring with study. We also found important instances of active family support.

Most of the continuing students told stories of more or less active support from their family of origin. Mothers appear to have played a particularly important role in caring for children, but the study threw up other examples of family support such as help with transport, paying bills and listening sympathetically to tales of woe. Where members of the family of origin were critical, it was either because they thought the student's aspirations were unrealistic (in all cases, this appears to have spurred students to succeed) or because they did not approve of the financial or childcare arrangements (one male and one female student in our sample had experienced such disapproval from a parent). Children themselves were cited by some students, male and female, as an important motivational factor and a source of support.

Partners were cited by some students as very supportive of their participation in HE. Emotional support and encouragement in times of difficulty (cited especially by female students), financial support, and/or taking on more responsibility for caring for children were sources of help that were crucial to some students' capacity to participate in HE. Children, too, were cited as an important source of motivation and encouragement for some students.

Most (though not all) of the students in our sample who had childcare responsibilities were female. The minority of males denied that they faced any particular difficulty as a result. For women, though, sustaining university study often meant re-negotiating responsibilities with partners and other family members. Sandra's narrative illustrates the guilt that this can provoke and also reminds us that adult women may have multiple caring roles:

> I've probably become a bit more selfish to be honest and that's not me at all.... I don't know if it *is* being selfish, if it's just trying to rake back some of me that I've let go. I don't feel as though I've been a whole person for so long because – I'm giving bits of me away to everybody... The children have bits of me, my husband has a bit of me, my Mum has lots of me. My Dad doesn't keep well so he has bits of me. My brother's gone through his second divorce and it's always me that he comes to... And I think, 'D'you know, what do I ever do for me? Absolutely bugger all. I do nothing for myself'. And now that I've made the decision to do *this*, I think: 'I think I need all of this back now, I need to reel it all in and I can give you all a little bit. But nobody can have as much as they've had. For another four years anyway. Because I need all of *me* now... to do the course that I'm doing'.

Sandra was not alone in experiencing conflict between her drive to achieve self-fulfilment through participation in HE and her socially defined role in focusing exclusively on the needs of others.

Other female students described difficulties in re-negotiating relationships with partners who were reluctant about or opposed to the changes in the division of household labour that were needed to sustain their participation in HE. For Ellie, who described her husband as having 'kinda been dragged along, a little bit kicking and screaming', and negotiating a change in her role – with her children, one of whom has a disability, as well as her husband – had been a significant challenge on top of the academic demands of her course, and this combination of pressures had led her to consider dropping out; support from friends at university had been crucial to her ability to keep going at this point. The need to re-negotiate relationships with children who had been used to unrestricted availability was also raised by other female students. Shirley, for example, described her husband as very supportive but was aware that her children were finding it difficult to adapt to her increased study commitments. Guilt and sadness about spending less time with children can be seen as an additional emotional burden of participation in HE for students who are accustomed to being the main carer:

> They enjoy the childcare. But they don't like the fact that they're there. Cause their mum hasn't picked them up from school... so we have had a few behavioural issues... It takes time to work through... It is a transition phase: it's different for them, it's different for me, and they haven't got mum – 100% of the time. You know, which my daughter – doesn't like. And – my son isn't so concerned; he deals with it a little better, but I feel

guilty that I'm not giving him as much time, especially with his hearing [difficulties].

The accounts of these students indicate, therefore, that as well as being a crucial source of support, relationships with partners and families entail responsibilities that can generate emotional and practical pressures, particularly for female students with children in view of the gendered division of household labour. In such cases, students had developed a degree of emotional resilience that was in turn reinforced by supportive peer relationships, and (in Shirley's case) a supportive partner.

Implications and discussion

Social connections provide an important resource for all students. Our research suggests that they may play a particularly important role in retention for non-traditional students and, particularly, those for whom HE is especially non-normative. This certainly includes mature students, single parents and students from working-class families, who often have to engage in serious identity work in order to see themselves as legitimate members of the imagined community of HE. This chapter reports the findings from interviews with those who have stayed on at university, rather than those who have left or never entered; among the stayers, social ties provide considerable support. While some of this echoes similar findings from existing research on family and peers, this study has also identified relationships with academic staff as an important feature of student identity formation. It has also noted the symbolic value that relationships with staff can have for students.

Clegg and Rowland (2010) have argued that economic pressures and policy choices in higher education have fostered institutional settings that are increasingly at odds with the 'kind' relationships with staff that we have identified as so important to student integration. While they argue against prescribing or requiring kindness from staff, seeing this as leading to 'a form of performativity through processes of routinisation', there are certainly ways in which institutions can avoid undermining or damaging the conditions that make kind relationships possible. This can include conventional mechanisms for intervention such as reward systems and (dis)incentives of various kinds, as well as more creative approaches to the design of systems and socio-physical spaces within universities. Our main findings, though, lead us to emphasise the critical role of staff in developing 'kind' relations with students. Clegg and Rowland recommend a professionalism based on notions of virtue; we would add that a clear reminder of HE as a public good might be timely, given increasing policy pressures to view a university education mainly as a private positional good.

Much the same argument applies to the development of peer support among students. The physical design of spaces within the university, support for student societies and associations, and a clear and virtuous definition of HE as a public good can all help protect the preconditions for meaningful sociable interaction among students inside and outside the classroom. The wicked problem here is the risk of ghettoisation. The tendency for non-normative students to socialise with one another is an understandable one; indeed, it is a specific form of a wider social pattern that is widely recognised in the social capital literature. But this raises the question of whether close bonds between mature students, or student parents, can inhibit the development of ties with younger students. In the social capital literature, it is sometimes suggested that such tendencies come at the cost of broadening horizons, intellectually and socially, that then penalise the non-traditional student both during their studies and when they enter the graduate labour market (Field, 2008). Our interviews with younger first-generation students suggested that they tended to value interaction with mature students, whom they saw as an educational and affective resource. This suggests that skilful facilitation of interaction in seminars and tutorials, as well as in informal interactions and generic employability programmes, has a part to play; but this is a difficult domain, and there are obvious risks of un-intended consequences from ill-conceived interventions.

Note

1. The 'Access and Retention: Experiences of Non-Traditional Learners in HE' (RANLHE) project was funded by the European Commission Lifelong Learning Programme. Further details are available on http://www.ranlhe.dsw.edu.pl/.

Bibliography

Action on Access (2009) *What Works? Student Retention and Success* [online] http://www.actiononaccess.org/index.php?p= 11_3_4 [accessed 25 August 2011].

Anderson, B. (1991) *Imagined Communities: Reflections on the Origin and Spread of Nationalism* (London: Verso).

Bourdieu, P. (1984) *Distinction: A Social Critique of the Judgement of Taste* (London: Routledge).

Clegg, S. and Rowland, S. (2010) 'Kindness in Pedagogical Practice and Intellectual Life', *British Journal of Sociology of Education*, XXXI: 719–735.

Ecclestone, K., Hayes, D. and Furedi, F. (2005) 'Knowing Me, Knowing You: The Rise of Therapeutic Professionalism in the Education of Adults', *Studies in the Education of Adults*, XXXVII: 182–200.

Field, J. (2009) 'Learning Transitions in the Adult Life Course: Agency, Identity and Social Capital', in Merrill, B. (ed.) *Learning to Change? The Role of Identity and Learning Careers in Adult Education* (Frankfurt-am-Main: Peter Lang, pp. 17–31).

Field, J. (2008) *Social Capital* (London: Routledge, pp. 17–31).

Fleming, T. (2011) 'Recognition in the Work of Axel Honneth: Implications for Transformative Learning Theory', in Alhadeff-Jones, M. and Kokkos, A. (eds)

Transformative Learning in Time of Crisis: Individual and Collective Challenges (New York: Teachers College, pp. 95–101).

Fuller, A., Heath, S. and Johnston, B. (2011) *Rethinking Widening Participation in Higher Education: The Role of Networks* (London: Routledge).

Gallacher, J. (2009) 'Higher Education in Scotland's Colleges: A Distinctive Tradition?' *Higher Education Quarterly*, LXIII: 384–401.

Higher Education Funding Council for England (2009) *HEFCE Strategic Plan 2006-11* (Bristol: HEFCE).

Jetten, J., Iyer, A., Tsivrikos, D. and Young, B. (2008) 'When Is Individual Mobility Costly? The Role of Economic and Social Identity Factors', *European Journal of Social Psychology*, XXXVIII: 866–879.

Jones, I. (2010) 'Senses of Belonging and Fitting In? Affinities and Emergent Identities', *Widening Participation and Lifelong Learning*, XII: 23–35.

Longden, B. (2004) 'Interpreting Student Early Departure from Higher Education Through the Lens of Cultural Capital', *Tertiary Education and Management*, X: 121–138.

McQueen, H. (2009) 'Integration and Regulation Matters in Educational Transition: A Theoretical Critique of Retention and Attrition Models', *British Journal of Educational Studies*, LVII: 70–88.

National Audit Office (2007) *Staying the Course: The Retention of Students in Higher Education* (London: NAO).

Ozga, J. and Sukhandan, L. (1998) 'Undergraduate Non-Completion: Developing an Explanatory Model', *Higher Education Quarterly*, LII: 316–333.

Quinn, J. (2010) *Learning Communities and Imagined Social Capital* (London: Continuum).

Reay, D. (1998) ' "Always Knowing" and "Never Being Sure": Familial and Institutional Habitus and Higher Educational Choice', *Journal of Education Policy*, XIII: 519–529.

Reay, D., Crozier, G. and Clayton, J. (2009) ' "Fitting In" or "Standing Out": Working Class Students in UK Higher Education', *British Educational Research Journal*, XXXVI: 1–18.

Reay, D., David, M. and Ball, S. (2005) *Degrees of Choice: Social Class, Race and Gender in Higher Education* (Stoke on Trent: Trentham).

Scottish Funding Council (2010) *Learning for All: Fourth Update Report on Measures of Success* (Edinburgh: SFC).

Scottish Funding Council (2005) *Learning for All* (Edinburgh: SFC).

Scottish Government (2010) *Building a Smater Future: Towards a Sustainable Scottish Solution for the Future of Higher Education* (Edinburgh: Scottish Government).

Stolk, Cv.an, Tiessen, J., Clift, J. and Levitt, R. (2007) *Student Retention in Higher Education Courses: International Comparison* (Santa Monica, CA: Rand Corporation).

Stuart, M. (2006) ' "My Friends Made all the Difference": Getting into and Succeeding at University for First-Generation Entrants', *Journal of Access Policy and Practice*, III: 162–184.

Tinto, V. (1987) *Leaving College: Rethinking the Causes and Cures of Student Attrition* (Chicago: University of Chicago Press).

Tinto, V. (1975) 'Drop-Out from Higher Education: A Theoretical Synthesis of Recent Research', *Review of Educational Research*, XVIV: 89–125.

Warner, R., Hornsey, M. and Jetten, J. (2007) 'Why Minority Group Members Resent Imposters', *European Journal of Social Psychology*, XXXVII: 1–17.

Part IV

Widening Participation in International Contexts

12
Widening Participation Trends in Sweden: Regulations and Their Effects, Intended and Unintended

Caroline Berggren and Christina Cliffordson

Introduction

Over the years, governments of various political persuasions have influenced all levels of the educational system from pre-school to higher education (HE). A majority of the Swedish higher education institutions (HEIs) are state-owned and state-regulated. However, the regulations also apply to private institutions.

In this chapter, we provide an overview of the regulations that have influenced the participation of different groups of students in HE. We consider not only regulations about admission to HE but also regulations that have influenced the pre-requisites for participation, including requirements in compulsory education. The steps that have been taken to increase participation in HE can be summarised in four broad areas:

1. Extending and reforming compulsory and upper secondary schooling to provide routes into HE and to provide more students with the required qualifications;
2. Extending educational opportunities to provide many older students with a second chance to obtain the qualifications needed to enter HE;
3. Changes in the admission and selection system to HE to facilitate attendance by under-represented groups of students;
4. Extending the number of HE study places and by increasing the number of HEIs, particularly in the smaller cities.

Students from less schooled home backgrounds have been the main target for widening participation (WP) in Sweden. More recently, this focus has been broadened to include a wider range of target groups depending on the area of education, for example, to attract more students from non-Swedish backgrounds into some programmes in law, or more men into pre-school teacher-training programmes. In this chapter, we focus on social class and gender.

The reasons for promoting WP and the ways of doing so have changed over the years since initial efforts that commenced in the post-war period and continue today. However, the ambitions for WP have diminished in recent years. Considering the most influential changes, we have divided the development into four periods, starting from the 1940s.

1940–1976: Increased educational accessibility

Widening participation

There have been two main reasons for widening HE participation. The first is for reasons of democracy. Discussions had already started in the 1940s and were further stressed in the 1970s and early 1980s, during Olof Palme's term as prime minister. Equality or equity was emphasised and phrased in terms of equal rights, opportunities and obligations across the entire social spectrum including education, working and private life (Jordansson, 2005). The focus was that lack of resources should not hamper a gifted person. The success of widening participation at this time did not happen in isolation but was connected with other social changes in society, such as the expansion of the public sector, with increasingly accessible child and elderly aged care, resulting in increased opportunities for women to study and work (SOU, 2005).

The second explanation was the influence of the human capital theory (Becker, 1964), which was predominant at this time. The idea was that investment in human capital, such as more education and training, would lead to financial returns such as higher income and thus improved standard of living for the individual and for society.

The ability reserve

In the middle of the 1940s, there was an idea that the ability to study beyond compulsory levels of school should be limited to a certain proportion of each birth cohort (Cliffordson, 2009). The group of able students coming from upper middle-class backgrounds and studying at upper secondary school was perceived as being saturated. Eyes turned to the lower socio-economic groups where it was expected there would be many able persons, but who had been excluded, mainly for financial reasons. The 'ability reserve' was the name given to these potential students. Husén (1946) was the first to estimate the proportion of able persons who would be able to complete upper secondary school. About 10 years later, Härnqvist (1958) completed a new estimation, based on grades in the compulsory school years. The able students were this time estimated to be about a quarter of each birth cohort[1]. These estimations led to an animated debate, and the results received international attention. The results also led to recommendations about increasing the size of the university sector.

Educational achievement and educational organisation

Educational results in compulsory schooling influence the type of study programmes that can be chosen in the subsequent educational level, which in turn influences future educational possibilities. We know from previous studies that students from less schooled home backgrounds obtain lower grades than their counterparts from more educated backgrounds (e.g. Erikson and Jonsson, 1993; Boudon, 1974). Moreover, in Sweden, since the 1960s, girls have achieved higher grades than boys in most subjects (Svensson, 1971). These structures were more apparent before the all-inclusive upper secondary school system, prior to which fewer girls and fewer students from less schooled home backgrounds (by tradition) followed the more academic upper secondary school track and, therefore, did not undertake studies that provided eligibility to undertake university studies.

In the early 1960s, compulsory schooling was extended to nine years with the aim of providing all pupils with basic schooling and to increase the proportion of students who could become eligible to undertake subsequent non-compulsory schooling (Skolöverstyrelsen, 1962; Erikson and Jonsson, 1993, 1996). A similar uniting idea was carried through in the early 1970s, by integrating the different forms of non-compulsory schooling into a single upper secondary system with a common curriculum (Skolöverstyrelsen, 1983; Erikson and Jonsson, 1996). Previously, the academic non-compulsory schooling that had prepared secondary students for university had been located in the cities. After this process of merging disparate school systems, preparatory education for future university students also became available in smaller towns and thereby became accessible to the less affluent families who had not been willing or financially able to send their children to the cities.

To make it possible to change track and to make up for previous school low attainment, *kommunal vuxenutbildning*, which translates directly as 'municipal adult education', was built up during the 1970s (SFS, 2004a). As used in Swedish, adult education is 'mature age' education, directed towards students aged 20 or older. It is a system built up on single subject courses, and it has been possible to study single courses and complete compulsory and upper secondary school programmes. It has also been possible to add on single subjects to an already existing degree from upper secondary school, meaning that it has been possible to 'transfer' from a vocational programme with less academic emphasis subjects into a degree equivalent to the academic route.

Expansion of higher education, tuition fees and financial aid

The university sector started to expand during the 1950s, but the real expansion took place during the 1960s. University studies have always been free of tuition fees, but what limited students from less affluent backgrounds was the increased living costs associated with moving to the larger cities, where universities were located. Financial aid was introduced in 1965. The eligibility to obtain financial aid was universal and not limited by parents' or other relatives' income, or based on private means. In the beginning, the aid consisted of a grant (one-quarter) and an interest-free loan (three-quarters). Financial aid has had positive effects on access to HE: it has levelled out social class differences, and it has also increased women's participation in the longer and more prestigious academic programmes in which men previously made up the majority (Reuterberg and Svensson, 1994). At this time, a university degree was a safe and reliable investment leading to a secure position in the labour market.

Summary of 1940–1976

Extensive reforms leading to a uniform compulsory and upper secondary school system was set in place. It led to increased accessibility to both upper secondary and HE for students from a less affluent home background. At university level, an increased number of study places were made available, and student aid was introduced. These changes were successful in levelling out social class differences.

1977–1990: A broadening university sector

Expansion of higher education and increased financial aid

The HE act introduced in 1977 (SFS, 1977) had a major influence on the organisation of the university sector and on the composition of the student population. This set of reforms included incorporation of the previous colleges, mainly located in provincial centres, into the university sector – simultaneously re-designating them as HE. The inclusion of such colleges within the ambit of an expanded HE was meant to be a way of levelling out social class differences (Kim, 1998; Bauer *et al.*, 1999). Originally, the former colleges had largely offered training programmes, such as compulsory teacher education or nursing education, attracting a majority of women. As these colleges were now included within HE, the student population changed from having a majority of men to a majority of women (HSV, 2008b).

During the 1980s, HE continued to expand not only by increasing the number of study places at existing institutions but also by establishing new university colleges in the less populated areas. Social class differences were less marked at the university colleges (SOU, 2003; Cliffordson and

Gustafsson, 2007). In particular, young students who still lived within the parental home and the mature students who had a family of their own were attracted by the increased accessibility, because they did not need to move from their hometown to undertake their studies (Wikhall, 2001).

Increases in the cost of living had led to an increase in the loan component of the student aid, while the grant part had been reduced (Reuterberg and Svensson, 1994). The financial aid programme was adjusted and the grant substantially increased.

Admission quotas

When compared with many other countries, Sweden has extensive admission regulations. Admission to all single courses and programmes became restricted in 1977 (SFS, 1977), and since then there have been general and specific entry requirements or eligibility. However, meeting entry requirements means that the applicant is eligible to apply, but there is no guarantee that the applicant will be admitted. The general requirement for eligibility to apply was to have successfully completed upper secondary school or its equivalent. The specific requirements were often linked to the area of study of the course or programme. For example, a programme in economics may require a certain standard of knowledge in mathematics. In addition to the eligibility, when there were more applicants than study places, the students with the highest grades were selected. Students from well-educated family backgrounds have been the most successful in this competition, as they traditionally have higher educational achievements. The admission regulation was a major instrument for the government to influence the composition of the student body. Students who had not been educationally successful previously, but who wanted to study as mature-aged students, were particularly assisted by the new regulations. General eligibility could now also be obtained by work experience. As an alternative to having completed upper secondary school, students aged at least 25 years who had four years' work experience, and with a general knowledge of Swedish and English, were eligible to enter HE. Moreover, students who had not completed upper secondary school (and thus were lacking the grades to allow them to compete for study places) could sit the Swedish Scholastic Aptitude Test, SweSAT – a test battery similar to the SAT in the United States. The test is administrated twice a year, and around 10,000 individuals each year took the test in the early years. A maximum of 2.0 credit points could be achieved in the SweSAT. Furthermore, mature students were assisted because they could earn extra 0.5 credit points based on their work experience to be added to the SweSAT results (Kim, 1998; Bauer *et al.*, 1999). Focussing on mature-aged students and acknowledging other competence measures helped students from less schooled home backgrounds, who have generally had a less-straightforward educational career (Balke, 2002).

Traditional educational choices

At the end of the 1980s, the common point of view was that a coherent educational system with a minimum of individual choices or tracks would improve equality (SFS, 2004a). Parents' educational aspirations for their children continued to have an impact on young pupils' early educational choices in compulsory schooling. This leads them to follow different tracks in upper secondary school, resulting in eligibility or not for HE studies. However, a more coherent and equivalent system of compulsory and upper secondary schooling was not introduced until 1994.

Summary of 1977–1990

More people became eligible to apply to undertake HE studies, largely because of the extension of upper secondary school (Härnqvist, 2003). The university sector expanded through inclusion of previous training programmes and through the establishment of new university colleges. Separate admission quotas were created to facilitate the entry of mature-aged students. Seen in a broad perspective, there was an increased equalisation of the student population with respect to gender and social class. However, the differentiation had moved from 'outside/inside' university to 'within' HE. From now on, a majority of the HE students were women but distributed unevenly across the disciplines, across the types of programme (men made up the majority in the prestigious study programmes), and across the type of HEI (more women studied at the university colleges). There is an interaction between gender and social class: fewer working-class men study within HE, resulting in similar patterns for working-class students and for women within HE. Despite the unintended outcomes within HE, this must be perceived as a very ambitious period with respect to WP.

1990–2004: Reducing the number of dead ends

Coherent educational system

The curriculum of 1994 for compulsory schooling gave no room for choice (Utbildningsdepartementet, 1994a), with all pupils studying the same subjects at the same level of difficulty. Moreover, all the upper secondary school programmes, including those aimed at a particular trade – the vocational programmes – became more theoretical, all providing the students with a general eligibility to undertake HE (Utbildningsdepartementet, 1994b). However, the different educational tracks in upper secondary school continued to be highly segregated according to gender and social class. In upper secondary school, some vocational programmes such as vehicle, electricity, energy and construction programmes had a majority of working-class background men. These programmes lead to traditionally male-dominated trades as painters, car mechanics, building construction workers and so on, trades which are also quite well paid. The vocational programmes that attracted women include those in child and recreation, health care, business and administration, hotel and restaurant, arts programmes and handicraft programmes. However, women's vocational programmes in upper secondary school often led to jobs within the health care or service sectors with high levels of part-time employment, inconvenient working hours and low pay. Because of the very limited variety of attractive upper secondary school vocational programmes for young women leading to jobs with adequate employment conditions, a majority of them chose academic programmes that were preparatory to HE studies. Around 50 per cent of women from a range of social classes had embarked on HE studies in the early 2000s compared with slightly below 40 per cent of men. The distribution among men is more skewed towards the upper middle class than it is among women (Berggren, 2008; HSV, 2008b; SCB, 2008b).

Expansion of municipal 'adult education'

During the 1990s, particularly from 1993, the government invested heavily in municipal 'adult education'. They did this not only for reasons of equality but also because it was also a way of alleviating the high numbers of unemployed after the dot.com bubble burst. Another reason for the increase in the number of students was the introduction of top-up grades, which allowed students to undertake the same course a second time, but this time within the framework of municipal 'adult education'. Despite men's lower general school achievements, the proportion of female students has been around two-thirds in municipal 'adult education' (HSV, 2008b). Women's majority can be explained by their larger share as employees within the public sector (SOU, 2003); a sector that has increased its requirements of qualifications. However, those who utilised the municipal 'adult education' to top up their grades and to gain entrance to HE tended to be upper middle-class men (Berggren, 2007). An explanation for this propensity is that women generally have higher grades than men and therefore have no need to top up their grades, and upper middle-class students are better informed about the educational system than working-class students are (Hutchings, 2003). However, at the beginning of the 2000s, overall enrolments started to decline. Explanations for the decline included reduced subsidies provided by the state to the municipalities in combination with improved job opportunities (Skolverket, 2007, 2009).

Changing admission quotas

In 1991, the regulations for the SweSAT were changed: all students, including those who had completed secondary education, could sit for the test. This provided an opening for tactically minded students who were inclined to seek entry into the prestigious HE study programmes that required the highest grades or test results. The number of test-takers increased from 10,000 to 140,000 per year. These students were usually from the upper middle class, and they were usually men. One explanation for this propensity is that not as many women from the upper middle class needed to be tactical because they already had grades from upper secondary school that were high enough. It is also possible that working-class students were hesitant about the costs of taking the test. Upper middle-class students soon realised that they could sit for the SweSAT test as many times as they needed and by the experience gained from the test, getting older, and becoming more knowledgeable, they improve their results and their competitiveness. Only the best result obtained was considered, so there was no risk taking involved in doing the test several times (Cliffordson, 2004b). Moreover, SweSAT is a multiple-choice test, and research has suggested that men tend to out perform women in this type of test construction (Willingham and Cole, 1997).

Providing bridging or preparatory courses was one suggestion from the HEIs in response to a government bill that aimed to increase recruitment (Utbildningsdepartementet, 2001b). Possible applicants who were not qualified for HE could get the necessary qualifications by undertaking preparatory courses. Introductory years had previously been available in science, but now they were also made available in other fields. However, most bridging courses were organised within science and teacher programmes, programmes with low or little competition for study places, which could be interpreted as a way for the institutions to fill their empty places (Johansson *et al.*, 2005; HSV, 2006).

As an early outcome of decentralisation, an unrestricted quota for admission was introduced in 2002. HEIs were given the option to decide on admission quotas for a small proportion of the study places. The argument was that alternative competence measures among the applicants should be acknowledged, to facilitate the admission of under-represented groups of students and to make it possible for local HEIs institutions to decide on specific needs of their student recruitment policy (Utbildningsdepartementet, 2001a).

Continuous expansion of higher education

In 1993, another HE reform was launched (SFS, 1993), which led to decentralisation of decision making to the individual HEIs, but at the same time allowed the government to keep a firm grip through increased financial control. Similar to other industrialised countries, the expansion of the HE sector was the most dramatic during the 1990s. The numbers of students increased, the variety of students also increased and this in turn influenced the institutions. The aim to maintain uniform standards for this sector seemed not to be possible. The university colleges were not able to compete with the traditional universities concerning research (fewer teachers at the university colleges had a doctoral degree, meaning that fewer could apply for external research funding), and the division of institutions into teaching universities and research universities was preserved. During this period, new HEIs had been established in the provincial areas. It was not until 2004 that the expansion stopped, to a large extent because of stagnation of funding, caused by a recession in the national economy (HSV, 2008b).

Summary of 1991–2004

There were both pros and cons concerning WP during this period. The coherent educational system was carried forward as a way of minimising the influence of family background that had continued to lead to 'traditional' educational choices (Erikson and Jonsson, 2002). It was also the period when the educational system was organised to reduce dead ends, to make it possible to change the educational track (Eriksson and Jonsson, 1998). However, when the option to take the SweSAT became available for all students, not only for those who were lacking pre-requisites, the equalising effects were counteracted. On the one hand, the social differences in participation in HE decreased, to a large extent because of the enormous expansion of HE. On the other hand, the differences based on social class and gender became evident within HE, as different educational 'choices'. The student composition in prestigious programmes had changed, with women now being in the majority, except for the programmes within technology, but social class differences remained with the majority comprising upper middle-class students (Erikson and Jonsson, 1993; Berggren, 2008).

2005 – Now, widening participation – A passed era?

Widening participation

The reasons for WP have changed. Reasons based on equality have faded and have been replaced by arguments based on efficiency. For example, the labour market and the educational system particularly needs people from all social groups; the labour market needs employees from a range of backgrounds to communicate with partners of diverse backgrounds, and the school needs a variety of teachers to be role models for students from different social groups (SOU, 2000). Moreover, the legitimacy of HE is expected to increase if the social composition of academically educated individuals corresponds with the composition of the population as a whole. Internationalisation has influenced reasons for WP for several reasons, including increased student mobility (Bologna Process, 2005; University of Gothenburg, 2006) and an increased need to understand international circumstances (SFS, 2004b). During recent decades, from the 1990s until now, the notion of democracy has increasingly been interpreted as individual freedom and rights in combination with decreased intervention by the state.

The Swedish government had been ruled by Social Democrats from 1936 until 2006, with only two short periods of exception. In 2006, the Liberals won the election, and neo-liberal tendencies that could already be seen before the end of the Social Democratic election period now came into full force.

Changing educational system

2011 saw the launching of a new curriculum in Sweden, under which the opportunity to choose subjects has been reintroduced in compulsory schooling levels. In upper secondary schools, the coherence of the previous policies has had to yield to increased diversity. The vocational programmes will consist of theoretical subjects that are less general; thus, students enrolled in these programmes will no longer have the prerequisites to enrol in HE programmes, unless they add extra courses. The difference between the vocational and the theoretical programmes will increase (SFS, 2010). A reason for the reduction of the teaching time spent on theoretical subjects is based on concerns about the higher dropout rates among boys (Murray, 2007).

Downsizing municipal 'adult education'

The opportunity to supplement and top-up grades in municipal adult education became restricted in 2010 (HSV and VHS, 2011). The reasons for restricting the capacity to top up was that it had led to grade inflation and unwanted pressure on the municipal 'adult education' and unreasonably prolonged education, particularly among the most ambitious students who absolutely wanted to enter the most prestigious programmes, such as medicine (Cliffordson, 2004a).

Changing admission quotas

The benefit of work experience in contributing to eligibility for HE has been removed. Work experience is no longer included with other general eligibility factors, and it does not add extra credit points to the SweSAT results (HSV and VHS, 2011). It is uncertain whether work experience had a positive effect for working-class students, because students from all social groups could add work experience to their score, and the extra credit points could only be used in addition to the SweSAT results – a SweSAT that favours some students over others, particularly those from the upper middle-class and men.

The changed regulations have made it difficult for students who lack the cultural capital to maximise their later educational opportunities at an early stage, particularly working-class students. The situation of students who know the direction they are aiming towards in HE has been improved since 2010 by appropriate subject choices at upper secondary school. Moreover, the government wishes to stimulate certain academic subjects in upper secondary school by favouring students who have studied languages and mathematics. Grades from these subjects provide extra credit points to students' total grade point average from upper secondary school, when these subjects are not a specific prerequisite. That is, it brings a general increased competitiveness for students who have studied these subjects, but who do not particularly need them for their specialisation within HE. A further drawback for students who have not planned to undertake HE, or who have not decided what to study, is that they will probably have to supplement their upper secondary school results. Students with supplemented grades are now directed to a specific admission quota.

The unrestricted quota, decided by individual institutions, gradually increased. The idea was that this quota could make up for the reduced alternative entrance options, such as work experience. Students could apply to the individual institution for recognition of their qualifications. However, it turned out to be difficult and expensive for HEIs to develop criteria and evaluate alternative qualifications, so that this quota has rarely been utilised. In 2008, this quota increased further, now comprising one-third of the study places. The reasons for the unrestricted quota also changed, and now the emphasis is on the freedom of individual institutions to decide on what regulations to apply, the possibility of creating a distinctive institutional image, and to attract students with specific qualifications (Utbildningsdepartementet, 2007).

Tuition fees and student aid

No students in Sweden had to pay tuition fees in the past, but in 2011 tuition fees were introduced for students from outside the European Economic Area. Institutions and departments decide on the size of the fee.

The grant component of the student aid has increased to one-third, but the loan is no longer interest-free (CSN, 2011). In contrast with earlier periods, the reliability of a degree as a safe labour market investment has diminished. Students without a degree that is in demand in the labour market may face difficulties (SOU, 2003).

Summary of 2005 to now

WP, in its original meaning, to increase the diversity of the student body in HE has been abandoned. Pupils will be required to make educational choices decisive about their future studies as early as in the sixth grade (age 12). The new regulations also imply that the vocationally oriented programmes in upper secondary school will not provide the student with eligibility to enter HE. Downsizing of municipal 'adult education' has led to reduced options for students to supplement the subject areas in which they are lacking. Efforts during the previous period to reduce the number of 'dead ends' have been replaced by policies that will reverse that trend. The admission quotas do not favour mature-aged students with work experience or students with supplemented grades.

We have not yet seen the effects of these recent regulations, but we fear that fewer students will choose the vocational programmes in upper secondary school in order to minimise the restrictions they face later on in life. This system will assist students from well-educated home backgrounds who have the knowledge to help them manoeuvre around the educational system.

Discussion

Policies around WP in HE in Sweden have resulted in an equalisation of the student population with respect to gender and social class – seen in a broad perspective. However, HE is strongly horizontally gender divided, meaning that some programmes attract a majority of men and some a majority of women. The gender division is as pronounced in Sweden as in most other countries (Leathwood and Read, 2009). This means that when women and men apply for different kinds of programmes, women with generally higher grades than men will compete with other well-achieving women, making it more difficult for women to enter HE than it is for men. In addition, when alternative quotas were used, that is, other than grade point average, the selection of men into HE programmes was additionally facilitated. The result was that among female applicants, 53 per cent were admitted, while among their male counterparts the share was 58 per cent (HSV, 2008b). Despite this, women now make up about 60 per cent of Swedish undergraduates (SCB, 2008a).

The share of working-class students is around a quarter, and they are also unequally distributed across programmes (SCB, 2008a). A system without 'dead ends' and a policy of giving people a 'second chance' has resulted in a larger proportion of mature students, with one-third being in the 26–40 years age groups. They are most likely to be women from working-class backgrounds studying within health care (HSV, 2008a).

The last decades of WP have been unsuccessful with respect to gender; women represent the majority in HE, including in most of the prestigious programmes, and there is no sign of a changing trend. The decision whether or not to enter HE is a question informed by gender, social class and the structure of the labour market. Concern has been raised about the increasing proportion of female students within HE, at the same time as there has been concern about the small proportion of students from less schooled home backgrounds. However, young working-class men in particular are not accessing HE; they are perceived largely not to feel the need to study beyond their vocational training – in Sweden, men in traditional male trades earn as much as women in traditional semi-professions with a HE degree (Ljunglöf, 2004). It is difficult, not to say impossible within a foreseeable period, to change these social structures. No political party would dare to decide that traditional male trades should be provided within HE with an additional three years of study without any financial compensation.

To have real impact, policies around WP need to include the whole educational system. All students need support through their whole education as well as in their career planning (University of Gothenburg, 2006). Since the middle of this decade, these ambitions have been abandoned. Governmental initiatives to counteract the effects of family background have been reduced by re-introducing early educational choices, favouring students who study natural science programmes in upper secondary school, and by reducing options to 'change track'. We foresee these new regulations leading to a younger HE student population and connected to that, a reduction in the number of students from the working class.

Note

1. Corresponding estimates (Härnqvist, 2003) some 40 years later showed that the proportion of individuals with the necessary adequate ability had doubled. This can be explained by the so-called Flynn effect (1984), which means that there has been a strong development of the general cognitive ability at the population level over these years.

Bibliography

Balke, G. (2002) *Olika bakgrund – olika uppfattning? [Different Background – Different Opinion?]* (Göteborg, Sweden: Avd f omvärldsanalys, planering och uppföljning [Dept. of Planning and Evaluation]).
Bauer, M., Askling, B., Gerard Marton, S. and Marton, F. (1999) *Transforming Universities. Changing Patterns of Governance, Structure and Learning in Swedish Higher Education* (London and Philadelphia: Kingsley).
Becker, G.S. (1964) *Human Capital; A Theoretical and Empirical Analysis, with Special Reference to Education* (New York: National Bureau of Economic Research).
Berggren, C. (2007) 'Broadening Recruitment to Higher Education Through the Admission System – Gender and Class Perspectives', *Studies in Higher Education*, 32 (1): 97–116.
Berggren, C. (2008) 'Horizontal and Vertical Differentiation within Higher Education – Gender and Class Perspectives', *Higher Education Quarterly*, 62 (1–2): 20–39.
Bologna Process (2005) *The European Higher Education Area – Achieving the Goals*. Conference of European Ministers Responsible for Higher Education, Bergen, Norway, 19–20 May.
Boudon, R. (1974) *Education, Opportunity, and Social Inequality* (New York: John Wiley).
Cliffordson, C. (2009) 'Från elituniversitet till masshögskola – utbildningsexplosionen och individuella förutsättningar för högre utbildning', in Wikande, L., Gustafsson, C., Riis, U. and Larson, L. (eds) *Pedagogik som examensämne 100 år [Science of Education as Subject for Examination 100 Years]* (Sweden, Uppsala: Uppsala University, pp. 143–164).

Cliffordson, C. (2004a) 'Betygsinflation i de målrelaterade gymnasiebetygen [Inflation in the Criterion-Referenced Grades from Upper Secondary School]', *Pedagogisk Forskning i Sverige*, 9 (1): 1–14.

Cliffordson, C. (2004b) 'Effects of Practice and Intellectual Growth on Performance on the Swedish Scholastic Aptitude Test (SweSAT)', *European Journal of Psychological Assessment*, 20 (3): 192–204.

Cliffordson, C. and Gustafsson, J.-E. (2007) 'Effekter av den grundläggande högskoleutbildningens expansion på studerandegruppens sammansättning [Effects of the Expansion of the Undergraduate Higher Education on the Composition of the Student Population]', in Askling, B., Foss Lindblad, R. and Wärvik, G.-B. (eds) *Expansion och kontraktion. Utmaningar för högskolesystemet och utbildningsforskare [Expansion and Contraction. Challenges for the Higher Education System and for Educational Researchers]* (Stockholm: Vetenskapsrådet, pp. 43–59).

CSN (2011) *Financial Aid for Studies* (Sweden, Sundsvall: Swedish Board for Study Support). [online] http://www.csn.se/en/2.135/2.624 [accessed 30 May 2011].

Erikson, R. and Jonsson, J.O. (2002) 'Varför består den sociala snedrekryteringen? [Why Does the Socially Uneven Recruitment Remain?]', *Pedagogisk Forskning i Sverige*, 7 (3): 210–217.

Eriksson, R. and Jonsson, J.O. (1998) 'Qualifications and the Allocation Process of Young Men and Women in the Swedish Labour Market', in Shavit, Y. and Müller, W. (eds) *From School to Work. A Comparative Study of Educational Qualifications and Occupational Destinations* (New York: Oxford University Press, pp. 369–406).

Erikson, R. and Jonsson, J.O. (1996) 'The Swedish Context: Educational Reform and Long-Term Change in Educational Inequality', in Erikson, R. and Jonsson, J.O. (eds) *Can Education Be Equalized?* (Boulder, CO: Westview, pp. 65–93).

Erikson, R. and Jonsson, J.O. (1993) *Ursprung och utbildning. Social snedrekrytering till högre studier [Origin and Education. Social Selection to Higher Education]* (Stockholm: Fritzes).

Flynn, J.R. (1984) 'The mean IQ of Americans: Massive Gains 1932 to 1978', *Psychological Bulletine*, 95: 29–51.

Härnqvist, K. (2003) 'Educational Reserves Revisited', *Scandinavian Journal of Educational Research*, 47 (5): 483–494.

Härnqvist, K. (1958) 'Beräkning av reserver för högre utbildning [Estimations of Reserves of Ability for Higher Education]', *SOU Statens Offentliga Utredningar [The Swedish Government Official Reports]* (Stockholm: Ecklesiastikdepartementet [The Ministry of Education and Ecclesiastical Affairs]).

HSV (2008a) *Vilka är studenter? En undersökning av studenterna i Sverige [Who Are the Students? A Study about Students in Sweden]* (Stockholm: National Agency for Higher Education).

HSV (2008b) *Women and Men in Higher Education* (Stockholm: National Agency for Higher Education).

HSV (2006) *Universitet and högskolor. Högskoleverkets årsrapport 2006 [Swedish Universities and University Colleges – Annual Report 2006]* (Stockholm: National Agency for Higher Education).

HSV and VHS (2011) *Applying to Higher Education in Sweden* (Stockholm: The Swedish National Agency for Higher Education, HSV and The Swedish Agency for Higher Education Services, VHS). [online] https://www.studera.nu/studera/1374.html [accessed 30 May 2011].

Husén, T. (1946) 'Intelligenskrav på olika utbildningsstadier', *Skola och Samhälle*, 27: 1–23.

Hutchings, M. (2003) 'Information, Advice and Cultural Discourses of Higher Education', in Archer, L., Hutchings, M. and Ross, A. (eds) *Higher Education and Social Class. Issues of Exclusion and Inclusion* (London: Routledge Falmer, pp. 97–118).

Johansson, M., Kim, L., Storan, J. and Sörlin, S. (2005) *Bridging the Gap: Widening Participation in Sweden and England* (Stockholm: SISTER and Continuum).

Jordansson, B. (2005) 'Jämställdhet och genusforskning [Gender Equality and Gender Research]', in SOU (ed.) *Forskarrapporter till Jämställdhetspolitiska utredningen [Research Reports for the Political Report about Gender Equality]* (Stockholm: Stadsrådsberedningen [Prime Minister's Office], pp. 239–281).

Kim, L. (1998) *Val och urval till högre utbildning [Choice and Selection in Higher Education]* (Uppsala, Sweden: Department of Education, Uppsala University).

Leathwood, C. and Read, B. (2009) *Gender and the Changing Face of Higher Education. A Feminized Future?* (Maidenhead, UK: Open University Press).

Ljunglöf, T. (2004) *Livslöner 2002 [Aggregate Lifetime Salary 2002]* (Stockholm: Saco). [online] http://www.saco.se/Global/Dokument/Trycksaker/Rapporter/2004_livsloner 2002.pdf [accessed 22 August 2012].

Murray, Å. (2007) 'Genomströmningen i gymnasieskolan. Före och efter gymnasiereformen', in Olofsson, J. (ed.) *Utbildningsvägen – vart leder den? Om ungdomar, yrkesutbildning och försörjning* (Stockholm: SNS, pp. 143–157).

Reuterberg, S.-E. and Svensson, A. (1994) 'Financial Aid and Recruitment to Higher Education in Sweden: Changes Between 1970 and 1990', *Studies in Higher Education*, 19 (1): 33–45.

SCB (2008a) *Utbildningsstatistisk årsbok [Yearbook of Educational Statistics]* (Örebro, Sweden: SCB [Statistics Sweden]).

SCB (2008b) *Women and Men in Sweden – Facts and Figures 2008* (Stockholm: SCB [Statistics Sweden]).

SFS (2010) *Gymnasieförordningen (2010:2039) [the Upper Secondary School Ordinance 2010:2039]* (Stockholm: Ministry of Education and Research). [online] http://www.skolverket.se/sb/d/2771 [accessed 30 May 2011].

SFS (2004a) *Education Act (1985:1100)* (Stockholm: Swedish Statute Book. Ministry of Education and Research). [online] http://www.sweden.gov.se/content/1/c6/02/15/38/1532b277.pdf [accessed 30 May 2011].

SFS (2004b) *Higher Education Act (1992:1434)* (Stockholm: Swedish Statute Book. Ministry of Education and Research).

SFS (1993) *Högskoleförordningen (1993:100) [Higher Education Ordinance 1993:100]* (Stockholm: Ministry of Education and Research). [online] http://www.notisum.se/rnp/sls/lag/19930100.htm [accessed 30 May 2011].

SFS (1977) *Högskoleförordningen (1977:263) [the Higher Education Ordinance 1977:263]* (Stockholm: Ministry of Education and Research). [online] http://www.notisum.se/rnp/sls/lag/19770263.htm [accessed 30 May 2011].

Skolöverstyrelsen (1983) *Lgy 70 Läroplan för gymnasieskolan, allmän del [Curriculumn for Upper Secondary School]* (Stockholm: Liber).

Skolöverstyrelsen (1962) *Läroplan för grundskolan. Allmän del [Curriculumn for Compulsory School]* (Stockholm: Kungliga Skolöverstyrelsen).

Skolverket (2009) *Beskrivande data 2009. Förskoleverksamhet, skolbarnsomsorg, skola och vuxenutbildning [Descriptive Data on Pre-School Activities, School-Age Childcare, Schools and Adult Education in Sweden 2009]* (Stockholm: The Swedish National Agency for Education).

Skolverket (2007) *Descriptive Data on Pre-School Activities, School-Age Childcare, Schools and Adult Education in Sweden 2006* (Stockholm: The Swedish National Agency for Education).

SOU (2005) *Makt att forma samhället och sitt eget liv – jämställdhetspolitiken mot nya mål [Power to Influence Society and Life – Gender Equality Politics Towards New Goals], Statens offentliga utredningar, 2005:66* (Stockholm: The Government Offices).

SOU (2003) *Utbildningens fördelning en fråga om klass [Distribution of Education a Matter of Social Class?], Statens offentliga utredningar, 2003:96* (Stockholm: Ministry of Finance).

SOU (2000) *Mångfald i högskolan – Refleksioner och förslag om social och etnisk mångfald i högskolan [Diversity in Higher Education], Statens offentliga utredningar, 2000:47* (Stockholm: Ministry of Education and Research).

Svensson, A. (1971) *Relative Achievement. School Performance in Relation to Intelligence, Sex and Home Environment.* Göteborg Studies in Educational Sciences, 6 (Göteborg, Sweden: Göteborg University).

Universtity of Gothenburg (2006) *Rapport from arbetsgrupp för alternativt urval [Report from the Working Team for Alternative Admission]* (Sweden, Gothenburg: University of Gothenburg).

Utbildningsdepartementet (2007) *Vägar till högskolan för kunskap och kvalitet [Paths to Higher Education for Knowledge and Quality].* Regeringens proposition 2006/07:107 (Stockholm: Ministry of Education and Research).

Utbildningsdepartementet (2001a) *Den öppna högskolan [An Open Higher Education System].* Regeringens proposition 2001/02:15 (Stockholm: Ministry of Education and Research). [online] http://www.regeringen.se/sb/d/108/a/1647 [accessed 30 May 2011].

Utbildningsdepartementet (2001b) *Reforms in Higher Education – A More Open System.* Summary of Government Bill 2001/02:15 (Stockholm: Ministry of Education and Research).

Utbildningsdepartementet (1994a) *1994 Curriculum for Compulsory Schools (Lpo 94)* (Stockholm: Ministry of Education and Research).

Utbildningsdepartementet (1994b) *1994 Curriculum for the Non-Compulsory School System (Lpf 94)* (Stockholm: Ministry of Education and Research).

Wikhall, M. (2001) *Universiteten och kompetenslandskapet: effekter av den högre utbildningens tillväxt och regionala spridning i Sverige [Universities and the Landscape of Competence: Impacts of the Expansion and Regional Decentralization of Higher Education in Sweden]* (Sweden, Lund: Lund University).

Willingham, W.W. and Cole, N.S. (1997) *Gender and Fair Assessment* (Mahwah, NJ: L. Erlbaum Associates).

13
Trends in Widening Participation in French Higher Education

Marie-Pierre Moreau

Introduction

During the second half of the 20th century, higher education (HE) systems significantly expanded in Europe and elsewhere (Shavit *et al.*, 2007). Whether these quantitative developments and the related widening participation (WP) rhetoric of many governments have been associated with the democratisation of HE remains a topical and much debated issue, including in France, the focus of this chapter.

France constitutes a unique terrain to explore WP in HE. The country experienced a shift to mass HE earlier than many of its neighbours, as the size of its post-compulsory student population increased sharply in the 1960s (for a comparison with Great Britain, see Deer, 2003). Despite the convergence of HE policies across Europe, French HE retains some distinctive features. In line with an equalitarian and universalist conception of education, access to universities is open to all those holding a *baccalauréat* or an equivalent title, and enrolment fees are kept at a low level. However, non-selective universities co-exist with a parallel system, the highly selective *Grandes Ecoles*. Entry to the *Grandes Ecoles* is often seen as based on merit, as it is granted to those who demonstrate the ability to succeed at national competitive examinations. Yet, these institutions have also been criticised for contributing to the reproduction of the French intellectual and political *élites* (Bourdieu, 1979, 1989). Moreover, as we shall see, the shift to mass HE has been associated with a strong differentiation of the available provision (Duru-Bellat *et al.*, 2011), with, in particular, the development of short and vocational programmes of studies.

Drawing on a review of national statistics and some of the key literature in the field, this contribution explores patterns of participation in French HE. Particular attention is given to how social class and gender shape participation in HE and to the tensions between these patterns and a meritocratic view of HE.

An overview of the French higher education system

A major characteristic of French HE lies in its tripartite nature. Universities coexist with the *Classes Préparatoires aux Grandes Ecoles* and the *Grandes Ecoles*, as well as a number of shorter vocational programmes. These parallel tracks are detailed hereafter.

Universities are the principal and oldest HE institutions. A distinctive feature of French universities is that entry at the undergraduate level is non-selective and is opened to all students holding a *baccalauréat* or an equivalent title. In 1985, the French Secretary of State for Education (*Ministre de l'Éducation Nationale*) decided that 80 per cent of each generation should gain a *baccalauréat*. To facilitate this, a vocational *baccalauréat* (*baccalauréat professionnel*) was established the same year, adding to the already in place *baccalauréat général* and *baccalauréat technologique*. Although this target was never reached, the proportion of *baccalauréat* holders among 18–19-year-olds went from 29 per cent in 1985 to 44 per cent in 1990, 63 per cent in 1995 and finally over 70 per cent for the first time in 2011. This implies that a university education is now accessible to the large majority of young adults. Another characteristic of French universities relates to tuition fees, which are kept at a low level in comparison with many western countries (i.e. in the area of 150 euros, with some minor variations depending on the institution and programme of study). In addition, means-tested grants are available for university and non-university-based students. However, despite the 'open' nature of entry procedures, it is worth noting that a large proportion of the university population will not gain a degree. For example, in 2009–2010, over a quarter of first-year students did not re-enrol at the end of the academic year, a proportion which was over a third in humanities and social sciences (Ministère de l'Éducation Nationale, 2010).

Despite the persistence of specific features, French universities have also grown closer to their European counterparts in many respects. As elsewhere, university educational provision has considerably diversified and a wider range of programmes are now on offer. Moreover, following the 1999 Bologna Act on the harmonisation of HE European systems, French universities have adopted in the 2000s the so-called LMD (*Licence-Master-Doctorat*) system, which distinguishes between three levels of qualification, rather than five as was previously the case. In 2007, the *Loi relative aux libertés et responsibilités des universités* (2007 Act on the Rights and Duties of Universities, also known as *Loi LRU*) anticipated that, by 2013, all universities should gain more autonomy, especially in relation to human resources and budget management. This suggests some convergence with other countries and may as well lead to further differentiation across institutions.

Another provider of HE are the *Classes Préparatoires aux Grandes Ecoles* (CPGE) and the related *Grandes Ecoles*. *Grandes Ecoles*, which were created much more recently than universities, in the 18th and 19th centuries, are by far the most prestigious form of HE schooling. The *Classes Préparatoires aux Grandes Ecoles* are two-year long classes that prepare for the *Grandes Ecoles* competitive examination. They are located in some of the most prestigious *lycées* (sixth-form colleges). Those studying in the state sector CPGE (that is, the majority of the CPGE population) do not pay fees. However, this parallel system is very selective (only students with the best academic results in the last two years leading to the *baccalauréat* can enrol). As a result, it has often been described as an élite system and compared with Oxbridge universities in the United Kingdom and Ivy League institutions in the United States. There are three types of CPGE, each with a different specialism: mathematics and sciences, humanities, and business and economics. In the humanities-oriented CPGE, most students will then continue their studies at university at the end of the two-year period, with only a small proportion entering the prestigious *Ecoles Normales Supérieures* (the most prestigious of all *Grandes Ecoles*, after which students usually take up a high-ranking position in the public sector, often in academia) or the *Instituts d'Etudes Politiques*. A significant share of those studying in the CPGE with a science or an economics specialism will then enter, respectively, the more numerous engineering schools (*Ecoles d'Ingénieurs*) or business schools (*Ecoles de Commerce*). While some *Grandes Ecoles* are free and, in some cases, even provide their students with a stipend (as do, for example, the *Ecoles Normales Supérieures*), others have a private status and can command high fees.

As the French HE system expanded, it also diversified. One aspect of this diversification has consisted in the development of a number of vocational programmes since the late 1950s. The *Sections de Techniciens Supérieurs*, created in 1959, offer some post-*baccalauréat* vocational training programmes, most of which are delivered within high schools and lead to a *Brevet de Technicien Supérieur* (a technical diploma, known as BTS). Other vocational programmes include those delivered by the *Instituts Universitaires de Technologie* (or IUT), mostly two-year long[1] vocational programmes, created in 1966 and delivered within universities, non-university-based actuary training programmes and programmes delivered by a wide range of vocational schools (for example, in institutions leading to a paramedical qualification). Most of these programmes do not have the élite status of CPGE, although some forms of selective procedures are usually in place.

The statistics collected by the Ministère de l'Éducation Nationale illustrate the shift to mass education and its association with the differentiation of HE provision. As evidenced in Table 13.1, the number of HE students has risen from 310,000 in 1960–1961 to 2,316,000, in 2009–2010. There are now 200 university centres in the country compared with 40 in 1968. The university student population[2] has multiplied by six, and the CPGE population by four. Although the increase of the university population accounts for the growth of most of the student population in absolute value, it is the more vocational programmes that have experienced an exponential growth. Indeed,

Table 13.1   Students enrolled in higher education since 1960 (in thousands)

	1960	1970	1980	1990	2000	2009
Universities	215	637	804	1,086	1,278	1,268
Instituts Universitaires de Technologie	N/A	24	54	74	119	118
Sections de Technicien Supérieur	8	26	68	199	239	240
Classes Préparatoires aux Grandes Ecoles	21	32	40	64	70	81
Other institutions and programmes	66	130	215	293	454	609
Total	310	851	1,181	1,717	2,160	2,316

Source: Ministère de l'Éducation Nationale (2010).

over the same period, the *Sections de Technicien Supérieur* student population multiplied by 30, while those of 'other institutions' (many of those with a vocational remit, such as paramedical schools) increased nine-fold. This means that while about two out of three HE students were university students in the early 1960s, this now applies to only about half, once the IUT population is counted separately.

Students' participation in HE in France: Exploring social class and gender issues

Patterns of participation in higher education and social class

There is a wealth of literature and policy intervention relating to socio-economic inequalities in education in France. Data from the French Ministère de l'Éducation provide a detailed overview of students' patterns of participation in HE by socio-economic background. However, a key limit of this data is that it usually relies on the occupational group of the father as a proxy for social class. This is obviously problematic as occupation is a rather partial indicator of social class and as maternal influences on children's education are then ignored (Crompton, 1989; Savage, 2000).

With the shift to mass HE, levels of participation have increased for all groups. However, students from socio-economic backgrounds with no history of participation in HE have struggled to catch up with other groups and levels of participation remain marked by social class. Students in the executives and intellectual professions category (*cadres et professions intellectuelles supérieures*) represent 29.8 per cent of the French HE population, yet, according to the *Institut National de la Statistique et des Etudes Economiques* (INSEE) data, this group represented only 14.4 per cent of the workforce in 2004 (INSEE, 2004). At the other end of the spectrum, students in the manual workers category (*Ouvriers*) represent only 10.3 per cent of the HE population, although this group constitutes 24.8 per cent of the workforce (Ministère de l'Éducation Nationale, 2010).

These overall figures hide some important variations across subjects and levels of study. For example, 40.1 per cent and 34.8 per cent of the medicine and law students, respectively, belong to the executives category, compared with only 5.2 per cent and 8.4 per cent of students from the manual workers category. The proportion of students from working-class backgrounds is the lowest at the most advanced levels of study. For example, those in the manual workers category represent 11.6 per cent of those studying towards a bachelor (*licence*), but only 6.4 per cent and 3.6 per cent of those studying at master's and PhD levels, respectively (Table 13.2).

Another imbalance relates to the type of track students embark on. As explained earlier, French universities co-exist with *Grandes Ecoles*, as well as with a number of vocational programmes. Because of the advantages associated with studying in and graduating from a *Grande Ecole*, equal access to such institutions constitutes a key social justice issue. Strikingly, over half the student population of the *Classes Préparatoires aux Grandes Ecoles* are from the freelance professionals and senior executives category (51.1 per cent). Even more strikingly, the same group represents 56.9 per cent of the *Grandes Ecoles* student population. In contrast, students from the *Ouvriers* category represent only 6.3 per cent of the CPGE and 2.3 per cent of the *Grandes Ecoles* population. The short, vocational programmes of study appear to be more popular with this group. For example, they represent 22.1 per cent of those enrolled in the *Sections de Techniciens Supérieurs* (Table 13.3).

Table 13.2 Socio-economic background of university students by level of study (2009–2010, in per cent)

	Bachelor	Master's[a]	PhD
Farmers (*Agriculteurs*)	1.9	1.6	1.4
Tradespeople, shopkeepers and business owners (*Artisans, commerçants et chefs d'entreprise*)	7.8	6.2	4.7
Freelance professionals and senior executives (*Professions libérales et cadres supérieures*)	28.0	32.7	31.4
Intermediate occupations (*Professions intermédiaires*)	13.1	11.2	8.0
Office workers (*Employés*)	13.5	9.0	6.2
Manual workers (*Ouvriers*)	11.6	6.4	3.6
Pensioners, not into paid work (*Retraités, inactifs*)	12.8	14.0	20.6
Unknown	11.4	18.9	24.2
Total	100.0	100.0	100.0

Note: [a]The IUFM (Instituts Universitaires de Formation des Maîtres), which are teacher education providers, are not included.
Source: Ministère de l'Éducation Nationale (2010).

Table 13.3 Socio-economic background and type of HE track (2009–2010, in per cent)

	Farmers, trades-people, shopkeepers, etc.	Freelance professionals and senior executives	Intermediate occupations	Office workers	Manual workers	Pensioners, not into paid work	Unknown	Total
Universities	8.9	29.7	12.2	11.6	9.4	13.6	14.5	100.0
Of which: general subjects	8.6	29.9	11.9	11.3	9.0	14	15.4	100.0
Of which: IUTs	11.5	28	16.3	15	14.2	9.2	5.8	100.0
STS	11.4	16.3	14.9	17	22.1	13.5	4.9	100.0
CPGE	10.8	51.1	12.9	9.3	6.3	6.4	3.2	100.0
Non-university-based actuary programmes	11.0	15.7	11.6	14.1	14.7	13.6	19.3	100.0
Non-university-based engineering programmes	11.8	48	11.2	6.5	4.6	6.5	11.4	100.0
Business and management schools	14.9	37.9	7.2	6.0	2.2	4.7	27.1	100.0
Ecoles Normales Supérieures	10.8	56.9	9.1	7.1	2.3	7.2	6.6	100.0
Arts and culture schools	11.6	31	10.7	9.3	3.3	5.5	28.5	100.0
Paramedical and social schools	11.9	18.9	12.1	19	17.6	2.1	18.4	100.0
Total	9.8	29.8	12.3	11.9	10.3	11.8	14.0	100.0

Source: Ministère de l'Éducation Nationale (2010).

Patterns of participation in higher education and gender

In France as in other European countries, women's access to HE on a large scale is a relatively recent phenomenon. As reminded in Lécuyer (2005), at the end of the 19th century, the word *étudiante* was used to refer to a young woman in a relationship with a male student (*l'étudiant*). Although the first French university was created during the 12th century, it is only in 1863 that one of these institutions, the Université de Lyon, started accepting women. Although the 1880 Camille Sée Act had created the *lycées de jeunes filles* (girls' upper secondary schools), only a few had access to such institutions, and it was not until after the Léon Bérard Act of 1924 that women were allowed to prepare for the *baccalauréat*. Until then, they only received an end of study certificate (Bard, 2001). Lécuyer recalls that, until 1913, the majority of the women studying at the Université de Paris were not French and came from abroad, in particular from Russia, Romania and Poland (Lécuyer, 2005). Yet, as shown in Table 13.4, by the early 1980s women represented the majority of university students in the country (57.6 per cent in 2009–2010).

Despite the statistical feminisation of the HE student population, some gender imbalances persist. In particular, subject choices remain highly gendered, both at compulsory and post-compulsory school levels. Women are significantly less likely to study sciences and engineering than men and, to a less extent, law and economics, but more likely to study humanities and medicine (Sautory, 2007; Duru-Bellat *et al.*, 2011). Another gender imbalance relates to the level of study. Women represent 56.8 per cent of university undergraduates and an even higher proportion of master's students, yet their proportion drops at the PhD level, where the majority of students are men (52.8 per cent).

Table 13.4 Proportion of women students in universities (in per cent)

Academic year	Proportion of women
1960–1961	42.8
1965–1966	44.0
1970–1971	44.5
1975–1976	47.6
1980–1981	49.8
1985–1986	52.2
1990–1991	54.3
1995–1996	56.3
2000–2001	55.6
2005–2006	56.6
2009–2010	57.6

Source: Ministère de l'Éducation Nationale (2010).

Another form of gender imbalance relates to the type of HE track on which men and women students embark. First, women tend to concentrate in universities rather than in the vocational programmes. They represent 40.2 per cent of IUT students and 51.0 per cent of STS students, compared with 57.6 per cent of the university population. There are, however, strong variations depending on the specialism. For example, in the STS sections, their proportion ranges from 2 per cent (in car mechanic) to 100 per cent (in hairdressing). Second, women are less likely than men to attend the *Classes Préparatoires aux Grandes Ecoles*: only 43 per cent of those doing so are women. Duru-Bellat and colleagues note that entering the CPGE or *Grandes Ecoles* track is mostly determined by previous academic results, but that, all things being equal, women are less likely than men to choose this track (Duru-Bellat *et al.*, 2011). As for IUT, there are major variations depending on the specialism of the CPGE, as well as, to a lesser extent, on the year of study. For example, only 31 per cent of those in science-oriented CPGE are women, compared with 55 per cent of those in economics and business CPGE, and 74 per cent of those in humanities-oriented CPGE. The proportion of women declines slightly (1–3 per cent points) between the first year and the second year. Their presence in the *Grandes Ecoles* tends to vary greatly depending on the specialism, although not to the same extent as can be observed in the IUT and STS. As evidenced in Tables 13.5 and 13.6, women represent only 39 per cent of the *Ecoles Normales Supérieures* population, 40 per cent of *Ecole Nationale d'Administration* students and 14 per cent of the *Ecole Polytechnique* population (these are usually considered to be the most prestigious *Grandes Ecoles*).

Statistics do not merely reflect reality, they also construct it. A key issue is that, in many ways, the production of statistics and indicators evidencing the existence and extent of inequalities, described in this section, is also

Table 13.5 Proportion of women in *Classes Préparatoires aux Grandes Ecoles* and *Grandes Ecoles* (2007–2008, in per cent)

Programme	Proportion of women
Classes Préparatoires aux Grandes Ecoles (CPGE)	43
Of which: science-oriented	30
Of which: economics-oriented	55
Of which: humanities-oriented	75
Ecoles d'Ingénieurs	27
Ecoles de Commerce	48
Ecole Normale Supérieure (ENS)	39
Ecole Nationale d'Administration (ENA)	40
Ecole Polytechnique	14

Source: Ministère de l'Éducation Nationale (2007–2008).

Table 13.6 Proportion of women by subject (2007–2008, in per cent)

	Proportion of women
Humanities	70.9
Medical sciences	61.9
Law and political sciences	64.6
Economics and management	51.2
Administrative sciences	59.8
Physical science	29.8
Life science	58.9
Sport	32.3
IUT	39.4
Total	56.9

Source: Ministère de l'Éducation Nationale (2007–2008).

part of the dominant discourse of WP and the dominant view of citizenship described in the next section. It is those discourses that we now turn to explore.

Research and policy discourses of widening participation

A vast scholarship exploring schools as the site of reproduction of social class divisions has developed in France since the 1960s (see, e.g. Bourdieu and Passeron, 1964, 1970; Baudelot and Establet, 1971). In the most recent period, research on HE and social justice has focused on whether or not the shift to mass education has led to some democratisation of HE. This has been explored mostly through large-scale, longitudinal data sets, going back to the period from after the Second World War and, sometimes, to the early 20th century.

Some, like Thélot and Vallet (2000), have concluded that there is a trend towards the democratisation of French HE. However, a more consensual position is that only a relative democratisation of HE has taken place and that Thélot and Vallet's findings result from a major flaw in their investigation, i.e. that they focused on access to undergraduate studies only. A common view among researchers is that only access to the lower levels of university studies and to the shorter programmes has democratised (Albouy and Tavan, 2007), even though over time, the relationship between socioeconomic backgrounds, and access to the different levels of the HE system seems to have weakened (Duru-Bellat and Kieffer, 2000). Another finding is that the élite tracks (CPGE and *Grandes Ecoles*) have not democratised to the same extent as other tracks and remain highly selective, with some arguing that the social selectivity of some of the *Grandes Ecoles* has even increased (Merle, 1996; Albouy and Wanecq, 2003; Jaoul, 2004; Duru-Bellat *et al.*, 2011).

In the French context, WP has been thought of mostly in relation to socio-economic inequalities, with gender and ethnicity less likely to be considered as legitimate objects of investigation and policy intervention (Moreau, 2011a, b). More recently, however, a number of authors have explored gender inequalities in the context of compulsory and post-compulsory schooling (e.g. Duru-Bellat, 1990; Baudelot-Establet, 1992, 2007; Zaidman, 1996; Mosconi, 1998). Yet, research focusing on gender issues has often been labelled as 'specific', and many sociologists of education continue to ignore the influence of gender at the individual and societal levels in their analysis.

Similar observations can be made at policy level, where most equality concerns in education relate to social class. This French focus on socio-economic inequalities in education has a long history. As documented by Allouch and van Zanten (2010), after the First World War and throughout the 20th century, a range of measures aimed to reduce inequalities of access to secondary schools were implemented. Yet, despite this intervention and formal barriers being broken down, inequalities remained, including in terms of academic performance. In 1981, the permanence of such inequalities led to the creation of the *Zones d'Éducation Prioritaires* (educational priority zones, known as ZEP), with additional resources allocated to the schools based in these areas. In HE, this shift away from the dominant republican paradigm equating fairness with equal treatment came only in the 2000s (ibid.). In 2001, the Institut d'Etudes Politiques (IEP) de Paris (also known as Science Po Paris) established a programme of positive discrimination, through the *Conventions Éducation Prioritaire* (Partnerships in Priority Education). A distinct procedure for entry was created for high school students from the ZEP, who do not sit the standard competitive examination and are recruited on the basis of their academic record and an interview. In 2003, ESSEC (a prestigious business school) launched the programme *Une grande école, pourquoi pas moi?* (literally, 'A Grande Ecole, why not me?'). In 2005, the, also prestigious, Lycée Henri IV, established a *Classe préparatoire aux études supérieures* (Preparatory class for HE) for high school students from deprived backgrounds. These WP initiatives attracted some resistance in a country where, despite their élite status, *Grandes Ecoles* are often seen as meritocratic as they recruit their students through national competitive examinations and criteria, which are perceived as neutral and universal (van Zanten, 2009). Yet, at the end of 2009, over 70 *Grandes Ecoles* had a WP programme in place (Allouch and van Zanten, 2010).

These programmes attracted some critique. As well as being in breach of the republican conception of equality, some have noted that promoting equal opportunities in HE by only targeting *élite* tracks may not be very effective as, by definition, *élite* tracks are quantitatively small (Duru-Bellat and Kieffer, 2008). The same also noted that an earlier intervention at *pre-baccalauréat* level would be useful, before students from working-class backgrounds are diverted from the general *baccalauréat* towards its not-so-well-regarded and less academic professional equivalent. Besides, positive discrimination, in its French form, is resource-based rather than outcome-based (thus, there is no requirement that the actions taken be effective, only for resources to be allocated).

It is also worth noting that positive discrimination actions have only targeted socio-economic groups, rather than gender or ethnic groups. In comparison, gender inequalities and, to an even wider extent, inequalities related to ethnicity, have been perceived as less legitimate areas of intervention. However, in recent years, concerns have been raised regarding gender equality in education. It has led to the publication of a number of regulatory texts, including the 25 February 2000 Interdepartmental Agreement, the 2004 Charter for Equality between Women and Men, and the 2006 Agreement for Equality between Boys and Girls, Men and Women in the school system. These texts and the increasing range of initiatives in this field have aimed to tackle students' gendered subject and career choice in compulsory and post-compulsory schooling, and its later impact on equality between men and women in the labour market. Girls and women have been a particular target of these actions, as they concentrate in a smaller range of subjects and career choices. Training actions, as well as prizes and awards, have been used to encourage girls to pursue science-based careers and to reward the excellence of woman scientists.

Further to the women's liberation movement and the entry of women into HE institutions, gender has increasingly become a legitimate category for research and policy intervention. However, it is worth noting here that other social divisions remain sidelined. One striking example is those of black and minority ethnic students. French statistics do not distinguish between ethnic groups, as concepts of ethnicity and 'race' have been described as opposed to republican principles and, sometimes, as possibly racist (Moreau, 2011a, b). As a result, very little is known about the participation of black and minority ethnic groups in HE, despite evidence that racism is a structural feature of French society (Silverman and Yuval-Davis, 1999). The collection of statistical data on ethnic background is only allowed under very strict conditions, and its relative absence from this chapter can be read as a reflection of this.

Conclusion

This overview shows that the shift to mass HE has opened opportunities for students from groups with no history of HE. However, it also highlights the persistence of classed and gendered patterns of participation. First, differences in overall levels of participation are not a matter of the past. Certainly, women have caught up with men and now represent the majority of HE students. But students from working-class backgrounds remain highly under-represented in HE as a whole. Second, the data examined show that the focus needs to shift from 'who is participating?' to 'who is participating in what?' In many ways, the tracks chosen by students suggest some form of social reproduction, as students from working-class backgrounds are more likely to choose the short, vocational programmes leading to the technical and maybe middle-management occupations, while those from middle-class backgrounds represent the majority of the CPGE and *Grandes Ecoles* population, most likely to lead to executive and senior management positions. The same can be said from women, who, despite their overall performance at school level and their over-representation in HE tend to be under-represented in the *Grandes Ecoles* and, ultimately, concentrate in the less prestigious segments of the labour market (Couppié and Mansuy, 2005; Duru-Bellat *et al.*, 2011). The imbalance by subject is not without its own problems either. Women are much more likely than men to concentrate in humanities subjects, whose returns in the labour market are less certain. Students from working-class backgrounds are also more likely to avoid medicine and law at university, despite the high potential returns of studying these subjects (especially as medicine is the only subject with a *numerus clausus* strictly regulating the number of graduates).

While the inclusion of working-class students and their access to the most advanced and elite segments of the education system have been a topic of interest and concern in French policy-making and research for some time (as exemplified by the work of Pierre Bourdieu), we need to interrogate the relative invisibility of gender and, to a wider extent, ethnicity, within French discourses of WP. The lack of legitimacy of these topics, both in terms of research and policy intervention, can be understood in the context of the French model of citizenship. The French modern state and model of citizenship take their root in republican, universalist and secularist values inspired by the 18th-century philosophy of enlightenment. These values still significantly influence policy intervention, especially in the field of education as a key function of schools and HE institutions is to form citizens. As we noted elsewhere,

In the French republican universalist view of citizenship, access to citizenship is granted on the basis of individuals' *intégration* into the mould of the universal individual. On paper, individuals are given formal equal rights, with equal treatment as the favoured form of equality policies. This concern for equal treatment has been translated into interventionist policies which are usually highly centralised and homogenous, so as to guarantee the equal (same) treatment of citizens across the national territory, although more recently positive discrimination has become a more acceptable form of intervention. According to French values of equalitarism and universalism, it is fair to treat all individuals the same (Planel, 2009) or morally unjustifiable to treat them differently.

(Osborn, 2009; Moreau, 2011b: 170)

Thus, this model has led to some extensive resistance to the acknowledgement of some differences. Its secular nature also implies a strong dichotomy between the public and the private. With educational institutions being associated with the former and gender and ethnicity, as well as religion, being constructed as private matters (contrarily to social class), discussion of gender and ethnicity are sidelined and seen as mostly irrelevant to being a student. Yet, as we have seen, this equalitarian model of citizenship excludes dominated groups from access to the most prestigious segments of the HE system.

Notes

1. It has become increasingly common for IUTs to offer some three- or five-year long vocational programmes, leading to a *licence professionnelle* or a *master professionnel*.
2. The *Instituts Universitaires de Technology* are part of universities but, in this case, are not included in university figures as they were created after 1960 and as the content of these programmes remains very distinct from other university programmes.

Bibliography

Albouy, V. and Tavan, C. (2007) 'Accès à l'enseignement supérieur en France: une démocratisation réelle mais de faible ampleur', *Économie et Statistique*, 410: 3–22.

Albouy, V. and Wanecq, T. (2003) 'Les inégalités sociales d'accès aux grandes écoles', *Économie et Statistique*, 361: 27–52.

Allouch, A. and van Zanten, A. (2010) *The Role of Knowledge in the Elaboration and Instrumentation of Policies of Widening Participation in Higher Education Elite Institutions in FRANCE* (Paris: Observatoire Sociologique du Changement, Sciences Po/CNRS). [online] www. knowandpol.eu/IMG/pdf/o22.franceeducation.pdf. [accessed 26 June 2012].

Bard, C. (2001) *Les Femmes dans la société française au vingtième siècle* (Paris: Armand Colin).

Baudelot, C. and Establet, R. (2007) *Quoi de neuf chez les filles?* (Paris: Nathan).

Baudelot, C. and Establet, R. (1992) *Allez les filles!* (Paris: Le Seuil).

Baudelot, C. and Establet, R. (1971) *L'école capitaliste en France* (Paris: Maspero).

Bourdieu, P. (1998) *La Domination masculine* (Paris: Le Seuil).

Bourdieu, P. (1989) *La noblesse d'Etat: Grandes écoles et esprit de corps* (Paris: Les Editions de Minuit).

Bourdieu, P. (1979) *La distinction* (Paris: Minuit).

Bourdieu, P. and Passeron, J.C. (1970) *La reproduction: Eléments d'une théorie du système d'enseignement* (Paris: Les Editions de Minuit).

Bourdieu, P. and Passeron, J.C. (1964) *Les héritiers* (Paris: Les Editions de Minuit).

Couppié, T. and Mansuy, M. (2005) 'L'insertion professionnelle des débutants en Europe: des situations contrastées', *Économie et Statistique*, 378–379: 147–165.

Crompton, R. (1989) 'Class Theory and Gender', *The British Journal of Sociology*, 40 (4): 565–587.

Deer, C. (2003) 'La politique d'accès à l'enseignement supérieur. Comparaison entre France et Grande-Bretagne', *Agone*, 29–30: 99–120.

Duru-Bellat, M. (1990) *L'école des filles: Quelle formation pour quelles rôles sociaux?* (Paris: L'Harmattan).

Duru-Bellat, M. and Kieffer, A. (2008) 'Du baccalauréat à l'enseignement supérieur: déplacement et recomposition des inégalités', *Population*, 63 (1): 123–157.

Duru-Bellat, M. and Kieffer, A. (2000) 'La démocratisation de l'enseignement en France: polémiques autour d'une question d'actualité', *Population*, 55 (1): 51–80.

Duru-Bellat, M., Kieffer, A. and Reimer, D. (2011) 'Les inégalités d'accès à l'enseignement supérieur: le rôle des filières et des spécialités. Une comparaison entre l'Allemagne de l'Ouest et la France', *Economie et Statistique*, 433–434: 3–22.

INSEE (2004) *Enquêtes annuelles de recensement de 2004 à 2006* [online] http://www.insee.fr/fr/themes/document.asp?ref_id=ip1117&reg_id=0 [accessed 22 July 2011].

Jaoul, M. (2004) 'Enseignement supérieur et origine sociale en France: étude statistique des inégalités depuis 1965', *Revue international de l'éducation*, 50 (5–6): 463–482.

Lécuyer, C. (2005) 'Une nouvelle figure de la jeune fille sous la IIIᵉ République: l'étudiante', *Clio*, 4. [online] http://clio.revues.org/index437.html [accessed 15 July 2011].

Merle, P. (1996) 'Les transformations sociodémographiques des filières de l'enseignement supérieur de 1985 à 1995. Essai d'interprétation', *Population*, 51 (6): 1181–1210.

Ministère de l'Éducation Nationale (2010) *Repères et références statistiques sur les enseignements, la formation et la recherche* [online] http://media.education.gouv.fr/file/2010/73/9/6_Les_etudiants_151739.pdf [accessed 15 June 2011].

Ministère de l'Éducation Nationale (2008) *Repères et références statistiques sur les enseignements, la formation et la recherche* (Paris: Ministère de l'Éducation Nationale).

Moreau, M.P. (2011a) *Les enseignants et le genre* (Paris: Presses Universitaires de France).

Moreau, M.P. (2011b) 'The Societal Construction of "Boys" Underachievement' in Educational Policies: A Cross-National Comparison', *Journal of Education Policy*, 26 (2): 161–180.

Mosconi, N. (1998) 'Réussite scolaire des filles et des garçons et socialisation différentielle des sexes à l'école', *Recherches Féministes*, 11 (1): 7–18.

Osborn, M. (2009) 'Être élève en Angleterre et en France', *Revue internationale d'éducation*, 50: 87–98.

Planel, C. (2009) 'Les pratiques de classe, partie émergée de l'iceberg des valeurs culturelles', *Revue Internationale d'Éducation*, 50: 75–86.

Sautory, O. (2007) 'La démocratisation de l'enseignement supérieur: évolution comparée des caractéristiques sociodémographiques des bacheliers et des étudiants', *Éducation et Formation*, 74: 49–64.

Savage, M. (2000) *Class Analysis and Social Transformation* (Milton Keynes: Open University Press).

Shavit, Y., Arum, R. and Gamoran, A. (eds) (2007) *Stratification in Higher Education: A Comparative Study* (Palo Alto, CA: Stanford University Press).

Silverman, M. and Yuval-Davis, N. (1999) 'Jews, Arabs and the Theorisation of Racism in Britain & France', in Brah, A., Hickman, M. and Mac an Ghaill, M. (eds) *Thinking Identities: Ethnicity, Racism and Culture* (London: Macmillan, pp. 25–48).

Thélot, C. and Vallet, L.A. (2000) 'La réduction des inégalités sociales devant l'école depuis le début du siècle', *Économie et Statistique*, 334: 3–32.

Zaidman, C. (1996) *La mixité à l'école primaire* (Paris: L'Harmattan).

van Zanten, A. (2009) 'The Sociology of Elite Education', in Apple, M., Ball, S. and Gandin, L.A. (eds) *International Handbook of the Sociology of Education* (London/New York: Routledge) pp. 329–339.

14
Widening Participation in Spanish Higher Education: Will the Current Reform Promote the Inclusion of Non-Traditional Students?

M. Teresa Padilla-Carmona

Introduction

The Bologna process aims to create a European Higher Education Area that will facilitate mobility and prepare students for their future careers and life, offering broad access to high-quality higher education (HE). In Spain, this process has meant a progressive and deep reform for universities, which affects not only the structure and profile of degrees but also teaching and assessment methods. The implications of Bologna go beyond the structural and didactic shift and call for the improvement of the social conditions of students, highlighting the importance of widening the participation of disadvantaged groups. Over recent years, the value of widening participation (WP) in HE has been stressed by highlighting the social and economic benefits for individuals, communities and nations (Merrill and González-Monteagudo, 2010). Besides the instrumental benefits of earning more or getting a better job, participation in education contributes to personal development, identity, family and community life, social networks and citizenship (Archer *et al.*, 2003).

Spain cannot avoid the WP agenda in HE, and its university institutions face the challenge that these politics and measures imply for the promotion of lifelong learning. As we near the end of Bologna reforms, it is necessary to review whether recent WP measures have been complemented with other mechanisms targeted to improve the social conditions of study, particularly those of the most disadvantaged students. The alternative possibility is that widening access measures answer to more self-interested aims by the HE sector – attracting new student groups when the demand of 'traditional students' is decreasing every year – and are primarily a matter of political opportunism. This leads us not only to review relevant policy, practice and the support system offered to students but also to understand non-traditional students' daily lives at university, their needs and specific proposals to improve their study experience.

Non-traditional students in Spanish universities

Literature on HE in Spain has paid little attention to the importance of developing understanding of the experience of university students. Beyond basic socio-demographic profiles and specific aspects such as the needs of disabled students, or the factors related to dropout, there is a huge lack of information about cultural and cognitive characteristics of students (Ariño *et al.*, 2008).

For instance, the term 'non-traditional students' is scarcely used in the Spanish context to refer to the ever-increasing non-conventional populations coming into HE. This lack of discussion of the groups' experience, added to the in-existence of official records on their characteristics, shows the invisibility of the students, both for those in charge of decision making and regulations, and for those researching in the field – an 'invisible majority' (McNair, 1998) if we consider the data we are presenting here.

Other related terms have occasionally filled the gap of more direct recognition of non-traditional students. Thus, *mayor de 25* (older than 25, mature) is the most frequently used term, referring to those who enter university via an access route designed for this age group: in Spain since 1971, applicants without admission qualifications can enter HE via an entrance examination. This entrance examination is only open to those 25 years old or more.

'Disabled' is also commonly used to describe all students with special needs. However, other circumstances, such as having a low educational and/or socio-economic background, being the first generation in the family to access HE, or having family commitments, do not exist as categories of non-traditional students in Spain. Hence, not being named, students with these characteristics are included in the general mass of students, regardless of the differences they might present.

According to Eurostudent (2008), 38 per cent of Spanish students are aged 25 years or older, in comparison with the European Union (EU) average of 34 per cent. This has been an ever-increasing trend during the last 10 years, as the age structure in graduate and postgraduate programmes has significantly changed, and the number of people under 30 years has doubled while the percentage of students below 25 has dropped 10 points since 1999–2000 (MEC, 2011). Thus, the number of traditional students accessing HE is decreasing, and this trend will continue in coming years (Angoitia and Rahona, 2007). The high percentage of mature students is seen as a direct consequence of the aforementioned special route of access. Other relevant features of non-traditional students in Spain are the following (Eurostudent, 2008; MEC, 2011):

1.9 per cent of students feel impaired in their studies by disability.

4.1 per cent of students have dependent children.

4.1 of graduate students come from overseas. Most of them (45.6 per cent) come from Latin America and the Caribes, but also from EU27 (30.7 per cent) and North Africa (7.4 per cent).

The percentage of students from a disadvantaged social background, according to parents' educational level, is 28.37 (father) and 33.85 (mother), and 3.5 per cent of students have parents with low incomes.

According to this data, a significant percentage of Spanish university students are seen to be non-traditional. For example, taking only age as a criterion, over one-third of students are mature, as well as almost 30 per cent coming from families with low levels of education. Given that existing statistics are scarce and limited – for example, only accounting for students of other nationalities but not those from other ethnic groups – they show a high percentage of university participation by non-traditional students, and more importantly, an upward trend in recent years.

However, statistics on dropout and continuation of studies provide little or no account of the rate of retention of non-traditional students, and the sparse existing data from international studies do not consider sociodemographic characteristics. According to Eurostat (2009), the completion rate in Spain is 74 per cent. This figure decreases drastically in the case of students of 25 or more years whose parents have low educational background, only 20 per cent of whom have completed tertiary education. This percentage is somewhat higher than the average EU (17 per cent for EU-25).

The most significant legal contribution to access policy is specified in the university access regulations (RD 558/2010 and RD 1892/2008). This is one valuable development in the establishment of some level of positive discrimination to improve access to university for traditionally disadvantaged groups, reserving a certain percentage of places in courses leading to official degrees. Some of the advancements that this regulation implies are as follows:

First, it unifies previously dispersed concessions into a single legal body.

It balances the access requirements for high school and vocational education students, in cases of high demand degrees. While high school students had to complete the entrance examination to access HE, vocational students were granted a reserve of 30 per cent of places. In certain degrees, the number of places applied for by students is greater than the number of places offered, and the different access conditions inform a slight advantage for vocational students.

It also expands the non-traditional routes to access to university by creating two new ones: access for people over 40 years – for which only professional experience is required – and for people over 45 years – for which an entrance examination is required.

Finally, the system provides a special reserve of 5 per cent of places for disabled students.

Some data offer estimation of the high demand for these new routes for mature students. For example, in 2010, 31,033 students were enrolled in the entrance examination for over 25-year-olds – 18.7 per cent more than the previous year, and 5,404 students carried out the first stage of the exam for the over 45-years route. Almost 60 per cent of both groups passed. Regarding those over 40 years, there is no available data on the number of students using this route, although the system specifies a maximum of 3 per cent of the university places to be reserved for them.

Despite the increasing volume they represent, there remain few studies that have delved into the characteristics of mature students in Spain. The vast majority of them enrol in social science degrees, and some surveys (Bermejo *et al.*, 2011) – working with non-representative samples – found a dropout rate of approximately 22 per cent, highlighting problems including the difficulty of combining paid work and studies, lack of effective study habits and the perception of a lower level of skills compared with younger peers.

In general, these students seem to have a more responsible attitude towards study and know better what they want and how to go about achieving this (Zabalza, 2004). However, they complain that teachers often do not acknowledge their presence in class, and, thus, their previous experience can rarely be drawn on in class (Adiego *et al.*, 2004).

Regarding social class, many Spanish academics do not perceive it as an important issue, despite evidence that university students bring with them structural factors related to their family origin, which impact degree choice, and the length of time spent to complete a degree (Solano *et al.*, 2004). It is sometimes supposed that, after having entered HE, there is equality among students, regardless of their social or family backgrounds (González-Monteagudo and Ballesteros-Moscosio, 2011). The main supposition informing this perspective is that students with fewer economic resources will have access to grants and financial support and that this is all they need to access university.

As to disabled students, some researchers (Castellana and Salas, 2005; Moriña, 2011) have focused on their particular needs, finding that teaching staff are perceived as the main barrier to participation, mainly due to inflexible attitudes and non-inclusive methodologies used in lectures. For this reason, commentators point to the need to provide specific training to teachers to address special needs effectively (Sánchez-Palomino, 2009).

A recent OECD report (Santiago *et al.*, 2009) suggested that little emphasis is placed on student progression through tertiary studies, with little special support or follow-up measures to assist those students who experience more difficulties. There is little evidence that students' progress is closely followed by teachers and that students for whom a disadvantaged background has been identified receive any particular attention.

Thus, policy emphasis in Spain has mostly focused on the expansion of overall enrolment while limited attention has been paid on the socio-economic background of students and widening access to HE (Santiago *et al.*, 2009). In addition, neither researchers nor theorists have paid attention to this ever-increasing group, and when they have, they tend to focus their interest on specific sub-populations (most notably, mature and disabled students). As a consequence, we lack detailed, in-depth information about how non-traditional students in Spain progress through university, what needs they present, what they demand from university institutions, or even, how they experience their daily lives on campus.

Exploring the needs and experiences of non-traditional students in the University of Seville

This is the first attempt to document the experiences of non-traditional students in Spain. Our research has been carried out at the University of Seville, and while its results cannot be generalised nation-wide, there are common patterns in most public HE institutions in Spain that credit broad transferability to the results.

A narrative approach is known to be effective in providing insights into complex and contextualised student experiences (Benson *et al.*, 2010). Written narratives were collected from 23 participants who were studying different degrees. Several criteria were taken into account in order to select or invite the respondents representing different groups of non-traditional students including 25 years old or more, disabled, low socio-economic background, family commitments, first-generation university students and other nationalities or ethnic groups. In addition to these criteria, students representing different degrees were selected.

The participants were given several topics to write about, including family background, school paths, access and adaptation to university, teaching and teachers, institutional environment, personal and educational identity, future motivations and suggestions to improve the situation of non-traditional students at the university. Each topic presented a guide of possible questions to consider but only as suggestions to foster inspiration. Respondents were encouraged to write in as much detail as possible about their experiences, opinions and needs.

The analysis of the stories showed a wide range of life experiences, and it became difficult to identify common patterns. What follow are initial observations in advance of more extensive analysis. To preserve anonymity, each participant chose a pseudonym, which appears in brackets at the end of the quotes.

The daily experience at campus

High lecture attendance is one of the most common patterns among non-traditional students, and it is considered by individuals as key to learning. Taking notes, asking for further explanation of concepts that are difficult to understand, participating and giving their opinions, help them to optimise their personal study:

> I need to attend lectures to understand the subject, if I don't attend, I feel I'm missing something.
>
> (Magister)

> I always attend 99.99 per cent of the lectures; if I miss one, it is really due to something serious.
>
> (Ananda)

However, tutorials (which are normally held individually or in small groups at the teacher's desk) are not considered as important as lectures and only a few students indicate using this resource. When they do attend, tutorials tend to be regarded as a problem-solving device and not as a mechanism for guiding their own learning:

> I haven't made much use of tutorials, I haven't had doubts to resolve through them.
>
> (Emma)

The use of tutorials is important to establish different kinds of relationships with teachers, but only one student demonstrated perceiving the full usefulness of tutorials.

> It's different, attending lectures involves listening to the lesson, making comments about what has been explained, doing activities...but going to tutorials is more direct...the relation between student and teacher..., one tutorial where you can talk about all the areas within certain limits, the tutor can help you, he [sic] can advice you, he can guide you...
>
> (Lidia)

The general trend in lecturers is delivering theoretical, non-participative teaching, almost exclusively based on taking notes. Non-traditional students have to adapt to this style, and if they cannot attend lectures, they have to rely on asking other students for their notes in order to pass exams:

> A typical day at the campus is...attending lectures, taking notes and listening to the teachers; only two or three teachers use a different dynamic

in class, in which we are the ones who talk most of the time, students, but overall we are still in school, where it is the teacher who gives the lesson.

(Lidia)

Good time-planning skills are very important for students to be successful. They spend many hours in lectures, but they also have to dedicate daily time to study and to do the practical tasks teachers usually set, many of which require teamwork. Taking into account that many of them need one hour or more to commute to campus, and some others have children and/or work responsibilities, they have long working days and need to plan and manage their time as best as possible:

I wake up around six in the morning everyday, and I end my working day at the campus about 9 pm

(Isabel)

I often make schedules to organise my time

(María)

As a result of the Bologna process, more and more teachers set practical assignments, which require teamwork. Although this is considered more enriching than individual assignments, teamwork raises new complications in non-traditional students' daily management of time, as well as requiring development of social skills that make that teamwork effective and fair:

When carrying out assignments, it's harder for me doing them in groups, because I don't think my mates really get involved the way and degree I would like them to.

(Hernán)

Personally, it usually takes me much more time to do the assignments than to study, and it is not because we don't have to study, but because those projects absorb much of my time.

(MJ)

Despite the difficulties posed by teamwork, most of the participants indicated a preference for this type of assignment, because it is perceived as more satisfying and allows learning from peers:

With regard to the subjects in which teamwork is used I have to say I have learned much more than in traditional lectures where there is no such relationship among students.

(Cristi)

Relationships with teachers

Participants' discussion of their relationships with teachers is limited to generalised aspects, providing only limited insight into their experience of these relationships. Non-traditional students do not expect special treatment, so when their non-traditional status remains unnoticed, individuals describe feeling that their teachers connect 'well' with them as they receive a 'normal' treatment.

> I don't think they treat me in a different way to that of my mates
>
> (Emma)

Where all classes consist of lectures, and there is no participation by the students, some feel unable to ask questions:

> Lecturers used a more advanced, more 'professional' language. New concepts, new vocabulary...I didn't want to interrupt them and ask what those words meant in front of hundreds of people, I became shy...
>
> (Alvarittocrack)

It seems, therefore, that non-traditional students avoid drawing attention to themselves in front of the teacher and fellow-students as being 'special' or different. However, when students do reveal their non-traditional status or this is directly observable – for example, in the case of mature students and some disabled students, some teachers showed sympathy and, in some cases, provided more flexible models to help students meet the requirements of the course.

> So far, I have found great support from the teachers since I re-entered university, finding in them some sympathy for the times in which my responsibilities prevented me from attending classes.
>
> (Man)

> Most of them understand and appreciate my situation, but obviously they cannot demand from me less than what they ask the others...
>
> (Mjose)

As evidenced in the quote from Mjose, some students believe that the academic context should be 'neutral' and not promote positive discrimination. Others feel that more flexible arrangements should be considered, but:

> always showing equity and applying the same criteria...so that there is no preferential treatment for anyone.
>
> (AlvarittoCrack)

Such views may result from common assumptions in the institutional culture, in some cases transmitted by teachers, that university requirements are the same for everyone, and it is the student who must adapt, no exceptions can be made.

Support

Government grants and part-time employment, as well as careful budgeting, are central for non-traditional students with low incomes. In Spain, this means that low-income students are impelled to attain good marks because, if they do not, they lose the right to grants:

> So, I'm hoping for the grant to come this year to save and to pay at least the first university registration fees, then I will have to work to continue paying for them by myself.
>
> (Noa)

The main sources of support cited by non-traditional students are family, spouse or partner, and classmates. This support takes different forms: providing motivation, helping economically and offering technical assistance to complete assignments (for example, assisting building concept-maps, power points and so on). Other research has also found that students value the importance of family and peer support (Wilcox *et al.*, 2005; Baptista *et al.*, 2010; Fleming *et al.*, 2010; Moriña, 2011).

> The relationship with my classmates ... is very important to me. We have become a family.
>
> (Yria)

It is very important to understand the role of family support in the context of Spanish culture. Young people tend to become independent at a later age, and also family support in critical situations explains how the Spanish economy and social system are surviving in this time of crisis and unemployment (20.89 per cent) according to the last Active Population Survey (Instituto Nacional de Estadística, 2011). When Spanish students discuss family and partner support, they reflect on the multiple ways they receive help from loved ones – not only the economic contribution, of course, but also help in looking after their own children to facilitate university attendance to class and encouragement during hard times.

Two main patterns of support are given by family, which relate to socio-economic background. In working-class families in which no other member has attended HE, the conception of education as a key pathway to social mobility prevails. The kind of support these families tend to offer is motivational, passing the importance of going to university on to their children 'to be someone with a future', which it is at times done in an authoritarian manner, like an obligation:

> Since my brother and I were young, our parents have instilled us with the significance of studies, and they have shown us they were working hard so that we could study and have a good future.... Moreover, sometimes my father was very authoritarian on this topic.
>
> (Cristi)

In contrast, in middle-class families, the importance of going to university is not something parents have to instil, given that they themselves frequently have HE qualifications, and they hence do not even question that their children will do the same. In these families, the support given is more 'instrumental': introducing children to culture, helping with homework, and providing books:

> My parents have influenced my learning, my father is an educated man and he likes talking about interesting topics, my mother helps me with my studies and she tries to motivate me and my brothers.
>
> (Carlos)

However, in some cases, family does not provide support and even becomes a constant source of trouble that prevents students from achieving higher attainment. One reason indicated for this is the louder call for attention by the more pressing issue of earning a living:

> My mother hardly asks me anything about it, because I think that she doesn't know what to ask about and she also has her mind on other, more important things... My father hardly ever knows what I'm studying.
>
> (Noa)

Discussion of support from outside the family by non-traditional students focuses on grants and other financial aid, as well as the classmates with whom they develop mutual help strategies:

> I was lucky to meet in first year a fellow student who is also non-traditional, and, as a consequence of her disability she deals with study in the same way than me. Since then, we have made a team.
>
> (MJosé)

> If I have an academic problem, there is always a fellow student that helps me and gives me advice.
>
> (Isabel)

University-provided support services did not emerge as an important source of support. Comments on such support came in response to a specific question and indicated that these services are not considered as a central source of support for study. The most surprising fact about non-traditional students' experience of universities' social and support services is their lack of knowledge about them:

> I use only few services, I better say none, because I do not know them; if we were given more information, maybe I would use them more.
>
> (Lidia)

> Above all, I would highlight the importance of providing information, because I'm so lost right now in some issues, like postgraduate option, the job opportunities of my degree...
>
> (María)

It would therefore seem that the support services offered by the university are failing in their objective, as they are not reaching the students who could benefit from them most. This may be the result of a 'remedial' policy from which such support services are offered as problem-solving devices, rather than delivered with a more preventive, needs assessment-based approach.

Resilience of non-traditional students

Traumatic personal situations emerged from the stories told by some of the non-traditional students: seven out of the 23 had suffered either family abuse, long periods of severe illness, extreme poverty or stress around gaining acceptance of their sexual identity amongst family and friends. But in these individuals, as in nearly all of the 23, a general attitude of resilience appears deeply rooted. Thus, in spite of encountering acutely challenging situations, these students did not question their intention to continue their degrees, setting up many strategies to resist and overcome difficulties in order to achieve their goals:

> One of the severest crises I have experienced at university was in the second year, when I didn't pass any subjects; this brought about a drop in my motivation, for a long time, I thought about giving up the degree. But I have always considered myself to be a girl who has fought very hard for what she wanted and I decided to keep trying, and that was right, the next year I passed everything.
>
> (Yria)

All respondents showed a high motivation to study at university despite the setbacks they encountered, and all of them were clear that their determination was the most important factor for them to continue their studies. Their ultimate belief in the potential for success is evidenced by their refusal to give up, and persistence in doing everything necessary to fulfil their goals. Similar studies (Murphy and Roopchand, 2003; González-Monteagudo, 2010a,b) have also highlighted the significance of personal initiative and eagerness to overcoming problems in order to develop successful learning careers.

> I've tried to not let these problems affect my degree, and I think I managed it, because I have passed all the subjects in the 1st and 2nd year with good marks, but it is very hard studying in a hospital or at the door of the intensive care unit, trying to keep your mind clear to study, having so many family and health problems, it's difficult and very complicated to also do well in the university.
>
> (Magister)

> Difficulties? Architectural barriers. I have been asking for the adaptation of the building for four years at university but they haven't done it [...]. I've been asking for building works for years but I am not being listened to. One time out of man, I went to complain about the lifts, the help they gave me was: 'we can give you a stick to press the buttons' [...] I am not going to stop until I get the building adapted, maybe it will happen by the last year of my degree, but, at least, it will be there for others in my situation.
>
> (Yria)

These findings lead us to question traditional notions of failure and dropout in HE, particularly considering that some participants described previous unsuccessful attempts at HE study. Some had begun studying other degrees but left after discovering that they were not what they had expected, as found by Cabrera *et al.* (2006). As suggested by Thunborg *et al.* (2011), dropping out is not always what it seems, as the system allows individuals to make alterations to their learner pathways; students' educational trajectories develop as they proceed through their life course. Thus, beyond finishing the degree successfully, participants speak of their desire to improve their capacity to stay afloat despite their circumstances, which in some cases leads to a higher performance in university than that of previous educational stages:

> Since I've been back at the university, my academic results have been outstanding, and I think that's due to the high motivation and joy I feel being able to complete my studies, and it's also due to the wonderful group of people I've met in my class
>
> (Man)

Challenges for Spanish higher education students

Many non-traditional students at university remain unnoticed, partly because they often do not want to be considered different to their fellow students. In many cases, they live and study under distinct conditions that are completely unknown by teachers. In addition, the way in which classes are delivered and the type of relationship often established between teachers and students does not help to identify their needs. Even when these needs are identified, a call for the need for 'neutrality' in university provision is often made, both by students and teachers.

There are many proposals for action suggested by non-traditional students that HE institutions should begin to consider if their commitment to the democratisation of the university goes beyond simply providing access. The insights provided by non-traditional students in this research can be summed up in one word: flexibility. This flexibility must begin with the timetables for classes and tutorials. Intensive course options during weekends or at night time are not currently provided.

> I also believe that there should be an adaptation of tutorials and revision sessions to the needs of students, as teachers do tutorials without taking into account our availability.
>
> (Noa)

In addition, the mandatory attendance requirement that most HE teachers in Spain set should be reconsidered. Current legislation determines that attendance is not mandatory, so that, theoretically, students can achieve a degree even with low attendance. However, in practice, there are different assessment systems for those who attend lectures and those who do not. While the former can opt for assessment based on the completion of practical work – the option preferred by the majority of students – exams are the only means of assessment for the latter group. This generates two separate sets of learning and assessment: one that consists of studying the contents that teachers provide in their course materials and sitting an exam on this material, and another that, while in some cases includes examinations, focuses on the carrying out of one or more practical projects with the support of teachers in practical classes and a potentially more formative assessment. There is a clear need to develop the assessment system for non-lecture-attending students to ensure greater standardisation with the alternative that attracts them most – practical work.

Finally, the flexibility required by non-traditional students should inform greater openness to other forms of knowledge and skills beyond what is traditionally considered as 'academic knowledge':

> I think some teachers should be more open to the contributions of foreign students and not only refer us to their texts and books to explain the contents, because just in this diversity of opinions lays [*sic*] the enrichment of the class and, therefore, of the study program.
>
> (Ananda)

Non-traditional students need to feel that they have something valuable to contribute and that they can bring their own life or work experience to bear on topics covered in classroom discussions (Bamber, 2010). Further, as suggested by Ridley (2004), academic staff in an HE institution must question whether expectations are fair and reasonable, whether dominant ideologies should be changed, and in what ways it is possible to learn from and build bridges with the different learning cultures students bring with them. This is a matter of attempting to break down the barriers that we experience through the separation we make between 'them' – the students – and 'us' – the academics (Coronel, 2006).

In general, we understand that the most significant change to be addressed by Spanish universities to promote the integration of non-traditional students is simply the actual and effective implementation of an active teaching-learning methodology based on student autonomy and the supervisory role of the teacher. This summarises most of the contributions of Bologna and, practically, means reducing the emphasis on traditional lectures progressively, in favour of greater student participation, properly addressed and monitored through tutorials. Although tutorials are a key element in any educational model based on learning, the truth is that there is great disparity in their development and use.

Tutorials can realise a vision for more personalised instruction, specifically based on the teacher–student relationship. As shown in the students' accounts, it is necessary to strengthen the channels of communication between students and teachers. However, in the assessment of the methodological renewal that is taking place after the implementation of the Bologna requirements, tutorials are the aspect that received the lowest rating by students (MEC, 2006).

It is clear that tutorials are under-utilised due to several reasons: first, a tendency for the teacher to offer them or to take a passive, minimal approach – expecting students to come to their office to ask about doubts. Second, perhaps as a reflection of this approach, students do not see tutorials as a useful instrument for learning. Moreover, the greater intimacy and student focus of tutorials compared with lectures may pose an increased and un-welcome risk of exposing non-traditional students' status to teachers and fellow students, threatening the desire of many not to be perceived as 'different' to their peers. HE policies must be reinforced to challenge assumptions by both teachers and students of tutorials as peripheral to the university learning experience and to assert their central role as a device for guiding and advising.

Likewise, given that peer support appears to be a cornerstone for non-traditional students and possibly for all students, strategies based on peer mentoring may be particularly useful. Peer mentoring has proved to be an effective tool to support first-year students' transition into university (Rísquez *et al.*, 2007–2008; Abbate-Vaughn, 2008). The skills developed by students further along their academic journeys to successfully overcome adverse situations are a valuable resource to support the transition to university in new students who may be dealing with similar circumstances. In recent years, some Spanish universities have developed guidance programmes based on peer mentoring (Sánchez-García *et al.*, 2011), which have demonstrated a significant impact. However, budgetary constraints of the current crisis are leading to cuts to funds for such projects despite their evident success.

In conclusion, there continues to be insufficient evidence that Spanish universities are investing sufficient resources in widening access for non-traditional students, indicating that the WP agenda in Spain remains, to a considerable extent, primarily restricted to being part of a hypocritical political discourse, rooted more firmly in opportunism rather than reality. The feasibility of a real shift in practices may be hampered by the reliance on cultural change amongst those who are part of the institutions: teachers, with their ideas about their own function and what constitutes valid knowledge in the university, and students, traditionally 'recipients' of this process of cultural exchange. Of course, cultural changes are not made through decrees and require time, but one way to initiate them is through opening the university to increasingly valuing diversity in the backgrounds and experiences students bring to university.

Bibliography

Abbate-Vaughn, J. (2008) 'Admisión, apoyo y retención de estudiantes no tradicionales en carreras universitarias', *Revista Iberoamericana sobre Calidad, Eficacia y Cambio en Educación*, 6: 7–36.

Adiego, V., Asensio, S. and Serrano, M.A. (2004) *Transformando espacios: el aprendizaje de estudiantes no tradicionales en la educación superior*. Paper Presented at the VIII Congreso Español de Sociología, Alicante, Spain, 23–25 September.

Angoitia, M. and Rahona, M. (2007) 'Evolución de la educación universitaria en España: diferentes perspectivas y principales tendencias (1991-2005)', *Revista de Educación*, 344: 245–264.

Archer, L., Hutchings, M. and Ros, A. (2003) *Higher Education and Social Class. Issues of Exclusion and Inclusion* (London: Routledge).

Ariño, A., Hernández, M., Llopis, R., Navarro, B. and Tejerina, B. (2008) *El oficio de estudiar en la Universidad: compromisos flexibles* (Valencia: Universitat de València).

Bamber, T. (2010) 'Toward a Sufficiency Model in Teaching Non-Traditional Students', in Merrill, B. and González-Monteagudo, J. (eds) *Educational Journeys and Changing Lives* (Seville: Digital@Tres).

Baptista, A.V., Santos, L., Bessa, J. and Tavares, J. (2010) 'The Journey of Non-traditional Students at the University of Aveiro', in Merrill, B. and González-Monteagudo, J. (eds) *Educational Journeys and Changing Lives. Adult Student Experience* (Seville: Digital@Tres).

Benson, R., Hewitt, L., Heagney, M., Devos, A. and Crosling, G. (2010) 'Diverse Pathways into Higher Education: Using Students' Stories to Identify Transformative Experiences', *Australian Journal of Adult Learning*, 50: 26–53.

Bermejo, B., Camacho, L.M., Fernández-Batanero, J.M. and García-Lázaro, I. (2011) *The Academic Study of Non-traditional Students at the University of Seville*. Paper Presented at RANLHE Conference on Access and Retention: Experiences of Non-traditional Learners in Higher Education, Seville, Spain, 7–8 April.

Cabrera, L., Bethencourt, J.T., González-Alfonso, M. and Álvarez-Pérez, P. (2006) 'Un estudio transversal retrospectivo sobre prolongación y abandono de estudios universitarios', *Revista Electrónica de Investigación y Evaluación Educativa*, 12: 105–127.

Castellano, M. and Salas, I. (2005) *Estudiantes con discapacidad en aulas universitarias*. Paper presented at I Congreso Nacional de Universidad y Discapacidad, Salamanca, Spain, 24–25 November.

Coronel, J.M. (2006) 'Technologies of Disciplinary Power in Action: The Norm of the "Good Student"', *Higher Education*, 55: 665–686.

EUROSTAT (2009) *The Bologna Process in Higher Education in Europe. Key Indicators on the Social Dimension and Mobility* [online] http://epp.eurostat.ec.europa.eu/cache/ITY_OFFPUB/KS-78-09-653/EN/KS-78-09-653-EN.PDF [accessed 26 June 2012].

Eurostudent (2008) *Social and Economic Conditions of Student Life in Europe* [online] http://www.eurostudent.eu/download_files/members/Spain.pdf [accessed 26 June 2012].

Fleming, T., Loxley, A., Kenny, A. and Finnegan, F. (2010) *Where Next? A Study of Work and Life Experiences of Mature Students (Incl. Disadvantaged) in Three Higher Education Institutions* (Ireland: Combat Poverty Agency).

González-Monteagudo, J. (2010a) 'Learning Careers of Poor University Students in the Dominican Republic: Cultural, Institutional and Personal Dimensions', in Merrill, B. and González-Monteagudo, J. (eds) *Educational Journeys and Changing Lives. Adult Student Experience* (Seville: Digital@Tres).

González-Monteagudo, J. (2010b) 'Biografía, identidad y aprendizaje en estudiantes universitarios no tradicionales. Estudio de caso de una mujer trabajadora', *Revista de Curriculum y Formacion del Profesorado*, 14: 131–147.

González-Monteagudo, J. and Ballesteros-Moscosio, M.A. (2011) *Social and Cultural Dimensions of Higher Education as Contexts to Understand Non-traditional Students*. Paper Presented at RANLHE Conference on Access and Retention: Experiences of non-traditional learners in Higher Education, Seville, Spain, 7–8 April.

Instituto Nacional de Estadística (2011) *Encuesta de población activa. Segundo trimestre de 2011* [online] http://www.ine.es/daco/daco42/daco4211/epa0211.pdf [accessed 26 June 2012].

McNair, S. (1998) 'The Invisible Majority: Adult Learners in English Higher Education', *Higher Education Quarterly*, 52: 162–178.

Merrill, B. and González-Monteagudo, J. (2010) 'Introduction to Educational Journeys and Changing Lives', in Merrill, B. and González-Monteagudo, J. (eds) *Educational Journeys and Changing Lives* (Seville: Digital@Tres).

Ministerio de Educación y Ciencia (2011) *Datos y cifras del sistema universitario español* [online] http://www.educacion.es/dctm/ministerio/educacion/universidades/esta disticas-informes/novedades/2011-datos-cifras-10-uv.pdf?documentId=0901e72b 809384a4 [accessed 26 June 2012]

Ministerio de Educación y Ciencia (2006) *Propuestas para la renovación de las metodologías docentes* (Madrid: Subdirección General de Informes y Publicaciones).

Moriña, A. (2011) *Barriers and Aids in the University: A Study from the Perspective of Students with Disabilities*. Paper Presented at RANLHE Conference on Access and Retention: Experiences of Non-traditional Learners in Higher Education, Seville, Spain, 7–8 April.

Murphy, H. and Roopchand, N. (2003) 'Intrinsic Motivation and Self-Esteem in Traditional and Mature Students at a Post-1992 University in the North-East of England', *Educational Studies*, 29: 243–259.

Ridley, D. (2004) 'Puzzling Experiences in Higher Education: Critical Moments for Conversation', *Studies in Higher Education*, 29: 91–107.

Risquez, A., Moore, S. and Morley, M. (2007–2008) 'Welcome to College? Developing a Richer Understanding of the Transition Process for Adult First Year Students Using Reflective Written Journals', *Journal of College Student Retention*, 9: 183–205.

Sánchez-García, M., Manzano-Soto, N., Rísquez-López, A. and Suárez-Ortega, M. (2011) 'Evaluación de un modelo de orientación tutorial y mentoría en la Educación Superior a Distancia', *Revista de Educación*, 356. DOI:10-4438/1988-592X-RE-2010-356–119.

Sánchez-Palomino, A. (2009) 'La Universidad de Almería ante la integración educativa y social de los estudiantes con discapacidad: ideas y actitudes del personal docente e investigador', *Revista de Educación*, 354: 575–603.

Santiago, P., Bruner, J.J., Haug, G., Malo, S. and Pietrogiacomo, P. (2009) *Review of Tertiary Education in Spain* (Paris: OECD).

Solano, J.C., Frutos, L. and Cárceles, G. (2004) 'Hacia una metodología para el análisis de las trayectorias académicas del alumnado universitario. El caso de las carreras de ciclo largo de la Universidad de Murcia', *Revista Española de Investigaciones Sociológicas*, 105: 217–235.

Thunborg, C., Edström, E. and Bron, A. (2011) *Motives for Entering, Dropping Out or Continuing to Study in Higher Education*. Paper Presented at RANLHE Conference on Access and Retention: Experiences of Non-traditional Learners in Higher Education, Seville, Spain, 7–8 April.

Universidad de Sevilla (2010) *Anuario estadístico de la Universidad de Sevilla 2009/10* [online]　http://servicio.us.es/splanestu/WS/Anuario0910/Present.pdf　[accessed 26 June 2012].

Wilcox, P., Winn, S. and Fyvie-Gauld, M. (2005) 'It Was Nothing to Do with the University, It Was Just the People': The Role of Social Support in the First-Year Experience of higher Education', *Studies in Higher Education*, 30: 707–722.

Zabalza, M.A. (2004) *La enseñanza universitaria. El escenario y sus protagonistas* (Madrid: Narcea).

15
Experiencing Higher Education in Ghana and Tanzania: The Symbolic Power of Being a Student

Louise Morley

Introduction

This chapter is based on findings from the project 'Widening Participation in Higher Education in Ghana and Tanzania: Developing an Equity Score-card' (WPHEGT).[1] An original feature of the study was the inclusion of 200 interviews with students from sub-Saharan Africa (SSA). They narrated experiences, aspirations and disappointments. Positive and enabling student accounts were evident in both countries and in all case study universities. These included supportive and accessible lecturers, enjoyable and well-taught programmes of study, good peer relations, independent learning and the development of social capital in the form of networks, self-confidence and self-efficacy. However, negative experiences were also widely reported including lack of, or poor quality facilities and resources, large classes, poor pedagogy, lecturers' lack of professionalism, problems with assessment, favouritism, corruption and lack of transparency in admissions procedures and student loan entitlements. In spite of many unsatisfactory experiences, the motivation for social mobility, status and employability drove students to enter, stay in and value higher education (HE). Social differentiation and the desire to 'become a somebody' meant that the symbolic power of being a student overrode many of the frustrations. This raises questions about whether a central impact of HE is dispositional and relates to identity transformation.

Revitalising African higher education

Undergraduate student enrolment worldwide rose from 13 million in 1960 to 137.8 million in 2005. It is predicted that the demand for HE worldwide will expand from 97 million students in 2000 to over 262 million students by 2025 (UNESCO, 2009a). SSA has experienced the highest average regional growth rate in HE. For more than three decades, enrolments have expanded by 8.7 per cent annually, compared to 5.1 per cent for the world as a whole, and have tripled since 1990, to almost 4 million students. Women's access has improved markedly in the region, from one out of six students in 1990 to approximately one out of three today (World Bank, 2009). However, the gross enrolment ratio (GER) for tertiary education – the main indicator of participation rates – was 5 for Ghana compared to 24 for the world and 71 for North America and Western Europe in 2005. Tanzania's GER was 1 in 2005 (UNESCO, 2009a). Both secondary and tertiary enrolment ratios for SSA are the lowest among the eight major geographical regions of the world.

Whereas previously, HE was positioned as a luxury product in low-income countries by the World Bank (Robertson, 2009), from 1994, HE became a development priority and part of the new global economic imaginary (World Bank, 1994). The 2009 World Bank Report expressed the desirability of accelerating quality-assured growth in sub-Saharan HE and working towards a more knowledge-intensive approach to development. The 2009 UNESCO World Conference on HE also gave special focus to the challenges and opportunities for the revitalisation of HE in Africa, now considered an important tool for the development of the continent (UNESCO, 2009b). Yet it seems that there is still much work to be done to ensure that widening participation (WP) is not just a question of 'a flood of students into increasingly dysfunctional institutions' (World Bank, 2009: 110).

Widening participation and structures of inequality

The project 'Widening Participation in Higher Education in Ghana and Tanzania: Developing an Equity Scorecard' (WPHEGT) is a new evidence base contributing to making HE more socially inclusive in SSA (Morley *et al.*, 2010). The project used a mixed-methods approach, allowing the qualitative data to illuminate the statistical data and provide textured information about enablers and barriers to participation and achievement for under-represented groups in HE. Life-history interviews were conducted with 200 undergraduate students across both countries including 119 students from public universities and 81 studying in private universities, from different programmes, and from a diversity of backgrounds including under-represented groups such as mature, poor and disabled students. Students were asked about primary, secondary and HE experiences, with questions about their motivations, transitions, support, decision making and first impressions relating to HE, its impact on them and their future plans. HE policy and research tend to be dominated by the messaging systems of the North. De Sousa Santos (2007) argues that we need to listen to the Global South, and that we need to develop a sociology of absences. The life history interviews captured experiences and aspirations of stakeholders' views that are often absent from research, particularly in low-income countries.

The semi-structured interviews with 200 academic staff and policymakers across both countries included 28 national policymakers as well as senior academics, lecturers and staff in the four case study institutions. Academic staff and policymakers were asked about policies, interventions, strategies and challenges for WP, and the part that their universities had played in working towards the Millennium Development Goals (MDGs). 100 Equity Scorecards were compiled largely from raw data on admission/access, retention, completion and achievement, for four programmes of study in relation to three structures of inequality: gender, socio-economic status (SES) and age. The interview data were compared with the statistical data from the Equity Scorecards.

A guiding theoretical construct was intersectionality. The multiple markers of identity do not act independently of each other. While gender has received some policy and research attention, it is rarely intersected with other structures of inequality in low-income countries. Intersectionality theory suggests that oppression and discrimination occur in varying configurations and in varying degrees of intensity, and that there are 'vectors of oppression and privilege' (Ritzer, 2007: 204). Poor women fall into two socially disadvantaged groups and, as such, can become the invisible 'other' in audits of gender or social disadvantage (Morley and Lugg, 2009).

Poverty, as a structure of inequality, was a focus of the study – both in terms of how it intersects with gender, or is eclipsed by gender gains in WP (Morley *et al.*, 2006), and also in relation to the part that HE can play in poverty alleviation. On average a student from the lowest socio-economic quintile in SSA has 15 times less chance of entering a university than one from the highest quintile (Brossard and Foko, 2007). Currently, a third of the world's poorest people live in SSA (UN, 2008), meaning that it has the highest levels of absolute poverty of any region in the world. The number of people living under the new poverty line of $2 a day has increased by 100 million between 1990 and 2005 (UN, 2008). Bernstein's famous caution that education cannot compensate for society (1970) has particular resonance in SSA.

Both Ghana and Tanzania have policy commitments for WP in HE. Although both countries have introduced HE loans policies to assist students from low socio-economic backgrounds, in practice WP has focused largely on addressing the gender gap in admissions. In Tanzania, HE post-independence in 1961 was perceived as a 'powerful strategic weapon in the fight against poverty, ignorance and disease' (Mkude *et al.*, 2003: 583). In Tanzania, it is estimated that only about one per cent of poor people as compared to 11 per cent of the economically advantaged complete secondary school and thus are eligible for HE (URT, 2004: 48).

In Ghana, a study of 1,500 students (Manuh *et al.*, 2007: 82–83) found that the majority of students in the five publicly funded universities in 2002 came from the five more developed regions in the south and centre of the country (24.3 per cent coming from the Ashanti region alone), while only between 4.2 per cent and 6.2 per cent of students came from each of the five less developed Northern and Western regions. Addae-Mensah's (2000) study revealed that at the University of Ghana, depending on the subject of study, between 60 per cent and 92 per cent of students came from the top 50 elite schools (less than 10 per cent of the country's schools) and about 43 per cent came from the top 18 schools (with 57 per cent of students admitted to science degrees being from these schools).

While gender is a major structural inequality, WP has tended to concentrate on counting more women into universities in general, and to Science, Technology, Engineering and Mathematics (STEM) in particular, with less emphasis on women's qualitative experiences once entered. During the 1990s, new policies for the reform of HE emerged in both Ghana and Tanzania (GoG, 1991, 2004; URT, 1999). Similar in form to the international policies emerging from UNESCO (1998) and the World Bank (2000) at much the same time, the Ghanaian and Tanzanian policies expressed commitment to the expansion of HE to larger numbers of students, and to a greater diversity of students, with a particular emphasis on attaining gender equity (GoG, 1991; URT, 1999). Female enrolments, as well as overall expansion, are noteworthy. In Ghana, the enrolment of women increased from 25 per cent in 2000 to 34 per cent in 2007. In Tanzania, women's enrolment grew from 13 per cent in 2000 to 32 per cent in 2007 (UNESCO, 2009b). The distribution of students by type of institution (UNESCO, 2006) reveals that in 2005/2006, in Ghana, women were making up 35 per cent of students in public universities and 41 per cent in private universities. In Tanzania, in 2005/2006, women made up 31.2 per cent of students in public universities and 38 per cent in private universities. Around ten per cent of students were in private universities in both countries (UNESCO, 2006).

A further structure of inequality that the project examined was age. Lifecourse theory implies telelogical notions of progression (Elder, 1998; Mortimer and Shanahan, 2003). Age, linearity and uninterrupted transitions through the educational system are not the norm in mainstream education in SSA where many students enter school at an age older than the official age of entry. Rates of grade repetition can also be high. Multi-grade and multi-age classrooms, and high rates of attrition all disrupt age-related norms in education (Little, 2001). Whereas mature students and off-time events have been theorised in HE in the West (Edwards, 1993), temporal theory and information about participation rates and the cultural experiences of mature students are often invisible in HE studies in low-income countries.

The public–private divide: Case study universities

The project undertook comparative research in public and private universities as the growing number of private HE institutions is a noticeable feature of expansion in SSA. The number of universities in the region is now approximately 650 (200 public and 450 private), and private HE has been perceived as a strategy for enhancing participation and easing the capacity challenge (Varghese, 2004). While there are publications on quality and standards in private HE (Bjarnason *et al.*, 2009), there is less information on the sociology of these institutions and how they are experienced by different constituencies. Furthermore, there is considerable diversity among providers. In this study, both private universities were Christian organisations.

The case study universities claimed above average female enrolments. In Ghana, female enrolments stood at 37.5 per cent in the public university in 2006–2007, and 54.8 per cent in the private university in 2005–2006 compared with 35 and 41 per cent in the public and private sectors, respectively, in 2005–2006. In Tanzania, in 2007–2008, female enrolment was 33.3 per cent in the public university and 42 per cent in the private university compared with 30.5 and 35 per cent in the two sectors, respectively (TCU, 2009). The higher enrolments of women may be in part due to affirmative action initiatives.

Affirmative action at the public university in Ghana included lowering of the cut-off point for entry into some programmes for female students by one or sometimes two points. There were also special entrance examinations and remedial programmes for mature entrants and those from schools identified as 'deprived'. Mature students were given a 6 per cent enrolment quota, while 200 slots were reserved for students from deprived schools. The private case study university attracted large numbers of mature students through its worker-friendly flexible delivery mode, with courses being offered in the morning, afternoon and at weekends (Morley *et al.*, 2008). In Tanzania, the public university's affirmative action initiatives include a pre-entry programme and scholarship scheme funded by the Carnegie Corporation of New York for women who wish to study on the BSc in engineering (Lihamba *et al.*, 2006). They also had a mature entry route for those aged 25 years and over,[2] and recognition of equivalent qualifications, as in Ghana.

Why widen participation?

The 2009 UNESCO World Conference on HE in Paris adopted the resolution that HE is a public good (UNESCO, 2009b). This value was evident in WPHEGT data. Staff and policymakers conceptualised and expressed the public good in the policy vocabularies of economic development and the needs of the labour market (Singh, 2001). Staff in both countries combined economic with social reasons for supporting WP. They prioritised national development in terms of economic development and producing a highly skilled workforce:

> The aspiration of Ghana to be a middle level income nation by a certain target set means that a certain level of manpower will need to be trained,

if you want to develop a nation you have to broaden for admission and enrolment into tertiary institutions and when this is achieved then the impact in national development can be greatly felt.

(male staff, private university, Ghana)

National development was sometimes overtly linked to poverty alleviation, assuming that there would be a public and private return on the investment:

A trained manpower is the best access [to development] a country can have... I believe that any initiative at all in education leads to a reduction in poverty.

(female government official, Ghana)

In Tanzania, policymakers discussed national labour market needs as well as the international policy imperatives to widen participation:

The basic qualification for a person to get employed at least you need to have a degree... a degree qualification, so it's not a policy per se but rather the demand for HE, which is being reflected to the requirement of the society, what the society needs now.

(male policymaker, Tanzania)

When it came to students' motivations for entering HE, as Figure 15.1 shows, they combined public and private factors. The main reasons cited in both countries were the labour market, e.g. career aspirations, employment

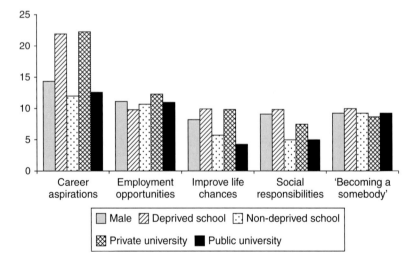

Figure 15.1 Students' motivations for entering HE

opportunities, entry into the professions and obtaining professional knowledge. Social status and social differentiation were also important to many students who saw graduate identity as a means of marking them as different. Many talked about 'becoming a somebody' (Wexler, 1992), or getting a 'good life' and were specific about their economic goals and enhanced life chances:

> I think that when you go there {University} you have to study and you will become somebody.
>
> (Female student, public university, Tanzania)

> Actually the first time I stepped into university I am no more myself... I realise I am somebody now.
>
> (Male student, public university, Ghana)

> My expectations were, I think I should go to the university, study; I wanted to be somebody, recognised as somebody in the society.
>
> (Mature, female student private university, Tanzania)

Students in all universities were motivated by the material and symbolic power of gaining a degree. The range of motivators was wider in Tanzania than in Ghana. In Ghana, the main motivators were employment and career, whereas in Tanzania, these were accompanied by social responsibility and escaping rural poverty. For women in the private universities in both countries and in the public university in Ghana, HE was considered essential as a route into employment and careers in the professions. As such, it was linked to financial and social independence and played a major role in transforming their status from objects to agentic subjects. While many students had high expectations of their university experiences, many were also disappointed by the poor quality of provision.

Supporting success

Students from non-traditional backgrounds are frequently constructed as a risk to universities and to the state that invests in them (Leathwood and O'Connell, 2003). A way of minimising risk is to install structured support mechanisms. Support in the WPHEGT study was seen as financial, including scholarships, loans or bursaries; academic, e.g. improved and student-centred pedagogy, practical, e.g. accommodation, and emotional, e.g. counselling. Some respondents in Ghana discussed organisational strategies to improve retention and achievement. These included the sexual harassment committee (sexual harassment was a major finding in the study; see Morley, 2011) and a quality assurance unit to monitor teaching in the public university and, in the private university, student placements in industry, and announcing names of students with good grades at graduation ceremonies. Strategies for retention in the public

Table 15.1   Percentage of students who mentioned lack of support

Percentage of respondents	Mature $N = 38$	Non-mature $N = 153$	Female $N = 103$	Male $N = 97$	Low SES $N = 53$	Non-low SES $N = 145$
Ghana private	0	6.45	4.54	5.26	0	5.71
Ghana public	10	6.52	0	13.79	14.29	7.31
Tanzania private	0	0	0	0	0	0
Tanzania public	0	8	3.23	9.68	12.5	4.54

university included allowing students to repeat papers that they had failed and to receive counselling on how to approach their studies so that they could return the following year. Retention and achievement strategies mentioned in Tanzania included study skills development, linkages with other departments and professional institutions, more time for disabled students to do their exams, accommodation, pedagogy, student groups, religious support, financial support, library services, time management and information literacy classes, discussion groups and practical training for students. Lack of support for disabled students was seen as a major problem by staff and students, particularly in Tanzania (Morley and Croft, 2012).

While the staff in all the universities cited a range of support interventions, its lack was reported by all categories of students, except in the private university in Tanzania. More male students than females complained about lack of support, as shown in Table 15.1.

Lack of support from lecturers and lack of services and facilities, e.g. libraries, information technology (IT), accommodation and social amenities, especially in the private universities, were the categories most frequently discussed. The capacity challenges and under-funded expansions were felt strongly by many students in both countries. Lack of, or poor quality, facilities, lack of infrastructure and overcrowding were widely reported (Table 15.2).

> Sometimes because our class is very large and some teachers are low speakers, so during that time we get difficult to hear them.
> (Female student, private university, Tanzania)

> Yes, this place, everything is about queue, queue... For our lecture halls, if you don't go early, you will stand outside and peep through before you can hear or listen to something.
> (Female student, public university, Ghana)

> Sometimes we have more than eight hundred students in the class.
> (Male student, private university, Ghana)

In lecture rooms...we are so many students...like seven hundred up to, up to one thousand and five hundred students in one lecture room. So somehow if you're late to come it means you will be studying standing or sitting on the floor where there are no chairs.

(Male student, public university, Tanzania)

Overcrowding has been documented by the World Bank:

The ratio of academic staff to students has fallen significantly, producing overcrowded classrooms and unrelenting workloads for teaching staff.

(World Bank, 2009: xxvii)

It is crucial that WP is not achieved by adding more students to systems that are already overloaded and poorly resourced. Access also needs to be accompanied by attention to retention and achievement.

Succeeding against the odds

In spite of the reported problems with the quality of student experiences in the WPHEGT study, once entered, many students completed. Mature students were at the highest risk of dropout in both countries. Women and men's completion rates were similar in both countries and low SES students represent a lower risk than imagined, (Morley *et al.*, 2010). However, the class of degrees awarded varied considerably between programmes and between institutions (see Tables 15.3, 15.4, 15.5 and 15.6). Poverty seemed to be the dominant structure of inequality in the study that worked against access to HE. Once students from low socio-economic backgrounds entered university, they often did better than average, and better than mature students. This can be seen by examining the degree classifications for the 2007–2008 cohort in each university. In the public university in Ghana (Table 15.3), low SES students achieved more first-class degrees than the cohort as a whole on the three programmes where they were present. On B. Commerce, 58.34 per cent of low SES students achieved either a first- or second-class degree compared with 52.29 for the whole cohort of students and 36.59 for the mature students. On BEd (primary), 82.70 per cent of low SES students achieved a first- or second-class degree compared with 80.75 per cent for the whole cohort and 77.78 per cent for mature students.

No student from the private university in Ghana gained first-class degrees on any of the selected programmes in 2007–2008.

In Tanzania, low SES students were more numerous than in the Ghanaian universities, and a higher proportion gained second-class degrees than the cohort as a whole on three programmes. On the BSc with education and the BEd Maths, all gained second-class degrees, and in the BSc engineering, five per cent gained first-class degrees and those with second-class

Table 15.2 Number of students who mentioned under-resourcing

	Mature N = 38	Non-mature N = 153	Female N = 103	Male N = 97	Deprived N = 53	Non-deprived N = 145	Ghana N = 100	Tanzania N = 100
Lack of/poor facilities	7	38	18	27	17	28	11	34
Lack of support	7	25	15	17	14	18	17	15
Overcrowding	3	17	9	11	7	13	14	6

Table 15.3 Equity scorecard: Student achievement in four programmes, by gender, age and socio-economic status at a Ghanaian Public University in 2007–2008

Programme	Total		Men			Women			Low SES students			Mature students		
	Percentage 1st class	Percentage 2nd class	Percentage on programme	Percentage 1st class	Percentage 2nd class	Percentage on programme	Percentage 1st class	Percentage 2nd class	Percentage on programme	Percentage 1st class	Percentage 2nd class	Percentage on programme	Percentage 1st class	Percentage 2nd class
B. Commerce	6.47	45.82	70.62	7.63	49.24	29.38	3.67	37.61	3.23	16.67	41.67	22.10	2.44	34.15
B. Management studies	2.80	48.76	54.35	4.57	53.14	45.65	0.68	43.54	1.24	25.00	0.00	17.70	0.00	19.30
B. Education (primary)	5.59	75.16	56.52	6.59	70.33	43.48	4.29	81.43	10.56	11.76	70.94	72.67	6.84	70.94
BSc Optometry	0.00	68.75	75.00	0.00	66.67	25.00	0.00	75.00	0.00	–	–	0.00	–	–

Table 15.4 Equity scorecard: Student achievement in four programmes, by gender, age and socio-economic status at a Ghanaian Private University in 2007–2008

Programme	Total — Percentage 1st class	Total — Percentage 2nd class	Total — Percentage on programme	Men — Percentage 1st class	Men — Percentage 2nd class	Men — Percentage on programme	Women — Percentage 1st class	Women — Percentage 2nd class	Women — Percentage on programme	Low SES students — Percentage on programme	Low SES students — Percentage 1st class	Low SES students — Percentage 2nd class	Mature students — Percentage on programme	Mature students — Percentage 1st class	Mature students — Percentage 2nd class
BSc Economics	0.00	79.17	83.33	0.00	80.00	16.67	0.00	75.00		4.17	0.00	100.0	0.00	–	–
BSc Human resources management	0.00	67.84	29.52	0.00	67.16	70.48	0.00	68.12		0.88	0.00	100.0	4.41	0.00	50.0
BSc Agri-business management	0.00	81.82	72.73	0.00	75.00	27.27	0.00	100.0		0.00	–	–	0.00	–	–
BSc Accountancy	0.00	85.09	57.76	0.00	83.87	42.24	0.00	86.76		0.62	0.00	100.0	3.11	0.00	80.0

Table 15.5 Equity scorecard: Student achievement in four programmes, by gender, age and socio-economic status at a Tanzanian Public University in 2007–2008

Programme	Total			Men			Women			Low SES students			Mature students		
	Percentage 1st class	Percentage 2nd class	Percentage on programme	Percentage 1st class	Percentage 2nd class	Percentage on programme	Percentage 1st class	Percentage 2nd class	Percentage on programme	Percentage 1st class	Percentage 2nd class	Percentage on programme	Percentage 1st class	Percentage 2nd class	Percentage on programme
B. Commerce	0.75	90.43	70.36	0.80	89.33	29.64	0.63	93.04	6.57	0.00	88.57	2.06	0.00	81.82	
LLB law	0.00	77.97	58.90	0.00	84.17	41.10	0.00	69.07	8.05	0.00	84.21	5.08	0.00	66.67	
BSc engineering	5.39	82.75	74.66	5.78	81.59	25.34	4.26	86.17	10.78	5.00	82.50	4.31	0.00	81.25	
BSc with education	0.00	93.51	61.04	0.00	91.49	38.96	0.00	96.67	10.39	0.00	100	5.19	0.00	100	

Table 15.6 Equity scorecard: Student achievement in three programmes, by gender, age and socio-economic status at a Tanzanian Private University in 2007–2008

Programme	Total			Men			Women			Low SES students			Mature students		
	Percentage 1st class	Percentage 2nd class	Percentage on programme	Percentage on programme	Percentage 1st class	Percentage 2nd class	Percentage on programme	Percentage 1st class	Percentage 2nd class	Percentage on programme	Percentage 1st class	Percentage 2nd class	Percentage on programme	Percentage 1st class	Percentage 2nd class
LLB law	0.00	34.83	55.14	55.14	0.00	31.10	44.85	0.00	39.41	7.65	0.00	34.48	12.40	0.00	44.68
B. business administration	13.33	74.00	71.33	71.33	12.15	72.90	28.67	16.28	76.74	6.00	11.11	77.78	25.33	13.16	60.53
B Ed maths	0.00	100	70.18	70.18	0.00	100	29.82	0.00	100	12.28	0.00	100	77.19	0.00	100

degrees were close to the figure for the whole cohort (see Table 15.5). It is of note that 5 per cent of low SES students and 4.26 per cent of women achieved a first-class degree in engineering – the programme with affirmative action. This suggests that, given the opportunity, women and students from disadvantaged backgrounds can excel in STEM subjects.

In the private university, a slightly higher proportion on the B. business administration and a slightly lower proportion on the LLB gained second-class degrees. In Tanzania, three programmes awarded a few first-class degrees, and a relatively high proportion gained second-class degrees in both public and private universities.

In conclusion, an examination of the achievement records for low SES students in terms of the proportion who gained first- and second-class degrees reveals that, for the 15 programmes for which figures were gathered, this group performed as well, or nearly as well, as the cohort as a whole in most programmes, although the numbers were very low, and support was perceived as inadequate.

Conclusion

To summarise, there are unequal geographies of knowledge and archaic patterns of participation in HE in the two countries studied in this project. In a globalised knowledge economy, WP in HE can be a force for democratisation and economic growth. However, it can also map on to elite practices and contribute to further differentiation of social groups. It is often claimed that those with social capital are able to decode and access new educational opportunities and that those without it can remain untouched by initiatives to facilitate their entry into the privileges that HE can offer (Crozier *et al.*, 2008; Heath *et al.*, 2008). It has been repeatedly argued that poverty and the uneven distribution of material, social and cultural capital influence those who have the capacity to aspire to HE (Appadurai, 2004; David *et al.*, 2009).

Globally, participation rates are rising, but not from a range of social groups in Ghana and Tanzania. For many, WP was seen in relation to quantitative change of one particular group – usually women-into STEM subjects. There was less engagement with qualitative experiences of students once entered, their support needs, or with monitoring educational outcomes including retention, completion and achievement, or with intersectionality of social identities. However, many students from under-represented social groups flourished when given the opportunity to enter HE. In spite of the numerous shortcomings, students with low SES or spoiled identities believed that their participation in HE transformed them from 'nobodies' to 'somebodies', providing the social differentiation that would be a lifelong positional good.

Acknowledgements

Thanks to the ESRC/DFID (RES-167-25-0078) for funding this project and to members of the project teams: Fiona Leach, Kattie Lussier, Rosemary Lugg, Duna Sabri, Amandina Lihamba, Rosemarie Mwaipopo, Linda Forde and Godwyn Egbenya.

Notes

1. www.sussex.ac.uk/education/cheer/wphegt.
2. Although in Tanzania, those aged 25 years and above could qualify for the mature entry route, our category of 'mature students' includes only those aged 30 years and above, this being the age for mature entry in Ghana.

Bibliography

Addae-Mensah, I. (2000) *Education in Ghana: A Tool for Social Mobility or Social Stratification?* (Accra: INSTI).

Appadurai, A. (2004) 'The Capacity to Aspire: Culture and the Terms of Recognition', in Rao, V. and Walton, M. (eds) *Culture and Public Action* (Stanford: Stanford University Press, pp. 59–84).

Bernstein, B. (1970) 'Education Cannot Compensate for Society', *New Society*, 15 (387): 344–347.

Bjarnason, S., Cheng, K., Fielden, J., Lemaitre, M., Levy, D. and Varghese, N. (2009) *A New Dynamic: Private Higher Education* (Paris: UNESCO).

Brossard, M. and Foko, B. (2007) *Couts Et Financement De L'enseignement Superieur En Afrique Francophone* (Washington, DC: World Bank).

Crozier, G., Reay, D., Clayton, J., Colliander, L. and Grinstead, J. (2008) 'Different Strokes for Different Folks: Diverse Students in Diverse Institutions – Experiences of Higher Education', *Research Papers in Education*, 23 (2): 167–177.

David, M., Bathmaker, A.-M., Black, L., Cooke, S., Crozier, G., Davis, P., Ertl, H., Fuller, A., Gallacher, J., Hayward, G., Heath, S., Hernandez-Martinez, P., Hockings, C., Parry, G., Reay, D., Smith, D., Vignoles, A., Wake, G. and Williams, J. (2009) *Improving Learning by Widening Participation to Higher Education* (London: Routledge).

De Sousa Santos, B. (2007) *Cognitive Justice in a Global World: Prudent Knowledge for a Decent Life* (Lanham: Lexington).

Edwards, R. (1993) *Mature Women Students* (London: Taylor and Francis).

Elder, G.H., Jr. (1998) 'The Life Course as Developmental Theory', *Child Development*, 69 (1): 1–12.

Government of Ghana (2004) *White Paper on the Report of the Education Reform Review Committee* (Accra: Ministry of Education).

Government of Ghana (1991) *Government White Paper on the Reforms of the Tertiary Education System* (Accra: GoG).

Heath, S., Fuller, A. and Paton, K. (2008) 'Network-Based Ambivalence and Educational Decision-Making: A Case Study of "Non-Participation" in Higher Education', *Research Papers in Education*, 23 (2): 219–229.

Leathwood, C. and O'Connell, P. (2003) ' "It's a Struggle": The Construction of the "New Student" in Higher Education', *Journal of Education Policy*, 18 (6): 597–615.

Lihamba, A., Mwaipopo, R. and Shule, L. (2006) 'The Challenges of Affirmative Action in Tanzanian Higher Education Institutions: A Case Study of the University of Dar Es Salaam, Tanzania', *Women's Studies International Forum*, 29 (6): 581–591.

Little, A. (2001) 'Multigrade Teaching: Towards an International Research and Policy Agenda', *International Journal of Educational Development*, 21 (6): 481–497.

Manuh, T., Gariba, S. and Budu, J. (2007) *Change and Transformation in Ghana's Publicly Funded Universities. A Study of Experiences, Lessons and Opportunities* (Oxford/Accra: James Currey Ltd./Woeli Publishing Services).

Mkude, D., Cooksey, B. and Levey, L. (2003) *Higher Education in Tanzania: A Case Study*. Partnership for Higher Education in Africa (Oxford: James Currey/ Dar es Salaam).

Morley, L. (2011) 'Sex, Grades and Power in Higher Education in Ghana and Tanzania', *Cambridge Journal of Education*, 41 (1): 101–115.

Morley, L. (2010) 'Gender Mainstreaming: Myths and Measurement in Higher Education in Ghana and Tanzania', *Compare: A Journal of Comparative Education*, 40 (4): 533–550.

Morley, L. and Croft, A. (2012) 'Agency and Advocacy: Disabled Students in Higher Education in Ghana and Tanzania', *Research in Comparative and International Education*, 6 (4): 341–347.

Morley, L., Gunawardena, C., Kwesiga, J., Lihamba, A., Odejide, A. and Shackleton, L. (2006) *Gender Equity in Selected Commonwealth Universities* (London: Department for International Development).

Morley, L. and Lugg, R. (2009) 'Mapping Meritocracy: Intersecting Gender, Poverty and Higher Educational Opportunity Structures', *Higher Education Policy*, 22 (1): 37–60.

Morley, L., Leach, F. and Lugg, R. (2008) 'Democratising Higher Education in Ghana and Tanzania: Opportunity Structures and Social Inequalities', 29 (1): 56–64.

Morley, L., Leach, F., Lussier, K., Lihamba, A., Mwaipopo, R., Forde, L. and Egbenya, G., (2010). *Widening Participation in Higher Education in Ghana and Tanzania: Developing an Equity Scorecard*. An ESRC/DFID Poverty Reduction Programme Research Project [online] http://www.sussex.ac.uk/wphegt/impact-outputs/report-summary [accessed 1 August 2011].

Mortimer, T. and Shanahan, M.J. (eds) (2003) *Handbook of the Life Course* (New York: Kluwer Academic).

Ritzer, G. (2007) *Contemporary Sociological Theory and Its Classical Roots: The Basics* (Boston, MA: McGraw-Hill).

Robertson, S. (2009) *Market Multilateralism, the World Bank Group and the Asymmetries of Globalising Higher Education: Toward a Critical Political Economy Analysis*. ESRC Seminar Series 'Imagining Universities of the Future' CHEER, University of Sussex, UK. [online] http://www.sussex.ac.uk/cheer/esrcseminars/seminar1 [accessed 1 August 2011].

Singh, M. (2001) *Re-Inserting the 'Public Good' into Higher education Transformation*. Paper Presented at the SRHE Conference 'Globalisation and Higher Education: Views from the South, Cape Town, South Africa, March 2001.

Tanzania Commission for Universities (TCU) (2009) *Basic Statistics* [online] http://www.tcu.go.tz/uploads/file/Statistics%20for%202009-2010.pdf [accessed 5 July 2012].

UNESCO (2009a) *Global Education Digest 2009* (Montreal: UNESCO Institute for Statistics).

UNESCO (2009b) *Communique. 2009 World Conference on Higher Education: The New Dynamics of Higher Education and Research for Societal Change and Development* (Paris: UNESCO).

UNESCO (2006) *Global Education Digest 2006* (Montreal: UNESCO Institute for Statistics).

UNESCO (1998) *World Declaration on Higher Education for the Twenty-First Century: Vision and Action. Adopted by the World Conference on Higher Education* (Paris: UNESCO).

United Nations (UN) (2008) *The Millennium Development Goals Report 2008* (New York: United Nations).

United Nations Development Programme (UNDP) (2006) *Human Development Report 2006/2007* (New York: UNDP).

United Republic of Tanzania (URT) (2004) *Higher and Technical Education Sub-Master Plan 2003-2018* (Dar es Salaam: Ministry of Science, Technology and Higher Education).

United Republic of Tanzania (URT) (1999) *National Higher Education Policy* (Dar es Salaam: Ministry of Science, Technology and Higher Education).

Varghese, N.V. (2004) *Private Higher Education in Africa* (Paris: IIEP/ADEA/AAU).

Wexler, P. (1992) *Becoming a Somebody: Toward a Social Psychology of School* (Basingstoke: Burgess Science Press).

World Bank (2009) *Tertiary Education and Growth in Sub-Saharan Africa* (Washington, DC: The World Bank).

World Bank (2000) *Higher Education in Developing Countries: Peril and Promise* (Washington, DC: Task Force on Higher Education and Society).

World Bank (1994) *Higher Education: The Lessons of Experience* (Washington, DC: World Bank).

16

Women and Students of Colour as Non-Traditional Students: The Difficulties of Inclusion in the United States

Anne J. MacLachlan

Introduction

Equity of access to post-secondary education for all groups in American society has been a focus of policymakers in the United States since the Second World War. Target groups have changed over time from veterans just after the War, women, then African Americans and members of other minority groups. Participation has increased for all groups, but unevenly, so that minority groups are now known in higher education (HE) as 'under-represented' since their share of earned bachelor's degrees is less than the representation of these groups in the total population. Women also remain 'under-represented' in many fields of study and in higher degree programmes. Because of this unequal distribution, women and students of colour are still considered as non-traditional students and all too often treated as outsiders. Current trends, of increasing poverty, under-funding of primary and secondary education and vitriolic attacks on HE with drastic cuts in funding of public colleges and universities, are intensifying exclusion. Women and students of colour will not only remain 'non-traditional' students, but 'standing on the outside looking in' at middle-class life, as Mary Howard-Hamilton and Merlon-Quainoo (2009) described it in the title of her compendium of studies on this phenomenon.

Today increasing numbers of Americans are excluded from educational opportunity and related economic mobility as a result of decades of poor public policy and more recent polarising politics (Carnevale and Strohl, 2010: 74–76). Those most affected are women of all ethnicities, American blacks, Latinos and American Indians, the poorest groups in the United States whose wealth accumulation and standard of living has never achieved that of white men (Deere and Doss, 2006; US Census Bureau-4, 2011, tables 689–691). Their poverty is sustained by low educational opportunities leading to low-paid employment. Increases in the educational level of the population generally since the Second World War and decades of expanding employment opportunity have not produced parity. Not only has uniform access to education never been achieved, it has declined since the 1980s (Carnevale and Strohl, 2010: 74).

Certainly, patterns in earned bachelor's degrees changed substantially between 1980 and 2008 – the latest available data. A total of 934,800 degrees were conferred in 1980, when compared with 1,563,069 in 2007–2008. In 1980, white students earned 807,319 degrees or 86.4 per cent of the total declining to 71.8 per cent in 2007–2008, less than their 74.8 per cent representation in the US population. Black students earned 60,673 degrees in 1980, 6.5 per cent of the total; in 2007–2008 they earned 152,457 degrees or 9.8 per cent of the total, but they represent 13.6 per cent of the US population. In 1980, Hispanics earned 21,832 degrees, 2.3 per cent of the total; in 2007–2008, they earned 123,048 or 7.9 per cent of the total. Hispanics are the second fastest growing population group comprising around 14 per cent of the total population but earn a far smaller share of degrees. These inequalities persist despite 30 years of programmes to increase the number of black and Hispanic graduates.[1] Asians are an exception, earning 7 per cent of all bachelor's degrees, but they make up only 5 per cent of the total population (NCES-5 and Snyder *et al.*, 2011 table 285; US Census Bureau-6, 2011). Racial and ethnic groups are increasingly difficult to classify, however, as there has been a 50 per cent increase of children of mixed race under 18 in the United States since 2000 (Saulny, 2011). It is also possible to list one's self as more than one race on the US census forms and other official documents such as college registration. This makes exact tracking very difficult.

The purpose of this chapter is to analyse how this situation developed and what is happening in the present to address it. I begin with considering the many factors that work to exclude students from educational participation and success. This includes high-school graduation rates, college choice in the face of a complicated system of HE and the heavy role played by poverty and other forms of 'disadvantage'. I then turn to programmes created to increase minority and female participation, discuss how they have been undermined and conclude with policy efforts to broaden participation.[2]

Overview of post-secondary education in the United States

HE policy is difficult to implement in the United States due to the variety of types of colleges and universities found. Today there are approximately 6,000 institutions ranging from highly prestigious research universities to open enrolment two-year community colleges, along with many less standard institutions (NCES-5 and, Snyder *et al.*, 2011: 19). The majority of undergraduates, more than 70 per cent, are enrolled at public colleges and universities. To provide a framework for HE analysis, the Carnegie Foundation in the 1970s categorised institutions by function, with the research university at the pinnacle. The system has become increasingly complex, employing multiple criteria.[3] Very broadly, there are full doctorate granting universities, more programmatically limited doctorate granting institutions, and master's granting institutions, which include extensive state systems enrolling the largest number of undergraduates. Another category, liberal arts colleges, has high academic standards, emphasises undergraduate teaching and are almost all private. Two-year colleges, known as community colleges, focus on teaching. They usually admit all who apply with or without a high-school diploma and have multiple teaching missions in remedial education, academic transfer to a four-year college and vocational technical certificate programmes. They charge very little for enrolment, and in some states these are administered by the local school district.

There are other specialised types of post-secondary institutions: professional schools, seminaries, technical colleges and adult and further education colleges. Since 1976 when the University of Phoenix was founded, for-profit training establishments for working adults have proliferated along with for-profit organisations promising to educate for achievement of credentials and academic degrees.

There still are separate colleges for women, mostly belonging to the liberal arts category. There are also separate higher education institutions (HEIs) largely for African Americans today, which were formerly part of a historical system. Until the 1960s, black children and young adults had been completely excluded from attending white schools and colleges in the South. In 1890, after a Supreme Court decision that 'separate' was 'equal', the federal government mandated a state system of colleges exclusively for black students in the 17 former slave-holding states. Now known as Historically Black Colleges and Universities (HBCUs) they number 105, span the spectrum of institutional type and enrol students of all ethnicities but retain a focus on African American education (NCES-1 and Provasnak *et al.*, 2004). The Supreme Court decision in 1954 that 'separate' was not 'equal' led to the integration of all educational institutions, including previously all black colleges. In addition, concentrations of particular ethnicities have produced what are called 'minority serving institutions (MSIs)', the most rapidly expanding type is 'Hispanic serving institutions (HSIs)'.

How institutional multiplicity affects student access and success

Where students attend college makes a huge difference in their chances of earning a degree. Commonly poor women and minorities attend the type of college in which they have a high probability of failing, or if in four-year colleges with high academic standards, are often viewed as outsiders (NCES-4 and Aud *et al.*, 2010; IHEP, 2011; Leonhardt, 2011). Getting into a four-year college at all is complicated, requiring as a minimum a high-school diploma (not necessary for a community college). Around 74 per cent of all high-school pupils in the United States leave school with this diploma by age 19 (NCES-4 and Aud *et al.*, 2010: 66). However, only 61.5 per cent of black students and 63.5 of Hispanic students earned high-school diplomas (NCES-2 and Stillwell, 2010, table 2). Of those who do not graduate high school, some eventually earn a general education development (GED) by attending a community college or special adult education programmes or in the military. Those who earn diplomas from poorer school districts with a high dropout rate may have other characteristics, which contribute to them being perceived as 'disadvantaged'. Their school is more likely to have low academic standards and not to promote a culture of college attendance, leaving pupils from uneducated families with little understanding of HE. (Thirteen per cent of US residents over age 25 have less than a high-school education, 5.3 per cent have less than an eight-grade education (US Census Bureau-2, 2011.) Additionally, individuals from this kind of school often lack the experience or support to evaluate programmes of study and knowledge of financial aid or how to manage money. They may not be native speakers of English. A most alarming trend is that women of colour especially are enrolling at for-profit colleges. Seven out of ten African American women in college now come from a poor background, and 26 per cent are enrolled at a for-profit institution (IHEP, 2011). Degree attainment is low at such places and recognition of the degree uncertain, but what is clear is that loans are commonly used to pay college fees so that a student can well end up with no bachelor's degree but up to forty thousand dollars in debt (Fry and Hinze-Pifer, 2010). Worse, for-profits enrol only 13 per cent of all post-secondary students in the United States but absorb 25 per cent of federal (Pell) grant money and generate 47 per cent of defaults on student loans (Lynch *et al.*, 2011: 7). Loans are all the more difficult to pay off since women in the United States still earn anywhere from 65 cents to 80 cents for every dollar earned by men at the same occupational level (US Census-2, 2011).

Among those who meet the criteria of attending a four-year college, the type they attend matters greatly to whether they will earn a degree (NBER, 2009). Choice is restricted by variability in admission standards, but students who are successful in any college tend to enrol full-time, do not live at home with their parents, have usually arranged their finances so as not to work more than 15 hours a week and have developed the focus necessary to master college work. Degree attainment is to some extent a self-fulfilling prophecy since to be admitted to colleges with rigorous academic standards a student has already demonstrated a high level of academic achievement, although this by itself is not enough to earn a degree.

Students from poor backgrounds who are often less prepared for college enrol in overwhelming numbers in the least demanding institutions, the majority enrolling in two-year colleges with no admissions criteria. Community college enrolment represents nearly 45 per cent of the college-going population, but only a small number of students will either earn a two-year associate's degree or transfer to a four-year college. This is the college of choice because it is cheap, close to where students live, classes can be scheduled at the students' discretion to fit work hours, and faculty are usually highly motivated to help students succeed. Unfortunately, the majority of all students will begin in remedial education classes; the lower the level, the greater the chances the student will never make it to college-level instruction. Community college students often attend part time, work up to 40 hours a week, live at home with their parents and are poorly integrated into college life. The upshot is that only 19 per cent of those beginning in college-level classes will transfer and 10 per cent will earn a two-year academic degree (associate of arts) in three years (NCES-3 and Horn *et al.*, 2009: ix–x). The numbers of those who transfer include the highly motivated, well-prepared students who also attend a community college for the same general reasons as less prepared students but are able to use their time to complete the course work for the first two years of a four-year degree, before transferring and earning a bachelor's degree.

The hallmark of community colleges is that they are able to give students a second chance: those lacking a high-school diploma, who have experienced unstable upbringings, or returning veterans, often find that community colleges give them the time to discover their interests and progress. So while community colleges can divert students with potential out of the HE system, or see unprepared students get bogged down, at the same time it also offers the opportunity for anyone to get a first chance at college success or a second chance later in life. In community colleges, fewer students can be considered non-traditional, as the majority, in one way or another, does not fit the profile of the usual 18–24-year-old college-going population. Unfortunately, there is a widely held misperception from the Obama administration on down that community colleges are the answer to broadening participation and post-secondary success in academic programmes. This will never be the case when a major portion of community-college resources go to remedial instruction, and the majority of students enter at such low levels of academic proficiency that they cycle right out of college altogether.

Ascending the ladder of institutional complexity, the next possibility for college enrolment is the four-year state colleges, which most often offer masters and professional degrees as well as bachelor's. Admission standards vary, but the practice is to accept those earning a high-school diploma in the top 25–50 per cent of their class. Most offer remedial classes and a wide array of academic majors as well as pre-professional programmes. The campuses tend to be large with the majority of students living off-campus, many working up to full time and attending college part time. Once in an academic major, courses can be as rigorous as those at colleges and universities with more restricted admission standards. Unfortunately, there is a stereotypic view that state colleges are not demanding. In a form of tacit structural racism, counsellors tend to direct students of colour, no matter how well prepared, to state colleges instead of to a university (Hernandez, 2010; MacLachlan, 2010). The large number of part-time students, the absence of a defined 'class' cohort for full-time students (which puts students on a scheduled path to graduation) and the paucity of student monitoring contributes to high dropout rates at state colleges.

In all public four-year institutions, a declining percentage (presently approximately 15 per cent) of students enrolled are from poor backgrounds and are often the first in their families to attend such institutions. More students from this group enrol in for-profit institutions (IHEP, 2011).[4] They are also much more likely to be students of colour. The bachelor's degree completion rate in five years is currently 39 per cent, and added years raise the percentage to nearly 60 per cent, but it does not go higher (ACT, 2010; NCES-5 and Radford *et al.*, 2010). Although the undergraduate population generally consists of many students of colour and women of all ethnicities and ages, once members of these groups enter some academic majors, particularly mathematics and the sciences, they are often seen as 'non-traditional', as there still are very few of either in most of their classes.

> Liberal arts colleges on the other hand have a very different profile. They are small, usually very expensive, have a demanding curriculum and are usually private not for profit. Students tend to be white, upper middle class, traditional college age (19 years old or younger) and academically very well prepared. Many are children of professors (Gonyea and *et al.*, 2008; O'Shaughnessy, 2011). Life is centred on the campus and on learning. Students are expected to read broadly and take courses in all of the liberal arts areas. These colleges mostly focus on bachelor's level instruction, a few also confer masters and an even smaller number, doctorates. Graduation rates are very high as students are high achievers and very closely monitored. Women represent more than half of undergraduate enrolment, some from relatively privileged long-established families with generations of college participation. Students of colour are also present, but often from families who have been middle class for a few generations. While they may well still experience reactions from others based on stereotypes, especially because there still are so few of them, they are less likely to be seen as 'non-traditional' as class usually trumps race (Mullen, 2010). Graduation rates are around 90 per cent at the best, 55 per cent in five years on average, and a large proportion of students go on to graduate or professional school.
>
> (ACT, 2010; O'Shaughnessy, 2011)

As every other institution type discussed in this chapter, universities, defined by offering several PhD degree programmes, come in a large variety of forms. Most undergraduates attend public state universities such as the University of Wisconsin or the University of Texas – every state has at least one, as they do public four-year colleges. Undergraduate admission standards are high. Two campuses of the University of California (UC) only accept the top 4 per cent of the state high-school graduating class, the remaining eight UC campuses, the top 12.5 per cent. The majority of such institutions were created under the Morrill Land Grant Act of 1862, whereby states were given large tracts of land to establish and pay for a university to serve the population of their state. Some are both public and private such as the University of Michigan or Cornell University and are expensive to attend. In 2011, the average parental income level at the University of Michigan was $200,000 (Leonhardt, 2011). Students at the undergraduate level are usually from the state in which the university is located and to some extent may reflect the population distribution in the state. If all things were equal, this would mean that in California over one-third of undergraduates would be Latino when in fact only 14 per cent are. The reality is that there is a much higher proportion of Asian students in attendance and a much lower proportion of African Americans, Latinos and native Americans – a reversal of the state's ethnic composition. Students from poor backgrounds tend not to enrol in undergraduate programmes at doctorate-granting universities because they may consider themselves insufficiently prepared or cannot afford to attend.

The percentages of undergraduates of colour in majority white institutions – as most universities are – reflect the small percentage of students of colour who excel in high school. Their small number in turn ensures that they will be seen as non-traditional and frequently subjected to forms of differential treatment and racist judgments. Common examples include expressions of faculty doubt that students of colour have independently authored outstanding papers or obtained high test-scores without cheating, even challenging students to prove they really did the work. The graduation rate of students of colour can be somewhat lower than that of their representation among the undergraduate population as a whole, not necessarily through any academic inability, but through discouragement and disillusion (Dowd *et al.*, 2011).[5]

Private universities such as Harvard, Yale or Stanford are still bastions of privilege. Few students from poor families attend, although if accepted, they receive comprehensive financial aid and pay less than at a state university (Lynch *et al.*, 2011). The culture is upper middle class and wealthy; students are provided with many academic and extra-curricular services, and graduation rates are similar to the rates of liberal arts colleges. Such institutions are called 'elite' not only for their current academic standards, but because the children of the very wealthy and powerful have been attending for generations. Indeed, children of alumni are given admission preferences.

College friendships are considered the basis of future networks that function in politics, finance, law and elsewhere. Women were only relatively recently admitted, two of the last holdouts were Yale and Princeton, which only admitted women in the late 1960s. Many of the elite men's colleges also had parallel women's colleges: Harvard had Radcliffe, Columbia had Barnard. They also had quotas for Jewish, black, and Irish Catholic students, and for others considered 'undesirable' until after the Second World War (Synnott, 1979). Today African Americans and Latinos attending as undergraduates may still be viewed with suspicion about their intellectual capabilities and treated as 'non-traditional' in this setting also.

The remaining forms of post-secondary education in the United States are too diverse to be considered here in relation to the acquisition of a bachelor's degree, and many do not confer first degrees in an academic field, such as theological colleges and law schools. What is significant is that the more prestigious the institution, the more likely women and students of colour will feel like, and be viewed as, non-traditional students, as they encounter forms of bias. At the undergraduate level, this is less likely to occur to women, except when in classes or majors in which women are still under-represented. In advanced and professional degree programmes such as law or medicine, as the stakes get higher, it is more likely that women will be made to feel strongly that they are non-traditional and do not belong. The same is true for students of colour. Graduate school can still be experienced by women and students of colour as 'Darwinian', fiercely competitive and hierarchical, with the sense of exclusion and discrimination documented in many studies, including those by the national academies (NAS-1, 2007; NAS-4 and Blank *et al.*, 2004). For women and faculty of colour this can be exacerbated.

Forms of exclusion since the Second World War and early attempts at broadening participation

The first real expansion in post-secondary participation after the Second World War arose from the aftermath of the war itself. In order to prevent massive unemployment as demobilisation occurred, the GI Bill was passed, which provided payment for tuition and living expenses for former military personnel. This Bill also provided low-cost mortgages and many other means of facilitating entrance to middle-class life. Because of the way in which it was administered, white male veterans profited most from this; women and black veterans had a much more limited opportunity to realise these benefits fully. As a result, from 1944, when the bill was passed, to 1955, 2,250,000 veterans – mostly white men – went to college, earned bachelor's degrees and, with new homes and good employment, moved into the middle class (Katznelson, 2005). College enrolment went from 1,100,737 in 1929–1930 to 2,653,034 in 1955 (NCES and Snyder *et al.*, 2011). But in this same period, the proportion of women enrolled dropped from a high of 40 per cent in 1930 to 32 per cent in the 1950s (Thelin, 2004: 267). Black students were still excluded from most US colleges and absolutely banned in the South. From this beginning, a great expansion in HE facilities was developed by states and the federal government to train more students and to create extensive research facilities supporting American science.

The current situation in post-secondary participation arose from the Civil Rights Movement of the 1950s and 1960s, as well as from the Women's Movement of the 1960s and beyond, in conjunction with a contemporary widespread drive for social justice. Until mid-century separate schools for black and white children in the southern United States were legally mandated, and formal segregation existed elsewhere, such as in San Francisco, where Mexican Americans and Asians as well as black students were prohibited from attending white schools. In 1954, the US Supreme Court ruling the 'Brown vs. the Board of Education of Topeka Kansas' that separate educational facilities for black students was inherently unequal, and that henceforth educational facilities of all kinds should be integrated. Most of the southern states resisted this ruling, leading to widespread protests by black demonstrators. The fight was not just for education, but for basic civil rights, particularly the right to vote, which had been sabotaged in local voting districts. In response to the protests, riots and murders taking place in the southern states as blacks demonstrated for their civil rights, the federal government responded by first sending US marshals and subsequently passing a large number of Civil Rights bills. During this period, many anti-poverty initiatives were also undertaken as President Johnson promoted his 'great society' programme. Emphasis was again placed on education as the vehicle to create citizens and provide the tools for successful employment as it had been until the Great Depression.

The cornerstone was the Civil Rights Act of 1964, which radically altered HE. It prohibited discrimination against students, employees and others on the basis of race, colour, national origin, religion and sex and applied to any organisation or institution receiving federal money. This was followed by the Higher Education Act of 1965. Its purpose as stated in Title IV was 'to assist in making the benefits of postsecondary education [available] to eligible students...in institutions of higher education'. The act provided grants to students, to the states for financial aid, and in particular paid for special programmes targeted at the poor – 'youths with financial or cultural need'. These included programmes to prepare students from low-income families for postsecondary education and programmes to provide remedial and other services to students (Texas: 1). Building on this foundation, many other laws and policies were put in place through the 1990s, which promoted college enrolment of students who were poor, members of minority groups and women. Of particular significance was President Johnson's administrative ruling enjoining institutions of higher education to take 'affirming action' to bring 'minority' students into HE.

There were many reasons why these programmes were initially very successful in promoting college success among women and students of colour. The US economy was expanding in the later 1960s, through the 1970s, and into the 1980s. While there were numerous federal agencies supporting college-level education after the War, including the National Science Foundation (NSF), the launch of Sputnik generated something of a frenzy of federal spending at all levels of education with the purpose of creating a scientifically proficient population capable of out-performing the Soviet Union. The real expansion of scientific educational programmes coincided with the well-funded and inclusive policies adopted in Congress in the 1960s and 1970s. Programmes were also started for 'minority' students – at the time mostly African Americans. Building on earlier programmes, the Louis Stokes Alliances for Minority Participation Program (LS-AMP) was founded in 1991 to increase under-represented post-secondary science graduates. This was an alliance of different types of institutions including high schools, colleges and graduate universities and worked to create a 'pipeline' of scientists and engineers. It is credited with supporting 24,642 bachelor's degree recipients in science in 2005 (Majesky-Fullmann, 2007). It is just one of the numerous federally funded education programmes intended to broaden participation in post-secondary education from kindergarten through to post-doctoral positions.

The impact of targeted programmes for women and students of colour was great, and the numbers of students of these populations steadily increased their enrolment in post-secondary education. The decade of 1980–1990 saw the highest proportional enrolment of students of colour at all levels, most noticeably at the PhD level. At the same time, however, affirmative action programmes were coming under attack by those who thought somehow poor students of colour and women were receiving 'unfair' advantages over whites, especially white men. A strong backlash against affirmative action resulted in several court cases, which essentially gutted such programmes. Misinformation about how affirmative action worked was widely believed, and many efforts were made to discredit it (Plous, 2003). This misinformation also affected excellent students who had to tolerate the assumption that they were dunderheads who were only enrolled because of affirmative action. The strongest stereotypical belief is that people of colour and women generally are not as intelligent as white men, and to this day this kind of prejudice drives students out of college and the professions. Assisting in potential failure is the phenomenon of 'stereotype threat' in which negative beliefs about one's intellectual capacity are internalised by women and minorities. When members of these groups are made aware of their minority status, they tend to perform poorly on tests and in other intellectual work

(Steele and Aronson, 1995). In this vicious circle, such students are still seen as non-traditional in far too many educational settings.

Impact of all programmes for broadening participation

The most successful programmes intended to increase participation in post-secondary education are those providing financial assistance and academic support for disadvantaged students whether poor, inadequately prepared for college or with a first language other than English. All these programmes such as the Pell Grants (free), the guaranteed student loan programme and several other forms of financial aid, including the Economic Opportunity Program, have widened participation greatly. As far as is known, the more focused affirmative action programs such as the LS-AMP were also successful but supported far fewer individuals. The population of qualified students of colour from disadvantaged backgrounds ready for college was small in the 1970s, and so in a way, any increase in their participation is a win. But the programmes were usually created as part of the federal affirmative action initiative and funded by the many federal agencies: NSF, Department of Education, Department of Defense, National Institutes of Health, Department of Energy and so on. They require one or more faculty members to compete for funding through a complicated grant application process for a programme, which may or may not be effective in broadening participation. Until recently, programmes created in the 1970s and later had virtually no evaluation of their effectiveness, no tracking of student participants and no sense of the money and effort being well applied. That has only changed in the last few years, but even now there is no overall picture of the degree of success. For example, NSF funds a ten-week summer research programme (Research Experience for Undergraduates (REU) intended to increase the number of minorities in Science, Technology, Engineering and Mathematics (STEM) by enabling them to work with a senior scientist at a research university and become enthusiastic about pursuing a research PhD. There are currently over 600 REU sites in the United States in all disciplines but the humanities, with around 10–15 students in each. This programme was designed for students 'under-represented in science' (minorities and women) who are the first in their family to attend college, attend an institution with few research facilities and who have an interest in a science career. It is likely that the programme initially functioned as intended, but if so, there is no general documentation. Today, the programme is being compromised by accepting students with educated parents: immigrants who look like African Americans but are, for example, Ethiopian, Nigerian, Trinidadian, or from other parts of the world as well as students from other research universities (Russell, 2005; MacLachlan, 2011). Few are of the population originally intended.

If students of colour, women and the otherwise disadvantaged are to merge into the educational mainstream, the educational system that now ensures their non-traditional status needs reform from the bottom up. Success in secondary education today still depends very much on class and race. Schools are being re-segregated by the more affluent congregating in predominantly white neighbourhoods, while the poor and children of colour are left behind in inadequately funded schools (Orfield, 2009). College access requires appropriate academic preparation which the 16,000 'poverty schools' (schools defined as having 75–100 per cent of pupils on the free lunch programme) do not provide (NCES-4 and Aud *et al.*, 2010). The socio-economic environment and disconnect from middle-class life for those who may want to go to college may lead them into making college choices in which they are disproportionately likely to fail. Programmes created to assist such students have helped to foster success, but as part of the current polarisation of American politics, cuts in educational funding of all kinds are occurring. Those public colleges and universities enrolling more than 70 per cent of all undergraduate students have had to reduce the number they can accommodate, cut majors and classes, raise tuition, end many student support and advising services and generally reduce academic quality as class size grows and more adjunct untenured faculty instruct those classes. Increasingly a college education is considered by a portion of the electorate, including many students, to be a workforce-training exercise, not a place where students are exposed to many and new ideas, taught to think analytically and to explore the fullness of intellectual endeavour.

Broadening participation

The United States led the world in broadening participation in post-secondary education after the Second World War when college enrolment increased from 2,444,900 in 1950 to 18 million by 2009 (NCES-5 and Snyder *et al.*, 2011: 112, 291). Enrolment expanded from a small elite to a broad cross section of the population. HE participation for the 18–24 cohort rose to 69 per cent in 2002 but has since dropped to 62 per cent. Today, colleges and universities enrol more than 50 per cent women and more members than ever before of ethnic groups long excluded from mainstream HE.

While these numbers reflect a social revolution, the disproportion in participation by various groups and the increasing gap between white, black and Hispanic degree acquisition point to deep structural problems. The gap between white and black bachelor's attainment has risen from 12 per cent points in 1971 to 18 per cent in 2009, with the white–Hispanic gap increasing from 14 per cent to 25 per cent points (NCES-4 and Aud *et al.*, 2010: vii). Efforts to address these problems take many different forms ranging from individual initiatives in schools and colleges, larger targeted programmes such as those privately funded by the Bill and Melinda Gates

Foundation in the Seattle school district, state-wide initiatives through state departments of education and a great many federally funded programmes. 'Broadening participation' is a current buzz word in education at all levels including many federal agencies. Of course, every activity that assists excluded students is to be applauded, and every single student who is enabled to attend college and succeed there needs to be celebrated. Efforts by individual four-year institutions to bridge the gaps in access and persistence can often be successful and should be taken seriously. Retention efforts do not have to be expensive, more so if it is an institution-wide approach in which faculty and staff are cooperatively working to bring about student achievement (College Board, 2011). At the present time, however, it is unlikely that any individual programme or the huge multiplicity of programmes will succeed even in the middle term in 'fixing' the national problem of deep economic and social inequality, which is the basis for uneven post-secondary participation. Broadening participation cannot be confined to educational initiatives, however, well designed and funded.

Nonetheless, there is a serious national effort at the level of the National Academies of Science and Engineering (NAS) to broaden participation. The focus is on the national scientific workforce keeping up with global standards by utilising all the talent of the United States. The seriousness of the concern is reflected in the title of their 2006 publication, *Rising Above the Gathering Storm, Energizing and Employing America for a Brighter Economic Future*. NAS has conducted and published studies on bias, discrimination, and unequal educational access with titles such as *Beyond Bias and Barriers* (2006), focusing on women, and *Expanding Underrepresented Minority Participation: America's Science and Technology Talent at the Crossroads* (2011). Execution of the recommendations in these studies is by federal agencies such as the NSF, which has put great effort into analysing existing educational and training programmes (NSF, 2008; NSF and Clewell, 2009). The approach is targeted at under-represented individuals, institutions and regions of the United States. Many other federal agencies are similarly engaged.

Yet, the likelihood of these efforts being very successful even in the next decade is highly uncertain. As we have seen, increasing numbers of young people of colour are not participating in post-secondary education or not participating successfully. Extensive gaps in high-school completion, poverty, rising college costs and changing financial aid policies work against success. These persons of colour and women generally still face substantial bias and discrimination even when successful in enrolling in college. Perhaps even more disheartening is that federal programmes devolve to individuals to implement them, individuals who may hold their own biases and through them undermine the intent of the funded programmes they run. It is a general pattern to consider immigrants of colour as US minorities (see Harvard's announcement of its 'diverse' entering class), admit them to programmes intended for US disadvantaged students and derive satisfaction from their success in terms of having met the federal mandate.[6] Immigrants are frequently highly motivated students and come from countries that may be poor, but which may have excellent secondary education, and such students are in many ways more tractable than US students (Bennett and Lutz, 2009). If this misappropriation of broadening participation strategies was not already a source of deep concern, the current political landscape has allowed the appropriation of educational priorities to a deeply anti-intellectual section of the electorate. The result is the widespread disparagement of going to college at all, serious cutting of HE funding in many states and at the federal level, and a climate actively hostile to the poor, minorities and women.

It should be an anomaly in 21st-century America that women and students of colour are still considered to be non-traditional students in some educational settings. Yet this is not likely to change in coming years. Truly, broadening post-secondary participation requires a different vision of civil society, not a tacit acceptance of growing income and educational disparities. Inclusion flows from a principled commitment to equality and a willingness to work towards achieving it.

Notes

1. Latino and Hispanic are both used in statistical sources and are used here interchangeably.
2. In the United States, 'broadening' participation is used instead of 'widening' participation.
3. See the Carnegie Foundation website for full information on 4,635 accredited institutions: http://classifications.carnegiefoundation.org/
4. There is great variation in student enrolment and graduation rates in four-year and master's granting institutions among the various states.
5. A full review of the impact of racism and differential treatment on undergraduates of colour can be found in Dowd *et al.* (2011).
6. The alarm sounded by Professors Lani Guinier and Henry Louis Gates Jr in 2004 about Harvard claiming immigrants as domestic minorities is confirmed in Bennett and Lutz (2009).

Bibliography

ACT (2010) *2010 Retention/Completion Summary Tables. Institutional Data Files* (Iowa City: American College Testing Program).

Bennett, P.R. and Lutz, A. (2009) 'How African American Is the Net Black Advantage? Differences in College Attendance among Immigrant Blacks, Native Blacks, and Whites', *Sociology of Education*, 82 (January): 70–100.

Carnevale, A.P. and Strohl, J. (2010) 'How Increasing College Access Is Increasing Inequality and What To Do about It', in Kahlenberg, R.D. (ed.) *Rewarding Strivers: Helping Low-Income Students Succeed in College* (New York: The Century Foundation Press, pp. 71–207).

College Board Advocacy & Policy Center (2011) *How Four-Year Colleges and Universities Organize Themselves to Promote Student Persistence* (New York: College Board).

Deere, C.D. and Doss, C.R. (2006) 'The Gender Asset Gap: What Do We Know and Why Does it Matter', *Feminist Economics*, 12 (1–2): 1–50.

Dowd, A.C., Sawatzky, M. and Korn, R. (2011) 'Theoretical Foundations and a Research Agenda to Validate Measures of Intercultural Effort', *The Review of Higher Education*, 35 (1): 17–44.

Fry, R. and Hinze-Pifer, R. (2010) *The Rise of Student Borrowing. Social and Demographic Trends Report* (Washington, DC: Pew Research Center).

Gonyea, R.M., Kuh, G.D., *et al.* (2008) *Expectations and Engagement: How Liberal Arts College Students Compare with Counterparts Elsewhere* (Bloomington, IN: Indiana University, National Center for Postsecondary Research).

Hernandez, A. (2010) 'Report: Poor High School Counseling Could Lead to Diminished Opportunities,' *Diverse Education*, 3 March 2010.

Howard-Hamilton, M.F., Merlon-Quainoo, C.L., *et al.* (eds) (2009) *Standing on the Outside Looking in: Underrepresented Students' Experiences in Advanced-Degree Programs* (Sterling, VA: Stylus).

IHEP (2011) *Initial College Attendance of Low-Income Young Adults* (Washington, DC: Institute for Higher Education Policy).

Katznelson, I. (2005) *When Affirmative Action Was White: The Untold History of Racial Inequality in Twentieth-Century America* (New York: Norton).

Leonhardt, D. (2011) 'Top Colleges, Largely for the Elite,' *New York Times*, 24 May 2011.

Lynch, M., Engle, J., *et al.* (2011) *Priced Out: How the Wrong Financial-Aid Policies Hurt Low-Income Students* (Washington, DC: The Education Trust).

MacLachlan, A.J. (2011) *Understanding the Impact of Interventions on Students in Summer Research Programs*. Understanding Interventions Conference, Vanderbilt University, 27 May 2011. [online] http://www.understandinginterventions.org/index.php/2011-oral-presentations/ [accessed 22 August 2012].

MacLachlan, A.J. (2010) *Student Experience with Counseling at an Urban Community College*. Unpublished, Center for Studies in Higher Education, UC Berkeley.

Majesky-Fullmann, O. (2007) 'Just the Stats: How Effective Are STEM Pipeline Programs?' *Diverse: Issues in Higher Education*, 21 June 2007.

Mullen, A.L. (2010) *Degrees of Inequality: Culture, Class, and Gender in American Higher Education* (Baltimore, MD: Johns Hopkins University Press).

NAS-1 (2007) *Beyond Bias and Barriers: Fulfilling the Potential of Women in Academic Science and Engineering* (Washington, DC: The National Academies).

NAS-2 (2007) *Rising Above the Gathering Storm: Energizing and Employing America for a Brighter Economic Future* (Washington, DC: The National Academies).

NAS-3 (2011) *Expanding Underrepresented Minority Participation: America's Science and Technology Talent at the Crossroads* (Washington, DC: The National Academies).

NAS-4, Blank, R.M., Dabady, M. and Citro, C.F. (eds) (2004) *Measuring Racial Discrimination* (Washington, DC: The National Research Council).

NBER, Bound, J., *et al.* (2009) *Why Have College Completion Rates Declined? An Analysis of Changing Student Preparation and Collegiate Resources*. NBER Working Paper Series (Cambridge, MA: National Bureau of Economic Research).

NCES-1, Provasnik, S. and Shafer, L.L. (2004) *Historically Black Colleges and Universities, 1976 to 2001* (Washington, DC: National Center for Education Statistics).

NCES-2 and Stillwell, R. (2010) *Public School Graduates and Dropouts From the Common Core of Data: School Year 2007-08: First Look* (Washington, DC: National Center for

Education Statistics).NCES-3, Horn, L., *et al.* (2009) *On Track to Complete? A Taxonomy of Beginning Community College Students and Their Outcomes 3 Years After Enrolling: 2003-04 Through 2006* (Washington, DC: National Center for Education Statistics).

NCES-4, Aud, S., *et al.* (2010) *The Condition of Education 2010* (Washington, DC: National Center for Education Statistics).

NCES-5, Radford, A.W., *et al.* (2010) *Persistence and Attainment of 2003–04 Beginning Postsecondary Students: After 6 Years. First Look* (Washington, DC: National Center for Education Statistics).

NCES-5 and Snyder, T., *et al.* (2011) *Digest of Education Statistics 2010* (Washington, DC: National Center for Education Statistics).

NPC National Poverty Center (2011) 'Poverty in the United States: Frequently Asked Questions.' [online] http://www.npc.umich.edu/poverty/ [accessed 21 July 2011].

NSF, Clewell, B.C., *et al.* (eds) (2009) *Framework for Evaluating Impacts of Broadening Participation Projects* (Arlington, VA: National Science Foundation).

NSF (2008) *Broadening Participation at the National Science Foundation: A Framework for Action* (Arlington, VA: National Science Foundation).

Orfield, G. (2009) *Reviving the Goal of an Integrated Society: A 21st Century Challenge* (Los Angeles: Civil Rights Project, UCLA).

O'Shaughnessy, L. (2011) *Where Professors Send Their Children to College.* CBS Moneywatch [online] http://moneywatch.bnet.com/spending/blog/college-solution/where-professors-send-their-children-to-college/4508/?tag=col1;blog-river [accessed 22 September 2011].

O'Shaughnessy, L. (2010) *25 Private Colleges with the Best Graduation Rates.* CBS Moneywatch [online] http://moneywatch.bnet.com/spending/blog/college-solution/25-private-colleges-with-the-best-graduation-rates/4426/ [accessed 27 July 2011].

Plous, S. (2003) 'Ten Myths About Affirmative Action', in Plous, S. (ed.) *Understanding Prejudice and Discrimination* (New York: McGraw-Hill, pp. 206–212).

Russell, S.H. (2005) *Evaluation of NSF Support for Undergraduate Research Opportunities, Survey of STEM Graduates* (Menlo Park, CA: SRI International).

Saulny, S. (2011) 'Census Data Presents Rise in Multiracial Population of Youths,' *New York Times*, 24 March 2011.

Selingo, J. and Brainard, J. (2006) 'The Rich-Poor Gap Widens for Colleges and Students', *Chronicle of Higher Education*, 52 (31): 7.

Steele, C.M. and Aronson, J. (1995) 'Stereotype Threat and the Intellectual Test Performance of African Americans', *Journal of Personality and Social Psychology*, 69 (5): 797–811.

Synnott, M.G. (1979) *The Half-Opened Door: Discrimination and Admissions at Harvard, Yale, and Princeton, 1900-1970* (Westport, CT: Greenwood).

Taylor, P., Fry, R., *et al.* (2010) *Minorities and the Recession-Era College Enrollment Boom. Social & Demographic Trends Project* (Washington, DC: Pew Research Center).

Texas Guaranteed Student Loan Corporation (2004) *Title IV-Student Assistance* [online] http://'www.tgslc.org/pdf/HEA_Title_IV_Oct02.pdf [accessed 12 June 2011].

Thelin, J.R. (2004) *The History of American Higher Education* (Baltimore, MD: Johns Hopkins University Press).

US Census Bureau-1, Getz, D.M. (2010) *Men's and Women's Earnings for States and Metropolitan Statistical Areas: 2009* (Washington, DC: U.S. Department of Commerce, U.S. Census Bureau).

US Census Bureau-2 (2011) 'Educational Attainment in the United States: 2010-Detailed Tables.' Retrieved 12 June 2010.

US Census Bureau-3 (2011) *2010 Census Shows America's Diversity. U.S. Census Bureau News* (Washington, DC: U.S. Department of Commerce).

US Census Bureau-4 (2011) *The 2011 Statistical Abstract: Section Income, Expenditures, Poverty and Wealth* (Washington, DC: U.S. Department of Commerce). Tables 689–705.

US Census Bureau-5, Bishaw, A., *et al.* (2010) *Poverty: 2008 and 2009* (Washington, DC: U.S. Department of Commerce).

US Census Bureau-6, Humes, K.R., *et al.* (2011) *Overview of Race and Hispanic Origin: 2010.* Census Briefs (Washington, DC: U.S. Department of Commerce).

17
Widening Participation and 'Elite' Online Education: The Case of the University of California

Sarah Earl-Novell

Introduction

This chapter focuses on the University of California's (UC) effort to become one of the first 'elite' institutions in the United States to deliver online undergraduate education *vis-à-vis* its Online Instruction Pilot Project (OIPP). The project is part of a wider initiative to evaluate the merits of online instruction to determine whether high-quality education can be offered through a digital medium. UC, California's flagship university system, constitutes one part of a three-tier higher education (HE) structure, which also includes the California State University (CSU) system and the California Community Colleges. While efforts to expand HE into a non-traditional online realm could increase revenue and student access (and eventually enable non-UC students to take UC-taught online courses prior to applying or transferring to a university within the system), there is widespread concern over the dilution of quality education.

Widening participation initiatives, including the OIPP in California, may contribute to efforts to diversify the undergraduate student body and increase the representation of minority and mature students and those from lower socio-economic backgrounds. The ramifications for the college gender gap, however, remain unclear; currently fewer men than women enrol, persist and graduate from university.

'Elite' online higher education

Public higher education in California

California's master plan for public HE, adopted in 1960, is a three-tier system – UC, CSU and the California Community Colleges – with a distinct mission for each tier. The most select tier includes the ten-campus, research-intensive UC system and offers undergraduate teaching through doctoral training. The second tier comprises the 23-institution-strong CSU network, which predominately offers undergraduate and master's degrees. The third tier of 110 community colleges offers vocational and workforce training leading to two-year associate's degrees as well as courses that prepare students to transfer to a university within the UC or CSU system (Douglass in Sengupta and Jepsen, 2006; Corbyn, 2011).

The Online Instruction Pilot Project at UC

Information and communication technologies are enabling the transformation of the learning process. While traditional learning methods are still used and valued by students, the means by which many undergraduates communicate, acquire and absorb information is shifting.[1] In response to this transformation, UC is launching the OIPP,[2] which will reach out to this technologically savvy student base. While the terms 'online learning', 'e-learning' and 'distance learning' are frequently used interchangeably, it is worth noting that distance learning often encompasses a wide array of methods and has a long pre-Internet history. On the other hand, e-learning and online learning can be purely Internet-based and/or include a hybrid of online and face-to-face instruction (Harley and Lawrence, 2006).[3] In fact, many on-campus undergraduate courses nowadays incorporate digital instruction into traditional face-to-face classroom-based teaching.

The UC, like many other state-funded universities in the United States, finds itself in unchartered waters. Faced with increased staff furloughs, cuts in student enrolment, rise in tuition fees and decline in state fiscal support, the OIPP may provide the university system with a way to reshape itself by widening student participation and creating much-needed revenue.[4]

Proponents have suggested that the OIPP is paving the way for the introduction of quality online education at top universities and that many other universities will follow UC's lead (Edley, 2010). While a number of the nation's most prestigious universities – including the Massachusetts Institute of Technology (MIT) and Yale – have provided free access to undergraduate course materials for a number of years, they do not offer online credit or bachelor's degrees (Walsh, 2011). Moreover, while UC has historically offered online courses to graduate students and through extension programmes, full-time undergraduates do not typically take these courses for credit.

Integral to the pilot project is developing and delivering online courses from all ten UC campuses to the currently enrolled UC students as well as a formal evaluation of the project itself. The pilot has been conducted in two phases. During the planning phase (from October 2010 to March 2011), faculty could submit course proposals for inclusion. UC is currently in the implementation phase (from March 2011 to December 2012), which involves the development, delivery and evaluation of twenty-nine selected online courses. The first courses will be on offer from early 2012.

The overarching goals of the OIPP are to (i) test whether online instruction can provide students with educational opportunities commensurate to the first-rate classroom instruction that has historically defined UC institutions and (ii) enable the university system to evaluate the merits and value of online instruction.

The pros and cons of 'elite' online education

Supporters of online HE emphasise the potential of new revenue streams created by widening student participation. They argue that as demand for a UC education rises, the OIPP would eventually enable the university system to expand student access and enrolment by offering high-quality online courses to a greater number of students than traditional means of instruction alone. Indeed, in a recent speech, Christopher Edley Jr, co-leader of the project, hypothesised that online degrees could accomplish the 'democratization of access to elite education' and, consequently, help diversify the student body.

Some research indicates that students in blended learning environments perform moderately better than those receiving only face-to-face instruction (Means *et al.*, 2010), although this is heavily contested by others (Figlio *et al.*, 2010). For some commentators, the advantage of online education over traditional classroom-based instruction is the emphasis on self-paced learning; learning is not a one-size-fits-all experience (Khan, 2011). Furthermore, it has been suggested that online instruction could speed up the trajectory to graduation. Interestingly, a recent survey produced by the Pew Research Center indicates that college presidents value online education more highly than the general public. Moreover, college presidents predict a substantial growth in online learning (Parker *et al.*, 2011).

Unsurprisingly, there is much faculty opposition to the introduction of online education within the UC system. There is concern that the UC's high-quality educational system could be diluted. Since online education is often associated with community colleges, some fear that the UC might be perceived as downscaling, particularly in light of (some well-funded, high-profile) failed attempts of blended learning offerings at other institutions.[5] Others are concerned that online education could ultimately lead to a de-skilling of university teaching. In addition, insufficient demand could result in limited enrolment alongside significant upfront costs for technology and faculty training, which could further stress the state's HE budget. A core concern is whether online versus face-to-face learning is really in the best interest of students in terms of academic development, particularly as withdrawal rates are typically higher for online instruction compared with traditional classroom courses (Levy, 2007).

The future of University of California's online education

The ultimate success of the project depends on its evaluation of the merits of online instruction. If deemed successful by faculty and administrators, UC will expand its offering of online courses. It is envisaged that, ultimately, UC will widen student participation by directly partnering with community colleges and high schools, which would enable non-UC students to take UC-taught online courses. These students could then transfer or apply to a college with already-earned UC credits. In terms of blue-sky thinking, UC could become one of the first 'elite' institutions to deliver online undergraduate education *vis-à-vis* the development of a 'virtual' university or an 11th UC campus.

The college gender gap

In recent years, trend statistics indicate that men, not women, are finding themselves positioned on the unfavourable side of the college gender gap (Riordan, 2003; CPEC, 2006a; King, 2010), a disparity echoed between the sexes in primary and secondary schooling (that is, kindergarten through to 12th grade) and fast becoming a global phenomenon (Goldin *et al.*, 2006). Research shows that women are more likely to attend university, persist with their studies and earn the majority of undergraduate degrees. Moreover, the college enrolment gender gap is expected to widen over the next decade (Gerald and Hussar, 2003; Sum *et al.*, 2003), with projections indicating that the average US campus will have two women graduates for every male (Whitmire, 2011). By contrast, some have suggested that while women represent the numerical majority, student enrolment has reached a plateau and stabilised, with the exception of the Hispanic undergraduate population (King, 2010).

Given the likelihood of a future move towards Internet-based learning within the UC system for non-UC students, it is worth considering the implications for the college gender gap in terms of student participation, retention and attainment.

Historical overview

Thirty to forty years ago, academics and practitioners flagged the ways in which education short-changed girls and women (for example, Sadker and Sadker, 1995; Margolis and Fisher, 2003). Scholarly research on gender inequity in education focused almost exclusively on women and frequently treated 'all aspects of education as disadvantaging women' (Jacobs, 1996: 156) The academic performance of the two genders converged in the early 1990s, followed by a 180-degree turnaround with more women forging ahead academically. In addition, there was a reversal in undergraduate participation and retention patterns.

To date, neither national nor state educational policymakers have seriously addressed the under-representation and under-performance of men at the university level. Moreover, suggestions that academic research concentrate on male participation, persistence and attainment in HE are met with some resistance. As Mead (2006) points out, a shift in the gender debate has tapped into public fear of changing gender roles and boys' so-called academic deficits. Furthermore, a refocus of scholarly attention may be seen as detracting from the gender inequity that continues to favour men, not to mention other inequities along social class and ethnic lines.

For universities, though, it is imperative that post-secondary education maintains a balanced male–female ratio in student enrolment figures (Riordan, 2003), not least to attract students of both sexes. Yet moves to minimise gender imbalances remain a challenge because affirmative action admission policies are illegal for public institutions.[6] Having launched an investigation looking into 'gendered' admissions favouritism, the US Commission on Civil Rights suspended the investigation after collecting incomplete data.[7] As men are viewed as highly valued applicants (given their fewer numbers in relative terms), some institutions are attracting male students through increased sports and academic opportunities, such as adding football teams or engineering programmes to their curricular offerings.

From an economic perspective, the growing college gender gap has serious implications for the future US labour force. As Sum *et al.* (2003) note, it is critical that colleges attract male students. Lower attainment rates among men result in a reduction in the size of a skilled, educated labour force and a subsequent decline in labour productivity and economic growth. Moreover, better-educated adult males are less likely to be unemployed and earn higher annual earnings than their lesser-educated counterparts. From a sociological and a psychological perspective, the educational marginalisation of men will undermine their ability to perform important social functions and roles – including 'father' and 'breadwinner' – that strengthen the very fabric of society (Sum *et al.*, 2003). Gauges of success look bleak for male adolescents: the Boys Project reports that young boys are less likely to be on the honour roll and more likely to be suspended or expelled from school, to withdraw from school and to commit suicide.[8]

Enrolment, persistence and attainment

The gender gap in HE can be observed using a number of indicators including college outcomes such as degree enrolment, persistence rates and educational attainment (that is, the receipt of a four-year bachelor's degree). The statistical picture is complex and diverse, though overall it indicates that women outnumber and outperform men in HE and have higher persistence rates. Since 1980, female undergraduate enrolment has risen to about 1.3 women for every man (Goldin *et al.*, 2006). A recent report indicates that men now represent 43 per cent of degree enrolment and earn 43 per cent of bachelor's degrees in the United States (King, 2010). In particular, women have increased their representation among younger, full-time students (Peter and Horn, 2005). It should be noted, however, that both sexes have made significant gains educationally, but those made by women have been far more pronounced. For instance, while the number of men attending college is increasing, the number of women is rising at a much faster rate.

Persistence can be measured by the number of students who start college and earn degrees within a specific time period. Using this measure, the growth in collegiate completion rates is very clearly higher among women than men (Buchmann and DiPrete, 2006). Figures produced by the National Center for Education Statistics show that in public four-year institutions, the six-year graduation rates for female students were higher than their male counterparts; 58 per cent of women seeking a bachelor's degree graduated within six years, compared with only 52 per cent of men (Aud *et al.*, 2010).

At most universities and in most academic disciplines, women continue to outperform men (Willingham and Cole, 1997; Mau and Lynn, 2001). At all levels of degree attainment, and particularly at the associate's degree level,[9] the rate of increase in college degrees conferred to women is several times higher than those awarded to their male counterparts. In 2000, women earned 151 associate's degrees, 133 bachelor's degrees and 138 master's degrees for every 100 degrees earned by men (Sum *et al.*, 2003). Moreover, women are now majoring in many disciplines that have been traditionally in the male domain (Adebayo, 2008), such as law and the biological sciences.

Women have also gained significant ground in their receipt of PhDs; women now earn slightly more than 50 per cent of the PhDs awarded by American universities (Mason and Ekman, 2007). In fact, they have achieved parity in the graduate programmes of law and business administration, though minority women continue to be under-represented in many academic programmes (MacLachlan, 2006). Since 1984, the number of women in graduate schools exceeded the number of males. Between 1997 and 2007, the number of full-time female graduate students increased by 63 per cent, when compared with a 32 per cent increase for their male counterparts (Snyder and Dillow, 2010), though such increases remain discipline-specific.

The interplay of ethnicity, social class and gender

Some have urged scholars to focus less on the college gender gap and more on social class and racial gaps in university enrolment and attainment. The HE system is failing certain segments of the population. In particular, African American and Hispanic men and men from lower socio-economic backgrounds fall into this category (Riordan, 2003; Peter and Horn, 2005; King, 2010). Specifically, a 2005 NCES report indicates that, for the academic year 1999–2000, women made up 63 per cent of all black undergraduates. It is clear, however, that men are trailing behind women academically,[10] a pattern further amplified by race or socio-economic class.

Enrolment, persistence and attainment in California

California higher education institutions (HEIs) reflect the national picture for student enrolment, persistence and degree attainment. Reports produced by the California Postsecondary Education Commission (CPEC) show that females in every major ethnic group are over-represented in HE relative to their representation in the state's population.

Since 1983, women have exceeded their male peers in undergraduate enrolment. By 2004, women in all ethnic groups superseded men in undergraduate enrolment. Among African Americans, more women than men have enrolled within the UC and CSU systems since 1976 (the first year that data became available). The same is true among Latinos since 1985, among Asian–Pacific Islanders since 1997 and among Caucasians since 1981 (CPEC, 2006a).

Persistence has also been greater for women than men across all ethnic groups in the UC and CSU systems. In 2000, the freshman gender breakdown within the UC system was 55.6 per cent female and 44.4 per cent male. Five years later, the proportion of students awarded degrees was 60 per cent female and 40 per cent male (CPEC, 2006a).

By 1981, more Caucasian women than Caucasian men were awarded bachelor's degrees and, by 2004, female students outpaced their male counterparts in degree attainment across all ethnic groups (CPEC, 2006a).

Explanations for male inequity in higher education

There are several explanations for 'gendered' patterns of participation, persistence and attainment at the bachelor's degree level. While some point to the success of policies aimed at promoting female educational prosperity or a chilly campus climate now experienced by male students, others highlight that young males have slipped behind in literacy skills just as society is becoming more verbal (Whitmire, 2010).

Some commentators have suggested that aggregate gender differences in enrolment and earned degrees simply reflect differences in the actual student population. In other words, there are more women than men of student age. This is heavily contested by CPEC; in California in 2004, men constituted about 51.3 per cent of the population between 18 and 34 years of age, while women made up 48.7 per cent. In particular, males outnumbered females among Latinos and Whites were roughly equal among Asian–Pacific Islanders, and trailed only among African Americans (CPEC, 2006a). Despite these figures, women continue to constitute the majority of university enrolments and earned degrees across all ethnic groupings.

Moreover, some studies show that males are simply disengaged; educational expectations, college preparation and academic engagement are higher among females than their male peers (Freeman, 2004; Sax, 2008), which may correlate with actual academic performance (Woodfield *et al.*, 2006). The National Longitudinal Survey of Youth indicated that, during 1997, women were significantly more likely than men to report that they expected to graduate from four years of college. Moreover, research indicates that women have improved their academic preparation with respect to men (Peter and Horn, 2005). Linda Sax (2008) shows in her study, using data from University of California, Los Angeles' (UCLA's) Higher Education Research Institute annual studies, that male students are more likely than females to miss classes, fail to complete or hand in their homework on time and spend less time studying and engaging in extra-curricular activities (such as volunteering and getting involved in students clubs and groups).

In their analyses of two large data sets,[11] sociologists Buchmann and DiPrete (2006) found that the female-favourable trend in college completion is attributable to a number of factors. In particular, they note a declining rate of college completion among male students from families with 'low-educated' or absent fathers. It is interesting that sons seem particularly vulnerable to academic failure in the absence of strong male role models, while daughters surge ahead in HE irrespective of family composition. Other factors, which could contribute to the growing female advantage in college completion, include the decrease of overt gender discrimination and growing incentives for women to attend university. There may be increased interest among young women to pursue educational opportunities as they witness improved schooling and employment among maternal role models. In today's society, women may work hard to provide 'insurance' for their futures (Buchmann and DiPrete, 2006).

Female inequity on campus and in the workplace

Significant educational advances made by the female student population must be understood in the context of gender inequities that continue to favour men (Sax, 2008), which colour the social and academic development of both sexes while at university. Female students can experience a chilly climate on campus often in the form of overt and covert discrimination; for example, male students may verbally dominate the classroom. Moreover, many high-achieving women fall prey to a leaky pipeline. A history of high grades and outstanding graduate work does not always translate into a successful academic career particularly as men continue to dominate the higher echelons of academia underpinned by a higher rate of promotion to the academic tenure track. Women are more likely than their male peers to be low income (Bobbitt-Zeher, 2007; Sax and Arms, 2008; Mason, 2009), older (aged 40 or older), have dependents or children or be single parents – all of which are characteristics associated with lower rates of degree completion (Berkner *et al.*, 2002).

Choice of undergraduate major and career aspirations remain 'gendered'; men continue to dominate computer and information sciences, engineering, mathematics and physical sciences (though the proportion of women increased in all these disciplines between 1976 and 2004), while women are over-represented in the social sciences, health professions, communications and the biological sciences (CPEC, 2006a). Female students continue to report higher levels of stress and lower levels of academic self-confidence than their male counterparts (Woodfield and Earl-Novell, 2006; Sax and Arms, 2008), despite their better academic performance. Post-secondary educational gains made by women are not necessarily transferred to the world of work, as flagged by American Association of University Women (AAUW) and others. Gender inequity remains evident in post-collegiate salary among men and women and in the over-representation of women in part-time positions.

'Elite' online education and implications for the college gender gap

Given what is known about gender inequities in California's HE system, the question remains: What are the implications for the college gender gap if 'elite' online education is made more widely available?

Pooling from the California Community Colleges system

Initially, a small selection of online courses will be available through the OIPP to currently enrolled UC students. If successful, however, it is anticipated that exclusively online courses will be on offer to non-UC students, including community college students seeking to transfer to a four-year college within the UC or CSU systems.

The California Community Colleges system is self-described as the largest post-secondary education system globally.[12] As illustrated earlier in this chapter, statistics show that the college gender gap is replicated at community college level (Mead, 2006). While UC currently accepts transfer students from community colleges, a move towards offering greater access to online 'elite' education could result in increased recruitment from this predominately female student pool, exacerbating an already existing college gender gap.

Over the last 30 years, there has been an increase in the enrolment of women at two-year community colleges, a trend not insignificant relative to men's enrolment (Gill and Leigh, 2000). In 1977, females comprised 53 per cent of the California Community Colleges intake. By 2003, this had increased to 57 per cent (CPEC, 2006a). While overall women outnumber men, this difference increases with age. When broken down, the representation of men and women in the 17–20 and 21–25 age groups are almost identical. It is the over-representation of women in the older age groups that skew the figures and create the overall gender difference. Moreover, while college transfer rates differ by age (that is, younger students are more likely to transfer than their more mature counterparts), they do not differ by gender (Sengupta and Jepsen, 2006). Consequently, because mature women at community colleges are less likely than their younger female counterparts to transfer to a UC institution, it may be that UC will not experience a female-heavy intake of students from this tier of public

HE. On the other hand, it could be argued that mature students (many of whom have families and jobs) may be more likely to benefit from the flexibility of online courses and use them as a conduit to a four-year bachelor's degree.

Gender differences in online versus face-to-face learning

It is worth considering whether there exists a 'gendered' uptake in and preference for online learning versus face-to-face interaction, which might exacerbate the college gender gap. Historically, non-traditional forms of education have appealed to students with family and professional commitments, those looking to resume their education following an interruption to their studies and those looking for a more cost-efficient education. In particular, distance learning has been evidenced to be attractive to women with dependents because of the greater flexibility afforded by online education over traditional education (Hinton-Smith, 2012).

There is a diverse and multi-dimensional body of commentary on gender differences in online learning. While it is suggested that men and women experience online learning in different ways (Herring, 1994; Weinman and Cain, 1999), there is some dispute as to whether a 'gendered' preference exists for online learning versus face-to-face interaction. Some scholars suggest that women flourish in a learning setting underpinned by face-to-face communication (Anderson, 1997). Studies from the early 1990s point to a 'locker room' atmosphere in the online learning environment (see Young and McSporran, 2001, for a detailed discussion), with men tending to 'hog' the cyber conversation and posting comments that are more forceful or aggressive than those posted by their female counterparts (Herring, 1994). As a result, women may feel alienated and without a voice and/or unmotivated and reluctant to participate in online conversational forums. More recent research, however, indicates that women who experience shyness or are reserved in a classroom setting may thrive in a more anonymous digital environment (Young and McSporran, 2001).

Several studies show that online learning favours the types of skills typically associated with women (such as self-regulation, an ability to manage time and organise material), and that women perform better than men academically in a digital environment (Young and McSporran, 2001), though such differences are often overstated (Yukselturk and Bulut, 2009). The workload associated with online learning is significant; the pedagogical approach, which is heavily tilted towards reading, combined with technical demands associated with online learning, do not make online learning an easy option over more traditional instruction.

In sum, it is unclear whether women have a greater preference than men for online learning and whether online instruction taps into a skill set typically associated with females. Given that withdrawal rates in online courses are greater than face-to-face classes (Levy, 2007; Xu and Jaggars, 2011), we can only hope that the growing male attrition rate is not worsened under the new system.

Conclusion

Widening participation efforts have important ramifications for non-traditional students, particularly with regard to diversifying the undergraduate student body. In the event that UC-taught online courses are offered to non-UC students, the move towards 'elite' online education will essentially provide access to groups of students historically estranged in large numbers from the more select UC HE system. The OIPP may, therefore, go some way in addressing equity issues around access – particularly among minorities, mature students and those from lower socio-economic backgrounds – and, in effect, maximise the benefits of college for all by democratising access to high-quality education.

It is paramount, though, that the ramifications on the college gender gap be considered in the context of expanding 'elite' online education. At present, a paucity of reliable empirical research prevents us from validating or discrediting the hypotheses on the 'boy crisis'. Is the gender gap in enrolment, persistence and achievement really a 'crisis' in California post-secondary education? What we do know is that gender disparities visible in high-school graduation are replicated at post-secondary level. Men are not flourishing in the HE environment relative to their female counterparts. It is, therefore, important that we address and monitor the educational needs of the former – though not to the detriment of latter; despite a growing representation of women in universities, the HE landscape is not yet one of gender parity.

It will be of particular interest to see the effect of 'elite' online instruction on gender differences in HE enrolment, persistence and attainment rates. With regard to enrolment, the student community college pool that feeds the CSU and UC systems is predominately female, a discrepancy largely attributable to an over-representation of mature female students. But as younger female students are more likely to transfer to the UC or CSU systems, it is unlikely that increased student transfers via online UC courses will deepen the existing college gender gap. In terms of retention and attainment, the picture is murky. Some research indicates that the gender gap can be explained, in part, by greater female engagement in the learning process, but how this will translate to an 'elite' online learning environment remains to be seen.

Acknowledgements

With special thanks to Shannon Lawrence for her copy-editing skills and invaluable feedback on this chapter.

Notes

1. Some students, however, voice significant concern over the role that technology plays in their lives and, in particular, the amount of time they spend online. See: http://chronicle.com/article/No-Cellphone-No-Internet-So/127391/.
2. An overview of UC's Online Instruction Pilot Project (OIPP) can be found at: http://groups.ischool.berkeley.edu/onlineeducation/.
3. See Harley and Lawrence (2006) for an excellent discussion of the regulation of e-learning.
4. The OIPP is funded in part by the Next Generation Learning Challenges (NGLC) award in the form of an external grant of $748,000 from the Bill and Melinda Gates Foundation and the William and Flora Hewlett Foundation. In addition, the project will take a loan out of $6.9 million from UC.
5. See, for instance, the University of Illinois's Global Campus: http://www.insidehighered.com/news/2009/09/03/globalcampus.
6. Title IX of the Education Amendments of 1972 bars gender discrimination in all education programmes at federally funded institutions.
7. For a more detailed discussion on the investigation, see: http://www.insidehighered.com/news/2011/04/11/qt#256529.
8. The Boys Project can be found at: http://www.boysproject.net/.
9. An associate's degree is equivalent to the first two years of a four-year university degree.
10. See, for example, the Boys Initiative at: http://www.theboysinitiative.org/index.html.
11. The authors used data from the General Social Surveys and the National Educational Longitudinal Survey (NELS).
12. For more information on California Community Colleges, visit: http://www.cccco.edu/Home/tabid/189/Default.aspx.

Bibliography

Adebayo, B. (2008) 'Gender Gaps in College Enrollment and Degree Attainment: An Exploratory Analysis', *College Student Journal*, 42 (1): 232–237.
Anderson, T. (1997) 'Integrating Lectures and Electronic Course Materials', *Innovations in Education and Training International*, 34 (1): 24–31.
Aud, S., Hussar, W., Planty, M., Snyder, T., Bianco, K., Fox, M., Frohlich, L., Kemp, J. and Drake, L. (2010) *The Condition of Education 2010 (NCES 2010-028)*. National Center for Education Statistics, Institute of Education Sciences (Washington, DC: US Department of Education). [online] http://nces.ed.gov/pubs2010/2010028.pdf [accessed 10 May 2011].
Berkner, L., He, S. and Cataldi, E.F. (2002) *Descriptive Summary of 1995–96 Beginning Postsecondary Students: Six Years Later*. National Center for Education Statistics (Washington, DC: US Government Printing Office). [online] http://nces.ed.gov/pubs2003/2003151.pdf [accessed 26 May 2011].
Bobbitt-Zeher, D. (2007) 'The Gender Income Gap and the Role of Education', *Sociology of Education*, 80: 1.
Boushey, H. (25 January 2011) 'The End of the Mancession', *Slate* [online] http://www.slate.com/id/2282340/ [accessed 15 June 2011].
Buchmann, C. and DiPrete, T.A. (2006) 'The Growing Female Advantage in College Completion: The Role of Family Background and Academic Achievement', *American Sociological Review*, 71 (4): 515–541.

California Postsecondary Education Commission (2006a) *The Gender Gap in California Higher Education*. Commission Report 06-08 [online] http://www.cpec.ca.gov/completereports/2006reports/06-08.pdf [accessed 17 May 2011].

California Postsecondary Education Commission (2006b) *The Gender Gap in California Higher Education: A Follow Up*. Commission Report 06-23 [online] http://www.cpec.ca.gov/completereports/2006reports/06-23.pdf [accessed 17 May 2011].

Corbyn, Z. (13 January 2011) 'The Fruits of Californication'. *Times Higher Education* [online] http://www.timeshighereducation.co.uk/story.asp?sectioncode=26&storycode=414846&c=2 [accessed 2 June 2011].

Edley, C.F. (20 April 2010) *UC's 'Eleventh Campus'?* Presentation Given at The Center for Studies in Higher Education, University of California, Berkeley, CA. [online] http://cshe.berkeley.edu/events/index.php?id=317 [accessed 17 May 2011].

Figlio, D.N., Rush, M. and Yin, L. (2010) *Is It Live or Is It the Internet? Experimental Estimates of the Effects of Online Instruction on Student Learning*. National Bureau of Economic Research, Working Paper 16089 [online] http://www.nber.org/papers/w16089 [accessed 7 June 2011].

Freeman, C.E. (2004) *Trends in Educational Equity of Girls & Women: 2004*. National Center for Education Statistics (Washington, DC: US Government Printing Office). [online] http://nces.ed.gov/pubs2005/2005016.pdf [accessed 12 May 2011].

Gerald, D.E. and Hussar, W.J. (2003) *Projections of Education Statistics to 2013*. National Center for Education Statistics (Washington, DC: US Government Printing Office). [online] http://nces.ed.gov/pubs2004/2004013.pdf [accessed 12 May 2011].

Gill, A.M. and Leigh, D.E. (2000) 'Community College Enrollment, College Major, and the Gender Wage Gap', *Industrial and Labor Relations Review*, 54 (1): 163–181.

Goldin, C., Katz, L. and Kuziemco, L. (2006) 'The Homecoming of American College Women: The Reversal of the Gender Gap in College', *Journal of Economic Perspectives*, 20: 133–156.

Harley, D. and Lawrence, S. (September 2006) *The Regulation of E-Learning: New National and International Policy Perspectives*. Research and Occasional Paper Series CSHE.1.07, Center for Studies in Higher Education [online] http://cshe.berkeley.edu/publications/docs/ROP.Regulation_of_elearning.pdf [accessed 7 June 2011].

Herring, S. (1994) *Gender Differences in Computer-Mediated Communication: Bringing Familiar Baggage to the New Frontier*. Keynote Talk at Panel entitled 'Making the Net*Work*: Is There a Z39.50 in Gender Communication?' American Library Association 113th Annual Conference, Miami, FL.

Hinton-Smith, T. (2012) *Lone Parents' Experiences as Higher Education Students* (Leicester: Niace).

Jacobs, J.A. (1996) 'Gender Inequality and Higher Education', *Annual Review of Sociology*, 22: 153–185.

Keller, J. and Parry, M. (9 May 2010) 'University of California Considers Online Classes, or Even Degrees', *The Chronicle of Higher Education* [online] http://chronicle.com/article/In-Crisis-U-of-California/65445/ [accessed 9 June 2011].

Khan, S. (March 2011) 'Let's Use Video to Reinvent Education'. *TED Short Videos* [online] http://www.ted.com/talks/salman_khan_let_s_use_video_to_reinvent_education.html [accessed 7 June 2011].

King, J.E. (2006) *Gender Equity in Higher Education: 2006* (Washington, DC: American Council on Education).

King, J.E. (2010) *Gender Equity in Higher Education: 2010* (Washington, DC: American Council on Education).

Levy, Y. (2007) 'Comparing Dropouts and Persistence in E-Learning Courses', *Computers & Education*, 48: 185–204.

MacLachlan, A. (2006) 'The Graduate Experience of Women in SMET Fields and How It Could Be Improved', in Bystydzienski, J.M. and Bird, S.R. (eds) *Removing Barriers: Women in Academic Science, Technology, Engineering, and Mathematics* (Bloomington, IN: University of Indiana Press, pp. 237–253).

Margolis, J. and Fisher, A. (2003) *Unlocking the Clubhouse: Women in Computing* (London: The MIT Press).

Mason, M. (2009) 'Creating Opportunities for All Women to Succeed in the Workforce', in Boushey, H. and O'Leary, A. (eds) *The Shriver Report: A Woman's Nation Changes Everything* (Washington, DC: The Center for American Progress, pp. 160–193).

Mason, M. and Ekman, E. (2007) *Mothers on the Fast Track* (Oxford: Oxford University Press).

Mau, W. and Lynn, R. (2001) 'Gender Differences on the Scholastic Aptitude Test, the American College Test and College Grades', *Educational Psychology*, 21: 133–136.

McSporran, M. and Young, S. (2001) 'Does Gender Matter in Online Learning?' *Association for Learning Technology Journal*, 9 (2): 3–15.

Mead, S. (2006) *The Evidence Suggests Otherwise: The Truth about Boys and Girls* (Washington, DC: Education Sector). [online] http://www.educationsector.org/usr_doc/ESO_BoysAndGirls.pdf [accessed 12 May 2011].

Means, B., Toyama, Y., Murphy, R., Bakia, M. and Jones, K. (2010) *Evaluation of Evidence-Based Practices in Online Learning: A Meta-Analysis and Review of Online Learning Studies* (Washington, DC: US Department of Education). [online] http://www2.ed.gov/rschstat/eval/tech/evidence-based-practices/finalreport.pdf [accessed 26 April 2011].

Parker, K., Lenhart, A. and Moore, K. (2011) *The Digital Revolution and Higher Education*. Pew Research Center, Social and Demographic Trends [online] http://pewsocialtrends.org/files/2011/08/online-learning.pdf [accessed 15 September 2011].

Peter, K. and Horn, L. (2005) *Gender Differences in Participation and Completion of Undergraduate Education and How They Have Changed Over Time (NCES 2005-169)*. US Department of Education, National Center for Education Statistics (Washington, DC: US Government Printing Office). [online] http://nces.ed.gov/pubsearch/pubsinfo.asp?pubid=2005169 [accessed 17 May 2011].

Riordan, C. (October 2003) 'Failing in School? Yes; Victims of War? No', *Sociology of Education*, 76: 369–372. [online] http://www.uiowa.edu/~c07b150/riorden_article.pdf [accessed 26 April 2011].

Ryu, M. (2009) 'Minorities in Higher Education: Twenty-Third Status Report: 2009 Supplement', *Education*. [online] http://www.acenet.edu/AM/Template.cfm?Section=CAREE&TEMPLATE=/CM/ContentDisplay.cfm&CONTENTID=34441 [accessed 31 May 2011].

Sadker, M. and Sadker, D. (1995) *Failing at Fairness. How Our Schools Cheat Girls* (New York: Touchstone).

Sax, L. (2008) *The Gender Gap in College: Maximizing the Developmental Potential of Women and Men* (San Francisco, CA: Jossey-Bass).

Sax, L. and Arms, E. (2008) 'Gender Differences Over the Span of College: Challenges to Achieving Equity', *The Journal about Women in Higher Education*, 1 (1): 23–48.

Sengupta, R. and Jepsen, C. (November 2006) 'California's Community College Students', *California Counts*, 8 (2). [online] http://www.ppic.org/content/pubs/cacounts/cc_1106rscc.pdf [accessed 24 May 2011].

Snyder, T.D. and Dillow, S.A. (2010) *Digest of Education Statistics 2009 (NCES 2010-013)*. National Center for Education Statistics, Institute of Education Sciences (Washington, DC: US Department of Education). [online] http://nces.ed.gov/Programs/digest/ [accessed 24 May 2011].

Sommers, C.H. (2000) *The War against Boys* (New York: Simon and Schuster).

Sum, A., Fogg, N., Harrington, P., with Khatiwada, I., Palma, S., Pond, N. and Tobar, P. (2003) *The Growing Gender Gaps in College Enrollment and Degree Attainment in the U.S. and Their Potential Economic and Social Consequences*. Prepared for the Business Roundtable (Washington, DC/Boston, MA: Center for Labor Market Studies).

Walsh, T. (2011) *Unlocking the Gates* (Princeton, NJ: Princeton University Press).

Weinman, J. and Cain, L. (1999) 'Technology: The New Gender Gap', *Technos*, 8 (1): 9–12.

Whitmire, R. (2011) Blog for Education Week [online] http://blogs.edweek.org/edweek/whyboysfail/ [accessed 14 June 2011].

Whitmire, R. (2010) *Why Boys Fail* (New York: Amacom).

Willingham, W. and Cole, N. (1997) *Gender and Fair Assessment* (Mahwah, NJ: Lawrence Erlbaum Associates).

Woodfield, R. and Earl-Novell, S. (2006) 'An Assessment of the Extent to Which Subject Variation in Relation to the Award of First Class Degree between the Arts and Sciences Can Explain the "Gender Gap" ', *British Journal of Sociology of Education*, 27 (3): 355–372.

Woodfield, R., Jessop, D. and McMillan, L. (2006) 'Gender, Attendance and Degree Outcome', *Studies in Higher Education*, 31 (1): 1–22.

Xu, D. and Jaggars, S.S. (2011) .*Online and Hybrid Course Enrollment and Performance in Washington State Community and Technical Colleges*. CCRC Working Paper, No. 31 [online] http://ccrc.tc.columbia.edu/Publication.asp?UID= 872 [accessed 18 July 2011].

Young, S. and McSporran, M. (2001) *Confident Men – Successful Women: Gender Differences in Online Learning*. UNITEC Institute of Technology [online] http://hyperdisc.unitec.ac.nz/research/edmedia2001_gender.pdf [accessed 17 May 2011].

Yukselturk, E. and Bulut, S. (2009) 'Gender Differences in Self-Regulated Online Learning Environment', *Educational Technology & Society*, 12 (3): 12–22.

18

Conclusion: Assessing Progress and Priorities in Widening Participation

Tamsin Hinton-Smith

This chapter draws on the insights provided by contributors throughout the volume to evaluate progress in widening participation (WP), including identifying key achievements and relative failures across the different dimensions of evaluation. This takes place alongside discussion of areas for future development and why such work remains necessary and will continue to become increasingly so. The diverse perspectives of the 22 commentators who have contributed to this volume represent a range of specific concerns in WP, from understanding historical developments (Berggren and Cliffordson in Chapter 12), charting contemporary progress (Padilla-Carmona in Chapter 14), or looking to predicting the future of higher education (HE) provision (Earl-Novell in Chapter 17). The book's contributors bring to the discussion their own unique areas of expertise, encompassing issues focused around facets of experience including gender, race, class, age, subject area, higher education institution (HEI) type and mode of study. These contrasting national, disciplinary, theoretical and ideological perspectives, and the rich empirical research that has informed them, collectively provide a broad and solid base for understanding key contemporary issues in WP. Despite such apparent divergence, these scholars of HE are united in their attempt to understand the factors supporting and impeding participation amongst previously excluded groups. This is informed by a shared belief in the right to participate in HE, the benefits of participation and the responsibility of governments to work towards equalising of access. The perspectives in this volume, however, reach further than this, representing a commitment to moving beyond identifying exclusion and increasing equality of access, as the WP agenda focuses on the third stage of ensuring equity of treatment and opportunity within HE for those drawn in through WP. These overarching concerns inform the perspectives of contributions to this volume, addressing the experience of WP students, who represent diverse demographics, once they arrive in HE; this includes experiences in terms of quality of teaching and resources, assessment, student support and recognition of the legitimacy of competing responsibilities.

What has been achieved?

Participation in HE has undoubtedly undergone a process of massive expansion over the last 50 years. In the United Kingdom, participation of around 6 per cent in 1960, as discussed by Yorke in Chapter 3, had grown to 43 per cent by 2008. This picture is even more striking globally. As described by Morley in her chapter on WP in Ghana and Tanzania (Chapter 15), UNESCO figures show worldwide undergraduate student enrolment to have risen from 13 million in 1960 to 137.8 million in 2005. This trend is projected to continue, with demand for HE worldwide predicted to expand from 97 million students in 2000 to over 262 million students by 2025 (UNESCO, 2009). Such massification of HE has inevitably entailed drastic alteration of the profile of HE students, leading to far wider casting of the student recruitment net by necessity. Expanding HE sufficiently to meet the changing needs of post-manufacturing knowledge economies would not have been possible without challenging the historical profile of the archetypal university student as the young, white, privileged, able-bodied, European male encapsulated in Edwards' conception of the 'Bachelor boy' student (1993). Nevertheless, as Morely warns in Chapter 15, while WP in HE in a globalised knowledge economy can be a force for democratisation and economic growth, it can also map on to existing elite practices and even contribute to further differentiation of social groups. As Morley suggests, those with increased social capital may be more able to decode and access new educational opportunities, while those without it are left untouched by initiatives to facilitate their entry into the privileges that HE can offer. Christie *et al.* have similarly counselled wariness as to 'the presumption that a greatly expanded HE sector automatically enhances social justice', pointing out that this 'is challenged by the persistent social-class gradient in participation' (2005: 4). Even when non-traditional students do participate in HE, they often occupy a relatively disadvantaged position in an education marketplace of autonomous individuals with marketable skills used to exercise choice (Zepke, 2005). One facet of this is the unequal spread of university places that sees the most valued young, privileged applicants offered places at a number of institutions, while less valued non-traditional applicants may be lucky to receive a single offer of a place.

In addition to the persistence of access inequalities in HE, despite several decades of WP initiatives, while successive rounds of policies may unquestionably have drawn in more students representing all those categories that contrast with the 'bachelor boy' ideal, the extent to which this has resulted in the dismantling of elitist assumptions of the academy as the rightful domain of societies' most privileged remains less clear cut. The way in which such power dynamics are experienced by WP students, as continuing to operate within HE, is expressed succinctly by one of Field and Morgan-Klein's interviewees in Chapter 11:

middle class people have a really interesting way of using language where they can say things that might come across that they agree with you or be gentle about things but where the power still remains wi' them. It's a really…I dunno how to describe it – you know, no passion – there's no passion in what they're saying, and this really cold distant calculated use of the English language that I have nae quite managed to grasp yet – thankfully.

Such experiences represent evidence of the way in which mechanisms of exclusion continue to marginalise WP students once they have gained access into the academy, and hence the ambitious project we face of dismantling long-established cultures of exclusion in order to reconstruct them as more egalitarian pillars of learning for all. The above quote also illustrates some student's not only exclusion from but ultimately also rejection of some of the particular values seen as persisting in HE, iterating the shortcomings of WP approaches that focus on attempting to assimilate non-traditional students into success within the existing dominant framework, rather than challenging and remodelling this.

Evaluating successes in widening participation

There are important contributory factors then around both initial access and experience of participation, informing the extent to which WP initiatives have been successful in making HE more equitable. A third key aspect of testing the success of such attempts at equalisation is that of outcomes from HE. In 1976, Levin put forward four criteria for evaluating the equalising influence of a nation's education system – equality of access, participation, results and effects on life chances. It has been suggested that the effects of HE participation for non-traditional students have remained relatively under-researched compared with other measures (Woodley and Wilson, 2002: 329; see also Wisker, 1996: 5). The 'success' of HE participation for WP students in terms of outcome is explored, by Merrill in Chapter 10, in terms of degree completion or dropout, and by Field and Morgan-Klein in Chapter 11. Previous research by Yorke has shown wider life responsibilities including paid work and family to contribute centrally to non-completion for many WP students (Yorke, 1999; Yorke and Longden, 2004). Further, in terms of HE outcomes for WP students, concern around whether or not mature graduates engage fully in the labour market has been couched in terms of potential lack of return on investment both for society and individuals (Woodley and Wilson, 2002). The return of investment in HE in terms of employment outcomes is explored in Chapter 6 by Woodfield with regard to mature women students. While Woodfield identifies that much research indicates mature students to experience significant disadvantage in the graduate labour market compared with their younger peers, and that their degree therefore represents less value for them in employment, her research provides a more affirmative story of employment outcomes for this group of graduates, pointing to the need for further research to understand the complex relationship between gender, age and graduate employment outcomes. While mature women HE students may be successful in securing graduate employment, this is suggested to exist alongside the persistent failure of women's out-performance of men in education to translate into greater equality in employment trajectories (Taylor, 2007: 36), with women continuing to earn substantially less than men for undertaking the same work, despite several decades of equal opportunity interventions.

While the 2009 Labour government White Paper, 'Higher Ambitions: The Future of Universities in a Knowledge Economy', highlighted the transformative potential of universities for policy purposes (David, 2009), both David's Chapter 2 as well as Chapter 8 of Stuart, Lido and Morgan discuss the relevance of the UK Government Cabinet Office 2009 Milburn Report's contrasting findings that in practice UK universities have in fact been limited in achieving social mobility especially into graduate professions and that access to professional careers has become more, not less, difficult for people from lower socio-economic backgrounds over time. The report in particular identified the persistence of a glass ceiling for women in graduate professions (Milburn Report, summer 2009). Thus, while governments including that of the United Kingdom increasingly place considerable weight on the importance of getting underprivileged students into HE, and while WP may indeed be a precursor to upward social mobility, as Stuart *et al.* warn in Chapter 8, it does not automatically create it.

Good and bad students?

The persistence of prejudices around legitimate ways of being a student are particularly important because they do not remain contained within the corridors of universities but are carried beyond them into workplaces by graduated employers who have absorbed and continue to implement such prejudices in their selection of employees. Stuart *et al.* remind us that although there may no longer be 'typical' graduates, many employers nevertheless maintain a rather blinkered view of what a 'good graduate' is. For example, BME graduates are evidenced to have both lower employment rates and average incomes after HE completion compared with white graduates (AGCAS, 2008; Li *et al.*, 2008). Individual students are not merely judged according to their own perceived merit by prospective employers and neither is this restricted to the making of assumptions based on lumping students into groups according to demographic characteristics including social class, gender, ethnicity, age and stereotypes about such 'types' of students. A further key dynamic by which employers and others sort and categorise HE students and graduates into status groups operates by the mechanism of HE type. Barber and Hill (2005) have highlighted that over-emphasis on graduates who come from a small pool of universities with certain characteristics both restricts employers' choice of employees and limits graduate opportunities. The creation of tiered systems of HE, while pre-existing WP in many countries (as discussed, for example, by Moreau with regard to France in Chapter 13 and by MacLachlan in the US context in Chapter 16) has nevertheless both extended as a feature of the massi-fication of HE and served as an effective mechanism of maintaining elite privilege within the context of vastly extended HE participation. Inequali-ties between the status of different types of HEI, and the qualifications they offer, act as a particularly powerful means of excluding some groups of learn-ers from the full social benefits of HE participation. In Chapter 10, Merrill addresses the concentration of both younger and adult non-traditional stu-dents in the UK HE system within post-1992 institutions, locating them in a disadvantaged position within the strict hierarchical division between privileged HEI, such as Russell group universities, and less privileged and lower-status colleges, as identified by David in Chapter 2. The operating of such mechanisms of exclusion are twofold, with pervasive evidence that as well as being selected into particular status points in HE learning hierarchies by admissions staff, students also 'self-select' according to factors includ-ing ethnicity, class and gender, drawing on implicit and often intangible assumptions about the types of HEI in which students 'like them' do and don't belong. The social significance of such racialised, gendered and class effects of tiered HE system are importantly identified in MacLachlan's dis-cussion of US HE. Finding ways and promoting policies to increase equalities in resources, recruitment, status and outcomes between universities within HE markets is one of the central projects in addressing the persistence of inequalities experienced between the most and least privileged students in HE participation.

Which inequalities?

The perspectives of international commentators identify the sharing of key elements of shared experience in global trends WP in HE. These include the persistence of access inequalities and the demographic characteristics along which these are drawn; unequal status of institutions, subject areas and the students recruited to them; and issues in promoting parity of partic-ipation experience and outcome. The chapters also, however, highlight the significance of important cross-cultural differences in priorities. For exam-ple, David and Moreau's chapters explain how in the United Kingdom and France, respectively, social class has dominated the focus of the WP agenda at the expense of gender or race. This stands in marked contrast to Sweden where, Berggren and Cliffordson argue, poverty has been eclipsed by gender as a WP priority. Similarly, with regard to Ghana and Tanzania, Morley explains that although both countries have introduced HE loans and policies to assist students from low socio-economic backgrounds, in practice WP has focused largely on addressing the gender gap in admissions. The way in which approaches to addressing WP are informed by broader political and cultural values is illustrated by Moreau's discussion of the development of WP discourse in France in Chapter 13, explaining how the French republican universalist model of citizenship has informed focus on formal equal rights and equal treatment as the favoured form of equality policies. Moreau explains how a shift in French HE away from this dominant paradigm through the introduction of positive discrimination in the 2000s met with resistance and critique as breaching the republican conception of equality in a country where, despite their élite status, *Grandes Ecoles* are often seen as meritocratic in recruiting students through examinations and criteria, which are perceived as neutral and universal. While many of the chapters in this volume explore the significance of issues of ethnic and gender inequalities in HE participation in different national contexts, Moreau explains how significantly, French HE positive discrimination actions have only targeted socio-economic groups, while inequalities related to gender, and, in particular, ethnicity have remained perceived as less legitimate areas of intervention. This has serious ramifications for the experience of BME students and the equalising potential of HE in France and other countries in which such a universalist model of citizenship dominates policy. Further, Moreau explains how such values have translated into homogenous WP policies that aim to treat all citizens the same. This represents a lag in WP politics, addressing issues of access while leaving unchallenged the increasingly acknowledged inequalities in participation experience and HE outcomes. Such homogeneous policy also stands at odds with the critique of lumping WP students together as one category, stemming from the acknowledgement that the distinct needs of diverse groups are not the same and resist being boiled down to one-size-fits-all solutions (Edwards, 1993; Reay, 2003; Laing *et al.*, 2005; Kingston, 2006; Taylor, 2007).

WP development as work in progress

Padilla-Carmona's chapter on the development of WP in Spain reminds us of how useful and important it is to chart the journeys and lessons of policies aimed at equalising HE access, experience and outcomes. While WP has been a developing concern in some countries for several decades (Delors, 1996), Padilla-Carmona explains how the experience of non-traditional students in HE remains barely discussed in Spain, rendering the 'invisible majority' of non-traditional HE students discussed by other commentators (McNair, 1998) a particularly direct and persistent reality. As the needs of non-traditional students and the benefits of addressing these continue to become increasingly recognised globally, and as countries develop and embark upon their own WP agendas, often within the context of shrinking public resources, it is vitally important to document and share stories of successes and failures in policies and practice.

While the WP discourse and policies that have developed over several decades have matured, refined and gained increasing acknowledgement, they now also face new uncertainties in the context of global recession and its repeated threat and political responses to this in terms of streamlining public resources. Several chapters throughout this volume discuss the centrality to WP of how, in the United Kingdom, the effects of fiscal resources coupled with regime change have informed unprecedented course fee rises widely predicted to threaten progress and exacerbate inequalities in patterns of HE participation. While the Organisation for Economic Co-operation and Development (OECD) figures showed the United Kingdom to have by far the highest HE fees in Europe even prior to the increases announced in 2010, UK graduates have been shown to reap a much higher return in future earnings compared with their counterparts in most other western countries' (Bawden, 2006). Nevertheless, contrary to the UK government White Paper 'Higher Education: Students at the Heart of the System' (BIS, 2011), which stresses that nobody should be put off HE because they cannot afford it and outlines a new framework for WP and fair access, many critics believe that potential students will be deterred by the size of the student loans required to pay increased fees, as Woodley discusses in Chapter 4. This is particularly significant for the most financially disadvantaged students, whom Taylor's research has shown to be the most debt aversive (Chapter 5, this volume, and 2007). As Taylor asserts in Chapter 5, for students from working-class backgrounds 'debt aversion' is a very real structural dis-incentive rather than something which they personally have to conquer and 'get over'. This illustrates one of the key shortcomings of HEIs in assimilating non-traditional students through attempting to remould them as learners more compatible with integration into existing structures rather than remoulding outmoded structures to fit the changing needs of diversifying student groups and experiences. As Frame *et al.* explore in Chapter 9, too much educational transition research has focused on the impact of new institutional structures on those who join them, rather than questioning the structure itself, perpetuating the implicit assumption that it is the student who must adapt, rather than the university. This paradigm of individual responsibility (Bostock, 1998) serves to obscure institutional shortcomings in facilitating access and support, enabling HEIs to blame WP students themselves for 'failing' to successfully manage HE (Jackson, 2004; Quinn and Allen, 2010), when more onus should fall upon HEIs to facilitate participation. Increasing understanding of how HE provision must change to meet the needs of non-traditional students is a key area for continuing research focus. Without doing so, HE markets are failing to tap into and make the most of the available resources in terms of the unrealised human capital potential of students excluded either from access or from the full benefits of participation once subsumed within the university.

Promoting participation

All universities and governments have a responsibility to promote the educational participation of previously excluded students; in the United Kingdom, this onus on individual HEIs has increased with the devolution of responsibility for WP Outreach work from Aimhigher to individual institutions in 2011. Contributors to this volume including Moreau and David identify how implementation of WP has been far from equal across institutions and disciplines, and it is arguably frequently the more elite HEIs that have the greatest distance to travel in addressing and implementing the ideals of WP (Reay, 2003). That WP learners experience benefits of an increased student-focused approach from HEIs oriented towards serving the needs of non-traditional learners is indicated through national student survey (NSS) results (Unistats, 2011). The Open University, with its high numbers of WP students attracted by focus on part-time, distance learning with online teaching delivery and out-of-hours contact timetabling, has consistently achieved NSS overall student satisfaction scores within the top three institutions, since the survey began in 2005 (OU Senate, 2010). Similarly, Birkbeck College, nearly all of whose students are part time, has formerly been ranked top in the country (Shepherd, 2006). The Open University's vice-chancellor has attributed the institution's success to a student-focused approach and constant focus on student support, assessment and feedback, as well as peer mentoring and small class sizes facilitating personal interaction between staff and students (Lipsett, 2007).

One of the key contributions of WP discourse has been to provide the vital resource of well-researched and documented insight into some of the most productive ways in which to support WP students operating within imperfect HE learning economies. While they should not be a substitute for increasing equalisation, in the context of barriers, pragmatic responses inevitably develop amongst both individuals and institutions. Hence, Woodley charts early indication of increasing Open University participation by school-leaver applicants, informed by the relative attractiveness of both fee levels and opportunities for part-time employment balanced against fee increases in the UK sector as a whole. From an institutional perspective, Earl-Novell explores the contemporary development of online course delivery at the University of Berkeley, USA, considering its potential to increase participation by disadvantaged groups and deliver affordable provision without compromising quality.

Why does widening participation matter?

Evidence from WP research shows a range of societal and individual bene-fits of broadening access to, and equalising experience and outcomes within, HE. At the individual level, there is a complex interweaving of instrumental (or employment-oriented) and intrinsic (personal development) benefits of WP, echoing the balance of intrinsic and instrumental motivations for HE participation by WP students explored in Chapter 7 of this volume. The balance of these HE outcomes varies across groups with, for example, male WP students perceiving enhanced career development and income gains resulting from HE participation compared with women (Brennan *et al.*, 1999: 9), while rich personal benefits in terms of developing confidence and self-esteem are also evidenced to be centrally important (also Hyatt and Parry-Crooke, 1990; Horne and Hardie, 2002). As Woodley and Wilson have identified, the benefits of HE participation for WP students extend beyond career to include increased community involvement, better health and improvements to children's educational attainment (2002).

Moreover, some of the key concerns facing WP students, including, for example, financial hardship and managing HE participation alongside paid work, are increasingly relevant to ever larger numbers of even tradi-tional undergraduate students, in the context of changing fee regimes and widespread financial insecurity. HE policy can no longer justifiably continue to implicitly assume education to exist in a vacuum, independent of com-peting responsibilities (Leonard, 1994). For WP students representing several traditionally excluded groups – for example, learners who are working class, from minority ethnic backgrounds and lone parents – inequalities can com-pound, feed into and reinforce one another (Reay, 2003). Chapters 2, 7 and 17 in this volume identify the resourceful determination of many mature women HE learners with children, informing successful degree outcomes compared with other groups of learners, despite the challenges associated with managing such dual responsibilities. Successive research evi-dences WP students frequently to make diligent HE students, motivated to make the most of the opportunity to capitalise on the benefits offered by HE participation. Their fundamental need from the education system as adult learners is the opportunity of what Wisker has suggested may be their first real chance at engaging with education (1996).

Institutionalising good practice

This informs questions about the level at which recommendations for WP work should be implemented. Opportunities for improved delivery of provi-sion may variously be addressed at a range of levels, from (but not reliant upon) good practice by individual staff, departments and HEIs, through to broader policy by government, unions within the sector, and umbrella bodies including UK universities, OFFA (Office for Fair Access), HEFCE (Higher Education Funding Council for England) and HEPI (Higher Education Policy Institute). Beyond this, implementation of equalising policies above the national level have further potential to spread good practice and improve HE opportunities and outcomes for more students. While the Bologna process, instigated in 1999 to make academic degree standards and quality assurance standards more comparable and compatible across Europe, has not been without criticisms, its contribution to equalising the experience of HE students in different European countries is identified in this volume with reference to Sweden (Chapter 12), France (Chapter 13) and Spain (Chapter 14). As Padilla-Carmona highlights, 'the implications of Bologna go beyond the structural and didactic shift and call for the improvement of the social conditions of students, highlighting the importance of widening the participation of disadvantaged groups'.

While the limitations of tightening public purses have inevitably compromised WP initiatives, leading for example to the end of Aimhigher in the United Kingdom in 2011, financial constraints should not be seen as vetoing the WP agenda. While effective WP work is unarguably dependent on adequate resourcing, and governments have a responsibility to invest in this, other factors facilitating participation are relatively cost-efficient or even cost-neutral, as also identified by Wisker (1996: 3). These may include, for example, focusing on respecting and validating non-traditional students' backgrounds, needs and perspectives. MacLachlan argues in Chapter 16 that retention efforts do not have to be expensive, suggesting that more important are institution-wide approaches in which faculty and staff co-operatively work towards supporting student achievement. The narratives of non-traditional HE students frequently indicate a key element of supporting their needs to be a willingness in extreme cases to 'bend the rules' usually applied to traditional students. This may mean, for example, providing advance access to timetables and first choice of seminar times to students who have to balance competing commitments or allowing those with young children to queue jump registration. Perhaps, what these stories illustrate is in fact the need for such recognition of students' needs to be applied more consistently to all students. The role of HE staff in validating the experience of those students who do not conform to traditional stereotypes of the ideal university student is central to supporting WP. In Chapter 11, Field and Morgan-Klein identify positive relationships with staff to emerge as highly significant in the narratives of WP students, particularly early on in their learner journeys, and later at moments of crisis. This contrasts with the worst examples of HE staff practice, in which WP students describe experiencing university staff as conveying explicitly or implicitly that the needs of non-traditional students are not a valid consideration, and that concessions will not be made. This is particularly problematic given that WP students' accounts of positive experiences in HE frequently focus on informal support from individual staff, rather than on positive institutional policies (Hinton-Smith, 2012). This conveys the need for WP-friendly practices to be embedded more strongly in policy, rather than leaving students mostly in need of support subject to a lottery of experience.

Supporting widening participation students in higher education

A key area of vital support for WP students is high quality, individually focused career guidance. This is particularly important given that many non-traditional students will not have benefited from privileged networks of social and cultural capital that provide informal guidance around learning and career decisions, through family contacts and inter-generational HE participation. Lack of clear, accurate information around, for example, the value placed by employers on particular institutions and degree pathways continues to disadvantage those students not privileged to insider knowledge. This is further compounded for many WP students who recount stories of negative experiences of career guidance provision in school and college, where subjection to negative stereotypes around career destinations based on classed, gendered and racialised assumptions continue to limit the potential of their HE participation. Ill-informed degree pathway 'choices' too often fuse with other practical limitations often placed on WP students by their wider life commitments to channel students into HE outcomes in semi-professional employment that maintains their exclusion from the fullest career benefits of HE participation. Long-term educational inequalities experienced around factors including race, class and gender can be further intensified for those WP students who participate in HE as mature learners, given evidence that this group faces particularly negative career outcomes from HE (Woodley and Wilson, 2002: 335), as a result of persistent ageism. Good quality career advice, preferably targeted to the pre-entry stage, has been identified as particularly important for this group (Gallagher *et al.*, 1993: 59). Similarly, evidence indicates the benefits of preparatory modules to assist students in successfully making the transition from further education (FE) to HE, identified as particularly beneficial for access route students and with the implementation of such programmes evidenced to result in positive outcomes (Knox, 2005). Non-traditional students describe feeling 'apprehensive', 'disorientated', 'frightened' and 'scared', as well as 'excited' by their initial experiences of university life, with the most commonly reported basis for negative feelings being feeling unprepared for the workload (Hinton-Smith, 2012). Once again, acknowledgement of the importance of pre-entry support work sits ill at ease with the discontinuation of Aimhigher in the United Kingdom. It has also been suggested that such stretching back of advice should include advising WP students about relevant issues including available financial support and flexible modes of study, as part of HE admissions interviews (Wisker, 1996: 31).

Providing adequate support for WP students is particularly important given the lack of self-esteem and academic confidence that many bring to HE (Murphy and Roopchand, 2003). Feelings of inadequacy, fraud and fear of being 'found out' as not being as capable as other students are commonplace (also Wisker, 1996; Jackson, 2004). Such feelings of intellectual inadequacy around the perception of not properly 'belonging' within the academy resonate with Clance's documentation of feelings of perceived 'imposterdom' described by women academics (1985). It is argued that individuals from middle-class backgrounds feel like 'fish in water' in HE and that university serves to 'certify' students from middle-class and upper middle-class backgrounds for privileged social and occupation positions in the world (Kaufman and Feldman, 2004: 464). Many WP students may have a tendency to feel more like fish out of water at university. The transitional phase of becoming a learner is identified as a complex process period of reflexivity and risk, confusion and contradiction (Brine and Waller, 2004: 97). Many WP students are indicated to have an increased fear of academic failure compared with their traditional student peers, partly because of the high-risk investment often required of them and partly because of poor previous learner identity. Providing WP students with adequate support to ensure that they are not held back by low confidence and self-esteem is vital to academic attainment, given evidence that academic confidence in HE impacts centrally upon attainment levels (Woodfield and Earl-Novell, 2006: 356). WP students can often feel isolated within the academy, further informing the need for adequate support. Evidence suggests that students from non-traditional HE learner groups feel less isolated when they are able to make connections with other students who share similar circumstances with them, informing recommendation for institutional assistance with supporting networking and mentoring programmes for WP student groups, as identified by commentators including Padilla-Carmona in Chapter 14 (also NUS, 2009: 66). Social integration into university life is far from a peripheral distraction from studies; it is demonstrated to fundamentally inform students' academic success and retention (Hussey and Smith, 2010: 159). While formation of sub-cultural groups may be experienced as essential to 'surviving' at university, Field and Morgan-Klein's Chapter 11 also identifies that participation by WP students in broader student social networks is vital not only to HE experience but also to graduate employment outcomes. Taylor's chapter, however, serves as a warning that activities such as student-mentoring programmes in HE must be approached with care in order to avoid replicating the very inequalities they seek to address.

Acknowledging students' wider lives

Alongside providing adequate support, one of the key areas in validating WP students' position in HE and ensuring that facilitating participation means more than just extending access lies in acknowledging the relevance of wider lives and the legitimacy of the way in which these impact on participation in HE. The stereotypical idea of a student's lifestyle, with its combination of independence, dependence, leisure and academic work, is likely to be alien to many WP students (Reay, 2003: 307). In contrast, while the main problem facing traditional students may be fitting into university, it is suggested that for many WP students, the chief difficulty is fitting university in, given the frequently higher life loads in terms of competing commitments (Scott *et al.*, 1996: 235). Such sharp contrast between ideals of studentship and WP students' own lives can leave them feeling like deviant tokens (Edwards, 1993: 102). Earl-Novell and Woodley's chapters support the relevance of ICT-mediated HE learning in facilitating participation by WP students whose wider responsibilities may conflict with fulfilling traditional models of studentship. This resonates with the suggestion of Open University's Pro-Vice Chancellor David Vincent that the opportunities afforded by Internet- and DVD- based learning have replaced the focus on evening and weekend courses to meet the needs of non-traditional students balancing multiple commitments (Shepherd, 2006).

Alongside delivery of learning, there remains a need for universities to increase their focus on the additional support services that facilitate participation by WP students. It has been suggested that without basic childcare provision, HEIs are effectively closing their doors to many WP students (Gallagher *et al.*, 1993). Contemporary policy development in the United Kingdom is leading away from such provision, rather than towards it, particularly amongst the most privileged HEIs that 'select' rather than 'recruit' their student numbers, informing a lack of need for working to meet the needs of non-traditional HE learners. Such unequal provision of essential facilities including childcare risks contributing towards a ghettoisation of WP, as WP students gravitate towards those universities that offer to meet their needs.

The balance is precarious between avoiding HE ghettoisation and supporting WP students in accessing those HE spaces that they may find most accessible and non-alienating. Franchising of HE courses to FE colleges has long been advocated as an effective means of supporting HE participation for non-traditional students (e.g. Wisker, 1996: 4). Franchising simultaneously addresses several problems including (i) travel distances, (ii) enabling WP students to benefit from participation in educational cultures that may be more attuned to their needs and (iii) predictions in the current UK course fee increase climate that degrees offered through franchising in partnership with FE colleges may charge less, and in doing so attract large numbers of WP students. Disproportionate clustering of WP students on franchised courses risks, however, building further on existing inequalities in tiered HE provision, with its ensuing ramifications for future employment prospects as discussed earlier in this chapter.

What are the priorities for the future of widening participation?

WP must continue to work towards developing further understanding of what constitutes the conditions under which HE participation can offer real opportunities for improved life chances, such as the improved prospects for participation in paid work described by Morley with regard to Tanzania. The emancipatory potential of WP must be separated out from those aspects that continue to contribute towards perpetuating the rigid traditional hierarchies present in HE as a system for the maintenance of social exclusion. We must continue to challenge systems of organization through which different groups of students are sorted, categorised and restricted to particular HE outcomes through both the constrained 'choices' that they make and the positions within the HE system to which they are selected.

A large part of the task in continuing to advance WP in HE globally undoubtedly pivots on adequate and effectively targeted financial investment in HE. This is a challenging task in the context of competition for resources and the tightening of public spending across many countries. Much of the immediate task in the United Kingdom at least is to observe and document the impact of contemporary policy developments. Contributions to this volume demonstrate that across other countries too, WP remains a constantly shifting work-in-progress to be charted, with the HE sectors of countries occupying varied positions along the pathway towards WP in HE. These diverse positions range from the as-yet newness of the WP discourse in Spain, through to Berggren and Cliffordson's assertion in Chapter 12, that in Sweden, 'widening participation, in its original meaning, to increase the diversity of the student body in HE has been abandoned'. We should not however deduce, as some of the harshest critics contend, that WP is dead. A key task in the context of new challenges to the ground fought so hard for over several decades of WP is to ensure that those advances made in equalising access are protected rather than retracted. Facing these challenges must take place alongside continuing to address the third stage of equalisation of participatory experience for WP students once in HE. Part of what is required is a shift in attitude to WP; this means overcoming, and rejecting as elitist, international fears over an assumed dilution of quality resulting from WP, as discussed by Earl-Novell and Yorke with regard to the United States and United Kingdom, respectively. In Chapters 3 and 12, Berggren and Cliffordson and Yorke, respectively, contribute to the dispelling of such fears through their challenging of the myth of grade inflation resulting from WP.

Alongside continuing the drives towards both breaking down elitist assumptions around what makes 'good and bad students' that have survived the development of WP, and supporting the participation experiences of WP students once in HE, it is suggested that to have real impact, WP may need to reach back much further than it currently does into initial schooling. Berggren and Cliffordson support such a more holistic perspective in their assertion that to have real impact, policies around WP must include the whole educational system, with all students receiving improved support through their whole education as well as in their career planning. Finally, as David suggests in Chapter 2, we must work to ensure that HE policy and practice values, respects and supports the participation and perspectives of individuals from diverse backgrounds. In order to protect and continue to advance the progress made in WP to date, a HE participation model based on such ethical principles must continue to call to account the dominant HE agenda within an increasingly individualistic marketised system of neo-liberalism, with its tacit emphasis on the maintenance of power and privilege.

Bibliography

AGCAS (2008) *What Happens Next? A Report on Ethnicity and the First Destinations of Graduates 2006* [online] http://www.agcas.org.uk/agcas_resources/49-What-Happens-Next-A-Report-on-Ethnicity-and-the-First-Destinations-of-Graduates [accessed 13 June 2011].

Barber, L. and Hill, D. (2005) *Is Graduate Recruitment Meeting Business Needs?* (Brighton: IES and CIHE).

Bawden, A. (2006) 'Study Pays Off for UK Graduates, Report Shows.' *The Guardian*, 12 September [online] http://education.guardian.co.uk/students/graduation/story/0,,1870488,00.html [accessed 25 July 2007].

BIS (Department for Business, Innovation and Skills) (July 2011) *Higher Education: Putting Students at the Heart of the System* [online] http://www.bis.gov.uk/news/topstories/2011/Jun/he-white-paper-students-at-the-heart-of-the-system [accessed 19 September 2011].

Bostock, S. (1998) 'Constructivism in Mass Higher Education: A Case Study', *British Journal of Educational Technology*, 29 (3): 25–240.

Brennan, J., Mills, J., Shah, T. and Woodley, A. (1999) *Part-Time Students and Employment: Report of a Survey of Students, Graduates and Diplomats* (London: DfEE/HEQE/QSE).

Brine, J. and Waller, R. (2004) 'Working-Class Women on an Access Course: Risk, Opportunity and (Re)constructing Identities', *Gender and Education*, 16 (1): 97–113.

Cabinet Office Strategy Unit (2009) *Unleashing Aspiration: Summary and Recommendations of the Full Report*. The panel on Fair Access to the Professions (Milburn report).

Christie, H., Munro, M. and Wager, F. (2005) 'Day Students in Higher Education: Widening Access Students and Successful Transitions to University Life', *International Studies in the Sociology of Education*, 15 (1): 3–30.

Clance, P.R. (1985) *The Impostor Phenomenon: When Success Makes You Feel Like a Fake* (Toronto, ON: Bantam).

David, M. (2009) *Transforming Global Higher Education: A Feminist Perspective*. An Inaugural Professorial Lecture Institute of Education, London.

Delors, J. (1996) *Learning: The Treasure Within*. Report to UNESCO of the International Commission on Education for the Twenty-First Century. [online] http://unesdoc.unesco.org/images/0010/001095/109590eo.pdf [accessed 7 October 2011].

Edwards, R. (1993) *Mature Women Students: Separating or Connecting Family and Education* (London: Taylor and Francis).

Gallagher, A., Richards, N. and Locke, M. (1993) *Mature Students in Higher Education: How Institutions Can Learn from Experience* (London: Centre for Institutional Studies, University of East London).

Hinton-Smith, T. (2012) *Lone Parents Experiences as Higher Education Students: Learning to Juggle* (Leicester: Niace).

Horne, M. and Hardie, C. (2002) 'From Welfare to Higher Education: A Study of Lone Parent Students at Queen Margaret University College', *Edinburgh Journal of Adult and Continuing Education*, 8 (1): 60–72.

Hussey, T. and Smith, P. (2010) 'Transitions in Higher Education', *Innovations in Education and Teaching International*, 47 (2): 155–164.

Hyatt, J. and Parry-Crooke, G. (1990) *Barriers to Work: A Study of Lone Parent's Training and Employment Needs* (London: The Council).

Jackson, S. (2004) *Differently Academic? Developing Lifelong Learning for Women in Higher Education* (Netherlands: Kluwer).

Kaufman, P. and Feldman, K.A. (2004) 'Forming Identities in College: A Sociological Approach', *Research in Higher Education*, 45 (5): 463–496.

Kingston, P. (2006) 'The Changing Face of Success'. *The Guardian*, 1 August [online] http://education.guardian.co.uk/higher/news/story/0,,1834155,00.html [accessed 16 February 2008].

Knox, H. (2005) 'Making the Transition from Further to Higher Education: The Impact of a Preparatory Module on Retention, Progression and Performance, *Journal of Further and Higher Education*, 29 (2): 103–110.

Laing, C., Chao, K.M. and Robinson, A. (2005) 'Managing the Expectations of Non-Traditional Students: A Process of Negotiation', *Journal of Further and Higher Education*, 29 (2): 169–179.

Leonard, M. (1994) 'Mature Women and Access to HE', in Davies, S., Lubelska, C. and Quinn, J. (eds) *Changing the Subject: Women in Higher Education* (London: Taylor and Francis, pp. 163–177).

Levin, H.M. (1976) 'Opportunity and Social Inequality in Western Europe', *Social Problems*, 24 (2): 148–172.

Li, Y., Devine, F. and Heath, A. (2008) *Equality Group Inequalities in Education, Employment and Earning: A Research Review and Analysis of Trends Over Time*. Equality and Human Rights Commission Research Report No. 10 (Manchester: EHRC).

Lipsett, A. (2007) '20% of New Students Dropping Out, Says Report.' *The Guardian*, 26 July [online] http://education.guardian.co.uk/higher/news/story/0,,2134548,00.html [accessed 26 July 2007].

McNair, S. (1998) 'The Invisible Majority: Adult Learners in English Higher Education', *Higher Education Quarterly*, 52: 162–178.

Murphy, H. and Roopchand, N. (2003) 'Intrinsic Motivation and Self-Esteem in Traditional and Mature Students at a Post-1992 University in the North-East of England', *Educational Studies*, 29 (2–3): 243–259.

NUS (2009) *Meet the Parents: The Experience of Students with Children in Further and Higher Education* (London: NUS). [online] http://www.nus.org.uk/PageFiles/5386/NUS_SP_report_web.pdf [accessed 17 May 2011].

Open University Senate (2010) *Minutes of the Meeting of the Senate Held on Wednesday 13 October 2010* [online] http://www.open.ac.uk/foi/pics/d126249.pdf [accessed 8 April 2011].

Quinn, J. and Allen, K. (2010) *Who Fits in the Creative World?* Friday 10 December 2pm – 5pm at London Metropolitan University.

Reay, D. (2003) 'A Risky Business? Mature Working-Class Women Students and Access to Higher Education', *Gender and Education*, 15 (3): 301–317.

Scott, C., Burns, A. and Cooney, G. (1996) 'Reasons for Discontinuing Study: The Case of Mature Age Female Students with Children', *Higher Education*, 31 (2): 233–253.

Shepherd, J. (2006) 'Shocked, Puzzled and Annoyed'. *The Guardian*, 18 September [online] http://education.guardian.co.uk/higher/news/story/0,,2171189,00.html [accessed 18 Sept. 2006].

Taylor, Y. (2007) 'Going Up Without Going Away? Working-Class Women in Higher Education', *Youth and Policy*, 94: 35–50.

UNESCO (2009) *Global Education Digest 2009* (Montreal, QC: UNESCO Institute for Statistics).

Unistats (2011) [online] http://unistats.direct.gov.uk/ [accessed 8 April 2011].

Wisker, G. (1996) *Empowering Women in Higher Education* (London: Kogan Page).

Woodfield, R. and Earl-Novell, L. (2006) 'An Assessment of the Extent to Which Subject Variation between the Arts and Sciences in Relation to the Award of First Class Degree Can Explain the "Gender Gap"', *British Journal of Sociology of Education*, 27 (3): 355–372.

Woodley, A. and Wilson, J. (2002) 'British Higher Education and Its Older Clients', *Higher Education*, 44: 329–347.

Yorke, M. (1999) *Leaving Early: Non-Completion in Higher Education* (London: Falmer).

Yorke, M. and Longden, B. (2004) *Retention and Student Success in Higher Education* (Maidenhead: Open University Press).

Zepke, N. (2005) 'Diversity, Adult Education and the Future: A Tentative Exploration', *International Journal of Lifelong Education*, 24 (2): 165–178.

Index

Note: Locators followed by 'f' and 't' refer to figures and tables respectively.

312